CLASS AND AMERICAN SOCIOLOGY:

From WARD *to* ROSS

CLASS AND AMERICAN SOCIOLOGY:

From WARD *to* ROSS

CHARLES H. PAGE

With a New Introduction by the Author

SCHOCKEN BOOKS · NEW YORK

ACKNOWLEDGMENT

ESSENTIAL to this research were the encouragement, tolerance, and stimulating criticism so generously given by my wife, Leonora, and my mother, Laura Hunt Page. They have also undertaken most of the wearisome mechanics of preparing the various editions of the manuscript. Nor could the volume have been completed without the critical guidance and the scholarly judgments of Professor Robert M. MacIver of Columbia University, who has followed the manuscript since its beginning; and of Dr. John W. Innes of Columbia and Professor Willard Waller of Barnard College, who have read and commented upon the entire work. I am greatly indebted to Professor Edward A. Ross of the University of Wisconsin for having read and criticized Chapter Seven; and to Dr. Henry David of Queens College for his similar aid with Chapter One. Professor Robert E. Chaddock, Professor Merle Curti, Professor Robert S. Lynd, Dr. Joseph Dorfman, and Dr. Bernhard J. Stern of Columbia have contributed helpful suggestions. My sincere thanks also to Messrs. Morroe Berger, Daniel Katz, Saul Blackman, Jack Alterman, Bernard Peck, Joseph Goldsen, and Isidore Landgarten, former and present students of the College of the City of New York, and to Miss Fuji Yanase, who have aided me in preparation of the study at different stages. The final stage, publication, has been eased considerably by the kindly cooperation of Mr. Stanley Burnshaw, who has also suggested important changes in method of presentation, and of Mr. Burton C. Hoffman.

1940   CHARLES H. PAGE

CONTENTS

INTRODUCTION

The student of the social sciences, in choosing to write on the concept of "class," responds to the changing life-scene of the times rather than to the prescriptions of formalized curricula. It is not an accident of the vagaries of academicians' interests that within the last few years "class" has been the core of several sociological volumes,[1] and the central theme of many other studies not strictly confined to this discipline.[2] The conditions which have given rise to this contemporary interest in class are of maximum significance for the student of American society, and demand more thorough treatment than the existing works provide. So broad an analysis, however, is beyond the scope of this investigation.

The fact of a growing concern with the subject matter of class is reflected, to put it conservatively, to a very slight extent in the various sociological "texts." F. N. House notes that since 1918 "social classes, class struggle, the sociological aspects or implications of socialism, and similar or related themes cannot be said to have had a prominent place." Professor House devotes less than seven pages to "Classes and Class Struggle in Pioneer American Sociology" in a historical survey;[3] there is no mention of class in his entire division on contemporary sociological research. The authors of *Trends in American Sociology* found no materials on class worthy of a chapter.[4] In outlining the

[1] For example: P. Sorokin's *Social Mobility* (Harpers, New York 1927); the Lynds' *Middletown in Transition* (Harcourt Brace, New York 1937); J. Dollard's *Caste and Class in a Southern Town* (Yale, New Haven 1937).

[2] For example: A. M. Bingham's *Insurgent America* (Harpers, New York 1935); L. Corey's *The Crisis of the Middle Class* (Covici Friede, New York 1935); A. N. Holcombe's *New Party Politics* (Norton, New York 1933); F. C. Palm's *The Middle Class, Then and Now* (Macmillan, New York 1936).

[3] F. N. House, *The Development of Sociology* (McGraw-Hill, New York 1936), ch. xxi.

[4] G. A. Lundberg, et al., *Trends in American Sociology* (Harpers, New York 1929).

"fields" of sociology L. L. Bernard omits social classes, and states that "the sociology of economic relations . . . has never appeared officially as a separate field of sociology. It is now assimilated in this country largely either to economics or to social work." [5] Many other statements could be arrayed illustrating the paucity of sociological materials in this particular problem area.

The principal exceptions to this general situation in American sociology today, excluding some of the most recent studies, are found in those texts either written or chiefly inspired by the older school of writers. E. A. Ross's latest edition of *Principles of Sociology* (1938), for example, contains an entire section on "Class and Caste," as well as several additional "class" chapters. The *Introductory Sociology* of Cooley, Angell, and Carr is marked by the same emphasis. As the greater part of this study illustrates, the prominent place afforded class in these works is a survival of one of the outstanding elements of pioneer sociology in this country.

While engaged in this research it struck the author rather forcefully that he was, in a sense, undertaking "pioneer" work. Not that interest in class theory is new; it is, in fact, as ancient as social literature. But to many Americans, including some professors of sociology, native class theory began and ended with Thorstein Veblen. The statement that a research was being conducted in the *American* materials often provoked the response—"There is nothing to be found," or "Of course, there is Veblen." Few persons deny the existence of classes in America (although there is considerable disagreement as to their criteria, causes, and social significance) but many are unaware of the amount or quality of the theoretical writings on the subject in American sociology. Too often "class" is identified solely with Veblen, or regarded as an importation from Europe. This is intensified by a traditional element of American folk-thought which Lewis Corey terms one of the "constituent ideals" of the

[5] L. L. Bernard, ed., *The Fields and Methods of Sociology* (Long & Smith New York 1934), p. 16.

"American dream": "No class stratification: the right to move freely from one class to another, including a disregard for class distinctions which colored American life and made it impatient of traditional restraint." [6] This "constituent ideal" which bulks so large in our lay ideology has left its mark on many of our scholars. It is significant, then, to attempt to stimulate class-theory consciousness among those who devote a share of their energies to the promotion of American social science.

The settlement of this continent partly destroyed the link with tradition; it prompted "the development and use of a realistic and functional standard of value." The older marks of rank and status lost a large share of their former importance.[7] This is one of the reasons why, in the United States, the word "class" is symbolic of stereotyped conceptions, and is apt to convey the impression that the person who speaks of "class" is moving outside the boundaries of American culture, or indicating an allegiance to the "foreign" doctrine of Marxism. Thus Samuel Gompers was reported to have once remarked: "Now just one thing I beg of you, don't use that word proletariat in talking with me or of me. My gorge rises at it. I do not think in terms of socialism, in terms of class consciousness." [8] Mr. Gompers' statement is not without its counterpart among American scholars. R. H. Tawney warns us against the pitfalls of this kind of verbal prejudice in words which deserve repetition: "The word 'class' is fraught with unpleasing associations, so that to linger upon it is apt to be interpreted as the symptom of a perverted mind and a jaundiced spirit. . . . If the word 'class' is one which everyone dislikes, it is also one which no one in practice can escape from using. The sensible attitude is neither to ignore the influence obviously exercised by the phenomenon which it describes, as though it were indecent to

<hr />

[6] L. Corey, *The Decline of American Capitalism* (Covici Friede, New York 1934), pp. 51-52.

[7] H. M. Kallen, *Individualism—An American Way of Life* (Liveright, New York 1933), p. 65.

[8] Quoted by B. E. Benjamin, *The Larger Liberalism* (Cambridge 1918), from *The New York Times Magazine*, March 24, 1919.

mention it in polite society, nor to erect that phenomenon, as by a kind of dreary parody of the Freudian psychology, into the unique reality to which all other aspects of social life are to be referred as their original source and all-sufficient explanation." [9]

The original plan for this study was set down in 1935. At that time it was hoped that a single volume could encompass the material presented here, as well as data which are now being gathered for a second, and perhaps a third, volume. The original schedule viewed three major divisions: the class thought of the "Fathers" of American sociology; an analysis of contemporary sociological research, either directly in the class area or specifically related to class phenomena; finally, a critical evaluation of the concept of class, its uses and methodological import. This schedule has not been discarded; in fact, the present study, in the author's mind, stands as the completion of the first and introductory task. A considerable amount of material has been collected for the second study, the "research" analysis; and the author's own views on class are becoming concretized to the extent necessary for the writing of the third.

This long-range plan, however, does not weaken the justification of its first division standing as a single book. In fact, it may be questioned whether the space allotted to Ward, Sumner, Small, Giddings, Cooley, and Ross is commensurate with the importance of the work of these scholars on class. Classes and their changes and conflicts afforded the pioneer sociologists common materials and problems; their several and dissimilar solutions form a body of thought worthy of collection and organization in a single document.

Confining the study to sociologists may be construed as a serious limitation. This self-imposed limitation is, however, the result of practical considerations. As "public opinion" has been an object of interest to several of the social sciences, so has "class" gained the attention of various disciplines. Economists,

* R. H. Tawney, *Equality* (Unwin, London 1931), pp. 65-66.

of course, technologists of social work, political scientists, occasionally psychologists, have contributed to class literature. The task of collecting and systematizing these materials would no doubt be scientifically profitable, but would demand the enterprise of a group of investigators. Nor would social science mark the limits of investigation: the novel, drama, poem, and the like would provide data of significance for this larger analysis.

A full-bodied exposition of class thought of the period under consideration would assign major rank, perhaps the major rank, to the work of Thorstein Veblen. Ward, Sumner, Small, and the rest were deeply concerned with class and class problems. But it is Veblen's name which is invariably associated with this field; not to include at least a chapter on his class theory may constitute a cardinal sin of scholarship. However, to render full justice to Veblen, claimed by economists and sociologists alike, would mean considerable expansion of the present volume. His principal concepts, furthermore, have occupied an imposing place in American social science and, consequently, have been given wide space in a number of volumes,[10] the most significant being Joseph Dorfman's *Thorstein Veblen and His America*. It is essential, of course, to consider Veblen's role in the development of American sociology. Later it will be shown that his relation with the early sociologists was reciprocal: his own theory was influenced by at least one of them, and he, in turn, sharpened their thought.

A further limitation of the study is the brevity of biographical material of the six figures with whom we are primarily concerned. It would be interesting and, we believe, important to know *why* William Graham Sumner, say, held certain views on class. But this is a problem beyond this volume's scope: it involves the task of probing the motivations of individual per-

[10] e. g. P. T. Homan, *Contemporary Economic Thought* (Harpers, New York 1928), pp. 105-192; W. Jaffé, *Les théories économiques et sociales de Thorstein Veblen* (Paris 1924); J. A. Hobson, *Veblen* (Wiley, New York 1937).

sonalities. To answer it would require a series of thorough and extensive biographical analyses. Here, motivations are not the central problem: the chief interest is with *how* certain concepts were used. The answer lies in an analysis of method, and in documentary investigation.

AN INTRODUCTION
THIRTY YEARS LATER

IN THE late 1930's, when this book about the views of pioneer American sociologists was being written, one might have expected that a good many social scientists would sufficiently follow the action of the times to focus upon the nature and functions of social stratification. But such was not the case; in fact, while working on *Class and American Sociology*, I was, according to my teachers and colleagues, something of a "pioneer" myself. For, in spite of such class-linked momentous events as the Great Depression, the emergence and militancy of organized labor, and radical political movements of both left and right, most sociologists, seemingly in keeping with a strong and pervasive cultural tradition in the United States, worked in other areas. In the 1920's and 1930's "class" was greatly underrepresented in research, publication, and curricula.

There were exceptions, to be sure, to this general neglect of a subject which had been of major interest to the Fathers of American sociology. For example: at the University of Chicago there was some spill-over from the famous seminars on Marxism and class conflict given in earlier years by Albion W. Small, and several of the well-known studies in urban ecology revealed a good deal about class divisions and their effects in American cities. In 1926, C. C. North had brought out an excellent theoretical treatise on *Social Differentiation*, and in the following year P. A. Sorokin's germinal *Social Mobility* was published. In *Middletown in Transition* (1937), Robert and Helen Lynd sharpened the ethnographic focus of their original study of Muncie, Indiana, by giving special attention to the class divisions and power structure of that community. John Dollard's *Caste and Class in a Southern Town* (1937), destined to become a classic, launched a series of studies of stratificational systems that emphasized the black-white division of American communities. Some empirical investigations of social mobility patterns were undertaken in the 1930's, notably F. W. Taussig and C. S. Joslyn's *American Business Leaders* (1932) and the later studies of occupational mobility by H. D. Anderson and P. E. Davidson (*Occupational Mobility in An American Community*, 1937, and *Occupational Trends in the United States*, 1940).[1] At Columbia University Bernard J. Stern offered a Marxist-oriented course on class structure and conflict—a curricular rarity. These worthy efforts, however, were deviations from the dominant trend: representatives of the sociological enterprise in the 1930's, for the most part, left the analysis of social stratification to journalists like Alfred M. Bingham (*Insurgent America: The Revolt of the Middle Classes*, 1935), to defenders of the Marxist faith like Lewis Corey (*The Crisis of the Middle Class*, 1935), and to a few scholars in sister disciplines, such as the political scientist A. N. Holcombe (*New Party Politics*, 1933) and the historian F. C. Palm (*The Middle Classes, Then and Now*, 1936).

Work on *Class and American Sociology* began in 1935 when, as noted in the original Introduction, I saw the project as resulting ultimately in a three-part volume. The initial part on the Fathers was to be followed by, first, an analysis of such research and writing on social stratification as that cited above and, second, a presentation of my own "developed" views on the concept of class and its theoretical utilities. This ambitious scheme was curtailed by the realization that the pioneers afforded ample material for a full monograph and by a four-year interruption of academic life by World War II; thereafter students and scholars became the gainers by reading Milton M. Gordon's *Social Class in American Sociology* (1958), which more than fulfilled my earlier aspirations for the second and third parts of the original project. My hopes for the study of the views of the early American sociologists—Lester F. Ward, William Graham Sumner, Albion W. Small, Franklin H. Giddings, Charles Horton Cooley, and E. A. Ross—included the following aims: that it would be a reminder of a highly important but long-neglected aspect of our sociological heritage; that the political dimensions of class structure and dynamics, in keeping with the practice of

[1] Several of these works are discussed at length in Milton M. Gordon, *Social Class in American Sociology* (Durham, N.C.: Duke University Press, 1958), Chapters 2–5.

the pioneers, would receive sociological attention; and that some push would be given to the theoretical analysis of social stratification. These particular aims were to be fulfilled in only slight measure, for reasons suggested recently by the English scholar T. B. Bottomore:

The interest of [*Class and American Sociology*] is not only that it draws attention to the deep concern of the fathers . . . with the class structure of their society in its political bearing, but that it was written at a time when this concern had revived very strongly as an accompaniment of the economic depression and the intensification of class struggles and ideological conflicts in all the great industrial countries. The book appeared, however, just at the close of that era, when American society was about to enter a period of sustained economic growth and more general prosperity. In the next two decades the study of social stratification took quite a different turn. . . . Instead of the opposition between major classes in a political struggle, it was now the manifestations of social prestige in the local community, evaluated in terms of consumption patterns and styles of life, or occupational prestige and individual mobility through the educational system, which absorbed the attention of sociologists. The underlying conception was that of America as a middle-class society in which some people were simply more middle class than others.[2]

Professor Bottomore overstates the concern of sociologists (but not of others) in the 1930's with class phenomena, I believe, but accurately describes the changed nature of that concern in the succeeding decades. Following World War II, social stratification became a growing field of sociological specialization, signaled by extensive research, the mushrooming of graduate and undergraduate courses, textbook production, the incorporation of the subject into the popular sociology of "best sellers" and mass media fare—and by some effort to develop systematic theory. Indeed, by the middle 1950's few sociologists, so it seemed, would have challenged the assumption that "class" is a strategic variable in the shaping of most social patterns.[3]

[2] *Classes in Modern Society* (New York: Pantheon Books, 1966), p. 105.
[3] For a notable exception and strong challenge to this view, see Robert A. Nisbet's essay on "The Decline and Fall of Social Class" in *Tradition and Revolt: Historical and Sociological Essays* (New York: Random House, 1968), Chapter 6, the original version of which appeared in the *Pacific Sociological*

Yet, as Professor Bottomore points out, most of the work in this field, in pursuit of a theme stressed long ago by most of the Fathers, took on a pronounced "middle-class" coloration in keeping with a still-powerful American cultural tradition. This quality is revealed in the large literature of recent decades by several of its features: by preoccupation with status hierarchies and status-seeking rather than the contours of economic and political power; by the focus upon the status systems of the local community—upon traditional "small town" America—rather than nation-wide class divisions; by investigations of occupational and social mobility, the results of which indicate the continuing—though limited—viability of the American Dream of success[4]; and, generally, by a strong emphasis upon empirical studies designed to test short- or middle-range propositions about American social structure rather than concern with broad theories of class and society.

From the viewpoint of a sociology of knowledge, it may be argued that the "middle-class" coloration of research and writing on social stratification—notwithstanding the relatively short-range effects of periods of depression and prosperity—is consistent with and partly a reflection of long-standing themes in American culture: an individualism that resists structural interpretations of social arrangements and processes, a voluntarism that rejects deterministic explanations of social action, a pragmatism that suspects abstract theories.[5] These are prominent themes in folk thought and folk sentiment, in popular culture, and in intellectual and artistic endeavor. These themes, clearly, significantly influenced the discursive theories of the pioneers of American sociology; and they have intruded, I believe, into the more objective and rigorous social science of recent years.

Review, Vol. II, No. 1 (Spring, 1959). For a discussion of the misuse of the concept of class, see Arnold M. Rose, "The Concept of Class and American Sociology," *Social Research*, Vol. 25 (Spring, 1958).

[4] For an excellent depiction of this theme, see Ely Chinoy, *Automobile Workers and the American Dream* (New York: Random House, 1955), Chapter 1.

[5] Roscoe C. and Gisela J. Hinkle have stressed (in the early 1950's) that "voluntaristic nominalism" has characterized a substantial part of the sociological enterprise in the United States from its earliest years; see *The Development of Modern Sociology* (New York: Random House, 1954), especially Chapter 4.

But the latter body of work on social stratification is impressive, both in terms of sheer amount and with respect to the high standards of scholarship that frequently have been attained. Since World War II, dozens of volumes have been published and many hundreds of pages of social science journals have been devoted to research reports and (far fewer) theoretical essays in this field. A complete bibliography of these publications would fill a sizable book, and only a small fraction of this literature can be cited here.[6] One can distinguish, however, the principal types of studies that make extensive use of empirical data. Eight such types are sketched in the following pages.

STATUS HIERARCHIES IN THE LOCAL COMMUNITY

As noted above, in 1937 the Lynds had brought out *Middletown in Transition*, the first important—and widely read—community study of *both* social class divisions and the local power structure (see below). Muncie's six developing social classes, ranging from a small and emerging upper class to a "ragged bottom" marginal stratum, were briefly described in a portrayal similar in many respects to those presented in several subsequent volumes, published largely in the 1940's and 1950's, which reported the status hierarchies of local communities.

The most ambitious of these studies was the series of "Yankee City" books, based upon field research carried out in the 1930's (some of which antedated the Lynds' research) by W. Lloyd Warner and his associates in Newburyport, Massachusetts. In the first two of these volumes—*The Social Life of a Modern Community* (Warner and Paul S. Lunt, 1941) and *The Status System of a Modern Community* (Warner and Lunt, 1942)—a diamond-shaped pattern of social stratification, similar in rough outline to Middletown's six social classes, and made up of "upper-uppers" through "lower-lowers," was displayed in microscopic detail; and in subsequent studies—*The Social Systems of Ameri-*

---

[6] For extensive, but by no means exhaustive, bibliographies, see, for example, *Current Sociology*, Vol. II, No. 1 (1953–54) on "Social Stratification," with a "trend report" by D. G. MacRae; and, more recently, Gerhard Lenski, *Power and Privilege* (New York: McGraw-Hill, 1966), pp. 447 ff.

can Ethnic Groups (Warner and Leo Srole, 1945) and *The Social System of the Modern Factory* (Warner and J. O. Low, 1947)—interconnections between this pattern of prestige and ethnic divisions, in the first case, and working- and business-class relationships, in the second, were analyzed. Throughout most of the Yankee City volumes (the factory study being something of an exception), the central focus was the *local* community and the methodological approach was primarily ethnographic, perspectives consistent with Warner's anthropological pedigree and with his earlier work on tribal life in Australia. For research "in depth," this orientation requires a community of limited size (Newburyport's population was about 17,000 at the time of the research) and yields, if the findings are as skillfully analyzed and presented as those of Warner, portrayals of "real life" of considerable human interest—so much so that, in the case of Yankee City, the community's status hierarchy was featured in *Life* magazine, and at least one novelist, John P. Marquand in *Point of No Return*, "immortalized" both this type of New England town and Professor Warner himself. But these gains of scale and publicity are offset, in my view, by the localistic focus which prompts over-preoccupation with the tactical details of social life and social arrangements in the small community and thus discourages careful consideration of strategic patterns of power associated with nation-wide class divisions.[7]

This comment holds, I believe, for most of the several studies of community status hierarchies published during the last three decades. Yet these books and articles, as in the case of the Yankee City series, bring out clearly the interrelations between local structures of social class and ethnic groupings, economic and political institutions, family life, and especially educational practices. The analysis of such relationships is a conspicuous virtue of Warner's *Democracy in Jonesville* (1949), which depicts a pattern of five social classes (the "upper-uppers" had not fully emerged in this Midwestern small city), and of *Elm-*

[7] For a perceptive discussion of the Yankee City series, within the context of an assessment of various types of community studies, see Maurice R. Stein, *The Eclipse of Community* (Princeton, N.J.: Princeton University Press, 1960), Chapter 3.

town's Youth (1949) by August B. Hollingshead (who had also contributed to the "Jonesville" volume), a meticulous investigation of the impact of this five-class system on adolescent life and the school. Indeed, these volumes show a large part of social life—as do Carl Wither's *Plainville, U.S.A.* (1945) and *Plainville Fifteen Years Later* (1961) by Art Gallaher, Jr., anthropological studies of a Missouri farming village—to be tightly intermeshed with the informal but powerful status system of the local community.

The impact of economic developments, especially of industrialized farming and the use of migrant labor, upon the social life of a rural community, is perhaps no more graphically portrayed than by the anthropologist Walter Goldschmidt in *As You Sow* (1947). This study of "Wasco," a California town of about 4,000 persons with a surrounding population of similar size, describes two large social classes: the "nuclear" group of businessmen, farm operators, professionals, and white-collar and skilled workers; and the "outsiders," mostly unskilled laborers of diverse ethnic backgrounds. The volume is less concerned with status hierarchies than with these basic socio-economic divisions, the social chasm and friction between them, and their pervasive influence in the community. In these respects, *As You Sow* stands in sharp contrast with the status-oriented investigations, including most of the studies of "caste and class."

"Caste and Class" in the Local Community

As early as 1909, in *Social Organization*, Cooley had stressed that the concepts of "closed class" or caste (rooted in the universal principle of "heredity" or, in modern usage, ascription) and "open class" (rooted in "competition" or achievement) are of central importance in the analysis of social stratification in any society, and had noted their special applicability to the complex structure of Negro-white relationships in the United States.[8] Not until the late 1930's and the following decade or so, however, did this structure become the target of intensive and theoretically guided research. Initiated in 1937 by John Dollard's

[8] See Chapter 6 in the present volume.

study of "Southern Town," referred to above, and inspired by Lloyd Warner's investigations in New England and the Midwest, the "caste and class" systems of several American communities were reported in close detail.

Dollard, an exponent of the life history and depth interview, had used these research methods in an effort "to grasp and describe the emotional structure which runs parallel to the formal social structure of the community,"[9] producing a superb functional analysis—to use the more recent and popular terms—of the social classes within the two racial "castes," the interrelations among and psychological "gains" within each of these strata, and the "caste patterning" of education, politics, and religion. Within a few years after the publication of *Caste and Class in a Southern Town*, the double-sided system of social stratification (with comparable but not parallel upper, middle, and lower classes in each caste) and its interconnections with the major institutions, informal social groups, and with personality formation were the subject of a large number of investigations. For example, the caste-class structure of "Old City," with a population of about 10,000 and the center of surrounding cotton counties, was delineated at length in *Deep South* (1941) by Allison Davis, Burleigh B. Gardner, and Mary R. Gardner, whose extended research was directed by Lloyd Warner.[10] At about the same time, with the sponsorship of the American Youth Commission, a series of volumes was published, based upon field and case research and focused upon the caste-class system's impact on personality among Negroes, including *Children of Bondage* (1940) by Allison Davis and Dollard, *Negro Youth at the Crossways* (1940) by E. Franklin Frazier, *Growing Up in the Black Belt* (1941) by Charles S. Johnson, and *Color and Human Nature* (1941) by Warner, Buford H. Junker, and Walter A. Adams, the research for which was conducted in Chicago. Chicago was also the site of the investigation by St. Clair Drake and Horace R. Cayton that resulted in the outstanding book

[9] *Caste and Class in a Southern Town* (New Haven: Yale University Press, 1937), p. 17.

[10] *Caste and Class in a Southern Town* and *Deep South* are discussed by Maurice Stein, *op. cit.*, Chapter 7.

Black Metropolis (1945), a large part of which treats class divisions within the Negro community (and includes a brief but excellent "methodological note" by Warner on the changing patterns of "social class and color-caste" in the South and metropolitan North).[11]

Of the many subsequent studies of the class structure within the Negro population, the similarities and differences between the latter and the "white" system, and of specific Negro strata, the work of E. Franklin Frazier is especially notable for its solid scholarship, as in *The Negro in the United States* (1949, revised 1957), and for its controversial and provocative analysis, as in *Black Bourgeoisie* (1957). The latter book anticipated, especially in its critical assessment of the Negro middle class, some of the substance and, in some measure, the ideological tone of black militancy, whose proponents of course are less concerned with sociological and psychological niceties of the "caste-class" structure than with the chasm between blacks and whites, with the creation of a viable Negro community, and with power.

POWER STRUCTURES IN THE LOCAL COMMUNITY

A repeated criticism of the investigations of status hierarchies and of "caste and class" concerns the putative over-preoccupation with patterns of prestige and the consequent neglect of patterns of power. This charge, as suggested above, cannot legitimately be levelled at the Lynds' *Middletown in Transition*, which gave top billing to the "pattern of business-class control" associated with the famous "X Family." Similar power structures have received a large amount of research attention, from sociologists

[11] It should be stressed that Lloyd Warner, from the beginning, played the major role—theoretically, methodologically, and as research director—in guiding and stimulating the studies of status hierarchies and of "caste and class" in the local community. See, for example, his early paper "American Caste and Class," *American Journal of Sociology*, Vol. XLII, No. 2 (September, 1936), pp. 234–37; and especially the "Manual of Procedure for the Measurement of Social Status," *Social Class in America* (Chicago: Science Research Associates, Inc., 1949), by Warner, Marchia Meeker, and Kenneth Eells. For an assessment of the "caste and class" approach within the context of a famous study of Negro Americans, see Gunnar Myrdal, *An American Dilemma* (New York: Harper & Row, 1944), Vol. I, Chapters 31–32.

and political scientists, during recent decades, as the following sampling of such research indicates.

Floyd Hunter's *Community Power Structure* (1953) launched —and, in a large number of cases, provided a model for—more than five hundred (according to one estimate) investigations of "power pyramids," "decision-makers," and informal systems of leadership and influence in small and medium-sized American cities. Most of these studies appeared as research articles in scholarly journals, but several sturdy volumes on community power patterns reached the shelves of social scientists during the 1950's and 1960's. Hunter's analysis of such a pattern in "Regional City"—a commercial, industrial, and transportation center in the Southeast of some half-million population—was based upon research that made central use of the "reputational approach" as a method of revealing the actual wielders of power in the community. Whatever the shortcomings of this method— and these have been the subject of an extensive critical literature[12]—Hunter's conclusion that Regional City's "real leaders," comprising a small power élite, are almost exclusively drawn from the "under-structure" of big business is consistent with the findings of both earlier (*Middletown in Transition*) and later investigations.

Hunter himself pursued the investigation of local (and national, as noted below) power structures in the 1950's and 1960's. Thus a large part of the volume *Community Organization* (with Ruth Connor Schaffer and Cecil G. Sheps, 1956), a study of civic "action and inaction" in Salem, Massachusetts, treats the hierarchy of influence and of decision-making in this city with a religiously and ethnically mixed population of over 40,000 persons. (As in Regional City, with respect to the Negroes, in Salem the Polish-Americans, as one of the minority ethnic groups, were studied as a partially separated sub-commu-

[12] See, for example, Nelson W. Polsby, "Three Problems in the Analysis of Community Power," *American Sociological Review*, Vol. XXIV (December, 1959), pp. 796–804; Raymond Wolfinger, "Reputation and Reality in the Study of 'Community Power,'" *American Sociological Review*, Vol. XXV (October, 1960), pp. 636–45; H. Herbert Danziger, "Community Power Structure: Problems and Continuities," *American Sociological Review*, Vol. XXIX (October, 1964), pp. 707–17.

nity.) Again, the reputational approach was used, producing results that support the contention that power is heavily concentrated in a predominantly Yankee, business-class élite. Hunter's most recent exploration of power and influence in the local community (and elsewhere), *The Big Rich and the Little Rich* (1965), is a collection of impressionistic essays, based upon general observations, and illustrated with vignettes of individual cases, in "Ivydale," a Southeastern university town, and in the Bay Area of San Francisco, in which the wealthy or "comptrollers" are viewed as greatly over-rewarded financially for their relatively simple economic tasks, over-rewarded psychologically as the recipients of largely undeserved prestige, and attempting with considerable success to maintain a closed élite. This controversial book, clearly, moves from research-controlled analysis of local power structures to a free-wheeling critique of business as a system of power on a national scale.

One criticism of Hunter's studies and of those of others who have used the reputational method is that, while it may produce a more or less accurate portrayal of reputation itself, this method does not bring out the realities of power. A second criticism, voiced by some sociologists and especially by political scientists, is directed toward Hunter's power élite thesis, in favor of the pluralistic view that effective participation in decision-making is sufficiently widespread to reject or substantially modify the élite thesis.

The research of Robert A. Dahl and his associates, conducted in New Haven, Connecticut, during the late 1950's, which resulted in several publications[13] including Dahl's *Who Governs?* (1961), exploits the pluralistic hypothesis. As a research site, New Haven was selected primarily for convenience, although its typicality in several respects of other American cities is claimed by Dahl—who also notes, however, the city's atypical, century-old, "highly competitive two-party system." The research methods included lengthy interviews with nearly fifty

[13] See especially Nelson W. Polsby, *Community Power and Political Theory* (New Haven: Yale University Press, 1963), which examines the use of "stratification theory" in Middletown, Yankee City, Elmtown-Jonesville, Regional City, and elsewhere, as well as the theory's "test" in New Haven.

active participants in decision-making concerning three important public issues (urban redevelopment, public education, and nominations for local office), reporting by a senior investigator who for a year occupied "two highly strategic locations in City Hall," and sample surveys of "subleaders" and registered voters. Dahl's interpretation of the resulting data—showing, for example, only minorities of "social notables" overtly or covertly influencing policy decisions—attacks the notion of a power élite that increasingly decides the community's fate and supports the view of the continuing viability of the democratic process. That such data are subject to alternative interpretations is illustrated by Floyd Hunter's assessment: the findings of the New Haven study, he has contended, are quite consistent with his own in Regional City and elsewhere. These rival interpretations of exponents of pluralistic and élite orientations suggest that, in some measure, social scientists find what they seek.

The competing models of power élite and pluralism (or polyarchy) have played a major role in several other community studies. In *Men at the Top* (1964), Robert Presthus, who had employed both the reputational and decision-making "complementary" techniques, as well as a sampling of "rank and file" opinion, reports the results of a comparative analysis of power structures in two small New York State towns. Presthus describes the decision-making activities of economic and political leaders in both communities, with the business class tending to dominate in the heavily Republican and overly consensual "Edgewood" and politicos having a more significant role in the socially diversified (ethnically and in terms of class) and highly conflictful "Riverview." He concludes, however, that there is more élitism than pluralism in both communities. Pluralism wins out in Aaron Wildavsky's *Leadership in a Small Town* (1964), an investigation of the college community, Oberlin, Ohio. Making extensive use of case studies, and following closely the political rivalry between the conservative "traditionalists" and the "planning faction," Wildavsky argues that such evidence as the absence of tightly integrated power blocs and departures from economic self-interest supports the pluralist model—and, indeed, that this model applies to "most American cities." A large-scale effort to compare power structures and decision-making in four communities is *The Rulers and the Ruled* (1964) by Robert E. Agger, Daniel Goodrich, and Bert E. Swanson. This huge volume depicts political developments in two small Western towns and two middle-sized Southern cities between 1946 and 1961; presents massive data from sample surveys of the general population, interviews with "manifest and latent" leaders, reputational studies, census information, and documentary analysis; elaborates types of ideological patterns, power structures, and "political regimes"; and describes the rise of both the civil rights movement and the radical Right. The principal yield of this mighty research exercise is twofold: that there is little or no evidence of a close relationship between economic and political trends; and that both the élite and polyarchical models are of limited use in revealing the actual power structure of the local community.

Both an advantage and limitation of the studies sketched above is their sharp focus on local power patterns, local issues, and local decision-making. The focus is broadened somewhat in Ritchie P. Lowry's *Who's Running This Town?* (1965), an investigation of a northern California city of 30,000. Aided by participant observation for several years in "Micro City" and by interviews with seventy-five of her leaders, Lowry divides the latter into "locals" and "cosmopolitans," and adds to this widely used dichotomy a third category of "mediators" who participate in both the local and larger communities. Much of this study is concerned with "conservative" and "utopian" ideologies, diverse leadership styles, and the alienation of leaders from the local community. Lowry, opting for the pluralist model, concludes that Micro City's power problem is not élitist but one of effective local leadership within the wider society.

The local community's shrinking autonomy is the central theme of *Small Town in Mass Society* (1958) by Arthur J. Vidich and Joseph Bensman, a study of an upstate New York township. This vivid account of "Springdale's" social and cultural life—which includes the depiction of a five-class system: a few "old aristocrats," the occupationally mixed "middle class," a "marginal middle class," "traditional farmers," and "shack people"—illustrates a third approach to the analysis of power patterns: the "mass society" model. Both élitist and polyarchical elements are to be seen in Springdale, to be sure, but the dominant trend is marked by the widespread influence of the mass media, the in-migration of both professional experts and commuting industrial workers, increasing involvement in the nation-wide economy and national politics, and the decline of the power and influence of local decision-makers.

ÉLITES AND POWER IN THE NATIONAL SOCIETY

"Class theory" and "élite theory" represent alternative and, in some respects, opposing orientations toward the study of societal structure. Both class hierarchies and differentials of power and prestige, however, are major and closely interrelated, but not identical, elements of the social systems of local communities and of the national society—and both must be considered in this survey of literature on social stratification.[14]

By all odds, the most controversial work on élites and power in the national society is *The Power Elite* (1956) by the late C. Wright Mills. This volume—or at least the image of the structure of power suggested by its title—has become a major canon of the radical critique of the New Left (with whose views Mills himself took issue). As a sociological study, however, its portrayal of a tripartite élite made up of the occupants of the "command posts" of big business, government, and the military —persons of similar social background and outlook, and united by informal ties—presented a bold challenge to the pluralistic conception of power and decision-making. In *The Power Elite*, to a greater degree than in his earlier books on labor leaders and the middle class (see below), Mills takes large strides away from his fairly extensive data—mainly biographies of leaders—

[14] Among omissions in this survey is the theoretical and empirical work of Harold D. Lasswell and his associates on power and élites, which bears upon but has not significantly influenced the study of social stratification; see especially Lasswell and Abraham Kaplan, *Power and Society* (New Haven: Yale University Press, 1950). For a quite different and a specifically sociological approach, see Richard A. Schermerhorn, *Society and Power* (New York: Random House, 1961).

in depicting a stratified social order, to be sure, but also a mass society of increasingly manipulatable citizens in which strategic policy decisions are almost monopolized by the power élite. Mills saw little hope for the realization of democratic principles in the foreseeable future, partly because intellectuals, including social scientists, have abandoned their responsibility to analyze power arrangements realistically—in the tradition of Marx and Weber and Veblen—and, like much of the larger public, have assumed an essentially conservative posture. Mills' own analysis of power patterns, together with his hard-hitting polemical unmasking, has provoked an extended critical response from prestigious—and "conservative"—social scientists.[15]

Social scientists have given far less attention to Floyd Hunter's *Top Leadership, U.S.A.* (1959), a work that provides some shaky support for Mills' central thesis.[16] This relative neglect, I believe, stems from the lack of either theoretical or polemical thrust in Hunter's book and from its methodological short-comings, resulting in what is essentially another "reputational" study. Hunter pursues the élite model of his earlier community investigations, in this case on the basis of interviews with and case studies of leaders and lesser fry in more than a hundred "influential" national associations, including, for example, the American Legion, AAUP, and PTA, as well as the American Bankers Association, the U.S. Chamber of Commerce, and the NAM. Noting conspicuous differences of interest and policy among these organizations, Hunter nevertheless contends that a few "top leaders," mostly from big business, control the society—although he does not explicitly refer to a "national power structure."

In *The Power Structure* (1967), the late Arnold M. Rose submits the Mills-Hunter claim of a single controlling élite

---

[15] Thus Talcott Parsons, for example, shortly after the publication of *The Power Elite*, gave the volume very serious attention in a lengthy essay on "The Distribution of Power in American Society," later published in *Structure and Process in Modern Societies* (New York: The Free Press, 1960), Chapter 6. A much more extensive critique forms a large part of Arnold M. Rose's *The Power Structure* (New York: Oxford University Press, 1967), a work described below.

[16] *Top Leadership, U.S.A.*, surprisingly, was not reviewed in the *American Sociological Review*.

to the most thorough critique to date, asserting at one point that Mills' volume is "a caricature of American society." Rooting his criticisms in a meticulous examination of the arguments of his adversaries and of the large body of research on local and nation-wide power structures, and illustrating his discussion with three case studies (drawn from Texas politics, John F. Kennedy's primary campaign in Kentucky, and the Congressional conflict over old-age medical care), Rose strongly advocates a multi-élite model and a "multi-influence hypothesis." With Robert Dahl and other political scientists, the sociologist Rose argues that the political realm (in which he had actively participated) enjoys a substantial degree of independence from both the essentially nonpolitical "warlords" and the business élite.

The study of élites takes a different turn, theoretically and methodologically, from the approach of Hunter, Mills, and their pluralistic critics in two provocative volumes by E. Digby Baltzell. In *Philadelphia Gentlemen* (1958), Baltzell employs the tools of historian and sociologist in a brilliant case study of Philadelphia's "aristocracy," composed of overlapping segments of an achievement-based élite and a hereditary upper class, identified, respectively, by appearance in the 1940 edition of *Who's Who in America* and the city's *Social Register* of the same year. These 226 persons represent "an American business aristocracy, of colonial stock and Protestant affiliations" who share a way of life—ecologically, educationally, recreationally, philanthropically—and who, it is claimed, are representative of a national "metropolitan upper class" (a claim inconsistent with the views of Mills and others). Baltzell contends, in functional fashion, that such an élite, if its ranks are open to those qualified by performance and if it is accountable to the larger public, is essential for effective democracy: a classless society, he notes, is a "sociological monstrosity." There is very little, however, in this otherwise excellent portrayal of "Proper Philadelphia" about *how* the "minority of leaders" exercises its power in either the city itself or in the nation. Limited concern with what is done by the powerful also marks Baltzell's more recent book, *The Protestant Establishment* (1964), a historical-sociological investigation of "aristocracy and caste in America."

Tracing the domination for many years of the WASP establishment in business, education, law, art, and politics, Baltzell shows that this group has long since held no monopoly of talent and accomplishment in these areas, but has nevertheless persisted in exclusionary practices, resulting in a widening gap between a closed upper class and the effective "working élites." Discrimination against Negroes, Jews, and "hyphenated-Americans," he holds, has robbed the traditional establishment, especially since 1930, of its leadership function and has greatly encouraged public susceptibility to demagoguery and extremist movements. Thus Baltzell, in both of his studies, develops an essentially conservative theory—in the tradition of Tocqueville—in support of open élites and ethnic equality.[17]

Changing relations between the "upper class" and élites, the principal concern of Baltzell, is also a major theme in Suzanne Keller's *Beyond the Ruling Class* (1963). This volume, in an impressive display of scholarship, reviews the work on élites by writers ranging from Aristotle to Harold Lasswell; brings together a considerable amount of empirical research on the class origins and career lines of the members of various types of élites (political, business, military, scientific, religious, intellectual, artistic); and attempts to demonstrate by theoretical deed the analytical utility of the conceptual distinction between "ruling class" and "strategic élites"—"those whose judgments, decisions, and actions have important and determinable consequences for many members of society." Strategic élites, Keller maintains, are misinterpreted as representatives of an exploitative ruling class, for they perform essential leadership and, indeed, moral functions in modern societies. Keller develops a typology of emergent élites based on Talcott Parsons' scheme of the basic functional problems of social systems (goal attainment, adaptation, integration, and pattern maintenance and tension management), and argues that these "specialists in excellence" are increasingly replacing a single ruling class in present-day society.

[17] There is some convergence between Baltzell's "conservative" theory and the nonconservative study of "mass society" by William Kornhauser—who *also* writes in the tradition of Tocqueville. See the latter's *The Politics of Mass Society* (New York: The Free Press, 1959), especially Chapters 1 and 6.

Although the utilization of Parsons' analytical concepts in depicting concrete groups is methodologically vulnerable, I believe, and the replacement thesis is muddied by what some critics view as the substitution for "ruling class" of such phrases as "social core group" and "élite of élites," Keller's volume presents students of social stratification with a provocative theoretical work of a kind all too rare today.

Clearly, the central thesis of *Beyond the Ruling Class* is pluralist or polyarchal rather than "monolithic" or neo-Marxist. In an extended and eloquent essay, *Elites and Society* (1964), T. B. Bottomore, writing in the Marxist tradition, examines much of the literature reviewed by Keller—the theories of élites of Pareto, Mosca, Mannheim, Raymond Aron, and Mills, for example, as well as empirical investigations from both sides of the Atlantic—and somewhat similarly describes the "plurality of élites" in modern society. Bottomore, however, offers a sharp critique of the principal exponents of the "élite school," points up the middle- and upper-class origins and orientation of most members of the élites, and stresses the persistent contradictions between élite *or* class domination and the realization of democratic values. Thus the works of Bottomore and Keller—which were written simultaneously but with no exchange at that time between the authors—provide a fine confrontation between interpretations of multiple élites in modern society anchored, respectively, in the general theories of Karl Marx and Talcott Parsons.

THE "CULTURE" OF CLASSES

Noted earlier was the preoccupation of many social scientists and other writers in recent decades with prestige patterns and status-seeking, the "tactical" details of local community life, and the "middle-class" coloration of a large part of the literature on social stratification. These features stamp, in varying degrees, several of the studies already considered, and are a chief characteristic of some of the principal works on the "culture" of classes. In the following paragraphs the focus shifts from divisions of prestige and power to the life-style and value orientations of the upper, middle, and lower strata.

Investigations of class and status in the local community bring out both cultural similarities and contrasts among the higher strata in different regions of the country. Thus the Yankee City volumes, notably *The Social Life of a Modern Community* (Warner and Lunt), portray the life-style of the small, prestigious, and lineage-rooted "upper-uppers," which includes the "cultivated" use of leisure, the inconspicuous use of influence, and considerable community service; these traits of an established upper class stand in partial contrast with those of the larger, increasingly influential, and often wealthier "lower-uppers" of more recent social pedigree whose mode of life is essentially a costly version of middle-class patterns. The latter group predominates in the upper class of the Midwestern Jonesville-Elmtown (Warner and Hollingshead), where only a tiny emerging "aristocracy" was reported in the 1940's. The life-style of the upper class also is portrayed in the Warner-inspired studies of "caste and class," most fully in *Deep South* (Davis *et al.*), where a more "decadent aristocracy" displays the patrician bent of New England's "upper-uppers" as well as the distinctively Southern exploitative but frequently protective role of "master." A different kind of "metropolitan aristocracy" is described in *Philadelphia Gentlemen* (Baltzell), based upon lineage *and* achievement, whose style of life is symbolized by the old school tie and the exclusive club, but whose ranks provide essential leadership in the community, polity, and economy.

Preoccupation with the life-style of the leaders of business and industry has a long-standing history in the United States (rivalled only, perhaps, by the public's interest in the celebrities of entertainment), and the voluminous literature on this subject ranges from popular fiction to scholarly tomes.[18] Of the sociological studies so far sketched, *The Power Elite*, to a greater extent than other books, describes the social life of business leaders—in "local society," among the "metropolitan 400," and, in pursuit of a popular theme, as part of the café society of

---

[18] Sinclair Lewis' *Babbitt* (1922) is but one of hundreds of novels, preceding and following this classic, that portray the life-style of business leaders. The extensive journalistic treatment of this theme is illustrated, partly in old-fashioned "leftist" and muckraking terms, by Ferdinand Lundberg's *America's 60 Families* (New York: Vanguard, 1937), and especially the same author's recent *The Rich and the Super-Rich* (New York: Lyle Stuart, 1968).

celebrities in general. Mills' lively account—based in part on his experience as a participant observer and quite a celebrity himself—tells us more, I believe, about the expensive segment of New York City's night life than about the modal life-style of American business leaders.

W. Lloyd Warner and James C. Abegglen's *Big Business Leaders in America* (1955)—a large part of which reports the principal findings of the same authors' companion volume on occupational mobility[19]—includes a suggestive treatment of the "private worlds" and personality traits of successful businessmen and, in appropriate recognition of marital teamwork, of their wives. This discussion, addressed to the general reading audience, makes use of more than 8,000 questionnaires, interviews with some of these men and women, and an undisclosed number of TAT profiles. The resulting data enrich a somewhat speculative and inconclusive analysis of the motivations of successful businessmen, and help to point up their energetic capacities—*both* their "self-directing" and other-directed bent, and the need to demonstrate by business accomplishment their adequacy and independence.[20] Although Warner and Abegglen do not develop the theme, their material on the personality modalities, parental background (including shadowy relations with their fathers and firm maternal ties), and the strategic role in occupational achievement of a firm break from parental families of business leaders and their wives brings into view behavioral features of the life-style of this division of the upper class.[21]

[19] *Occupational Mobility in American Business and Industry* (Minneapolis: University of Minnesota Press, 1955); this volume is discussed below in the section on Social Mobility.

[20] Warner and Abegglen do not explicitly make the point, but this observation is consistent with neo-Freudian theories of sex and character. See, for example, Erich Fromm, "Sex and Character," in Ruth Nanda Anshen, ed., *The Family: Its Function and Destiny* (New York: Harper & Row, 1959), Chapter 19.

[21] The professed values of business leaders concerning economic and related political affairs, and the psychological (but not the social) functions of this "ideology," are analyzed in the excellent volume by Francis X. Sutton, Seymour E. Harris, Carl Kaysen, and James Tobin, *The American Business Creed* (New York: Schocken Books, 1962). This work, although not a study in social stratification, should be consulted by students of the "culture" of classes.

This mode of life, aspects of which are described in the works of Baltzell and Mills and Warner, is the theme of a large and growing literature of "popular sociology," written without disciplinary restrictions or restraint. A well-known example of this genre is the trilogy by Cleveland Amory—*The Proper Bostonians* (1947), *The Last Resorts* (1952), and *Who Killed Society?* (1960)—a kind of culture trend report of upper-class folkways, kinship relationships, recreational patterns, social leadership, and the rise and decline of lineage based status; all of this has been carefully "researched" and is presented with wit —and a modest measure of sensational journalism. Exposé moves to front stage in the nevertheless informative *The Private World of High Society* (1960) by Lucy Kavaler, whose sprightly account includes brief sketches of the "private world" of affluent suburbanites and high-status Negro Americans. In more sober terms, the life-style of two upper-class groups is described in Stephen Birmingham's recent volumes: *"Our Crowd"* (1967), which stresses kinship and other social ties among established families of Jewish Americans, and *The Right People* (1968), a depiction of child and adult socialization practices, local community life, and costly recreational centers of the social élite. This popular sociology, although innocent of the demands of social science, is a useful source of information and suggestive interpretation for the more rigorous study of the culture of the upper classes.[22]

The life-style and cultural values of the middle classes, representing both the modal pattern of and model for most Americans, are the subject of an enormous literature—historical, sociological, journalistic, and fictional. Of the sociological studies, two widely read books, with contrasting orientations but some similar conclusions, are preeminent: C. Wright Mills' *White Collar* (1951) and David Riesman's *The Lonely Crowd* (with Reuel Denney and Nathan Glazer, 1950).

Perhaps the least controversial of Mills' several volumes,[23] and

[22] On this type of "sociology," see Ely Chinoy, "Popular Sociology," Chapter 5 in Charles H. Page, ed., *Sociology and Contemporary Education* (New York: Random House, 1963).

[23] Probably less controversial as a scholarly work of distinction is the joint

supported in substantial degree by his own research and that of other scholars, *White Collar* encompasses much more than the "culture" of classes. Following an analysis of the economic and ideological characteristics of the "old middle classes" and of their decline, the diversified occupational makeup of the "new middle classes," ranging from top-level managers to salesgirls, the impact of technology and bureaucracy upon all white-collarites including professionals, their "styles of life," and their "ways of power" in unionism and politics are described at length in Mills' characteristically vivid and frankly evaluative terms. There are several "white-collar worlds," as Mills makes abundantly clear, but increasingly they share a way of life marked by the manipulation of symbols rather than the older craftsmanship, the replacement of the sale of commodities and services by the sale of "personality," the ascendancy of technical prowess over intellectuality, alienation from work, ever-growing dependence on the "educational elevator," and the ubiquitous concern with status. This cheerless portrayal, to be sure, reflects Mills' populist and radical background (he was a great admirer of Thorstein Veblen) and his pronounced pessimism about the twin trends of mounting bureaucracy and power concentration. But *White Collar* remains a stimulating and important analysis of significant dimensions of the life-style of the American middle classes.

This life-style is a major theme of *The Lonely Crowd*—although Riesman and his collaborators might be surprised to find their work included in a review of contributions to the literature on social stratification. For only slight attention is given, systematically, to patterns of class, status, and power in this "study of the changing American character." Yet an important reason for the powerful appeal of *The Lonely Crowd*—for more than a decade it became something of a sociological bible for thousands of readers, especially non-sociologists[24]—is the book's

---

volume by Hans Gerth and C. Wright Mills, *Character and Social Structure* (New York: Harcourt, Brace & World, 1953). On this point, see the cogent observations of Robert K. Merton in his *Social Theory and Social Structure* (New York: The Free Press, 1968), pp. 65–66, note 48.

[24] The influence of *The Lonely Crowd* among sociologists themselves has been considerable—and long-lasting. Eleven years after its publication, in

extended and graphic portrayal of "other-directed," middle-class styles in child-raising, peer-group life, consumption, work, play, sex, and politics: readers have the narcistic pleasure of viewing themselves. Of course *The Lonely Crowd* contains other riches, including a challenging but questionable hypothesis relating character types to stages of population growth,[25] the delineation of the now-famous ideal types of tradition and inner and other direction, a brief analysis of power and leadership in which a pluralistic conception of "veto groups" is arrayed against the theory of a power élite or "ruling class," and a libertarian advocacy of autonomy in work and play. Interwoven with all of this, however, is Riesman's unsurpassed field report on the culture of middle-class America.

During the 1950's, *The Lonely Crowd* was joined—on the "best seller" lists and as reading assignments in hundreds of college courses[26]—by several volumes focused on the life-style of the middle classes. One of these, *People of Plenty* (1954) by the historian David M. Potter, exploits effectively the social and psychological sciences, including the work of Riesman, in analyzing the role of ever-growing economic abundance and consumption orientation in shaping that life-style and American character itself. A second and highly popular book, unblessed by the imprimatur of the academy[27] but replete with scholarly references, *The Organization Man* (1956) by the distinguished journalist William H. Whyte, Jr., pursues the same

---

the series on "Continuities in Social Research," appeared S. M. Lipset and Leo Lowenthal, eds., *Culture and Social Character: The Work of David Riesman Reviewed* (New York: The Free Press, 1961); see especially the contributions of Paul Kecskemeti, S. M. Lipset, William Kornhauser, and E. Digby Baltzell.

[25] For Riesman's own estimate of this "shaky" hypothesis, see "The Lonely Crowd: A Reconsideration in 1960," with Nathan Glazer, in Lipset and Lowenthal, *op. cit.*, Chapter 19.

[26] In history, American civilization, and even literature, as well as sociology—providing evidence, it may be argued, of the "narcistic" appeal referred to above of detailed and homely depictions of middle-class culture. To be sure, this literature has other appeals, including its exposé function for unsophisticated readers and, perhaps, its exploitative possibilities for middle-class readers of a "masochistic" bent.

[27] In a curious inversion of intellectual criteria, the *American Sociological Review* published no review of *The Organization Man*, although it has been frequently cited in scholarly contributions to that and other journals, but did so in the case of Vance Packard's *The Status Seekers* (referred to below), a work rarely given serious attention by sociologists.

theme, emphasizing the decline of individualism and the Protestant Ethic in the middle classes and their replacement by "collective" trends: by the value of "togetherness" (the individual "is not only other directed . . . he is articulating a philosophy which tells him it is right to be that way") and by the bureaucratization of business, science, and indeed much of community and family life. Finally, as a commercially spectacular example of popular sociology, Vance Packard, in *The Status Seekers* (1959), making extensive—and sometimes questionable —use of sociological studies, portrays the changing status lines and especially the patterns and strains of status striving that characterize the middle-class way of life, concluding that the United States, in objective but not psychological fact, is becoming increasingly "a more rigid society." These three books, whatever their shortcomings as works in social *science*, like the volumes by Amory and Birmingham for the upper class, put on display important features of middle-class culture.

The culture of the working class has received less attention from writers of popular sociology and, until very recent years, from sociologists themselves. This relative disinterest may be due in part to the widespread assumption (which appears to be the fact) that the predominant norms and the paradigmatic lifestyle of a substantial segment of blue-collarites, as suggested above, are essentially "middle class"—or become so with economic advance and stability in an American version of *embourgeoisement*. This process, linked with the rise of "mass" standards in a consumption economy, was foreseen at the turn of the century by Veblen and Cooley; since then the transition from first-generation cultural enclosure to a middle-class mode of life, often accomplished in two or three generations, has been documented by numerous sociological and historical studies of nationality groups and their accommodation to modal norms.[28]

---

[28] This process was analyzed in the classic *The Polish Peasant in Europe and America* (1918–20) by W. I. Thomas and Florian Znaniecki, the forerunner of a large number of studies of nationality groups published in the 1920's and 1930's. Recent excellent volumes include, for Italian Americans in Boston, Herbert J. Gans, *The Urban Villagers* (New York: The Free Press, 1962); for Italians, Irish, and Jews (as well as Negroes and Puerto Ricans) in New York, Nathan Glazer and Daniel Patrick Moynihan, *Beyond The Melting Pot* (Cam-

As these studies show, however, and as underscored by a large body of research on such diverse phenomena as child-raising techniques, sexual behavior and taste, courtship and marriage, educational aspirations and practices, organizational affiliation, and recreation and entertainment,[29] the life-style of even regularly employed or "stable" workers and their families continues to differ in several respects from that of the white-collar classes. Working-class culture—distinguished from middle-class patterns by more familial authoritarianism, less "deferral of gratification," a more limited range of sexual practices, earlier marriages and more frequent separation and divorce, fewer organizational memberships, and a relatively restricted social life—has not yet been portrayed with the insight and imagery of Mills' *White Collar* or Riesman's *The Lonely Crowd*. But the findings of a large number of investigations of various aspects of the working-class way of life have been brought together in *Blue-Collar World* (1964), edited by Arthur B. Shostak and William Gomberg; and, in a more recent volume, Shostak describes and evaluates the principal features of working-class culture in *Blue-Collar Life* (1969). The distinctiveness of this life-style persists in considerable measure as more and more blue-collar families move to what frequently is viewed as "middle-class" suburbia, as clearly shown in *Working Class Suburb* (1960) by Bennett M. Berger, *Class in Suburbia* (1963) by William M. Dobriner, and *The Levittowners* (1967) by Herbert J. Gans.

Such volumes are mainly concerned with the largest segment of the working class: blue-collarites of "upper-lower" and "lower-middle" social status, to use Warner's categories. The way of life of the "lower-lowers," far removed from middle-class norms, had been briefly depicted in several of the earlier community studies, for example, by the Lynds in their account

---

bridge, Mass.: M.I.T. Press and Harvard University Press, 1963); and, as a more general study, Milton M. Gordon, *Assimilation in American Life* (New York: Oxford University Press, 1964).

[29] See, for example, Arthur B. Shostak, *Blue-Collar Life* (New York: Random House, 1969); Lee Rainwater, *And the Poor Get Children* (Chicago: Quadrangle Books, 1960); Lee Rainwater, Richard P. Coleman, and Gerald Handel, *Workingman's Wife* (New York: Oceana Publications, 1959); Mirra Komarovsky, *Blue-Collar Marriage* (New York: Random House, 1964); Murray Hausknecht, *The Joiners* (New York: The Bedminster Press, 1962).

of the "ragged bottom" marginal group of Middletowners, by
Carl Withers' sketch of those who "live like animals" as seen
by other residents of Plainville, by Vidich and Bensman's description of the "shack people" in Springdale, and, for both
black and white "lower-lowers," in the studies of local structures of "caste and class." Only quite recently, however, has
the "discovery" (or rediscovery) of poverty and its culture, as
an anomalous but highly significant feature of our affluent society, taken place and been added to the agenda of social science
for thoroughgoing analysis. This development, of course, has
been prompted by the dismal conditions of life in the urban
ghettos and in the rural slums and by the ameliorative efforts—
however financially limited, programmatically unrealistic, and
unrewarded by positive results—of federal and local government.
Thus, the "culture of poverty" has become a matter of both
public and social-scientific concern.

The view that severe poverty and deprivation generate a
mode of life that permits people to cope with such conditions
without complete loss of humanity has ancient status; it is to
be found, for example in the Book. But in recent years, the
formulation of this view in sociological (and essentially functional) terms can be attributed largely to the anthropologist
Oscar Lewis, whose well-known studies of a few Mexican families not only report their lives in rich and literal detail—with
the aid of edited tape recordings—but do so as a confirmation
of a distinctive culture of poverty, which presumably is not
peculiar to Mexico but may in fact be found in all societies having a capitalistic economy or colonial history or both.[30] In the
widely acclaimed *La Vida* (1966), Lewis—again using taped interviews, supplemented by conventional research techniques—
pursues the lives of Puerto Ricans (primarily but not exclusively
the members of one family) in San Juan and New York City.
Noting similarities and differences between poverty-bound

[30] Lewis' Mexican studies include *Five Families* (New York: Basic Books,
1959); *The Children of Sanchez* (New York: Random House, 1961); and
Pedro Martinez (New York: Random House, 1964). The concept of the "culture of poverty" is briefly discussed in these volumes.

Mexicans and Puerto Ricans, the Introduction to this volume includes an extended discussion of the culture—or, "more accurately," the "subculture"—of poverty as a "conceptual model": "an adaptation and a reaction of [some] of the poor to their marginal position in a class-stratified, highly individuated, capitalistic society." For the very poor, this subculture is an agency of survival; it is socially inherited and self-perpetuating—its values are internalized by the age of six or seven; and it incorporates or encourages expressiveness, spontaneity, sociability, generosity, and sexuality, as well as the elimination of childhood, multiple consensual marriages, prostitution, and violence. These traits and behavior patterns are beautifully illustrated by Lewis' case materials, but the latter neither confirm the hypothesis of complete rejection of middle-class values nor specify those dimensions of the subculture that are rooted in poverty itself.

The rediscovery of poverty in the 1960's—as an economic reality, the principal source of a distinctive subculture, and perhaps the basis of an American *lumpenproletariat*—had been anticipated in the preceding decade by a few social scientists.[31] But poverty and its cultural correlates gained wide attention in both governmental circles and the academy, and at least some public recognition, following the publication of *The Other America* (1962) by Michael Harrington, a socially concerned and highly able journalist.[32] Harrington reaffirmed the economic

---

[31] For example, Herman P. Miller's statistical analysis of the *Income of the American People* (New York: Wiley, 1955) indicated that about one-fourth of the population lived below the "poverty line"; John Kenneth Galbraith's *The Affluent Society* (Boston: Houghton Mifflin, 1958) included a discussion of the persistence of both "case" and "insular" poverty; in *Social Class Influences Upon Learning* (Cambridge, Mass.: Harvard University Press, 1949) and other publications Allison Davis analyzed the violent and gratificational aspects of socialization among the very poor; and such scholars as S. M. Miller, Frank Riessman, and Walter Miller suggested alternative theories of lower-class culture. A sample of the periodical literature is reprinted in Arthur B. Shostak and William Gomberg, eds., *New Perspectives on Poverty* (Englewood Cliffs, N.J.: Prentice-Hall, 1965).

[32] *The Other America*, which helped to stimulate the "war on poverty," was not reviewed in the *American Sociological Review*, and it was depicted as "not intrinsically a very important" but "a very necessary book" in the *American Journal of Sociology* (William Simon, Vol. LXIX, No. 1, July, 1963, p. 103)—a case, I believe, of sociological provincialism.

fact that about one-fourth of the population lives below the "poverty line."[33] The main sociological interest of *The Other America*, however, lies in the two interrelated themes of the social invisibility and unique culture of poverty. "Insular poverty," as John Kenneth Galbraith had termed the pockets of deprivation in rural and urban America, promotes a "web of disabilities"—bad housing, inadequate schooling, lack of skills, apathy, poor health, mental distress, joylessness—that largely defines the mode of life of an unknown but substantial segment of the nation's poor.

This mode of life, with its mutually reinforcing disabilities and its persistence from generation to generation, became in the 1960's a major target of the government's "war on poverty" (with no large victories as yet in sight). And a growing number of social scientists turned their attention to various dimensions of poverty which, like black militancy and radical youth, became a "hot" field. Three volumes are illustrative: The realities of income distribution, the widening income gap while "the pie gets bigger," and the implications of these economic facts for housing, occupational changes, working wives and family life, and minority ethnic groups are described in popular terms in *Rich Man, Poor Man* (1964) by Herman P. Miller, an outstanding specialist in this field. Miller and such scholars as Gardiner C. Means, Ben B. Seligman, Harold L. Sheppard, and S. M. Miller are contributors to *Poverty as a Public Issue* (1965, edited by Seligman), a book that focuses upon policy problems but includes informed discussions of the social and cultural features of poverty. Most recently, S. M. Miller and Frank Riessman, leading sociologists in this area, in *Social Class and Social Policy* (1968), present a critique of the "culture of poverty" formulations of Lewis, Harrington, and others; stress the social variations within the "new working class" (increasingly com-

[33] Estimates of the amount of poverty vary between a fifth and a third of the population. See, for example, Miller, *Income of the American People*; Conference on Economic Progress, *Poverty and Deprivation in the United State* (the "Keyserling Report") (Washington, D.C.: 1961); James N. Morgan *et al. Income and Welfare in the United States* (New York: McGraw-Hill, 1962) Gabriel Kolko, *Wealth and Power in the United States* (New York: Praeger 1962); and especially Herman P. Miller, *Rich Man, Poor Man* (New York Crowell, 1964), which is briefly discussed below.

posed of the "colored": Negroes and Spanish-speaking Americans); and indicate how these structural patterns and trends are related to technological changes and to policies and practices in education, mental health, and community action programs. Studies such as these, of course, are more concerned with social problems and their amelioration than systematic analysis of social stratification.

THE "PSYCHOLOGY" OF CLASSES

The "culture" of classes, as noted earlier, refers to their life-style and value orientations. The latter are not only closely related to the differentiation of power, privilege, and status but are intermeshed with the psychological aspects of social stratification: with the attitudes and sentiments of group identity, class consciousness, and outlook toward other strata. This dimension of class, of major concern to European scholars writing in the tradition of Marx or Max Weber or Sombart, generally has been neglected in the United States. The meager treatment of the psychology of classes, evident since the years of the pioneer sociologists, is in large part a reflection of the predominance of competitive class feeling and the limited development of corporate class consciousness[34] in an expanding society lacking a hierarchical tradition. Class-based militant movements, however, illustrated by the Knights of Labor in the 1870's and 1880's and the IWW in the early decades of this century, periodically have marked the nation's history.

During the 1930's—with the prolonged Depression, the spectacular emergence of organized labor, and the intense activities of the numerically limited but influential political parties of Marxist orientation—the seeming possibility of substantial growth of corporate class consciousness among American workers prompted a few social scientists to study the psychology of classes. This effort was encouraged by the rapidly expanding field of public opinion research; thus survey data on class iden-

---

[34] For explication of this conceptual distinction and its application to the American scene, see Robert M. MacIver and Charles H. Page, *Society* (New York: Holt, Rinehart & Winston, 1949), pp. 358 ff.

tity and the attitudes of members of different economic strata toward political programs, governmental policies, unionism, property rights, and the like were collected and analyzed. Important examples of such research conducted during the Depression decade include the several reports in *Fortune*, especially "The People of the United States—A Self-Portrait" (February, 1940), in which more than one-fourth of a national sample's respondents—understandably—declined to identify themselves with any class when asked to name "upper," "middle," or "*lower*" membership[35]; the ground-breaking work of Arthur W. Kornhauser on "The Psychological Bases of Class Division" (in George W. Hartmann and Theodore Newcombe, eds., *Industrial Conflict* [1939]), in which the majority of respondents at all economic levels in a Chicago study declared their belief in the persistence of opportunity, a finding consistent with those of several subsequent investigations; and Alfred Winslow Jones' *Life, Liberty, and Property* (1941), based upon research in Akron, Ohio, in the late 1930's, which confirmed the "paradoxical" coexistence of sharp economic differentiation and widely shared conventional attitudes and values concerning property rights. These studies helped to support the thesis of a "disequilibrium" in the social structure, evidenced by the pronounced lack of fit between economic divisions and "middle-class" patterns of attitudes and aspirations.[36]

Since the 1930's, the most ambitious empirical effort to delineate psychological dimensions of social stratification is Richard Centers' *The Psychology of Social Classes: A Study of Class Consciousness* (1949). Based upon a survey of a quota sample of 1200 white adult males, Centers defends the "interest group theory of class structure" of Marxist derivation by establishing a fair degree of association between socio-economic position and both class identification and political attitudes and behavior. The latter two variables, he holds, are the major components of class consciousness; although each is positively

<hr>

[35] See below for Richard Centers' modification of the *Fortune* study method and his somewhat contrasting findings.

[36] This thesis and some of its wider implications are developed in MacIver and Page, *op. cit.*, pp. 370 ff.

correlated with economic status, the statistical relationship *between* class identification and political orientation is weak. But Centers clearly demonstrated the antipathy of Americans toward the designation "lower-class" by presenting respondents (in contrast with the earlier *Fortune* survey) with the self-ranking options of "upper," "middle," "*working*," and "lower," which yielded class identification percentages of 3, 43, 51, and 1, respectively—a finding consistent with later surveys. Such data suggest that about a half of American (white) adults, in our "middle-class" society, do not hesitate to declare themselves "working-class" when given this kind of choice. This indication of "class affiliation"—confined to self-rankings and thereby uninformed by external classificatory ratings—provides little evidence, however, of the growth of corporate class consciousness in the United States. Nor do the partial correlations between economic position and class designation, political preference, and voting convincingly support the interest theory of class structure. Nevertheless, Centers' study, including the author's perceptive evaluation of earlier research in this area and his informed discussion of relevant theoretical literature, remains a suggestive source for students of the psychology of class.

The exploitation of this source has been skimpy since the publication of Centers' work twenty years ago, notwithstanding the popularity of survey research among sociologists. The disinterest in the investigation of class consciousness has been paralleled by a persistent concern with the manifestations of competitive class feeling: status awareness, status striving, and status ranking. This is a major theme in the community studies of the Warner school (discussed earlier), and Warner himself has stressed the disutility of the concept of class consciousness in the analysis of social stratification. Referring to invidious status designations used by members of local communities, Warner declares:

The informants who give these [ranking designations] are explicitly class-conscious, and their presence in a society clearly demonstrates the existence of a class system; but class consciousness, as a critical concept for determining the presence or absence of social class, is largely unsatisfactory. More often than not, its use causes confusion and error. The term has more than one reference; the latter half of it, consciousness, may mean that an individual is explicitly conscious of class, that his behavior indicates the consciousness of class differences, and, consequently, that he makes such distinctions in his daily life in categorizing people. On the other hand, it may mean that the individual is not explicitly conscious of class differences but is implicitly aware of them and acts accordingly. Such a person sometimes actually denies the existence of class. Is such a person "conscious of class" or not, and, if he isn't, must we thereby deny the existence of class in his society even if others like him should agree verbally with him? Obviously, it would be nonsense and poor science to do so.[37]

This statement seems to imply that status awareness is identical with, or is perhaps an American version of, class consciousness —a view (if this reading of Warner is valid) that raises conceptual and theoretical questions of the kind to be discussed shortly. Whatever the theoretical issues, however, in recent decades status and its attributes, in the Warner school and elsewhere, have been the dominant theme in the study of the psychological aspects of social stratification.

SOCIAL MOBILITY

Competitive class feeling, I have noted, overshadows corporate class consciousness in the United States. Historically, the former pattern of attitudes and sentiments has been closely associated with the geographical and economic expansion of a "new nation," the tradition of individualism, and opportunity and egalitarianism as prominent elements of the American creed. During the depression years of the 1930's, however, when this creed faced heavy attack and the viability of our "open" society was seriously questioned, a few empirical studies of social mobility were undertaken, notably those of H. D. Anderson and P. E. Davidson, cited earlier. But only since World War II—a period of economic growth and increasing affluence, together with persistent poverty—have creed and myth been matched against the objective realities of opportunity and social movement in a large-scale effort to ascertain the actual amount of

[37] *Social Class in America*, p. 69.

upward (and downward) mobility, the latter's generational dimensions, and long-range mobility trends. Much of this research is reported in the sociological journals; the present discussion concentrates on four especially influential volumes. These include both "direct" and "inferential" analyses: the first seeking "to compare directly the social origins and career patterns of members of each class at different times in order to establish the frequency or rate of mobility and to discover any changes or trends"; while inferential analysis focuses upon institutional, structural, and demographic changes and their implications for types and rates of social mobility.[38]

Following the earlier work of Anderson and Davidson in the 1930's, several other direct studies compare the occupational levels of fathers and sons in an attempt to establish mobility trends. Of these, Natalie Rogoff's *Recent Trends in Occupational Mobility* (1953) for more than a decade stood as the most meticulous statistical analysis of these trends. Rogoff, using data obtained from marriage license applications in a single Indiana county, found no significant differences in mobility rates between the two periods 1905–12 and 1938–41. Moreover, her findings generally support the conclusions of preceding and subsequent investigations: that, in fact, considerable upward occupational mobility and a lesser amount of downward skidding take place; that, although about 70 per cent of the sons (in both periods) moved from the occupations of their fathers, occupational inheritance is the most frequent pattern; that most such moves are limited to occupational levels adjacent to those of the fathers; that there is less occupational inheritance among blacks than among whites, with the strong likelihood of the former becoming unskilled workers; that (in 1940) sons of foreign-born fathers outpace Americans of older pedigree in rising to professional and proprietory positions and in avoiding manual and service jobs; and, inferentially, that mobility, whether confined to adjacent occupational levels, as in most cases, or of greater

---

[38] Ely Chinoy, "Social Mobility Trends in the United States," *American Sociological Review*, Vol. XX, No. 2 (April, 1955), p. 181. This article is an excellent discussion of the contributions and limitations of social mobility studies prior to the mid-1950's, and remains a useful bibliographical source.

span, reflects in some indeterminate degree both the changing occupational structure and class differentials in fertility.

Rogoff's volume is a major example of an intergenerational study of all class and occupational levels. With a shift in focus to the largest élite, W. Lloyd Warner and James C. Abegglen's *Occupational Mobility in American Business and Industry* (1955) is concerned, primarily, with the social origins and careers of business leaders and, secondarily, with changes in the business system itself and their effect upon career patterns in this group; this volume is an outstanding illustration of both direct and inferential research on social mobility.[39] In large part a replication of Taussig and Joslyn's *American Business Leaders* of a quarter of a century earlier, Warner and Abegglen's analysis of some eight thousand questionnaires permits comparison of data obtained in 1928 and 1952 and thus some grasp of long-range trends. Information about the respondents, their fathers, paternal grandfathers, and their wives provides the basis for a detailed portrayal of the class recruitment of business leaders, their educational and family backgrounds and those of their wives, the latters' roles as career mates, and their geographical mobility and its relation to occupational movement. The comparative analysis supports the authors' contention that, rather than a growing rigidity of the occupational structure (as Taussig and Joslyn had predicted), high positions in business are no less available today than they were a half-century or more ago and, for persons of lowly class origin, there is somewhat greater opportunity to achieve such status[40]; moreover, as Rogoff had suggested, more sons of immigrants—disengaged from locality and tradition—enjoy long-range up-

---

[39] *Occupational Mobility in American Business and Industry* (and its companion volume, *Big Business Leaders in America*) also helps to illustrate the major role of Lloyd Warner in the study of social stratification since the mid-1930's—in investigations of status hierarchies in the local community, "caste and class," the "culture of classes" (as brought out earlier), and social mobility. This is a remarkable record, whatever the theoretical and methodological criticisms of Warner's work, some of which are made in this survey.

[40] This claim is consistent with recent historical studies. See, for example, William Miller, ed., *Men in Business* (Cambridge, Mass.: Harvard University Press, 1952), especially the essays by Frances W. Gregory and Irene D. Neu and by Miller.

ward mobility than do their "native" contemporaries of similar economic status. Such career advantages as high prestige of the father's occupation, regional location, family and friendly influence, and especially formal education (which increasingly compensates for disadvantageous family background) are examined. Lowly social origins, nepotism, traditionalism, and Ivy Leaguism, as the authors demonstrate, play a much larger role in the smaller and slowly expanding firms than they do in burgeoning big business, in which bureaucratic rationality encourages open top ranks for demonstrated talent. Warner and Abegglen do not use the findings reported in this book (in contrast somewhat with their comments in its more popular companion volume, *Big Business Leaders in America*) in support of a political or ideological stance—they do not, for example, laud the virtues of individualism or "our land of opportunity" or those of big bureaucracy—but their work contains little ammunition for the declaimers against such views.

Interconnections between mobility and political behavior and ideology are only one of the themes of *Social Mobility in Industrial Society* (1959) by Seymour Martin Lipset and Reinhard Bendix, the most ambitious book on the subject since Sorokin's pioneer work in 1927. Lipset and Bendix bring together several of their earlier publications (some of them written in collaboration with other scholars), report the findings of an investigation of occupational movement in Oakland, California, review and evaluate a large number of mobility studies undertaken in this country and elsewhere, and, most significantly, analyze and compare mobility patterns and their principal correlates in some dozen modern industrial societies.[41]

The Oakland study, based on a secondary analysis (a method extensively used by Lipset and his students) of the full job histories of 935 wage earners as reported in 1949, points up the large amount of both inter-job and geographical movement at

[41] Since World War II, important studies of social mobility and class structure have been made in several countries in Western Europe, for example, by D. V. Glass and his associates in Britain, Karre Svalastoga in Denmark, and Gösta Carlsson in Sweden. For a review of such studies and a secondary analysis of mobility in eighteen countries, see S. M. Miller, "Comparative Social Mobility," *Current Sociology*, Vol. IX, No. 1 (1960).

the same occupational level, the frequent shifting between socio-economic levels (for example, at least a third of the unskilled
workers at some time had held lower white-collar jobs), and
the stability of professionals and relative instability of people
in small business. But this occupational fluidity, as the authors
stress and as other studies confirm, has lowered only slightly
the traditional barrier between white-collar and manual work:
more than 80 per cent of the working time of the Oakland in-
terviewees had been spent in one or the other social division.
Lipset and Bendix show that the manual or nonmanual status
of fathers strongly influences their sons' educational attainment
and their—often critical—choice of the first job, and therefore
helps to perpetuate the inheritance of class position.

Manual and nonmanual origins have somewhat similar functions, Lipset and Bendix report, in other countries. Their review
of several intergenerational mobility studies, undertaken especially in Western Europe, supports the claim that the amount
and kinds of opportunity and upward movement are fairly uni-
form in many, if not all, modern industrial societies—a thesis
inconsistent with a long-standing American popular belief. Social Mobility in Industrial Society also challenges two other
widely held views: that mobility declines as industrial societies
"mature"; and that access to the upper reaches of the business
world, at least in the United States, has decreased during the
past century or so. The latter criticism, resting in part on the
findings of Warner and Abegglen and a careful evaluation of
other studies of business leaders, takes into account the changing nature of successful careers brought about by the bureaucratization of business and industry.

The value of Lipset and Bendix's volume is enhanced by their
treatment of the principal correlates of social mobility, including urbanization, education, differential birth rates, and class
differences in intelligence and motivation—again, utilizing investigations made in various industrial societies. And, to a greater
extent than in any publication since Sorokin's earlier work, they
analyze the cultural and ideological contexts of mobility and its
political consequences. In the case of the United States, the ab-

sence, historically, of large-scale, class-based radical movements is attributed largely to "ideological equalitarianism," non-rigid ascriptive patterns, extensive public education, and a relatively high standard of living. This book, then, is a many-sided and provocative contribution to historical and comparative sociology.

The largest research attack to date on the problem of social mobility is *The American Occupational Structure* (1967) by Peter M. Blau and O. Dudley Duncan. In this study, the authors' theoretical sophistication and methodological expertise are brought to bear on a critical review of earlier investigations, a depiction of modal patterns of occupational movement, a re-examination of historical mobility trends, a skillful deployment of techniques of measurement, and a detailed analysis of the job careers of more than 20,000 males between the ages of twenty and sixty-four (drawn from a national sample obtained from the Census Bureau in 1962). Generally, their conclusions are consistent with those of other sociologists: most mobility is short-range; high barriers against upward and especially downward mobility exist between blue-collar and white-collar and between blue-collar and farm occupations; mobility is associated in varying degrees with ethnicity, education, geographical movement, expanding industries and occupations, parental family size and sibling position, and differential fertility; there is no evidence that the American class system has become more rigid —a finding in keeping with the studies by Rogoff, Warner and Abegglen, and Lipset and Bendix. Blau and Duncan agree with Lipset and Bendix that the (limited) amount of mobility between the manual and nonmanual occupations is about the same in most industrial societies, but they argue strongly that long-range movement from working-class to élite status takes place with greater frequency in the United States than else-where—"there is a grain of truth in the Horatio Alger myth"— and that this structural fact, together with widespread material well-being, sustains egalitarian ideology and discourages class-based political movements.

This brief sketch gives little indication of *The American Occupational Structure*'s impressive scholarship and, particu-

larly, of its demonstration of the utility of able statistical analysis.[42] Although Blau and Duncan do not fully exploit this
analysis in their discussion of alternative theories of class structure and dynamics, they show convincingly that our society's
system of social stratification, in spite of its rigidities with respect to black Americans and a few other groups, is sufficiently
"open" to support the folk belief in opportunity, competitive
class sentiment, and disinterest in class action.

MULTI-CORRELATES OF CLASS

Political and economic activity is of course only one indication of the role of class divisions in social life. The salience of
that role in the view of a few sociologists in the 1930's is illustrated by the Lynds' *Middletown in Transition*, Sorokin's *Social Mobility*, the earlier work of Warner and Dollard on "caste
and class," and by a series of polling surveys of voters' preferences initiated during that decade. In the years following World
War II, however, most American sociologists, as noted early
on in this review, assumed or at least hypothesized in their
studies the strategic function of class position in the structuring
of a wide variety of behavior patterns, attitudes, and values.
These "multi-correlates" of class include, for example, organizational membership and participation, religious affiliation and
belief, dating customs and marital choice, family life and socialization, fertility and mortality, marital discord and divorce,
sexual tastes and practices, consumption patterns and use of
leisure, educational performance and opportunity, delinquency
and crime, physical and mental illness, prejudice and discrimination, modal personality and character—as well as political attitudes and behavior. None of these diverse social phenomena
reflects the class structure without distortion, to be sure, but
all of them, in some measure, are (or have been) correlated
with class divisions—a situation that in recent decades has pro-

---

[42] The statistical aspects of Blau and Duncan's research are evaluated by
H. M. Blalock, Jr., and W. Lee Hansen in the Review Symposium on *The
American Occupation Structure* in the *American Sociological Review*, Vol.
XXXIII, No. 2 (April, 1968), pp. 296–300; and by A. P. M. Coxson in the
British Journal of Sociology, Vol. XIX, No. 4 (December, 1968), pp. 454–58.

vided vast exploitative opportunities for sociologists and others engaged in social research.[43] Only a tiny part of this research can be cited here. The following paragraphs refer to investigations in five fields: organizational affiliation, socialization of children, sexual patterns, mental illness, and politics.

The traditional and popular view of the United States as a "nation of joiners," held by so perceptive an observer as Tocqueville long ago, has been revealed as a misconception or gross distortion of the facts by a number of research investigations conducted during the last twenty years.[44] These studies show that affiliation with voluntary associations—with the notable exception of the not-so-voluntary labor unions—is heavily concentrated in the white-collar, middle, and upper classes, and that income, education, and residence in towns and smaller cities are significantly correlated with both membership and participation in these organizations. The fact that no more than about half of American adults belong to organized groups of any kind and that affiliation and activity are fairly closely linked with class status has important implications in a society in which a large part of the business of the polity is conducted by voluntary associations. There are thousands of such groups, of course, representing specific interests of many kinds—ranging from the promotion of home gardening to the promotion of native fascism —but some organizations, including political parties and labor unions, are agencies of countervailing power and of intervention between governing élites and the citizenry. Therefore, the "mass apathy" suggested by nonaffiliation and scanty participation, and the relationship of both with class position, are matters of concern to proponents of democracy and the maintenance of an open society.

Our "land of opportunity," as the discussion above of social mobility indicates, is a society in which life chances are a relative matter, again a situation strongly affected by the class (and

---

[43] Several excellent examples of such research are reprinted in Reinhard Bendix and Seymour Martin Lipset, eds., *Class, Status and Power* (New York: The Free Press, 1966), Part IV; and Celia S. Heller, ed., *Structured Social Inequality* (New York: Macmillan, 1969), Part IV.

[44] Most of these studies have been reported in the sociological journals; for an analysis of their principal findings, see Hausknecht, *The Joiners.*

"caste") structure. Of major importance in this situation are modal patterns of socialization which characterize different strata, especially those found in white-collar and middle-class families, on the one hand, and in the families of the lower and less stable ranks of the working class, on the other. A large body of empirical research carried out by Bernard C. Rosen, Melvin L. Kohn, William H. Sewell,[45] and others makes clear that values and behavior associated with achievement motivation and conventional success are correlated with the class position of parental families: here, as in the extreme counter-case of the "culture of poverty," social inheritance and socialization increase or frustrate the individual's exploitation of social opportunity. Middle-class children, particularly those of parents of advanced educational attainment, are much more likely to internalize the value of accomplishment, to give career goals priority over immediate gratification, and to extend their formal schooling—itself an increasingly traveled avenue to upward mobility.

The sociologists who have documented this partially self-perpetuating institutional pattern have not yet (1969) used their research expertise to examine carefully the current rejection of the "achievement syndrome," including the deferral of gratification, by what appears to be a growing segment of middle-class youth. The revolt against the parental generation, convention and civility, and the "establishment" in general is in part a consequence of conspicuous and grave social problems, a hated war, and youthful idealism, but it may also incorporate a boomerang effect of overindoctrination of the presumed virtues of what such youth term the "middle class."

Also partly a product of differential socialization are contrasting class patterns of behavior, attitudes, and sentiments concern-

---

[45] Of the many journal articles by the authors cited, see, for example, Bernard C. Rosen, "The Achievement Syndrome: A Psychocultural Dimension of Social Stratification," *American Sociological Review*, Vol. XXI, No. 2 (April, 1956), pp. 203–11; Melvin L. Kohn, "Social Class and the Exercise of Parental Authority," *American Sociological Review*, Vol. XXIV, No. 3 (June, 1959), pp. 356–62; and William L. Sewell and Vimal P. Shah, "Social Class, Parental Encouragement, and Educational Aspirations," *American Journal of Sociology*, Vol. LXXIII, No. 5 (March, 1968), pp. 559–72.

ing sex. Once more, as several investigations bring out, the principal contrast is—or at least has been—between the higher status and better educated strata and, in this case, a fairly large part of the working class. Notwithstanding the universal, powerful interest in erotic experience, class position is associated with the age at which premarital coitus takes place, definitions of "natural" sexual behavior, repertoires of sexual conduct, reciprocity and mutuality in passionate love relations, and, it would seem to follow, common achievement of sexual fulfillment. This association should not be exaggerated, and indeed may be weakening significantly, but the available data show that working-class persons, in comparison with those of higher status, usually begin coitus earlier (and of course marry earlier), tend to define "sex" more narrowly, disapproving and avoiding "perversions," and experience greater frustration in their marital relations.[46] By far the most ambitious study of these differences is reported in *Sexual Behavior in the Human Male* (1948) and *Sexual Behavior in the Human Female* (1953) by Alfred C. Kinsey and his associates. The data of the "Kinsey Reports," although underrepresented for the working class and possibly slanted in favor of the more sex-preoccupied members of higher classes, confirm the behavior contrasts depicted above and, largely by inference, give support to the noted differences between classes in psychological orientation toward sex.

Psychological illness—so often interwoven with the individual's sexual history—provides another illustration of the ubiquitous influence of class. For the prevalence (and possibly the incidence) of mental illness and the manner of its care are correlated with social and economic status—with the advantages on both counts once again resting with members of the higher strata. This relationship had been suggested, though not pursued, by the ground-breaking work of Robert E. L. Faris and H. Warren Dunham, *Mental Disorders in Urban Areas* (1939),

---

[46] To repeat, these contrasts should not be overdrawn. For variations among working-class marriages, see Komarovsky, *Blue-Collar Marriage*, especially Chapters 4–8; and, among high-status marriages, John F. Cuber and Peggy H. Harroff, *The Significant Americans* (New York: Appleton-Century-Crofts, 1965), especially Chapters 2–3.

a study of the ecological distribution of psychoses in Chicago, which established an inverse correlation between the grade of residential area and the rates of most types of severe mental illness (manic-depressive psychosis, often found in the middle classes, was an important exception). The relationship between class position as such and psychological health, however, was not intensively investigated until the early 1950's, when research in New Haven by August B. Hollingshead and Frederick C. Redlich formed the basis of their *Social Class and Mental Illness* (1958). Whatever this study's methodological shortcomings—which, according to some critics, prevent firm conclusions about the class distribution of the *incidence* of mental illness—Hollingshead and Redlich's findings indicate considerable variation in the prevalence of such disorders among the different strata and, especially, contrasting class patterns of treatment. The therapeutic disadvantages of lower-class patients are also documented in a later study of the New Haven sample, *A Decade Later: A Follow-Up of Social Class and Mental Illness* (1968) by Jerome K. Myers and Lee L. Bean. The most extensive investigation to date seeking to establish interconnections between mental illness and socio-cultural conditions, which generally supports the view that class position significantly affects psychological health, is the interdisciplinary "Midtown Manhattan Study" by Leo Srole and his colleagues, reported in *Mental Health in the Metropolis* (1962) and in subsequent volumes. None of these studies, it should be stressed, pinpoints the causal role, if any, of socio-economic status in the production of mental illness. But all of them (and others) clearly demonstrate that the prevalence of and the type of care in psychological disorders—as in the case of physical illness—are strongly influenced by the class position of their victims.

No such easy generalization holds today concerning the influence of class on politics, our final example of the former's "multi-correlates." Of course, during the 1930's and continuing in the following decades, substantial majorities of working-class voters have supported the Democratic Party, while the Republican Party has remained the political home of a very large part of business and industry and, more recently, of middle-class suburbia, a situation amply documented by polling studies and survey research. But there have long been class renegades from both major parties (in keeping with the principle of their multi-group doctrines). The depression-created Democratic coalition of organized labor, minority groups, and urban political machines has been greatly weakened, especially by the desertion of fairly large numbers of workers; some of the latter are the American version of Britain's working-class Tories and support Republican candidates, while others favor (or did so in 1968) the racist and extremist George Wallace. Conversely, upper-class liberals—again going back to Franklin Roosevelt and earlier—more frequently have joined Democratic ranks than they have pursued their reformistic or even radical goals within the Republican Party. Moreover, both parties, although their class leanings are well established, are marked by wide political spectrums ranging from ultra-conservative to ultra-liberal, and periodic third parties often have strong elements of *both* radical rightism and populism. And the recent growth of the New Left, largely but not exclusively among radical youth, has introduced a politics of "confrontation" dominated by well-educated and affluent young people whose principal targets are bureaucracy, the "establishment," and alienation rather than class domination, the system of production, and exploitation. Given this complex situation, class is only a rough indicator of political attitudes and behavior.

The study of class and politics, however, is a thriving enterprise in present-day American sociology. Historically shifting voting patterns, the class composition of political parties, class differentials in political apathy, the persistent conflict between equality and inequality, and, generally, elections viewed as "the democratic class struggle" are overlapping themes that have received wide attention, particularly in the writings of Seymour Martin Lipset and his students, and with the aid of survey research data and "secondary analysis." Thus in *Political Man* (1960) a number of Lipset's papers, including the controversial essay on "Working-Class Authoritarianism," were brought together; and in later volumes—*The First New Nation* (1963) and *Revolution and Counterrevolution* (1968)—problems of class and politics (among others) are analyzed by Lipset in historical and comparative terms. These volumes underscore the continuing political significance of class divisions, but they also illustrate, I believe, the growing importance, politically and otherwise, of other components of the social structure.

Without neglecting or minimizing the role of class and class conflict in many areas of social life, the social sciences currently face the problem of identifying and analyzing other major structural and cultural developments in contemporary society. These "master trends"[47] include at least the following: the bureaucratization of more and more spheres of human activity, in keeping with the historical thrust of rationality; the ever-expanding state, for both welfare and warfare; the increasingly strategic role of science and technology—the rise of the "technological society"; spectacular innovations in communication, making possible the "mass society"; mounting conflict on the basis of racial division; a widespread and growing youth movement, incorporating both a radical critique of the social order and new life-styles. These are closely interconnected trends, of course, and each of them, though in different measure, is related to the changing class structure. These trends, moreover, pose important questions about power and social control, long-time preoccupations of those concerned with theories of social stratification.

The earlier neglect of *the theoretical analysis of class structure and change* by American sociologists not only reflected the conventional ideology of an open and dynamic society but was reenforced by the antitheoretical bias and the strong empiricism of the 1920's and 1930's. During the latter decade, however, Marxist theory—sometimes viewed as *the* theory of class—attracted a few sociologists, and the "discovery" of Marx (and, later, of Max Weber) by students and younger scholars, abetted by refugee social scientists newly arrived from Europe,

---

[47] This phrase was used by Hans Gerth and C. Wright Mills in *Character and Social Structure* (New York: Harcourt, Brace & World, 1953), Chapter 16, to refer to the "coordination of political, economic, and military orders"; bureaucratization; "the decline of liberalism"; and changing "character structure in a polarized world." Some of these trends, as well as others, are noted in the discussion above.

stimulated theoretical interest. At the same time, the limitations of "raw empiricism" and the advocacy of the interplay between theory and empirical research were increasingly stressed, a development that affected almost all sociological fields including social stratification. The growing interest in this area following World War II was signaled by the publication of the first widely used "text," *Class, Status and Power* (1953), a collection edited by Reinhard Bendix and S. M. Lipset,[48] the theoretical part of which includes readings ranging from Aristotle's classical statement on the virtues of the middle class to Talcott Parsons' functional formulation stressing the virtues of general analytical theory.

Functionalism—the general theoretical orientation and perhaps most notably its application to social stratification—has been a conspicuous trend in American sociology during the last twenty years or so, with Parsons as its chief spokesman. To be sure, functional propositions have long been a prominent part of the sociological enterprise and are found in the writings of such otherwise dissimilar scholars as Comte, Spencer, Marx, Durkheim, Max Weber, Pareto, Sumner, Veblen, and Robert MacIver—all of whom have produced theoretical analyses of class structure and change. But functional interpretation of social stratification is principally associated with the work of Durkheim and Pareto in the earlier period (and, by those few who read the book today, with Sumner's even earlier *What Social Classes Owe to Each Other* [1883]—an ideologically disguised functional analysis *par excellence*) and, in recent years, with the writings of Parsons, Kingsley Davis, Wilbert Moore, Bernard Barber, and Robert K. Merton.

The functional orientation is explicated—and criticized—in a large and expanding literature[49]; only its most general features

---

[48] Thirteen years later, a second edition of this volume was published, the theoretical section of which was substantially expanded by the addition of several selections on functional theory, discussed below; cf. Bendix and Lipset, eds., *Class, Status and Power* (New York: The Free Press, 1966).

[49] The functional approach is very ably presented in Merton, *Social Theory and Social Structure*, Chapter 3; Marion J. Levy, Jr., *The Structure of Society*, (Princeton, N.J.: Princeton University Press, 1952), Chapter 2; and Percy S. Cohen, *Modern Social Theory* (New York: Basic Books, 1968), Chapters 2–3.

need be noted here, especially three interrelated characteristics
of particular relevance for the study of social stratification.
First, functionalism is holistic, viewing societies (or smaller
units) as more or less integrated systems or "going concerns,"
and a major theoretical task is the specification of the structural
requirements of such systems. This systemic focus directs attention to the way in which social structures and cultural patterns
help to maintain, or to disturb, social systems—"social order" is
a central problem. Secondly, functionalism is concerned with
the interrelations or "exchanges"—manifest and latent—among
the structural and cultural elements of social systems, for example, between kinship and class structures or between the
class system and the polity. Thirdly, functionalism, in keeping
with holism, is interactional and multi-causational, rejecting all
monistic explanations of social structure and social change.
These features, clearly, have a direct bearing on functionalist
theories of social stratification.

These theories vary considerably from one functional sociologist to another, but their starting point is generally shared. It
stands in contrast with the orientation of those scholars—whether
of Marxist or other persuasion—who are *primarily* interested in
the role of class in social change, or in questions of exploitation
and justice, or in both. Functionalists, in accordance with their
systemic focus, are *primarily* concerned with how social stratification, with its hierarchy of material and symbolic rewards,
motivates qualified people (often, if not always, in short supply) to assume and carry out the diverse social roles that the
social system—any system—requires. From this viewpoint, social
stratification, as Durkheim observed, serves to maintain the social division of labor and thus to promote some degree of social
stability. An important function of differentiated rewards, of
social inequality, then, is to get the business of society done.
This functionalist approach was succinctly presented twenty-
five years ago by Davis and Moore in "Some Principles of

For an excellent collection of readings on the "debate over functionalism,"
see N. J. Demerath and Richard A. Peterson, eds., *System, Change, and Conflict* (New York: The Free Press, 1967).

Stratification,"[50] an essay which has been republished many times and retains, as noted below, a significant position in the "debate over functionalism."

The stress upon the need for a hierarchy of rewards does not, of course, explain how individuals and strata are ranked in different societies. The functionalist answer to this question, especially as it has been elaborated by Parsons,[51] follows a lead of Weber's by pointing out that, universally, there is a scarcity of *status* and that the basis of status varies from society to society. Parsons names "possessions," "qualities," and "performances" as the principal grounds of status ranking, indicating that concrete stratification systems, although they give emphasis to one or another ground (as in capitalist, feudal, and communist societies, respectively), involve all three of these "ideal types." This theoretical concern with diverse status arrangements, in contrast with a central focus upon economic divisions or power structures, has encouraged the analysis of the multiple dimensions of social stratification in complex societies, illustrated most fully by the work of Bernard Barber[52]—a major contribution of the functional approach.

This all too brief sketch runs the risk of suggesting that functionalists are disinterested in questions of economy and power, conflict and change, and the dysfunctions of social stratification. That such is not the case is amply illustrated by Parsons' writings on power and structural "strains," Moore's theoretical work on social change, and Barber's treatment of the historical role of class conflict. A striking example of the analysis of the functions of institutionalized inequality for social change is Merton's brief but persistently influential "Social Structure and Anomie"

[50] Kingsley Davis and Wilbert E. Moore, "Some Principles of Stratification," *American Sociological Review*, Vol. X, No. 2 (April, 1945), pp. 242–49.

[51] See especially "A Revised Analytical Approach to the Theory of Social Stratification" in Reinhard Bendix and S. M. Lipset, eds., *Class, Status and Power* (New York: The Free Press, 1953), pp. 92–128; this essay is not included in the revised edition of Bendix and Lipset, *op. cit.*

[52] See Barber's comprehensive textbook, *Social Stratification* (New York: Harcourt, Brace & World, 1957); and for a recent statement, "Social Stratification: Introduction," *International Encyclopedia of the Social Sciences* (New York: Macmillan and The Free Press, 1968), Volume XV, pp. 288–95.

(1938, 1949, 1957, 1968).[53] Referring to the discrepancy in American society between culturally prescribed and widely shared "success" goals and "socially structured avenues for realizing these aspirations," Merton analyzes several behavioral patterns that represent adaptive responses to this inconsistency between ends and means; two of these patterns—"innovation," involving new and frequently illegal avenues to success, and "rebellion," the call for both new cultural goals and new institutional methods—are (or should be) of major interest to students of class structure and social change. Although "Social Structure and Anomie" has been most frequently—and fruitfully —exploited by specialists in "deviant" behavior, Merton's essay also is a highly suggestive discussion of the dynamic aspects of social stratification.

The functionalist theory of social stratification, since the publication in 1945 of Davis and Moore's article cited above, has been under attack by several American and European scholars. One criticism is directed against the view that social stability requires institutionalized inequality; this universal feature of complex societies is more realistically explained in group-interest terms as a reflection of the concentration of power in the upper strata—the functional needs of the latter, not those of the "social system," account for the hierarchical distribution of wealth and status. This point and its ideological implications have been developed by Melvin Tumin, among others; while Walter Buckley and Dennis Wrong also have noted that functionalist theory fails to explain either the division of labor ("social differentiation") or the persistence of inequalities along family lines. Wrong, in addition, criticizes the theory as being so general as to preclude effective analysis of concrete patterns of inequality and their specific determinants (a charge that may be extended to functionalist theory in general), and cites the neglect, by both proponents and critics of

[53] The original essay appeared in the *American Sociological Review*, Vol. III, No. 5 (October, 1938), pp. 672–82; in expanded form it was included in the first edition of Merton's *Social Theory and Social Structure* (1949); the 1957 and 1968 editions of the latter volume also include "Continuities in the Theory of Social Structure and Anomie": see Merton, *op. cit.*, Chapters 6 and 7.

functional interpretation, of the possibly disruptive effects of extensive opportunity and social mobility.[54]

The extended controversy about functionalist theory reached a high point of intellectual exchange in 1963, when Moore, in the paper "But Some Are More Equal Than Others," conceded that advocates of the theory had neglected or downgraded dysfunctional and other dynamic aspects of stratification (all hierarchical reward systems generate "equity strains"), but argued effectively that performance differentials demand inequality and that dysfunctional elements would inhere in equalitarian systems themselves. Tumin, in a companion piece, "On Inequality," also made concessions by specifying the bases of seemingly unavoidable differentiation of rewards (in persisting societies) as "role specification," intrinsic characteristics of roles, and functional contributions, but nevertheless held that only a "minimum" of social inequality is essential for societal survival and that most existing systems of stratification are "probably seriously dysfunctional for social productivity." Clearly, significant theoretical differences remain between these major spokesmen of functionalist and counter-functionalist views, but, as Moore points out in a concluding rejoinder to Tumin's paper, they share important analytical problems in the sociological study of social stratification.[55] And clearly, too, if theoretical problems are still to be resolved, ideological and moral questions of equity, justice, and exploitation are matters of concern to the heirs of *both* Durkheim and Marx.

Questions posed by functionalist theory have been taken very seriously by scholars of the Marxist tradition, especially (and understandably) in Europe. Indeed, a confrontation and, in

---

[54] See Melvin M. Tumin, "Some Principles of Stratification: A Critical Analysis" (and the responses by Kingsley Davis and Wilbert E. Moore), *American Sociological Review*, Vol. XVIII, No. 4 (August, 1953), pp. 387–97; Walter Buckley, "Social Stratification and the Functional Theory of Social Differentiation," *American Sociological Review*, Vol. XXIII, No. 4 (August, 1958), pp. 369–75; Dennis H. Wrong, "The Functional Theory of Stratification: Some Neglected Considerations," *American Sociological Review*, Vol. XXIV, No. 6 (December, 1959), pp. 772 82.

[55] Wilbert E. Moore, "But Some Are More Equal Than Others," Melvin Tumin, "On Inequality," and Moore, "Rejoinder," *American Sociological Review*, Vol. XXVIII, No. 1 (February, 1963), pp. 13–28.

some degree, a reconciliation of aspects of functionalist and Marxist orientations mark the recent writings of four distinguished European sociologists: the Poles, the late Stanislaw Ossowski and Wlodzimierz Wesolowski; the German Ralf Dahrendorf; and the Englishman T. B. Bottomore. Ossowski's *Class Structure in the Social Consciousness* (1963; originally published in Polish, 1957), a study in both the sociology of knowledge and social stratification, analyzes the images of the class structure held by members of different groups including functionalist and Marxist sociologists, elements of truth and error in both of the latter conceptions, the existential sources of such views, the affinity between dichotomous depictions of the class structure and radical criticism and between multiple-strata portrayals and support of existing regimes (in Soviet Russia as well as the United States), the utilities and disutilities of the various meanings of "class," and the limitations of *any* theoretical model of social stratification. Wesolowski, in a critique of functionalist theory (1962),[56] and taking a different tack, agrees with the proposition that social stratification is an inevitable feature of complex societies—based, however, on the need for a hierarchy of authority positions rather than being a role-filling motivational system of differentiated rewards; class distinctions, then, can be greatly reduced or eliminated, but a division of command, as Engels had noted, is a functional necessity in industrial societies. Dahrendorf, in *Class and Class Conflict in Industrial Society* (1959), argues that large-scale structural changes, especially mounting bureaucracy and the separation of ownership and management, require revision of Marxist theory: class divisions and class conflict today, he holds, are anchored not in the ownership relation to the means of production, but in the distribution—again—of *authority*; "class," in this view, becomes something of a shotgun concept, but Dahrendorf develops a strong case for the functional contributions of authority-based class conflict in an effort to redress the balance with Parsonian integration theory. Finally, in a characteristically graceful and

[56] "Some Notes on the Functional Theory of Stratification," *The Polish Sociological Bulletin*, 3–4 (5–6), (1962), reprinted in Bendix and Lipset, *Class, Status and Power*, pp. 64–68.

informed essay, *Classes in Modern Society* (1966), Bottomore explores the possibility of realizing equalitarian goals in industrial societies by reviewing Marxist theory and the Weberian critique in the light of class developments in Britain and the United States, on the one hand, and Soviet-type societies, on the other; in both cases he finds monolithic *and* pluralistic trends and class-based conflict, and with respect to the former countries (with which he is primarily concerned) emphasizes the inconsistency between the *embourgeoisement* of the working class in leisure-time pursuits and life-style and the continuing subordinated and frustrated working role—which remains, Bottomore suggests, a basis of alienation and class conflict.

Although there have been relatively few theoretical efforts of this kind in the United States, the most ambitious attempt to develop a new theory—or meta-theory—of social stratification is the impressive volume *Power and Privilege* (1966) by the American scholar Gerhard Lenski. In a review of various answers to the question of "who gets what and why?" as they have been formulated from pre-Christian times to the present, Lenski distinguishes between conservative-functionalist and radical-conflict orientations, and cites the "emerging synthesis" of the two approaches in the work of such otherwise dissimilar sociologists as Sorokin (in his analysis of mobility), Parsons, Kingsley Davis, Ossowski, Dahrendorf, and C. Wright Mills.[57] Lenski himself, with an assist from Hegel's dialectic, recasts elements of both traditional orientations into a "single integrated theory of social inequality." The first part of *Power and Privilege* elaborates this synthetic theory which, as Lenski explains fully, rests upon several (familiar) postulates about the nature of man and society; generally, human life reflects *both* societal and individual interests *and* the conflict between them. Both types of interest are at work in "the dynamics of distributive systems": cooperation and the sharing of wealth to the extent required for "sur-

[57] Lenski pays special tribute for advancing this synthesis to Ossowski's *Class Structure in the Social Consciousness*, and to the more general treatment by Pierre L. van den Berghe, "Dialectic and Functionalism: Toward a Theoretical Synthesis," *American Sociological Review*, Vol. XXVIII, No. 5 (October, 1963), pp. 695–705.

vival"; power-seeking and conflict in activities involving a "surplus" of goods and services—privilege in the latter situation is largely a function of power, and prestige is largely a function of power and privilege. These propositions are illustrated in a discussion of classes, castes, estates, status groups, and élites, all manifestations of "the structure of distributive systems." Whether or not Lenski goes beyond illustration of his theory in the lengthy treatment (eight sturdy chapters) of stratification in hunting and gathering, horticultural, agrarian, and industrial societies is problematic; but this mighty exercise in historical and comparative scholarship is consistent with his Hegelian model. In contrast with Hegel, however, Lenski assigns technology the strategic role in the determination of "surplus" and thus of stratification—until the recent period, when "the appearance of mature industrial societies marks the first significant reversal in the age-old evolutionary trend toward ever increasing inequality." This "reversal" is documented convincingly, but the explanation of present-day *decreasing* inequality (encouraged by growing administrative efficiency, for example) does little, I would argue, to save the evolutionary component of his theory. This all too elliptical observation is hardly a weighty criticism of *Power and Privilege*, for Lenski's book, surely, stands as a major—and splendidly provocative—contribution to the literature on social stratification.

This literature, as these pages have illustrated, has reached huge dimensions during the last thirty years in the United States. Its most conspicuous single feature is the emphasis upon the multi-dimensionality of stratification, a reflection in part of the concern with the multi-bases of *status*, strengthened by the functional approach, and in part an indication of the powerful influence of Max Weber upon American sociology. Weber's tripartite analysis of class, status, and power is the starting point of a large amount of writing and research on stratification—and, I believe, this scheme "fits" the realities of American social life more neatly than does what often seems to be the one-dimensional class approach of Marx and his followers. Multi-dimensionality is stressed in several excellent textbooks—for example, Bernard Barber's *Social Stratification* (1957), Joseph A. Kahl's

The American Class Structure (1957), Leonard Riessman's *Class in American Society* (1959), Melvin M. Tumin's *Social Stratification* (1967), and Kurt B. Mayer and Walter Buckley's *Class and Society* (1969)—in which the discussions of institutionalized inequality pursue the interrelated topics of class, status, power, life-chances, life-style, class consciousness, and social mobility.

All of these dimensions of social stratification were matters of considerable interest to Ward, Sumner, Small, Giddings, Cooley, and Ross, the principals of *Class and American Sociology*. To be sure, none of these earlier scholars displayed the conceptual rigor and analytical prowess of a Weber—all of them (least so in the case of the systematic Small) were markedly discursive theorists. But most of them, as the concluding chapter of this book indicates, were sensitive to the multi-dimensionality of social stratification and were deeply concerned with both the structural manifestations and dynamic role of "class." The re-publication of this account and interpretation of their writings in this field will, I hope, prompt readers to visit—or revisit—the works of the Fathers themselves.

Charles H. Page

Northampton, Massachusetts
March, 1969

I am grateful to E. Digby Baltzell, T. B. Bottomore, Marvin Bressler, Ely Chinoy, Alfred A. Clarke, Jr., Lewis A. Coser, Joseph M. Goldsen, Everett S. Lee, Dennis C. McElrath, Wilbert E. Moore, Ilya Neustadt, Robert A. Nisbet, and Irving M. Zeitlin for their helpful comments on an earlier draft of this review. Several of the specific suggestions of these scholars have been exploited; that they all have not been pursued reflects my biases and limitations. I owe a special debt to Philip Rieff and Hanna Gunther of Schocken Books. Of course, the form and content of the essay are my responsibility.

CHAPTER ONE: THE FATHERS AND THEIR TIMES

THE FATHERS AND THEIR TIMES

1. THE AMERICA OF THE PERIOD

MEN's thoughts should be understood with reference to the cultures in which they take shape. This is true of the views expressed by the Fathers of American sociology: their theories, prophecies, and prejudices cannot be separated from their own world-scene.

In the battalions of America's great Civil War was a young ex-farmer, Lester F. Ward, the first of our pioneer sociologists, who, before his death, saw the science he helped found firmly settled in this country's academic institutions. The intervening years, from 1865 until the beginning of the second decade of this century, were stamped by the most profound changes in America's social history; note must be made of the high points of the period. Within the matrix of the fast-moving historical processes of post-Civil War America were molded the theories of the sociological Fathers. The war itself served as a spur to the kind of thinking that Small and Giddings and Cooley were later to garb in the terminology of their new science. There is no doubt that sociology owes part of its birthright to America's second revolution: "The Civil War and its after-results disturbed the settled status of classes and raised questions concerning settled opinions, and to thinking minds presented the challenge of re-examining some of our fundamental notions." [1]

---

[1] For the convenience of the reader, documentary footnotes appear at the end of the volume. Others are in the text.

The whole period, of which the Civil War marked the beginning and the World War the close, was both laboratory and inspiration of the new science.

This half-century "witnessed the refashioning not only of American industry, but of the whole structure of American society." Manufacturing freed itself from its commercial base; technology made great strides. Industry and business assumed the institutional pattern of the corporation and trust. Unprecedented fortunes were made. America was rapidly becoming urbanized, and in the new cities an industrial proletariat was forming. New problems arose with the influx of hundreds of thousands of workers from Europe.—The class lines of this country were being reshaped.

Economically, it was an epoch of rapid development, patterned by the fluctuations of the business cycle. Between 1866 and 1897 there were, according to Corey, five depressions, totalling seventeen years, and fourteen years of prosperity: there were "long-time factors of economic expansion, which provided increasingly larger markets for goods and capital, and insured, until temporarily limited by depression, the making of increasingly higher profits and their conversion into capital." Increased production, advances in real wages, and the great growth of consumers' goods were outstanding trends.

To these trends was closely linked the mechanization of economic functions. Veblen, a product of this milieu, had good reason to point up the causative role of technological factors: the impetus of advancing techniques in industrial life was profound. The introduction of the machine to manufacture, agriculture, and extraction was paralleled, perhaps excelled, in transportation; the story of the rise of the railroad is one of the most exciting chapters in American history. The society of small producers and farmers of the eighteen-thirties and 'forties, to which has been attributed the creation of the "American Dream," was invaded by a new technology. With some justification Horace Kallen has argued "that industrialization has aborted 'Americanism' as an ideal and has thwarted workers as individuals."

Mr. Spencer's "industrial society" was in the making in America—but not quite as he viewed it. The economic superman—the trust, the monopoly—was coming to maturity. In 1860 there were some 500 millionaires in the United States; by 1892 there were over 4,000. Three years before the turn of the century 82 industrial combinations were capitalized at 1,000 million dollars, and in the succeeding years these figures pyramided. A. M. Simons, writing before the World War, stated that "the panic of 1873 marked the climax and collapse of expanding and competitive industry. . . . The period between the panics of 1873 and 1894 was still fiercely competitive, but it was the beginning of the competition of cannibalistic absorption, not for the conquest of new fields." By 1910, the process of concentration of control was the dominant note in railroads, in steel, in sugar, in copper; this in spite of the series of regulative legislative acts of the Federal government.

As a concomitant of trustification evolved the intricate structure of finance capitalism, with the institution Veblen was to portray so pointedly, absentee ownership. By 1900: "The land of Washington, Franklin, Jefferson, and John Adams had become a land of millionaires and the supreme direction of its economy had passed from the owners of farms and isolated plants and banks to a few men and institutions near the center of its life." "Money power," personalized in the adventurous, but ruthless, activities of Daniel Drew, Commodore Vanderbilt, Jim Fisk, Jay Gould, and Russell Sage, was the central theme of the financial operations described by one author as the "Great Barbecue." By the end of the period the "picturesque rascality" of these earlier titans had grown into the smooth-functioning financial control of the modern vested interests.

These business leaders, aided by a "beneficent government," and often regarded as "heroes" by the populace, "marched from victory to victory in the decades that followed the triumph at Appomattox." These years witnessed the rise to power of a distinct class of the American population; even the settlement of the great western regions, which did benefit large numbers of farmers, primarily served the interests of our big bourgeoisie. Nor was this group's control confined to the economic sphere: it reached into the widest social activities of the American people in ways which Professor Ross set down in his first sociological study, *Social Control*.[2] In 1911, A. M. Simons, viewing American history through the Marxian lens, argued: "At no other time in this country, and never in any other land, has this class [of capitalists] enjoyed such complete domination. Its ideas and ideals made and modeled social institutions. It created a society after its own image, and looked upon its work in bombastic spread-eagleism and pronounced it good."

"In the swift transformation of the whole economic order, the very texture of American society had been recast." Recast: but not without strongly felt discontent and conflicts of serious proportions. A part of labor (and a larger part of agriculture) was on the march; the struggles in which it took part often reached the point of property-destruction and bloodshed. By the time of the infamous Haymarket Affair in 1886, America's economic structure had reached the stage where harmonious industrial relationships and a contented working class were not possible. This discontent was sounded most sharply on those famous battle-grounds of our industrial history: Pittsburg, Haymarket, Homestead, Leadville, Coeur d'Alene.

As early as 1866, the establishment of the National Labor Union reflected the attempt of American workers to solidify their ranks. Superseded, first by the Knights of Labor, and finally by the Gompers-led American Federation of Labor in 1886, the hopes and aspirations of the leading trade-unionists took significant organic form by the 'nineties. But the expansion of organized labor was not a smooth-flowing development: the terrorism of the Molly Maguires in the early years and the struggles of the railroad workers later were but high points in a half-century of labor strife. The pioneer sociologists, living

[2] See Chapter VII, Division 4.

through those tumultuous years, naturally centered a large share of their attention on the problems of class conflict.

This conflict produced its revolutionary elements. By 1860, Marxism had won a few followers in the United States; in 1874, the Social Democratic party was formally organized. Socialism, however, bolstered and diffused by the vast numbers coming from European shores, made little headway among native-born workers. Samuel Gompers, almost from the beginning of his power as leader of the American Federation of Labor, emphatically rejected the doctrine of class-struggle. The social-revolutionary movement of this period, largely a foreign and primarily a German importation, contrasted with the diametrically opposed, but equally radical native anarchism of men like Josiah Warren and Benjamin R. Tucker. Their anarchism, essentially individualistic and indigenous to local traditions, was closer, fundamentally, to the philosophical framework of, say, the distinctly American I.W.W. than the Marxism of the famous *Arbeiter-Zeitung* of Chicago's German workers. Socialism itself, in fact, was cast in the individualistic pattern: "Socialism became a symbol of rebellion, the flag of defiance which every vigorous, independent and courageous personality at odds with the social order unfurled in its face. To say, So-and-so is a Socialist was to say, So-and-so is a fighting, self-assertive, demanding individual, who shouted Socialism as his battlecry of individual freedom."

The rise of labor and the sporadic development of various radicalisms took place in a setting unlike that of the Old World. For this was the half-century during which the frontier found its limits, and during which more and more of the population moved towards the fast-rising cities. It was a period of expansion: in agriculture, in industry, no less than in city-building. The last waves of immigrants found themselves in a society which was turning "its face inward": a society which inspired Frederick Turner's striking treatise, first presented in 1893.[3]

[3] "The Significance of the Frontier in American History," read before the American Historical Association in Chicago.

In terms of economic class, Turner argued, the frontier had served as an expanding area of vertical mobility. The dispossessed, radically individualistic for the most part, won the opportunity of private enterprise: the settlement of the western regions was, in fact, a bulwark of the American Dream.

The farmers of these new lands, together with those who shared their occupation in the older states, represented "an older agrarian America," which could not avoid clashing with the new capitalism. The "eastern plutocracy," with its economic ramifications which stretched across the continent, forced the farmer into conflict with an elaborate middleman organization. In addition, the technological revolution, compelling agrarians to buy new equipment, crop specialization, pyramided land values, the influx of cheap labor, ex-slave and foreign, spurred America's rural people to their last great revolt.

From the 'seventies until the "tremendous Bryan push" in 1896, America witnessed its agrarians marshal their ranks—in the Grange, Greenbackism, the Free Silver movement, Farmers' Alliances, and Populism. Their advocacy of free-silver and a new currency policy, and their desire for railroad regulation, sprang from the pressing need to either increase the prices of their products or reduce their cost. Moreover, the farmers used the tools of "dynamic capitalism itself": they established cooperative associations in an attempt to control prices, and endeavored to use the instrument of the state to promote their own economic interests. Gains were made: a bureau of agriculture, finally organized into an administrative Department, a rural free delivery act, and other legislation favoring the agrarian population. But the force exerted by this great section of American society could not cope successfully with the fast-maturing capitalism of industry and finance. This period, from 1860 to 1920, marked the triumph of our *haute bourgeoisie* and the "final defeat of the traditional agrarianism."

The economic class lines of America had undergone a revolution; but this was not true of the social classes.[4] The economic distance between the nation's economic strata was unparalleled by correlative social distance. Thus John Chamberlain, in discussing the various reform programs towards the close of the period, states: "Class distinctions had not been drawn in hard and fast lines; because of this the prophets of discontent sounded a Babel of conflicting tongues." Their audience was largely a middle class-minded group knit together by the ideological threads of the Common Man. Regardless of the great extremes of wealth and poverty, this country "was still the land of the 'petite bourgeoisie." The middle class attitudes characteristic of the majority of workers, and of those for whom they worked, dominated the agrarian sections as well. These attitudes were highly individualistic, highly competitive: they were epitomized in the latter years, say from 1880, by Horatio Alger's "Rags to Riches." The conscious ties of this great "middle class" were rooted in no common ancestry, but in its individualized hopes and aspirations. This was the "class" quality of the human material which William Graham Sumner eulogized in his "Forgotten Man," [5] and which, it can be argued, inspired Thorstein Veblen's ironic analysis of competition, emulation, and display.[6]

The lack of corporate class lines was one factor accounting for the political trend between the Civil and Spanish-American wars. The presidents of the period were Johnson, Grant, Hayes, Garfield, Arthur, Cleveland, and Harrison; all but Cleveland were Republicans. This party dominated the executive branch

[4] By "economic class" is meant a section of the population which occupies a distinct position *vis-à-vis* the system of economic production; "social class" refers to an intracommunal group possessing a distinct *status* and a consciousness of kind. See Chapter VIII.

[5] See Chapter III, Division 5.

[6] According to some authorities this "middle class" is still the largest class group in America; since 1890, in fact, it has increased in size, according to their argument. See, for example, A. N. Holcombe, *The New Party Politics* (New York 1933); A. M. Bingham, *Insurgent America* (New York 1935). Compare this view with the Marxian analysis of L. Corey in *The Crisis of the Middle Class* (New York 1935).

and the Senate, while the Democrats maintained, for most of the half-century, majorities in the lower house of Congress. The Republican control of the "upper" national ticket resulted from the support of several groups: most of the vested interests, a large share of the established agrarians (note the selection of presidential candidates from the Middle West), veterans of the Union Army, the newly created freedmen of the South, the "spoils" office-holders. Furthermore, the ideological appeals of the Republican party were neatly linked to the events of the time. For their party was Lincoln's; it was the party of "emancipation"; most significantly, it had "saved the union." In the last, was the powerful appeal of national patriotism; it was important that all the Republican candidates, except the unsuccessful Blaine, were war "heroes."

The Republican party used the state to aid the development of economic enterprise through the maintenance of laissez faire on the one hand, and the control of tariffs and the securing of land and financial aid on the other. The Democratic party, without the leadership of the defeated southern aristocracy, and also pledged to laissez faire, found few major issues upon which to base their political campaigns. Until 1896, there was little economic difference in the national platforms of the two parties. But both had their "left-wing" elements: a short-lived Liberal Republican movement appeared in 1872, while the Democratic ranks included many of the militant farm group.

The Democrats gained some victories. Eight of the twelve popularly elected lower houses were Democratic majorities. They placed the "safe and sane" Cleveland into the White House twice. In the South, they defeated the intent of the Fourteenth and Fifteenth Amendments, first through extra-legal measures, and later through such "legal" devices as literacy tests, thereby depriving Negroes of the vote and gaining a solid Democracy below the Mason-Dixon line. Moreover, in many of the rising cities they outdid their Republican opponents in the creation of powerful political machines, the most notable example being Tweed's Tammany Hall in New York.

The corruption and spoils which marked the machine politics of urban life carried into the national sphere. From time to time the exposure or strong suspicion of graft, bribes, and "sell-outs" shocked part of America into a realistic political consciousness. The mail-frauds and the accusations made against people like James Blaine and William Belknap, Grant's Secretary of War, were events bound to be reflected in the critical writing of the period. And the tie between corruption and the powerful economic interests could not be completely hidden; it mattered little to the vested groups which party was in control "as long as the requirements of their political economy were met in a satisfactory manner."

Protests took shape in third-party movements. The Greenbackers polled a million votes in 1878, and the Populists the same number in 1887. Further left were the United Labor party, and the Socialist Labor party which entered the field in 1892. Without political success, they forwarded clear-cut economic criticism, and no doubt were partly responsible for the "concessions" granted the lower income groups. The concessions were few enough, and had little effect on the main trend of economic events. In 1883 a Civil Service Act was passed, but large-scale spoils continued; nor did the Interstate Commerce Act of 1887 and the Sherman Anti-Trust Act of 1890 check the growth of corporations. The Income Tax law of 1894 met very early defeat in the Supreme Court. Not until the Wilson regime of the second decade of the new century did this kind of legislation gain any important vestige of power.

The hectic presidential campaign of 1896 was "the most clearly defined struggle of economic groups" since Lincoln's first election. McKinley, guided by the master politician, Mark Hanna, was elected on a platform of the gold standard and anti-populism. His Democratic opponent, William Jennings Bryan, crusaded in the name of free silver, the income tax, labor, and farmer; his defeat symbolized a triumphant victory for America's business leaders. Before the close of McKinley's years as president, America fought a war with Spain, and started on new political and economic ventures as one of the world's "empires." And in 1900, the death of Bryanism was signalized by the passage of the gold standard law.

The economic and political changes of a society, the new alignments and conflicts, are always mirrored to some extent, at least, in the activities of its intellectuals. As the Beards stress, America was no exception: "the rhetorical discourses associated with the contest were embroidered by new logical, scientific, and factual designs." The social philosophers of the period, both professional and literary, could hardly escape the clash of events: some of them rushed to defend the *status quo* (the Beards name Sumner a leading example); perhaps as large a group assumed the task of social criticism.

Of the widely known figures, the most severe critics of America's growing capitalism were Henry George, Henry Demarest Lloyd, and Edward Bellamy. George, the author of *Progress and Poverty* (1879), which remains today the bible of single tax advocates, was a typical product of traditional American life. Member of a poor family, he fought his way up the "success" ladder: he was sailor, frontiersman, journalist, author, and candidate for New York's mayoralty. Impressed during his stay in California by the effects of the rocketed land values and the monopolization of industry—George witnessed the rise of the Southern Pacific Railroad—he utilized the Ricardian analysis of rent as a weapon against Manchester economics. The attack was bitter, but, he was convinced, in the interest of the greater good: he "humanized the dismal science and brought it home to the common interest." George's advocacy of the single tax was based upon a criticism of capitalism as "radical" as that of socialism, but, unlike the followers of Marx, he visualized no inherent conflict between capital and labor: his framework of reference included no rigid conception of a class dichotomy. But his was "a passionate sympathy for the exploited," a sympathy that won thousands.

Henry Demarest Lloyd was probably more influential than George in laying bare the abuses of the nation's economy. This "father of the muck-rakers," reared in the rigid morality of a Calvinistic home, fought for the amelioration of our social order from the days of his youthful support of free-trade until his first acceptance of socialism. But essentially he was a reformer: "he wanted to reform the social system which we then possessed and toward that end he dug at its cancerous spots." As a journalist and lawyer in the Chicago of the 'seventies and 'eighties, Lloyd surveyed the process of urbanization in its full beat; he saw labor organize economically, and politically in the Socialist Labor Party. As an enemy of injustice, he took the side of labor and struck out against Standard Oil and California's railroad "Big Four" (Huntington, Stanford, Hopkins, Crocker). The Haymarket Affair of 1886 sent him, no doubt, further to the left; during his later years he joined the socialist ranks, although he never fully accepted their doctrines. His *Wealth Against Commonwealth* (1894), unmarked by the interpretive qualities of the works of George or Bellamy, was "a reporter's book of facts," which anticipated the following decade's famous exposures by Ida Tarbell and Lincoln Steffens. And it was in these years, from 1880 to 1910, that Lloyd's social criticism was paralleled in the sociology of Lester Ward, E. A. Ross, and Albion W. Small.

The conditions which inspired *Progress and Poverty* and *Wealth Against Commonwealth* produced Edward Bellamy's classic, *Looking Backward* (1888). A million copies of this utopian novel were sold before 1900, and its publication resulted in the organization of a nation-wide "Nationalist" society. Even so, Bellamy's ideas had less influence in shaping America's social thought than those of George and Lloyd. Bellamy, the son of a clergyman, was dominated by an anti-individualistic ethics from his youngest years; Parrington names him an "incorrigible idealist." His sympathies with the underprivileged are clear in an early novel, *The Duke of Stockbridge;* his much later social treatise, *Equality* (1897), vigorously attacks capitalistic society and seeks the extension of democracy into our economic life. There is little reason to believe that Bellamy was influenced by socialist theory, although his *Looking Backward* portrays a highly-regimented industrial society—one great trust was the logical result of economic forces. This "horrible cockney dream," as William Morris labeled Bellamy's utopia, was unique in its abandonment of the ideals of the older agrarian individualism. But *Looking Backward* stands as an example of the works of those individuals "who were concerned for a juster social order than the Gilded Age dreamed of. . . ."

Bellamy's almost revolutionary attack on America's acquisitive society was the most extreme protest of its *literati*. The others, however, were not silent: "Their protest was usually aimed at little more than minor alterations of the rules of the game, but it was a protest, and it grew as time passed." Those great figures of the period, Walt Whitman and Mark Twain, each reflected, far differently to be sure, the social dynamics of a changing society. Whitman was "the poet and prophet of a democracy that the America of the Gilded Age was daily betraying." His bold, full-blooded poetry wedded the individualistic Jacksonian radicalism of his youth with the growing collective radicalism of his last years; he was a rebel all his life and advised rebellion in the interests of "selfhood" and brotherhood. His faith was in democracy, but even his boundless poet's faith was troubled by the events of the 'eighties. In 1888, Whitman announced: "I seem to be reaching for a new politics —for a new economy, I don't quite know what, but for something."

Mark Twain, "the very embodiment of the turbulent frontier," was less sure of his feelings. But, like Whitman, he loved democracy; his love took a twisted form in his later books, *The Mysterious Stranger* and *What is Man?*—"a fierce satire of disillusion." His works, taken together, combine the qualities of the changing west that produced Twain: admiration of the "gaudy frontier spirit," an idealism linked with the personal ambition of the adventurer, a contempt for conscious dishonesty, a disregard for *institutional* problems, rebellion against the mores of tradition, a robust individualism, a "passionate republicanism." (His republicanism was that of Lincoln's: of the man, not property.) And, finally, the disillusioned acceptance of a mechanistic fatalism. In Twain's life ran the birth, youth, maturity, and death of America's frontier individualistic democracy.

A more articulate social criticism came from the pens of the intelligentsia of literature: from Wendell Phillips, who was deeply concerned with the problems of the worker; from George William Curtis, who decried political laxity and urged drastic civil service reforms; from Godkin, liberal and founder of the *Nation*, whose criticism of the rising plutocracy was the result of his strong faith in laissez faire and confidence in the man of learning. Even James Russell Lowell, the most fêted bard of the period, asked in 1876 if America had become a "Kakistocracy." And especially William Dean Howells, the "reporter of his generation." Howells, with his "realism of the commonplace," was sensitive to the individualistic arguments of the majority of Americans and the collective doctrines of socialism. He appreciated the significance of both in interpreting his nation's changes.

These changes were placing their mark on the novels, even as early as the 'eighties. The political sphere was fictionized in Twain's *Gilded Age* (1873), Crawford's *An American Politician* and the *Democracy* (1881) of Henry Adams. Labor on the march provided John Hay the theme of *The Bread-Winners* (1882), an "economic novel" written from the vantage point of capital. Boyesen and others began to frame their writing in a deterministic sociology: the "sociological novel" was in its genesis in this country.

In 1883, E. W. Howe's *The Story of a Country Town* anticipated the novel-theme that Sinclair Lewis seized upon several decades later. The "agrarian crusader," Hamlin Garland, stated the interests of the farmers of the West in powerful fiction until the agrarian movement itself was defeated. M. A. Foran's *The Other Side* (1886), a pro-labor novel, stressed the theme of class division in industry. In *Through the Eye of a Needle*, Howells, shortly after 1900, voiced his reaction to the social order in semi-utopian terms. These works, and others, cleared the way for the clearly pronounced indignation of the new "realists." The harshest treatment accorded the nation's economic rulers came with the muckraking novels: Frank Norris' *The Pit* and *The Octopus*, and *The Financier* and *The Titan* of Theodore Dreiser.

Among the writers whose function was amusement were several who sensed the social upheavals of the times. Eugene Field's pointed humor did not hide his awareness of the "conspicuous" values of the new ruling class, or the doubtful practices of politicians. "Under the lackadaisical bantering and uproarious explosions of Artemus Ward often lay piercing observations on the paradoxes of the American republic." More "piercing," and with far greater insight, spoke Peter Dunne's "Mr. Dooley" at the end of the century—a Lincoln Steffens in the guise of a jester.

In the stream of social criticism which flowed during the second half of the nineteenth century, expressed implicitly and, at times, explicitly, a special quality stands out: most of the writers were *reformers*. "To the reformer," unlike the revolutionist, "the *status quo* is essentially healthy but a little out of gear in this spot or that." The reformism of this group was "middle class"; a large share of it was framed in the Christian faith. "The middle classes and the church," remarks F. C. Palm, "united in common opposition to the radicals." But a large segment of this united front also turned its attack on the ruling classes; this was especially true of American "Social Christianity." For the most part, the philosophy of Social Christianity assumed "an underlying harmony of interests between the working class and the owning class," and looked upon the function of the church as that of "impartial arbitrator" in the conflicts between economic strata.[7] The Christian reform point

---

[7] There were exceptions: men like Wendell Phillips and W. D. P. Bliss who viewed economic strife as a form of war and gave their support to the side of

of view colored a sizeable share of academic social science, including much of early American sociology. In this connection, Albion W. Small remarked in 1890 somewhat typically: "Jesus was, after all, the profoundest economist."

Reformism, in its strongest tones, however, appeared in the decade following 1900 with the revelations of the muckrakers. The development of journalism from independent enterprise to "big-business" status—a development correlated with technological advance and the growing dependence of the press upon advertising—was symbolized by the papers of Joseph Pulitzer and William Randolph Hearst. During the 'eighties and 'nineties these two publishers had introduced "yellow journalism" to the American public, which combined sensationalism with a frank attack on money-plutocracy. Pulitzer spoke in the name of the "aristocracy of labor" and the middle classes, and, with Hearst, advocated heavy income taxation and political reform. These years also witnessed the innovation of the semi-popular magazine: *Harper's Weekly*, *The Ladies' Home Journal*, and, most significantly, *McClure's*.

For it was S. S. McClure, "the greatest magazine genius America has produced," who, perhaps inadvertently, gave muckraking its start. McClure knew that the most important issue of the day was the trustification of business life; the persons he chose to probe this sphere were superlative selections: Ida Tarbell, Ray Stannard Baker, Lincoln Steffens. Tarbell's story of Standard Oil is now a classic. Baker uncovered the inner activities of the railroads and the practices of "labor" organizations. Steffens set down the mechanisms of the political machines of St. Louis, Minneapolis, Cleveland, Cincinnati, Chicago, Philadelphia, and New York. McClure's model soon had its imitators: *Everybody's Magazine* featured Charles Ed-

---

labor; later, the Reverend George D. Herron, who "accepted the class struggle as a fact of history" and reworked his theology into something closely akin to Marxian philosophy. The most extreme religious reaction to the class conflict of the day was the short-lived Christian Commonwealth Colony (1896-1900) which renunciated an economically divided society by establishing a classless community.

ward Russell's analysis of the beef trust; Samuel Hopkins exposed the patent medicine "racket" in *Collier's*. This muckraking was thorough: it was "always documented, sane, 'proved' to the last fact." (There were many, of course, as Hearst in the *Cosmopolitan*, who sensationalized muckraking by injecting it with the popular "yellow journalism.") No wonder that the sociologist, E. A. Ross, could publish in 1907 *Sin and Society: An Analysis of Latter-Day Iniquity*.

Ross was but one of many academicians whose interests were shaped by the new social events: "The *sturm und drang* of that gusty pre-War period had its inevitable impact . . . on a widely diversified group of scholars who were, nevertheless, united in their common feeling for the pathology of the American spirit." Albion Small, in reviewing a half-century of American sociology (in 1926) spoke of "the revolution which has taken place within the last twenty-five years, in all thinking about human experience, through shifting the emphasis from the assumed individual agent to the *group* in which persons are now seen to be subordinate factors." In the same article Small listed the various organizations, scientific, reform, and action, which were created between 1865 and 1912 to consider, essentially, the new social problems caused by changing class lines. The Beards include "the haunting queries of academic economists" among the factors leading to the formation of the Social Democratic Party in 1900.

The most important of these queries were found in the investigations of the social scientists who taught and studied at Johns Hopkins University. Herbert B. Adams and Richard T. Ely who came to this institution (established in 1876) stimulated an interest in social phenomena and the *facts* of history in a large number of prominent scholars; the socio-economists, Patten and Veblen, and the sociologists, Small and Ross, were among them. Ely himself was dominated by a moral reform point of view, but, with most of the others, he understood the history of his times in terms of economic class divisions.

These scholars at Johns Hopkins, in so far as they were investigating society on a level more in keeping with its contemporary qualities, were anticipating the wealth of studies which appeared after 1900. The philosophers of the new America, inspired by the changing conditions of their nation on the one hand, and, on the other, by the works of the European theorists, boldly declared in favor of new approaches. In 1899 appeared Thorstein Veblen's *Theory of the Leisure Class* and John Dewey's *School and Society*, the one at least implicitly directed against the "conspicuous" values of the new plutocracy, the other a scholarly plea for education geared to service in a democracy. The following thirteen years witnessed the publication of Gustavus Myers' *History of the Great American Fortunes* (1909) and *History of the Supreme Court* (1912), Herbert Croly's *The Promise of American Life* (1909), and J. Allen Smith's *The Spirit of American Government* (1907). Between the years 1912 and 1914 followed Walter Weyl's *The New Democracy*, Charles Beard's *An Economic Interpretation of the Constitution*, Walter Lippmann's *A Preface to Politics*, and Louis Brandeis' *Other People's Money*. This country's political and economic institutions met with severe criticism by these authors. But, like their contemporaries, the sociologists Small, Giddings, Cooley, and Ross, they were seeking the best in our industrialized democracy, which they hoped could be channelled for the broadest social uses.

With all its faults, this period of our history released a large number of scholars from the close ties to church or class found in an earlier age. "Provincial America had been theological-and political-minded; but with the staying of the dispersion and the creation of an urban psychology, the ground was prepared for the reception of new philosophies that came from the contemplation of the laws of the material universe." The heaviest impact of these new philosophies was upon the social sciences, which, in breaking away from the "academic sterility" of the older economics and political science, made their way into American universities through the "back door."

Moreover, many of the younger social scientists were studying in European centers in the 'seventies and 'eighties, where they were confronted with the provocative theories of Comte, Spencer, Bagehot, and others. They were especially influenced by the evolutionary doctrines of Darwin and Spencer, which "offered the starting point for dynamic speculation in every department of thought and action." Parrington has stated that Herbert Spencer and John Stuart Mill, but not Comte, shaped the thinking of American scholars; the point is supported by Dr. Barnes and Professor Becker in their recent work.[8]

Spencerianism, however, was not all-dominant. For many of the "masters" studied in Germany under such teachers as Mommsen, von Ranke, Wundt, and Wagner. Veblen, at least, was considerably influenced by Marx; and the theories of Ratzenhofer and Gumplowicz found their place in the works of Ward and Small. It was his contact with Schmoller and Sombart in Germany, in fact, that aroused Small's interest in the problems of class and class conflict. Herbert Spencer had his adherents in John Fiske and Sumner and Giddings, but Spencerianism, which was often linked with laissez faire economics (even as Spencer would have it), became the object of attack for many others, including Ward, Small, Cooley, and Ross. To them, Spencer's evolutionism was too often used as a bulwark of the *status quo* which, in their various ways, they hoped to alter. The sociologists of this period have sometimes been aptly described as "the left wing of the new economists."

There is no doubt of the "left wing" quality of the sociologists, if by that is meant their recognition of the significance of class divisions and conflicts in community life. The dominant characteristic shared by these six authors is their obvious con-

[8] "The chronological order of Comte and Spencer was, as it were, reversed . . . the pre-Civil War fruits of Comte's teaching withered because they were the outgrowth of a social system that was soon uprooted, whereas Spencer's evolutionary and individualistic doctrines coincided with the vogue of Darwinism, the growth of biological science, and the tremendous birth of expansion through private enterprise that characterized the period between the spanning of the continent by rail in the middle 'sixties and the 'passing of the frontier' in the 'nineties."

cern with class phenomena. In this they stand out sharply from most of their fellow academicians in the other social sciences.

2. THE FATHERS OF AMERICAN SOCIOLOGY

Something has been said of the conditions which surrounded the genesis of the notions and theories of the authors whose views are discussed in the six remaining chapters of this study, and of the other thought-phenomena which sprang from the same general social milieu. A. W. Small, one of the Fathers, has suggested such a treatment: "American sociology has been one expression among many" which should be viewed as "part of the orderly unfolding of native conditions." Before examining the specific ideas of these men, a few points must be noted concerning the general qualities of this group of pioneer sociologists.

None of the Fathers was a specialist. They were all social scientists in the broadest sense, their interests ranging over philosophy, history, economics, and politics. Most of them considered sociology a general science, at least with respect to its data. Ward, trained in the natural sciences and a contributor to them, surprised his colleagues by describing one of his courses at Brown as "a survey of all knowledge." Sumner and Small added an intensive study of history and economics to an early preparation in theology; their religious training left its mark on their later sociology. Giddings, Cooley, and Ross began as economists (Giddings also taught political science) before adopting the newer discipline. A wide erudition typified all of them: to the greatest extent in the cases of Ward and Giddings, perhaps least so with Cooley; though Cooley compensated with a thorough knowledge of literature.

The breadth of scholarship of each man was the result of long study. The Fathers all, sooner or later, had wide European contacts; at least Ward, Giddings, and Ross gained high prestige in European academic circles. Sumner and Small studied in Europe; the former's *Social Classes* won the attention of outstanding British scholars. The years these sociologists devoted to study had their results in extensive publication: the length of their bibliographies would discourage many young students today. Each found time to write several volumes, as well as numerous articles for the social science periodicals; Small was almost personally responsible for the growth of the *American Journal of Sociology*.

Three of them came to academic social sciences from other fields: Ward from his work in several governmental bureaus in Washington (his last position there was that of chief paleontologist of the United States Geological Survey); Sumner from the clergy and religious newspaper work; Giddings from a wide experience in journalism. Small, Cooley, and Ross were academicians from the beginning, though Small had studied theology, and Cooley and Ross had taken their advanced degrees in economics. But these masters by no means confined their activities to university life and scholarly pursuits. Except Cooley, who seldom ventured outside the academic sphere, they carried their theories and convictions into a diversity of civic activities: Ward in political articles and speeches; Sumner in public debate and political office; Small in religious and civic organizations; Giddings in extensive journalism and lectures, and in public educational posts; Ross in articles and books, and in energetic participation in the affairs of the day. They were all keenly aware of the changes taking place in our political, economic, and social institutions, and they all hoped that their science would aid in the solution of the nation's social problems. The problems provoked by class shifts and conflicts gained their earnest attention, which resulted, according to J. L. Gillin, in the beginnings of an adequate analysis of social classes.

These six pioneers possessed certain similar interests and characteristics, but the differences among them are of as much importance in presenting their respective views. Their methodologies differed; so did their specific foci of attention.[9] With

[9] These differences are discussed in the following chapters.

respect to their interest in class and social problems, their differences in sympathy and background are as important.

Of the six, Sumner and Giddings can be classified as the most ardent defenders of the *status quo*. These two, both of whom paid major allegiance to the notions of Herbert Spencer, were products of New England. Dogmatism and extreme conservatism, which have characterized this section of the nation, combined in Sumner and Giddings with the values of work, thrift, and snobbishness, also typical of New England. Both men expressed great admiration for the works of Benjamin Franklin, who has been named "the father of American bourgeois concepts." Sumner, more so than Giddings, was motivated by the "Protestant ethic" and faith in individualistic enterprise; he has been listed with J. B. Clarke as a leading representative of the academic "counter-reformation" of the late nineteenth century.

Small's early training and general background were similar to Sumner's and Giddings'. He expressed, however, during his long stay at Chicago, quite a different point of view and range of sympathies. No doubt Small's first-hand experiences with the dynamic events of Chicago itself and his thorough knowledge of the European social theorists led him to a position far left of his more conservative fellow-sociologists. His faith was in a democracy which, he argued, must go beyond the political, into the economic life of the national community.[10]

The most ardent exponents of a broad democracy were Ward, Cooley, and Ross. Their viewpoint was unquestionably linked with the fact that they were all of the Middle West. "The Middle West," state Odum and Moore, "is still largely classless and democratic. All men are equal (except the Mexican, Negro) economically and socially. Hence out of these states come the protests against trusts and monopolies, the plea for a reformistic return to economic equality." Such pro-democratic protest characterized the writings of these three: in bold tones in the statements of Ward and Ross, and somewhat milder in

[10] See Chapter IV, Division 4.

Cooley's works. Plutocracy of any kind, they declared, can not be tolerated.

The most penetrating analysis of plutocratic control was provided by a contemporary of these sociologists, also a product of the agrarian Middle West, Thorstein Veblen. Veblen's experiences touched those of the masters of sociology at several points: he studied at Johns Hopkins, and at Yale under Sumner; he taught at Chicago with Small and W. I. Thomas, and at Stanford where Ross had been. At Chicago, he became acquainted with Ward and Ross.

Veblen was an evolutionary social philosopher whose several volumes drove home the contrast and conflict between the "predatory" and "industrious" classes. His root distinction was the dichotomy between "business," "vested interests," and "kept classes," on the one side, and "industry," "common man," and "working class," on the other. He found the basis of this division in society's traditional property rights, and the causation of the separation of classes in its technological understructure. Exploitation, Veblen argued, stems from the state of the industrial arts. He set down the intricacies of the class domination of "culture": of leisure, art, philosophy. And he emphasized the vested interests' manipulation of the state. He believed that the machine produced in the worker an ideology of quantitative discipline and skepticism, while "business" practices kept the absentee owners conservative; the latter found their rationale in the "traditional rights" of history.

These major themes were provocative, but Veblen's influence on his contemporaries was limited by his unique style and peculiar erudition. Many of the historians, philosophers, and sociologists, however, were stimulated by his theories. Ward, for example, became acquainted with Veblen through Small at Chicago, and as a result of the laudatory remarks of E. A. Ross. Ward considered his review of Veblen's *Theory of the Leisure Class* the best one of his career; he recommended Veblen for an important government post and for membership in the exclusive Institut International de Sociologie. Veblen admired

Ward's scholarship, praising the latter's *Dynamic Sociology* and *Pure Sociology*. They did not accept each other's theories completely, but their mutual influence is apparent. Ward's early treatment of class "deception" anticipated Veblen's analysis of the leisure class, which, in turn, was employed by Ward in his later books.

Veblen's strongest support, in this group, came from Ross. Ross made extensive use of the former's leisure class materials and of the distinction between the "pecuniary" and "industrial" employments. Ross also praised Veblen's arguments favoring the emancipation of women. Sumner, one of Veblen's teachers at Yale, inspired in him "a deep and unqualified admiration," though Sumner's economics met his withering attack. Sumner copied Veblen's language in later years in describing leisure class values. Small and Cooley also utilized his "conspicuous" concepts; Small likewise took over his analysis of fashion. Veblen, however, found little of value in Small's works, regarding him, while at Chicago, as an administrative official rather than an "intellectual equal." Giddings and Veblen had little sympathy for each other, the latter finding Giddings' Darwinism and imperialism highly distasteful.

The force of Veblen's thought, which has been widely recognized only in recent years, was felt by most of the Fathers, although none of them was prepared to fully accept his views. All of these scholars, however, like the author of *The Theory of the Leisure Class*, recognized the significance of the study of class for social science. The following chapters present their attempts to deal with class phenomena.

CHAPTER TWO: LESTER FRANK WARD
(1841-1913)

LESTER FRANK WARD

1. INTRODUCTION

LESTER F. WARD, perhaps the most distinguished of the Fathers of American sociology, is associated with certain well-known doctrines: an energetic attack on the Spencerian evolutionary thesis; emphasis on the role of the "intelligence" of the individual in social history; elaboration of the "social forces"; the concept of "telic" change; the importance given to the Gumplowicz-Ratzenhofer thesis of race conflict; formulation of the concept of "collective telesis" and its social end, "sociocracy"; and, most importantly, the faith he placed in the socially therapeutic value of education. These doctrines are so much a part of the history of the discipline of sociology that their elaboration is not necessary. The essential task here is to discover Ward's conception of social class: to abstract from his voluminous writings the materials directly related to the subject at hand.

An author's major theses, the core of his writings, can be easily warped into misconception when a part is removed from the whole and presented for consideration out of context. And such procedure is imposed on the student interested in Ward's ideas on class. For, while he wrote much on the subject, he did not for the most part give it special treatment. One must seek materials which are interwoven with the many doctrines that made up his elaborate system of sociology. It is necessary, then, if distortion is to be kept to a minimum, to place some emphasis upon the relationship between Ward's class ideas and his entire system.

Ward was a unique product of the American life of his times. "A product of the frontier, born and bred in poverty," he rose to intellectual heights that placed him among the foremost thinkers of his day. He has been named, with Comte and Spencer, one of the founders of sociology, and one of Europe's leading sociological figures, his contemporary, Gumplowicz, wrote of him an "appreciation" which amounted to an eulogy. It is true that by the time Ward reached his later years he was surrounded by scholars of equal stature, but, as a younger man, he towered above his countrymen in the social sciences. It required several years and devoted work on the part of his early disciple, Albion W. Small, to secure a reading audience for *Dynamic Sociology*. Ward's breadth of scholarship, his keen insight, were the necessary qualities of his progression from an unknown student of no means to high rank in a new and important science. He gave sociology, in this country at any rate, a good send-off.

During these years Europe, especially Germany, was providing content and stimulus to Americans working in the social sciences. Ward, however, did not follow the rather common pattern of absorbing the philosophical and economic doctrines of strictly foreign scholars. His erudition was great but it was "learned at home." This essentially native background and experience help to explain one aspect of his writing. Gumplowicz says, "the practical American crops out in Ward, in the fact that he cannot think of a science, even the most abstract, without application. Ward is not willing to entertain the idea of a 'pure' science as an end in itself." This utilitarian quality, so pronounced in all his works, led Ward into the field of class. Growing up in America's new West, and under conditions of near poverty which demanded of him manual as well as mental work, he was a strong advocate of equality of opportunity for all. Ward's first forty years were marked by

early contact with rough frontier life, with participation, un-
happily concluded by severe wounds, in the Civil War, and
with the acquirement of a hard-earned self-education.[1] The
value he later ascribed to education as the major ameliorative
process in society, and his insistence that it should be universally
provided, very likely derived in part from his own struggle.
During these years, he supported his family, served for a time
as editor of the *Iconoclast*, and attained advanced academic
degrees. This post-war period contained a psychology of revolt
and general skepticism concerning the established order. Unquestionably such an environment helped provide direction for
much of Ward's thinking about class and social problems.

Stratification, economic and social, necessarily demanded
consideration from those interested in the structure and changes
of the current society. The America of the last three decades
of the nineteenth century was marked by conflicts that could
not escape Ward. His sympathies were never hidden: he "re-
peatedly indicated his awareness of class exploitation and expressed his sympathy with the rising proletariat." He recognized that the great majority of his countrymen had little
opportunity for development in the face of economic exploitation and educational restrictions. He endorsed, for the most
part, the attempts of the lower ranks to better their lot. The
awareness and sympathy of Ward concerning class and class
change have been thoroughly presented by Walter Bodenhafer,
who otherwise places Ward in the "individualistic" school.

Although his *Dynamic Sociology* was destroyed by the
Russian censors and his name has on occasion been linked with
Marxism, Ward's "socialism" was a brand of its own. Professor
Ross emphasizes the point: "While many policies that are
called 'socialistic' find their justification in Ward's philosophy
of progress, he was no Marxist. . . . He declined to recognize
changes in the technique of production as a prime motor of

---

[1] He subsequently worked for the federal government in the division of
geology, and became a recognized authority in paleontology. His training in
natural science no doubt partly accounted for the synthetic and genetic evolutionary quality of his sociology.

progress, nor was he willing to stress class struggle as Marx did. While attaching great importance to economic factors in history, he was no historical materialist. To him, not the better distribution of wealth but the better distribution of knowledge is a first essential to social betterment." Neither Marx nor Engels appear in the selected bibliographies of any of his major works, and only once is Marx's name found in the general indexes. There seems to be justification in Dr. Bernhard Stern's accusation as to his "surprising ignorance of Marxian socialist literature." His knowledge of Marxian theory, so far as his writings indicate, was based upon the essays of John Stuart Mill. Statements can be extracted from his work that, standing isolated, would seem to place Ward in the broad camp of socialism, but examination of any of his major books denies him fellowship with the exponents of the class struggle and demands a more careful analysis of his own class theory.

2. Origins of Class, Caste, and State

Ward's discussion of "origins" serves well as an introduction to his more general treatment of class. Systematic presentation of this topic was a relatively late development in his life and work as we find no thorough analysis of class origins in his earlier books (*Dynamic Sociology, The Psychic Factors of Civilization, Outlines of Sociology*). But, dating from the publication of *Pure Sociology* (1903) the topic received attention. Gumplowicz and Ratzenhofer had been elaborating the group-conflict concept, and Ward seized upon race-conflict and conquest as the explanatory theory of the origins of caste, class, and state. He confronted the problem of weaving the conflict theory of the "pessimists" into the pattern of his own system, and this he solved even to the satisfaction of one of its exponents. "I have never looked for very considerable results from any sort of collectivism. I have never given myself over to hope that collectivism could bring freedom and happiness to mankind. . . . Before Ward's arguments, however, I was obliged to lay down my arms." Thus, after several hours of discussion with Ward concerning the problems of group origins and changes, Gumplowicz stated this appraisal. Ward reciprocated in kind by declaring that Gumplowicz and Ratzenhofer had unquestionably established the origins of social organization, including class, caste, and state, in race struggle. This doctrine, indeed, Ward considered the most significant contribution thus far made to sociology. He did not claim to add to the theory, but viewed his own analysis as a reemphasis of the "truth" of race conflict and a demonstration of the fact that such conflict illustrates the operation of the "cosmic principle" of "synergy" in social life. When specifically devoting an article to social classes, Ward argued in his introductory remarks that "approaching this problem from the new point of view we find that it constitutes an integral part of the general social process inaugurated by the race struggle."

Typically, he borrowed from biology and conceived of a process of *social karyokinesis* which purported to describe the steps in the origin and development of class, state, and national community. Following carefully Gumplowicz's *Rassenkampf* and Ratzenhofer's *Sociologische Erkenntnis*, Ward outlined the following steps: "1. *Subjugation* of one race by another. 2. Origin of *caste*. 3. Gradual mitigation of this condition, leaving a state of great individual, social, and political *inequality*. 4. Substitution for purely military subjection of a form of *law*, and origin of the idea of legal *right*. 5. Origin of the *state*, under which all classes have both rights and duties. 6. Cementing of the mass of heterogeneous elements into a more or less homogeneous *people*. 7. Rise and development of a sentiment of *patriotism* and formation of a nation." An explanation was also presented for the cultural antagonism, the high degree of social distance, that prevails between the castes; for conquering groups view "with contempt" those they have subjected. Conquest necessarily breeds inequality and disdain on the part of the victors, for before the conquest the races were "thoroughly heterogeneous," possessing entirely different cultures. This now well-known historical theory was extended by Ward to include even contemporary class systems. He suggested that the four "estates" of European history "correspond well to the four great castes of India"; that the ancient Greek class order was the result of conquest; that the same phenomenon took place in Polynesia; that, in fact, all the present-day classes are the outgrowth of race conflict. This conflict is a constant dynamic of history (with results both "fruitful" and evil): "Races, states, peoples, nations are always forming, always aggressing, always clashing and clinching, and struggling for the mastery, and the long, painful, wasteful, but always fruitful gestation must be reviewed and repeated again and again." A cessation of race struggle means a cessation of "progress," and, in early society, the absence of race struggle betokens social decay.

Fortunately, perhaps, for his argument, Ward used "race" in a sense that, today, would hardly bear ethnological scrutiny. For him the term was "sufficiently vague and comprehensive" to be used as a general term for the great variety of social groups that were formed "during the process of social differentiation." The period of "social differentiation" was an early one in human history, and yet those groups born in prehistoric times were the conflicting elements that led to the caste and class organization of society. While there is no doubt that conquest and consequent subjugation has played a role in the formation of certain class systems,[2] it is difficult to employ this principle to account for all such systems. Little is known, in fact, of the beginnings of caste. When restricted to an early period of social development, "social differentiation" is an unfortunate expression. As Ward pointed out emphatically, the process of differentiation is continuous, and the factors involved in the process cannot be restricted to race, or even be referred to race as the basal item in the process.[3] Ward's own works illustrate this criticism; it was unfortunate that he was so influenced by the European doctrine of race conflict.

[2] See, for example, F. Oppenheimer, *The State* (New York 1914).
[3] See, for example, C. C. North, *Social Differentiation* (Chapel Hill 1926).

The process of *social karyokinesis*, the conflict of early groups, brings into existence not only an order of caste, but the most important of social organizational forms: law, the state, and national community. While historical anthropologists might question the simplicity of Ward's explanation of these developments, his reasoning on the surface is convincing. The problem of maintaining the conditions of inequality, the "difficulty, cost and partial failure attending the constant and unremitting exercise of military power over the acts of the conquered race ultimately becomes a serious charge upon the conquering race." When it is discovered that "authority must be generalized," that taboo acts may be classified, and that the "economy" of the situation demands this kind of general regulation, the basis is laid for the institution of law and law's resultant, a "degree of liberty." The creation of the legal institution leads to its associational agent, the state. The latter is, in a sense, a synthesis resulting from the conflict between conquered and conquering. Both groups are dominated by "egoistic" interests, but they "equilibrate each other": the "economy" of the governing class and the "resignation" of the governed. "Concessions" from the former and "assistance" from the latter produce the state association.

This process makes of the state the product of a kind of social contract, an agency of the community which, to a degree, is the arbiter of the disputes which arise between the classes of society. This is obviously a conception remote from the Marxian teachings, is, in fact, a doctrine which has served often as an object for their attack. Ward extended this argument to his analysis of the contemporary state, and blended it with his "applied sociology" in which the "sociocracy" of the future was conceived.[4]

The state is not the end object of the synthetic process described above. But the state plays a role in the inter-assimilation of the conflicting races which allows the creation of a "people,"

---

[4] Note that the state, following this argument, is not the instrument of a class of society

which is a "synthetic creation" rather than a "mechanical mixture." The most important agent in this stage of the synthetic process is "interest," and among the various interests the economic dominates. Irrespective of race lines, division of labor involving the formation of specialized economic groups founded upon business skills takes place. The advance of intra-associational contacts furthers the assimilation. The physical and moral interdependence of the two groups, conquered and conquerors, particularly in time of danger from outside attack, and finally, "social chemistry" (biological intermixture), also aid in the formation of a people. This stage reaches its final form with the development of national community sentiment, marked by value symbols of common interest, by attachment to a place of living, and by patriotism.

Systems of classes, states, and peoples are also structured through the operation of *social forces*—the latter one of Ward's best known doctrines. In the revised classification of these forces in *Pure Sociology*, the major categories are the physical and spiritual, the former being divided into "ontogenetic" (seeking pleasure and avoiding pain) and "phylogenetic" (sexual and consanguineal). The detailed discussion of the ontogenetic forces reveals the origins and functions of exploitation, slavery, labor, property, production, and social distribution. These phenomena are so directly related to the origins and development of classes that a special consideration of them is required.

Ward believed that all economic processes originate in exploitation. Cannibalism was one of the earliest forms of exploitation, but accompanying race conflict more efficient exploitive means were devised, including the enslavement of women, warriors, and workers. The caste order converted the conquered race into a servile group and the victors became the "leisure class." Slavery was essentially economic, and the part played by this institution was a necessary and useful force of social evolution. (The modern remnants of slavery earned Ward's condemnation: he referred to them as "social vestiges.")

Slavery, in fact, was responsible for the innovation of labor: the latter appeared as a relatively late accomplishment of man. "In a word, nothing short of slavery could ever have accomplished this. This was the social mission of human slavery— to convert mere activity into true labor." "True labor" is not dependent upon any inborn capacity of man: that capacity is the result of centuries of learning in the school of slavery. It is important that the "ruling classes" were but a small part of the population; the slaves, the laborers, were the many. And it was *by virtue of* countless generations of the exploited becoming trained to labor that modern industrialism became possible. Ward, insisting that conflict-produced slavery was the first great step in the "regime of status," and that militarism provided the foundations of industrialism, offered an evolutionary theory of historical change which qualified considerably Herbert Spencer's famous thesis.

Stemming also from exploitation in the line of economic developments is property. Ward, like others of his time, conceived of an early communal system of property ownership— the "protosocial" form. But, with the coming of race conflict and subjugation, the "metasocial" system of individual possession began. First, the ownership of women and land, and then the various other "properties," live stock, technical equipment, etc., fell into the hands of the conquerors, the ruling class. In this connection, Ward criticized the conception of a simple dichotomy of classes. "Both these classes must also be conceived as thoroughly heterogeneous." Large segments of both classes enjoy the same status with respect to property ownership, and together comprise the element which, with its constant intermingling, forms the basis of a "common people." At this stage, also, the state performs one of its essential functions: the protection and guarantee of possession.

Property, considered as a social force, wields its greatest influence as an incentive to accumulation. Without the latter, the division of labor is impossible: man must remain in a "primitive" condition. The pursuit of wealth becomes a means of attaining pleasure, and this new desire finally becomes an end in itself: "the supreme passion of mankind." Ward guarded against an ethical condemnation of such a materialistic conception. "All the good there is in material civilization" is due to this force. The moralist may frown upon it but the sociologist must assign it primary importance in history. Nor did Ward predict or urge a social order lacking the incentive of accumulation, though his analysis of production and social distribution, the creations of the property force, reveals him as a "reformer."

Consistently, he opposed the Spencerian evolutionism which made of the contemporary social order a "natural" product of forces outside man's control. He was eager to refute those writers who considered the present system of classes as being simply the end result of a process which had placed the fit above and the incompetent below. While arguing that conflict and conquest initiated caste and class, he emphatically denied that military success could be considered an index to superiority. Such a view was inconsistent with his "applied sociology" and his plea for universal education. The belief that class differentiation is a "natural" situation provoked the remark that "this idea still clings to the mind of man, and modern social classes are conceived to be marked off from one another by nature." Ward used strong language in condemning Sumner's *What Social Classes Owe to Each Other*, a book which emphasized the "natural order" viewpoint and pleaded for a strict laissez faire procedure. Born in conflict and conquest, social classes were the result of man's action, and Ward believed that man's action could also destroy this differentiation.

It has been shown that Ward opposed schemes that divided society into only two major classes. In his treatment of the origins of law, the state, and the "people" he emphasized the role played by those segments of the conquered and conquerors that did not correspond to the ideal types of either of the groups. We are reminded here of the oft-repeated principle of the Aristotelian mean: the middle group which possesses the virtues of both and the vices of neither of the two extreme divisions of society. In one place, at least, in discussing origins, Ward frankly stated that the economic affairs of newly created societies are conducted by "the intelligent elements of both the conquering and conquered races," and that the continuance of the community depends upon this middle class element. This confidence placed in the "middle class" is typical of many contemporary American scholars,[5] and is to be found more than once in Ward's discussion of contemporary society.

3. The Class Structure of Society

Ward was considerably preoccupied with the phenomenon of social differentiation. Not a volume failed to stress the fact that society in general, as well as the particular society of which he was a member, is stratified into groups designated as classes. If one follows chronologically from *Dynamic Sociology* (1883) through his works to *Applied Sociology* (1906), it is clear that the class order, which commanded his attention and led to Ward's program of educational reform presented in his original two volumes, remained the object of major consideration in his last full book. Similarly, a number of his shorter articles reveal the same interest.

Dynamic Sociology warns its readers in the first few pages of what is to follow: "the condition of society is at all times . . . bad, the degree of suffering everywhere witnessed is . . . great." And a few pages later: "There still remain the overworked millions on the one hand, and the unemployed millions on the other. There are still all the depths of ignorance, poverty, drudgery, and nameless misery that have ever been the baneful concomitants of human civilization." Class society, he argued, ruthlessly subjects the mass of men and confines the chances of contentment to a few. There are many similar statements which indicate Ward's conception of a class-divided world. Even in his milder-toned text he spoke of the ruling classes enjoying privilege and power at the expense of the "toiling

[5] See, for example, A. N. Holcombe, *New Party Politics* (New York 1933).

millions." His *Psychic Factors* placed emphasis on the "barriers" which separate class groups, and, while he denied being interested in the nature of the barriers, a considerable portion of the book is devoted to an explanation of the devices (e.g., the "principle of deception") used by the ruling groups to maintain power. *Pure Sociology*, in which Ward thoroughly discussed the origins of class, lays stress upon the fact that, although slavery and feudalism have been overthrown, the new economic order is one of narrow minority control: that class distinctions remain characteristic of both Europe and America.

While his other works display the class emphasis, the subject is given its broadest treatment in *Applied Sociology*. Here Ward used his heaviest artillery in an attempt to reveal the foundations for the application of his "principles." In this volume a clear picture is presented of his conception of a society class-dominated. His "pure sociology" had taught that social structures resisted change but were always actually changing; his "applied sociology" was to teach the methods of facilitating change in the direction of desired goals. Here the advocates of laissez faire received their severest condemnation because, he claimed, they represent only a class of society and not society itself. In this world those who have been rewarded have simply enjoyed the accidental fortune of ranking position in a poorly organized society, in which they are able to profit at the expense of others. Ward again traced the race-struggle history of society, showing how "national freedom" and, later, "political freedom" have been won. But *social freedom* remains to be achieved: "The forces that prevent social freedom . . . are hidden and universally diffused through the social fabric. They are largely economic forces guided by the acute sagacity of individual interest. . . ." The condition of social freedom is to be one unmarked by social classes. Although Ward did not adhere to the simple dichotomy of a two-class system, several pages of *Applied Sociology* contrasted the "elite" and the lower classes, implying that, basically, the traditional two-way division of society was most important. Shortly, consideration will be given to Ward's criteria of class, but here the emphasis is his ever-present conception of a stratified social order.

Notwithstanding his preoccupation with the subject, he failed to name class specific subject matter of sociology. Unlike the Marxian writers who would describe sociology as "historical materialism," [6] Ward omitted class when discussing the "data" of sociology. In view of his emphasis upon the subject, this omission is strange. Ward, it is true, insisted that he had "no idea of attempting an enumeration of the data of sociology." But, in developing his synthetic approach, illustrations of enumerations are many and among them we fail to find class.

This is understandable in consideration of Ward's philosophy of history. He has been named a "rank materialist" on the basis of such declarations as: "All interest is essentially economic, and seen in their true light religious interests are as completely economic as the so-called material interests." But, out of context, such statements are misleading. The psychological emphasis which marked his sociology led Ward to view history in the light of the Weltanschauung of a people. His plea for universal and compulsory education is an excellent illustration of his conception of historical change: teach the masses, he argued, and their economic interests will be cared for in turn. Education was the means, the institution which could be manipulated by man; the economic complex was the "superstructure," the reflection of the knowledge of the people. He was convinced that ideas are potent forces in social change, and that if proper ideologies can be diffused, the solutions for economic and political problems will follow automatically. *Pure Sociology* indicates a certain liking for "historical materialism," but even that volume qualifies the doctrine to the extent of reversing it. In discussing T. N. Carver's article, "The Basis of Social Conflict," Ward was frankly critical: "the more I look at the general doctrine of historical materialism, or the

---

[6] See, for example, N. Bukharin, *Historical Materialism* (New York 1933). Most European sociologists have considered class phenomena central data, and have named them so. See Chapter VIII.

economic interpretation of history . . . the more it narrows down relatively to the other motives and factors of history." Those "other motives and factors" were the ideologies, the *idées-forces*, and Ward's own efforts were pointed to their change. He brought this conception of the nature of historical development to the question of the basic determinants of class stratification.

Any number of factors have been singled out, and sometimes combined, as the criteria of class. Income, degree of leisure, relation to a system of production, birth, religion, and others have from time to time been considered the indices of class position. To Ward many of these factors were significant, but occupying most prominence in his system were two: the *economic* and the *educational*. The America of Ward's lifetime threw on the social screen the reflection of a society in which economic and educational differentiation were vividly marked. He did not clearly separate the one criterion from the other; in fact, an overlapping of the two was consistent with his theory of social change.

A picture of economic cleavage was drawn in the first volume of *Dynamic Sociology* in which Ward traced the genesis of society and social relations. It is in the economic sphere that the "morals of Nature" prevail: "the 'struggle for existence' has its true counterpart in society in the industrial struggles of men." The acquisition of property became an end of social life and the "genesis of avarice" characterized economic activity. Success in acquiring is the quality of uppermost importance.[7] Those who succeed economically do so at the expense of the great majority whose acquisitive powers are less developed. This process is natural: man obeys a universal law, and the "pseudo moralists" are mistaken in their condemnations. "Deception," for human beings, is the "normal form of intellectual action."

But Ward was not content to stop here. Society becomes

[7] As noted above, this desire for possession played a most useful role in social development.

divided into two classes in terms of ownership of wealth by virtue of this process involving "natural justice" or the "law of force." Man, however, is distinguished from other animals by the "intellectual" element, and it is this factor which guides him, necessarily, from the natural to the "civil" state. Operating in the process of change and stemming from the intellectual quality are an "increase in the susceptibility to sympathy," an "increase in the capacity for foretelling effects," and a "decrease of the power to perform desired acts." These three factors have taken humanity, or sections of it, a short way along the road to civil justice.

The distance has not been great enough, however, to change the class picture: society remains divided between those who own and the poverty stricken. Intelligence grows, it is true, but the material circumstances permit only the economically fortunate to gain knowledge; they use it to promote their own class interests. Moral considerations play little part in business transactions, which are largely governed by extreme selfishness. Government should provide protection against class abuse, but even the civil code is class controlled: in these matters classes with little or no representation are deprived of their rights. "The tendency of civilization itself is to 'make the poor poorer and the rich richer.'" Ward refused to admit that the economic division is indicative of any differentiation of abilities. The poorest are "the most enterprising and energetic," while among the wealthy the number of the industrious is a small fraction of the indolent rich. All this is right and proper "from the standpoint of Nature," but not from the standpoint of man. Circumstances and, to a considerable extent, mere luck, produce pecuniary inequality.

Acquisition, the major force of economic life, is the basis for Ward's economic class categories. He named three primary classes of this type: producers, accessories to production, and parasites—the last two classes constituting the non-producers. Thus, the "two great classes of society" are those who produce and those who do not.

This economic criterion, which was first extensively presented in *Dynamic Sociology*, appears in Ward's other volumes.
Psychic Factors in the discussion of the "principle of deception," *Outlines* in the elaboration of "sociocracy," *Pure Sociology* in the discussion of origins and functions of classes, and
almost all of *Applied Sociology*, repeat the original economic
distinction. Ward was always conscious of the capitalistic control of society.[8]

The economic division had always to be considered, but this
was not all, not the sesame to an understanding of the social
order. For the economic chasm between the vested groups and
workers parallels the division between intelligence and ignorance. The distinction between capital and labor is significant,
but its true importance, to Ward, is to be understood in the
light of the inequality of education. Leisure and material means
are afforded the capitalist group for the attainment of the best
of knowledge; the workers remain ignorant. The intellectual
monopoly which the former enjoys is used for its own protection, and even to manipulate in its own interest the less intelligent workers. Many acts of the upper group receive moral
sanction which, when performed by the workers, are tabooed.
The intelligent class realizes the value of cooperative methods
and uses them, but similar attempts of the working class are
"loudly denounced as a sort of crime against society." [9] Ward
guarded against the "self-made-man" thesis, as propounded by
the successful to reassure the workers, by pointing out that the
proportion of the lower class which rises from obscurity is
"next to infinitesimal."

The criterion of education was stressed most extensively in
Applied Sociology. In the most developed communities, Ward

[8] The well-known break that occurred in his friendship with Albion Small was
perhaps explained in terms of this control. In a letter to a friend he said:
"A change has come over the spirit of his [Small's] dreams and I can only
account for it on the hypothesis that he is under instructions from the capitalistic censorship that controls the U. of C."

[9] This "theoretical" conception places Ward on the side of organized labor.
He maintained this position in his more "practical" writings. See Division 5
of this chapter.

stated in this volume, the ignorant number about four-fifths of the population. Political democracy harms as well as aids the lower class, for it allows the rulers to manipulate the vote for their selfish interests. Only an enlightened populace can prevent this. The intelligent, that is the educated, are usually conservative and satisfied with the status quo. Possessing control of the social mechanisms, they exploit the much larger, unintelligent groups. Of course, there are "exceptional spirits" among the "élite" who do not correspond to the usual pattern, but they are very few. Moreover, not only does ignorance prevail among the members of the lower class, but also "error." "Fake ideas" in religion, undue faith in upper class leaders, and mistaken notions concerning his own condition mark the thinking of the worker. This cleavage of society into the intelligent and ignorant, Ward argued, must result in exploiting and exploited classes.

Although Ward often used the term "intelligence" to qualify the upper class, he held no conception of an innate intelligence as the special gift of the successful members of society. He protested against the "law of nature" argument that would place the intellectually fit at the top, and emphasized the material conditions that permitted the fortunate few to gain the fruits of civilizational achievement. Intellectually, the classes of society are equal: the differentiation of innate abilities is approximately the same among all groups. Intelligence is the result of intellect *plus* opportunity; and opportunity, for the most part, is restricted to the members of the upper classes. Ward insisted that native capacity for acquiring knowledge was distributed equally among the social strata, and that with a similar distribution of opportunity, this would become apparent. The distinction between intellect, or capacity, and intelligence first appeared in *Dynamic Sociology*, and was carried through all of Ward's volumes. *Psychic Factors* devotes a chapter to the distinction, and *Pure Sociology* considers it an important aspect of "social dynamics."

The basis of the social program which Ward demanded in *Applied Sociology* is exactly this distinction. Culture is not inherited via the germ plasm: "Social heredity is not a process of organic transmission." The nature of the social organization has always and everywhere meant that the transmission of the "products of achievement" favored only a small fraction of society. Indeed, the most fundamental problem of applied sociology is that of evolving a system permitting an equitable inheritance of culture. While there is a cleavage in terms of intelligence, there is none due to differences of native capacity: "class distinctions in society are wholly artificial": a monopoly is exercised over the social heritage by the few.

In his detailed analysis of those environmental factors which shape the intelligence of man, Ward's emphases are apparent: the economic and the educational. Several sources were used to establish the argument that the surroundings of an individual determine, to a great extent, his achievement. Particular importance was assigned to the elaborate studies of M. Odin. "Genius is in things, not in man," Ward quotes Odin, and here, at least, lauds this doctrine of "historical materialism." Although Odin's conclusions gave greatest weight to the economic factors, Ward almost allowed his argument to stand. But he had to build for his own program, and Odin's results could have been used to support any reform or revolutionary movement. Hence, he argued rather obviously, all environments, local, economic, and social, are, in a sense, educational. Of course, to Ward, "education" meant more than formal schooling, included, in fact, "all influences that react upon the mind."

The stress upon education is consistent with many of Ward's doctrines: the faith in the intellect, the conception of telic change, the schema of social forces, the plea for the advancement of womankind. Give to man knowledge and he will organize a splendid society. Education is the great means which permits attainment of our desired ends. Even on the basis of his broad definition of "education," Ward's argument appears over-balanced in favor of his own plea. His portrayal of a world which favors a small proportion of its members with educational opportunity is valid enough, but his singling out the one factor of education disregards, though not completely, the interaction, the reciprocal relations, among the economic, political, and cultural spheres. Ward did speak of the "intimate connection between the economic and social environment" and pointed out that the "higher social classes" are the "higher economic classes." His thesis, however, at this point, remained the almost monistic one of educational causation. Perhaps it was his realization of the inadequacy of such a conception that led Ward to expand his reformatory program to include political and economic change.[10]

The social world to Ward was one basically divided into two groups: the economically and educationally fortunate but small group, and the much larger class, poor in wealth and learning. These two criteria, education and wealth, can be considered objective or material; they are, to some extent, measurable, and lend themselves to forms of statistical analysis. When we speak of class, however, another range of factors must be included: the "subjective," the "consciousness of class," the values that dominate the thinking of social beings. Ward did not neglect this aspect of the problem.[11]

The "third proximate end of conation" or the "direct means to progressive action," as discussed in *Dynamic Sociology*, includes an extensive analysis of "opinion" and "ideas." After assigning primary importance to the material "circumstances" upon which opinion basically depends, Ward presented the "subjective influences." The latter are comprised of the "ante-natal" and "post-natal," and among the various post-natal subjective influences which shape opinion the consciousness of class finds its place. "The normal condition of the great mass of mankind . . . is one of complete indifference to the sufferings of all beyond the circle of their own immediate experience." Thus, throughout history, all peoples have established systems

[10] See Division 5 of this chapter.
[11] Ward's educational criterion of class, in the broad sense in which he used it, can be interpreted to include class "consciousness." However, the materials specifically devoted to class attitudes deserve special analysis.

of "dual morality" which have given to the upper classes a kind of ethnocentrism with respect to those beneath them in the social hierarchy. Ward recognized the distinction between those countries marked by a corporate class consciousness, particularly the European, and such communities as America, where competitive class feeling dominates. The attempts of the visiting European to adjust his class values to the American scene "often become very amusing." Both religion, which lends support to the rigid caste barriers of India, and custom, which strengthens the class consciousness of Europe, usually become confused with "morality": class differentiation is considered intrinsically "good," and attempts to weaken the barriers are "bad."

Ward's description of the special qualities of class ideology in modern societies was Veblen-like. Long before *The Theory of the Leisure Class* was published, he emphasized what was later to become associated with Veblen's "emulation" and "conspicuous consumption." [12] The "principles of deception," elaborated in *Psychic Factors*, describe that quality which marks all classes in capitalistic society—the desire to make an "appearance": to establish before one's fellows the fact of economic success. Obtaining and increasing wealth becomes the "criterion of worth." "Artifice, counterfeit, simulation, disguise, sham, and imposture" are devices used by all groups to support and enhance their status, a status measured by wealth. This quality, emulative and competitive, is most characteristic of a community like America, where a break from the old class lines, coupled with the vertical mobility of an expanding capitalism, increases the competitive class feeling.

Veblen's keen analysis of these phenomena was later utilized by Ward in *Pure Sociology*. In the discussion of "innovation," "property," "moral indirection," and the "conquest of nature," *The Theory of the Leisure Class* was the major citation.

[12] This is not to imply that Ward was the first social scientist to stress these conceptions. History affords many examples of writers who were conscious of the "conspicuous" elements of class behavior.

Veblen's notions of the instinct of workmanship, conspicuous consumption, and the predatory leisure class were used to support Ward's conception of competitive consciousness. Finally, in *Applied Sociology*, Ward quoted freely from Veblen, and noted the great contrast between the two major social classes marked by "sharply contrasted words and phrases." Instinct of workmanship versus instinct of sportsmanship, exploit versus industry, honorific versus humilific, futility versus utility, all stamp the opposing classes both in activity and psychology.

Although *Psychic Factors*, *Pure Sociology*, and *Applied Sociology* reveal Ward's interest in the psychological aspect of class, his major analysis of group psychology omits class consciousness. He pictured "social consciousness," a national community sentiment which erases class lines and induces a feeling for "the whole" which will finally lead to "sociocracy." Even the old organic analogy was brought into the picture: this social consciousness is the "nation or state," the "brain" of the social organism. The "science of meliorism" is to cope with social frictions; thus, class consciousness will give way to a truer feeling of social cohesion.

In Ward's discussion of class consciousness lies a striking inconsistency. He desired and predicted a world devoid of class lines, a world dominated by a consciousness of the whole. He described the earlier rise of the bourgeoisie and then, from the middle of the nineteenth century, the *political* emancipation of the proletariat as steps in the direction "of a great levelling up of mankind." Almost always, he favored the current democratic ideology which refused to recognize class lines. At the same time, Ward welcomed "the rising consciousness of the proletariat": he approved of the growth of trade-unionism and condemned the anti-union policies of business and government. It is apparent that he considered the growing consciousness of the workers as a step in the direction of his sociocracy. On the one hand, he praised the classless feeling of Americans, and, on the other, he lauded the conscious identification with a class that was beginning to mark the thinking of

American workers. However, there is an implicit reconciliation of this seeming contradiction in Ward's remedial program.[13]

The relationship between material conditions and ideas, the "dual morality" of the classes, and some of the features of class feeling in capitalistic communities were recognized by Ward. However, these questions were never consistently followed through. Class, in its objective aspects of income and education, was portrayed at length, but the consciousness of class leaves room for more extensive analysis.

The classes of society differ not only in "intelligence," in income, and in consciousness, but in *function*. They perform separate tasks in the business of running the social world. Ward pointed up this differentiation of function, including the biological roles performed by the different classes. *Dynamic Sociology* stated that those groups which are lacking in wealth and education contribute the larger number of children to the world. Those most able to provide their children with education are alarmed by the rapidly increasing population, and refuse to augment it; while the laboring masses whose children need education and protection add most to population growth. Ward considered this a reversal of the proper order, recommending legislation, as well as universal education, as a corrective. In *Applied Sociology* this theme was extended considerably, based largely upon the statistical data of Mulhall, Conrad, Casper, and Charles Booth. The system of "privative ethics," which has dominated the social scene throughout history, creates "inhuman conditions" which destroy the surplus population. "Reproduction is in the inverse ratio to intelligence." The poor marry early and breed plentifully, while the wealthy follow the opposite program. Birth-control practices aid somewhat, but only the adoption of a "positive ethics" will fully correct this situation.[14]

Causally related to the difference in biological function of

---

[13] See Division 5 of this chapter.
[14] Recent population studies indicate a levelling off of this class differential in western society.

the classes is the difference in economic roles. It has already been noted that in the first volume of *Dynamic Sociology* Ward conceived of a functional classification of classes: the producers, the accessories to production, and the parasites. The first group, the producers, includes all those persons who *by means of labor* make available any desired commodity or service. Ward followed the principle that all value results from labor, in this volume, tracing the steps in "primary" and "secondary" production. The "middle-men," standing between the producer and consumer, function in the process of distribution; they are the "accessories to production." Distribution for the financier becomes a method of acquisition, while the returns often far surpass the value rendered. The actual producer, the "poor mechanic," is taught to regard the merchant and financier as "superior beings"; the latter have profited enormously by merely handling the former's produce. "A firm footing on the globe" has been won by the labor of the producers and the accessories to production: by their efforts civilization's greatest achievements have been realized.

Another class, the "parasites," also performs important functions. This non-producing, non-industrial group is often the most active and energetic. Usually the most highly educated element of society, it is amazingly successful in establishing itself as the stratum of top rank. The dominating interest of this parasitic group is acquisition of wealth, an interest which is pursued through the institutions of robbery, theft, war, government or statecraft, hierarchy or priestcraft, and monopoly. Not all individuals engaged in such activities are parasites, but most of those occupying the highest positions fall into this group. Particular emphasis was given to monopoly, a device which was receiving much attention during Ward's lifetime. He discussed in some detail the monopoly of transportation, of exchange, of finance, of labor, of manufacture. The last is the "least objectionable," and can be remedied by the cooperation of the workers. The parasites are the "true aristocracy" in the organic world, but in the social world it becomes necessary to distribute the rewards on a more equitable basis in keeping with the value-services of the various groups. And by far the greatest value is the result of the labor of producers. This picture of two basic classes [15] functioning in the capacities of producer and parasite resembles a socialist interpretation. But Ward never subscribed to any rigid economic doctrine; in fact, his "economics," as Giddings has pointed out, fails to emerge from his writings with any clarity.

The description of the parasitic group suggests a further function of the upper class, the intellectual. Ward described the historically traditional monopoly exercised over intellectual activities by the ruling groups. The results of cultural accomplishments are spread through the upper ranks, and are beginning to be diffused down into the lower classes. The toil of the latter permits the former to function in the intellectual and artistic sphere. But Ward desired a world which would allow the potentialities of all to be fulfilled. In *Applied Sociology*, the intellectual function of the favored class is given greater stress: literature, for example, is described as a class and not a national product.[16] The very purpose of applied sociology, as Ward viewed it, is to create a method of eliminating such cultural inequalities by a general levelling upward of the masses of men.

4. CLASS AND STATE

There are at least three theories of the state that have gained the attention of writers in the social sciences: the Hegelian conception of an ideal totality, the Marxian doctrine of the state as a class instrument, and the liberal-democratic view of the state as a limited agency of the community. Ward refused to subscribe fully to any one of these theories, although certain of his statements may be taken to support each of them.

In the first volume of *Dynamic Sociology* Ward launched

---

[15] Those who "produce" and those who do not.

[16] One wonders how Ward would react to the contemporary situation in literature in which a share of it is *lower* class both in source and sympathy. This trend was under way during his lifetime. See Chapter I.

his attack on the advocates of laissez faire, stating that the limits of state regulation can only be set by the "circumstances" of time and place. Government is "but a system of control" and legislation, therefore, must be reduced to as exact a science as possible. Later in the same work government as a "social agency" was described as both benefiting and hindering communities. Government not only restrains, but has the other functions of "protection," "accommodation," and "amelioration" of society. Its success as an agent of progress has been exceedingly limited; we must look to the future for the state to become a really useful agency.

This failure on the part of the state is explained in Ward's discussion of its control by class. Here he came close to Marxian teachings. "He recognized the exploitation of the proletariat by the owners of wealth but he never fully admitted the extent of the latter's control over the powers and agencies of the state." Dr. Stern's comment is essentially correct. Ward did, however, stress the control of state by certain "class" elements.

One element of the "parasites," the important government officials, is pictured using the state for its own class ends. Governments "always emanate from the few seeking power, never from the many seeking protection"; they have been "a yoke upon the necks of the people." His original conception of the origin of the state was that of a class-controlled agency devised by the dominating few. The unpopularity that most governments have experienced has been due to the continual domination by the ruling class. Ward conceived of an ideal government which would, in most respects, be the "opposite of the existing ones." Such a government would truly represent society, not a segment of it: class control would be eliminated from the political scene. In *Psychic Factors*, his plan of a "sociocracy" expands this theme. Emphasized here is the notion that the present economic system has been produced by generations of shrewd manipulation on the part of a small group, which secures, through legal measures, most economic control. The policy of laissez faire voiced by the vested interest group is itself a device to keep political control in its own hands. Again, in *Outlines*, the famous "collective telesis" chapter points out that the "self-seeking class" strives, usually with success, "to enlist government . . . in its service," and thus to guarantee its control over the social processes.

This argument, much the same as that of, say, Engels or Kropotkin, did not, however, lead to Ward's endorsement either of a proletarian revolution for the seizure of the state or an era of anarchism. Rather, he looked to education as the process which will remove the state from the control of a single class. He believed that state-imposed restraints upon the people, theoretically benefiting the community as a whole, were, in fact, largely designed to aid the ruling classes in their exploitation. This situation will be corrected, he argued, only with the general raising of intelligence.

Ward never lost his faith in political democracy, nor did he finally give his allegiance to the cause of socialism. In fact, *Pure Sociology* and *Applied Sociology* picture the state quite differently from one dominated by class. It has already been shown how *Pure Sociology* explains the origin of the state as a neutral agency, based upon the institution of law, and serving as mediator between conflicting classes. In this volume, the political agency is presented as the most important and useful of all human inventions which serve in controlling the social forces. "The state becomes an instrument of morality as the ethical effect of the social process; out of the construction of society there results the conscious sacrifice of the individual in behalf of the community." Ward approved this semi-Hegelian statement of Ratzenhofer's, and condemned the extreme critics of the state. Almost all people, and particularly the members of the lower classes, believe that the state supports their interests, and welcome its activities as beneficial to all. He quoted at length the writings of Comte, Spencer, De Greef, and Ratzenhofer to help establish the thesis that freedom is largely the result of the state's activities; liberty, therefore, is the combination of restraint and privilege. At times, states may be class controlled, but such control results from community sanction: a "general will" lies behind the existence of all political systems. The state "has but one purpose, function, or mission, that of securing the welfare of society"; it is "essentially moral or ethical." The state has been the chief condition of "all achievement" and, while it has often erred, it remains the greatest agency of human advance. Its method is telic: the further development of the democratic state is based upon the extension of "collective telesis." The essential correctness of the democratic processes prevents class-control, claimed Ward in his later writings. The state always reflects the dynamic elements of society, and only under strict monarchical forms is the guarantee of class interests uppermost. But democracy changes the institutional structure so that the advantage of all society becomes the major interest of its political agent.

The relationship between class and state bulked large in Ward's thinking. He believed, certainly, that the privileged groups had and were to a considerable extent, using the political institutions for their own interests. But, for Ward, the problem did not resolve itself into the seizure of the state by those oppressed, or its overthrow and the establishment of a new and better political system. True, he desired that the state be used for the benefit of all society, with a particular emphasis on society's largest segment, the working class.

The plea for the extension of the sphere of state activity was typical of American "liberals" and "native radicals" of Ward's day, as indeed, is the case at present. A rationalization of those demands characterizes his somewhat eulogistic treatment of the state in his later writings. It is difficult to reconcile this inconsistency between Ward's earlier argument that the state is essentially the tool of the vested groups and his later theme that the state is a community agency. Probably it is fair to conclude that the earlier analysis was based upon his observation (he was a government employee for years) of the manipulations of the government agencies by economic interests, and that his later thesis pertained to his notion of the *duties* of the state. It should be remembered, furthermore, that Ward believed that extensive education would erase from the state its class qualities.

5. SOCIAL AMELIORATION

All of Ward's writings, including "pure" and "applied" sociology, point to a plan of remedial social action. His chief aspiration was to create a social science which could form the proper basis of intelligent social action; this is true of all of his theoretical work. Although he was critical of the "ethical" reformism of Small and others, Ward himself was essentially a reformist, placing his faith in the "scientific" control of society. He did not view science as an end in itself. Truth "for the sake of truth" or "knowledge for its own sake" were, he held, unwarranted principles. Science has "always an ulterior purpose, and that purpose is ethical. . . ." Sociology, even pure sociology, must be viewed as the science of welfare.

Social improvement for Ward included, as an essential element, the adjustment of class differentiation: "it is the duty of society . . . to prevent, as far as possible, the advancement of a small class at the expense of a large one." "Human happiness" is the ideal end of all social effort, but the system of classes stands as a great barrier in the way of its attainment. It becomes the task of a dynamic sociology to develop appropriate means for the gaining of this ideal end. Progress, being synonymous with the increase of human happiness, is in large part the result of the elimination of class barriers. "True civilization" should "render the great proletariat comfortable"; an important method is to "rationally change the environment." It was claimed, moreover, that, in the economic field, sociology is concerned with the "destination" of wealth: a plea for a more equitable distribution. In discussing methodology Ward stated that "a true sociologist will scarcely have an opinion on a current question," but in the same volume, *Pure Sociology*, he offered decided opinions on contemporary problems. The material achievements of western civilization have bettered and continue to better the lot of the oppressed; the sociologist must concentrate on the distribution of wealth and the phenomenon of consumption. Concern with social betterment is, indeed, the foundation of his sociology.

While to a considerable degree all of Ward's sociology is "applied," the volume thus designated describes those devices most directly aimed at improvement and reform, the major problem being the equitable distribution of the intellectual heritage. Ward always insisted, however, that applied sociology "is a science, not an art." ("Art" is the quality he assigned to political party programs which call for reform.) He criticized the "pessimists" of social science, Schopenhauer, Hartmann, Gumplowicz, etc., attributing to them the "disease called *Weltschmerz.*"

Political and civil justice have, to some extent, been won; continued Ward in *Applied Sociology,* society must establish *social justice.* The "new ethics" goes to the root of social inequality and introduces change or modification; the utilitarian principle of the greatest happiness of the greatest number is basic to the scientific control of society; the claims that social and economic inequalities are natural and inevitable are unwarranted in the light of scientific sociology. Ward clung to the form of individualism which demands a social order allowing individual achievement: this is true social achievement. Real knowledge, possessed by but a small group, must be "socially appropriated" to stimulate progress and, consequently, applied sociology must work for the intellectual "general levelling of all classes." The existing competitive system has refused to grapple with the social forces as it has the material; sociology must undertake this task. "Privative ethics" has sustained the illusion of the necessity for an economic stimulus: a hollow part of leisure-class philosophy. A "positive ethics" will become the corrective—so ran Ward's arguments.

"Meliorism" and "collective telesis" form the theoretical web into which Ward's specific remedial threads were woven. The first of these, meliorism, sounds the reformist note of *Dynamic*

Sociology. It is the true "means to progressive action." Moral ideas become more efficient as social forces to the degree that they become intellectualized: man has traveled from "mere impulse" to "true sentiment" to reason. Reason, introducing humanitarian schemes, paves the way for *meliorism*, "which may be defined as humanitarianism *minus* all sentiment." Meliorism is dynamic, not ethical, and calls for the improvement of social conditions "through cold calculation." It must, moreover, sacrifice the wish of a few for that of the many. In other words, meliorism is concerned, in part at least, with rational, scientific devices aimed at the abolition of the class order.

The same principle was extended in *Psychic Factors*. Ward emphasized the point that schemes of social reform are as much a part of the normal evolutionary development as all other social phenomena; the strict advocates of laissez faire who base their arguments on "let nature take care of herself" are themselves anti-evolutionists. Human evolution, "civilization," is "artificial": as civilization proceeds so does artificiality. All society must be made the recipient of the products of art, industry, and labor. The biological sociologists, who assume that the processes operating "in nature" (in human society, economic competition) are correct for man, overlook the evolutionary role played by the intellect. Not an ethical conception, insisted Ward, meliorism is the science of the amelioration of society.

Allied with meliorism is the conception of "collective telesis": together they point the proper direction of social change. In discussing the purpose of sociology, Ward summarized this doctrine's major features. "The study of sociology is calculated to enlighten the individual purposes of men and harmonize them with the good of society. It will tend to unify action, to combine the innumerable streams of individual effort and pour their contents into one great river of social welfare. Individual telesis thus verges into collective telesis." The purpose of sociology being to speed social evolution, it is the mental, intellectual factor that must promote the reform of the future. And it must be recognized that group, not individual, achievement is the key to advance. Thus telesis must be social or collective.

Meliorism, with its stress upon the rational selection of adequate means, and collective telesis, emphasizing group welfare, form the basis of the program to which Ward contributed innumerable pages. It is a program aimed at social reconstruction containing specific educational, political, and economic elements. What Ward labeled "art, not science" occupied a good part of his "scientific" writings.

It has already been noted that Ward believed education to be an important criterion of class. Social differentiation's most significant aspect is the division of society into the educated few and the ignorant mass. The need for a program of social reconstruction allowing the general spread of fundamental knowledge was continually emphasized in *Dynamic Sociology*. The educational monopoly of the élite furthers the cleavages and dissatisfactions in society, the existing social system being unable to assimilate adequately scientific advancements because they are confined to one small class. This group regards the "common herd" as if it was on its "way to the slaughterhouse." The masses are "like children": they are told how to act and what to think. Thus, it must be educational reform which is to remedy the class antagonisms of society. This theme is the central note of most of Ward's sociology.

Even a small class of uneducated, he maintained, imposes upon the government a great burden, for governments must always adjust themselves to their lowest strata. Education is not, like most forms of human enterprise, susceptible to the economic laws of supply and demand. It can and should be socially controlled, society as a whole being its chief beneficiary. *Applied Sociology* develops the idea of "intellectual egalitarianism," elaborating the Helvetian doctrine that "all truth is within the reach of all men." The "latent four-fifths of mankind," potentially as able as the best, can contribute to civilization's advance only when it has been given knowledge. Genius is present in all classes, and the extension of educational opportunity to all will allow its development. The failure to assimilate achievement is due to exploitation by the intelligent few; so long as society refuses to allow all classes to share the cultural benefits, this condition will remain. Knowledge is power: if the lower classes receive the first, they will achieve the second.

The theoretical concept upon which the educational argument rests Ward named "synergy": the "interaction of man and his environment." The proponents of a strict hereditary explanation of human achievement failed, of course, to gain Ward's sympathy. A good many pages were devoted to analysis and attack of Galton's *Hereditary Genius*. Cooley's well known article on genius [17] was praised by Ward as "the most consistent and satisfactory answer" to Galton ever published.[18]

Equality of opportunity, he believed, would result from equality of knowledge; any remaining inequalities would reflect native individual differences. Thus education becomes the chief agent for the attainment of a more perfect society. An adequate system of universal education would "increase the average fecundity in dynamic agents of society one hundred-fold." Education is the means, economic and social welfare the end, of social reform. There is no point in planning the equalization of wealth until humanity has provided itself with the means of its realization. Socialists and other reformers are, unfortunately, concerned with the end, not the means which is susceptible of human manipulation. Many people, said Ward, had expected his *Applied Sociology* to offer a remedy for the conflict of capital and labor. He had no solution, but he was convinced that if labor were as informed as capital, the conflict

---

[17] "Genius, Fame and the Comparison of Races," *Annals, American Academy of Political and Social Science*, Vol. IX (1897).

[18] Ward did stress the function of "great men" in history: they are the chief "agents of civilization." Emphasizing the significance of the educational environment, he attributed achievement to the "strong and brilliant minds in the world and not any vague, impersonal environmental conditions." The mental factor in which he had such great faith, and to which he attributed progress, becomes both the result of environment and an independent force operating in social change. Perhaps this paradox is the dialectic of synergy.

would solve itself. Even the "odium of labor," which Ratzen-hofer and Veblen had shown to be a matter of class, would be removed by the equalization of intelligence. The universal diffusion of knowledge would result in a greater sharing of a positive ethics demanding a great improvement in living standards, would, in fact, lead to a society free of classes.

In 1873 Ward wrote an extended treatise on education which, in abridged form, became the famous last chapter of *Dynamic Sociology*. The "indirect method of conation" receives its highest application: the "organization of happiness" is given a program for attainment. Happiness and progressive action are ends and cannot be directly legislated or instituted. On the other hand, the opinions that men possess determine their general conduct; opinions can be changed, truth can be inculcated, but only by giving knowledge to all members of society. The method involves a drastic social reconstruction to be accomplished by the "education of information": the provision to all of the "most important" of extant knowledge. This function can only be intrusted to "society itself," whose agent is the state. Hence, the state must provide universal education. Ward described the state as the most efficient of all administrative organizations, particularly in the field of scientific endeavor. In its administration of education, the state stands in a particularly unique position to gain its ends, for it is able to provide knowledge to the class most in need of it, the workers, whose educational requirements cannot be met by private agencies. Furthermore, public education requires the democratic process: the "lowest *gamin* of the streets" is on the same footing with the son of riches. Women, moreover, must be educated as well as men. The state can and, Ward hoped, will "equalize" and "compel" education.

Considerable weight was given to the class results that may be anticipated from this educational program. Cooperation and association, which have always been used by the intelligent capitalists, will become useful weapons for the lower class. The latter will recognize its own exploitation and will oppose the ruling class with its own devices. In fact, both economic classes will benefit because each will be able to prevent, when equipped with adequate knowledge, usurpations of its domain by the other.

This argument, the diffusion of knowledge resulting in the amelioration of class antagonisms, was continued in less elaborated form in Ward's other works, particularly in *Applied Sociology*. Slums, broken health, criminality, the danger of violence on the part of the uneducated mass, these and other social problems can be prevented by society setting for itself the task of educating all its elements.

Professor Ross has evaluated Ward's program of educational reform as "the most elaborate and fundamental argument ever made for universal public education as the preparation for solving the social problem and the basis for a continuous social progress." Certainly Ward's argument is forceful, but hardly conclusive. What, for example, is the exact nature of "informational education"? Ward described it as being the "practical," basic knowledge, not the techniques of research or the methods of the arts and sciences. Would such basic knowledge include the writings of, say, Ward and Spencer? Would both Kidd and Marx be on the required list? Apparently, Ward neglected the latter in his own education. Opinion is the dynamic agent of social change, claimed Ward, and it must be formed in the mold of "truth." What constitutes the latter? Surely the semi-materialist, Ward, did not consider truth to consist of certain basic Platonic ideas. At times, as noted earlier, he stressed the relationship between social conditions and social beliefs. But, in driving home his educational plea, he passed too lightly over this very problem.

A more important criticism involves Ward's argument for state-controlled education. He was careful to point out that governmental activities are, to a great extent, carried on in the interest of the capitalist class. But, apparently, the administration of education would not involve control by this group. Society "must simply wait until the state sees fit to adopt" an ideal educational program. The lengthy passages on the relation of state to class were mostly overlooked when the educational program was presented. The critics of the left have ample room to declare that he was "naively" convinced that education could serve as the lever for fundamental social reconstruction.

"Education is Mr. Ward's panacea for all the ills that flesh is heir to: the cure for our curse of overworked millions on the one hand, and unemployed millions on the other." Grant Allen thus summed up a commonly held opinion of Ward's thesis. Mr. Allen admitted that the logic of his thesis is almost "as rigorously deduced from given premises as a proposition of Euclid." Education held first place in his remedial scheme, to be sure, but it was supported by both political and economic arguments.

Such terms as "collective telesis" and "sociocracy" fail to conceal the very practical reforms that Ward desired. He was aware of the abstract nature of his terminology, informing his readers when developing the collective telesis theme that he was essentially concerned with the problems of government. For Ward distinguished between positive government and mischannelled political power. A severe critic of the latter, he was convinced that the former was potentially an important agency of social reform, given a scientific basis. He believed that the democratic political processes should benefit the community.

The legislative process, in particular, was the medium through which a broad reform program could be instituted. But legislation, to Ward, must be something far different from the party dominated decisions of contemporary parliaments. For the most part, the rulings of such bodies are "individual dynamic actions": they represent the desires and activities of individuals or small, self-interested groups. The present method of legislation does not allow "even an average expression of the intelligence of the body." Ward sought true *deliberation* unattainable under present partisan conditions. The legislator must be able to approach his problems as a scientist; legislation itself must be the result of applying the methods of science. Legislators will, of necessity, function according to the scientific method when the intelligence of their constituencies is raised through education to the level of science. Again the argument rests upon the major educational thesis. For one who revealed a somewhat realistic understanding of the political operations and the economic nature of parties Ward was surprisingly "idealistic" in his conception of possible legislative procedure. A sociological brand of "technocracy" is suggested by Dr. H. E. Barnes: "Ward's legislators, like the priests of the Positivist regime, were to be trained sociologists."

The method of legislation was to be scientific, the object of legislation comprehensive. "Government is becoming more and more the organ of social consciousness. . . ." As the servant of the community, it must expand its own functions. General social welfare is the only limit of state activity, and were it not for the pressure exerted by a minority of the influential, a series of important national reforms would be enacted. These would include broad governmental provision for education so as to prevent class control of intelligence in society, and a gradual extension of governmental control and ownership in the industrial fields. The latter should not be too rapid, for the public must be prepared and desirous of each further advance. But it had already been proven, Ward believed, that railroads, for example, are more efficiently administered by the government than by private owners. In fact, the state is almost always able to render better service for the community as a whole than any other group or individual.

The label of "state socialism" could be given such a program, but it would have met with objection from Ward. He described "collectivism" or "socialization" as the process through which "all esthetic, moral, and intellectual influences" are working. Collectivism took on a rather general meaning in Ward's writing, but in the section specifically devoted to this subject in *Pure Sociology*, he clearly indicated that his concern lay with the advance of governmental control in the economic field.

Spencer, Lecky, and Sidney Webb were cited to support the thesis that the state's powers and activities have gradually grown and will continue to grow. In America, he believed, the lower classes were becoming politically conscious, and were moving towards collectivism. Their freedom, and that of all members of society, are the objectives of the collective activity of the state. Mr. Spencer, claimed Ward, failed to realize the collectivistic implications of his own thesis of simultaneous differentiation and integration. Echoes of Rousseau were sounded in Ward's article on political parties: "We have the somewhat remarkable paradox, a true paradox, and not a false one, . . . viz., that collectivism, instead of being opposed to individualism, is the only means of securing it."

This collectivism is a *process* that operates in society; it does not necessarily mean a revolutionary change in the ownership of economic means, nor is it a name for any particular type of society. But Ward did desire a specific kind of social organization: "sociocracy." Sociocracy implies a government socially controlled and socially directed, as contrasted with the present party and class exploitation. Sociocracy is "stronger" than autocracy, aristocracy, or democracy: it is society ruling itself. It was never suggested exactly how this ideal was to be realized. Apparently, an educated mankind will necessarily think and act only for the welfare of the social whole. Classes, parties, and all self-interest groups will vanish; there will be left only the individual on the one side, and society on the other, interacting in the interest of a harmonious sociocracy.

Ward stated, in this connection, that Marxian socialism is based upon "pure theory and a priori deductions." He claimed that socialism would impose artificial equalities and an equal sharing of awards. Both socialism and sociocracy oppose individualism, which has created artificial inequalities. But sociocracy "recognizes natural inequalities," and aims to abolish the artificial: it "would confer benefits in strict proportion to merit, but insists upon *equality of opportunity* as the only means of determining the degree of merit." [19] These distinctions between socialism and sociocracy imply that both are programs of social action, qualitatively different, but of the same general type. However, in his last volume Ward offered a different kind of distinction: socialism, like misarchism and anarchism, is an "art," not a science. The socialist parties in all countries are increasing their power and may enjoy general success. Sociocracy, on the other hand, is a *scientifically* conceived program. Ward forgot that political "art" is required to place even "scientific" principles into operation and scientists into control. His reply to this criticism would be that an educated world will act rationally.

Ward did not support any specific political party in the United States, but he did indicate the direction of his sympathies. As early as 1887, in the *Forum*, he argued for a "people's government" which would truly represent the "public will," negating class or personal control of the state. Several years later, in *Psychic Factors*, he hailed the newly formed "distinctively industrial party" as an indication of the proper kind of reform movement; and he considered the growing Socialist party, particularly in Europe, as a move in the direction of sociocracy. In 1908, when writing on the sociology of political parties, he condemned the Republican party for carrying on a strictly "capitalist" policy, and maintained that the working classes had gained political sympathy, although the rank and file of both major parties was dominated by upperclass leadership. There is no doubt that he regarded this leadership as symbolic of a class-controlled society, and that his allegiance was continually pledged to the radical and "progressive" political movements of his day.

Ward's positive appraisal of the left-wing parties was consistent with his plea for the social distribution of wealth. He believed it impossible for the ruling class to maintain complete

[19] One is reminded here of Ward's apparently limited knowledge of socialist theory.

control over labor in its own interest, and stated that social distribution had already begun to occur. "It is more and more the interest of the proprietor of goods" to allow the laborer "to share in their consumption." Free competition leads to monopoly, which prevents proper social distribution: even the economists are beginning to recognize this fact. A well-regulated distribution would necessarily rid society of poverty and want. The phenomenon of over-production is only possible in an "unorganized state of society." In fact, greatly increased production is desirable: there can never be too much produced if a more equitable distribution of the world's goods were realized. It only waits for the "assimilation of achievement," the education of the masses, to accomplish this end.

A complete picture of Ward's program of action must include his evaluation of trade-unionism. The full discussion of labor organization in *Psychic Factors* pointed out that until recently the employers have monopolized the use of the "rational method" in their economic role. Combination and co-operation have always characterized capital, while labor has only competed. The recent attempts of the workers to use collective methods are often refused the legal sanction that is usually extended to the capitalist group, indeed, are often regarded as criminal. As the lower classes gain more education, and thus increase the use of the mental factor, the more they will utilize collective action, and the greater will be the role played by labor unions. Ward welcomed this "combination" that "is growing more and more universal, powerful and permanent." Similarly, the immediate objectives of unionism, higher wages, shorter hours, and the like, received his praise and theoretical sanction. In this, he concurred with the opinions of E. A. Ross and Simon Patten.

We have outlined the practical reform program conceived by Ward which clearly pointed to class changes. He desired a world in which legislation would be created in the interest of all, a sociocracy devoid of class control or conflict. He argued for a greater sharing of wealth by the vested group. At the same time, he welcomed labor's attempts to organize for its own gain, and praised both the political and economic activities of the left-wing. His sympathies are apparent, but a last word should be said of his hesitations.

Ward's ideals were fundamentally those of a "middle class" intellectual. In *Dynamic Sociology*, the economic "middlemen" were lauded for the significant function they contribute in production and distribution; they are "a very large and influential element in society." They are, in fact, the people of the type Ward would have us all be. The conflict between capital and labor "greatly reduces the productiveness of both." Ward desired the elimination of this conflict, but not the elimination of either group. In a word, the capitalists should become similar to the workers, the workers similar to the capitalists: again the ideal of the Aristotelian mean. The two great economic classes "constantly overlap, interlace, and interpenetrate each other, serving as a sort of leaven for the generation of a common people." Earlier, it was noted that Ward stressed the notion of the state as a community rather than a class agency. Again, in his discussion of party activity, he criticized the measures of the extreme left-wing of the Democratic party as "ill-considered and of doubtful propriety." The desire for "propriety" is, perhaps, characteristic of the middle class. One cannot condemn a writer for being motivated by the values of the group of which he is a member. But to analyse the relationship between an individual's social surroundings and his theory is, we feel, essential to the complete understanding of the latter.[20] This relationship, were it fully examined, would constitute an important contribution to American *Wissenssoziologie*.

The core of Ward's "pure sociology" is the central position given to ideas and values. His "applied sociology" describes the kind of ideas and values which will lead mankind to shape a

[20] Ward shared the ideal of a "middle class" society with most of the other Fathers of American sociology, especially Ross and Cooley; but to some extent the same conception appears in the works of Small, Giddings, and Sumner.

better social world free of class antagonism. Such an attainment rests upon the process in which he placed supreme faith —education. What Marx and Engels envisioned as the outcome of the historical dialectic found its counterpart in Ward's sociocracy, the result of the telic action of man's knowledge.

CHAPTER THREE: WILLIAM GRAHAM SUMNER
(1840-1910)

WILLIAM GRAHAM SUMNER

1. INTRODUCTION

WARD's contemporary, William Graham Sumner, presents a striking contrast. Product of the same general social milieu, a teacher of greater influence, preacher and prophet as dogmatic and unswerving, Sumner arrived at conclusions which were in many respects the antitheses of Ward's. But, whatever their differences, they shared an intense interest in the study of class and class change.[1]

Important aspects of American society of the nineteenth century are exemplified by Sumner's biography. The son of an artisan-worker father, member of an immigrant family of Anglo-Saxon traditions, young Sumner witnessed the rise of this family group from obscurity to a position of relative security. Independence, ambition, and common sense were highly valued by the Sumners, and the qualities of thrift, family solidarity, and Christian virtue (which were later to characterize Sumner's "Forgotten Man") formed a significant part of Wil-

[1] A number of evaluations have been made of Sumner's general position. These range from Horace Kallen's statement that "Sumner is the only realist among our sociologists who ever set his observations down on paper," to Bernhard Stern's comment that "his was a stark, drastic, social Darwinian philosophy unrelieved by any concession to humanitarian sentiments, which he ridiculed." The validity of these or similar judgments need not be considered here, but it is interesting to notice from which ideological directions they come. The exponent of "individualism" (Kallen) implies praise; the sympathizer with "collectivism" (Stern) suggests the opposite.

liam Graham's primary group experiences. There is little doubt that, at an early age, he associated these qualities with economic success. His biographer emphasizes the American social and economic conditions which freed Sumner from traditional class ties: he "owed much to the economic forces which he spent his life in studying and describing. By the exercise of an indomitable will he made himself what he was, but they gave him his opportunity."

Two influences played a telling role during his formative years: reverence for the feeling of independence, and for the ethics of the Protestant religion. "By birth and early association he was of the common people . . . his sympathy was always with the hard-working, self-respecting wage earners . . . *who minded their own business.*" (Author's italics.) This stress upon independent action, particularly in economic activities, remained dominant throughout his life. Likewise, from boyhood to old age, Sumner placed a high worth upon ethical-religious values typical of the Protestant faith; he was conventionally religious, tending towards serious puritanism. His views on class and class conflict, it will be shown, were considerably influenced by both of these factors.

Though Sumner displayed an early interest in economics and social problems (before entering college he had carefully studied H. Martineau's *Illustrations of Political Economy*), he decided upon a religious career and studied for the ministry at Yale and in several European centers. (Consequently he had no direct contact with the Civil War.) Returning to this country, he taught the classical courses in his Alma Mater before becoming rector of the Episcopal Church of Morristown, New Jersey.[2] Preaching and editorial work on a church publication failed to satisfy his intellectual interests, which were especially centered upon economic problems, and he was finally offered a chair in the somewhat reformed Yale University in 1872. Sumner remained at Yale until his death, but his activities en-

[2] It is interesting to note that he favored the Episcopal Church as it was "taking the best classes of society."

compassed a variety of functions: local alderman, member of the Connecticut School Board, professor of both political economy and sociology, administrative official of the college.

His own life had convinced him of the significance of the individualistic virtues: self-discipline, rugged perseverance, and industry. From the time Sumner joined the Yale faculty, these values were to play a principal role in his economic and sociological writings. This was a period in which "labor disturbances were beginning, and the excesses of the International Workingmen's Association had given many people a well-founded terror of the possibilities of Trade Unions." That his writings and lectures should be pointed, in the main, toward "the social problem" was not strange. Particularly were his essays and shorter writings, his most characteristic work, thus oriented. The number of these is amazing, ranging in subject matter from "pure" economics to history and sociology. Throughout the several volumes the emphases are apparent: individualism versus collectivism, the trade-union question, free-trade versus protectionism, the role of capital in civilization, the "forgotten man."

Sumner maintained a position that is usually described as individualistic and laissez faire. Even in his great sociological contribution, *Folkways*, this is apparent. Perhaps because of his advocacy of laissez faire, his favorite sociologists were Spencer, Lippert, Gumplowicz, and Ratzenhofer. Sumner himself stated: "I believe that my conceptions of capital, labor, money, and trade were all formed by those books which I read in my boyhood." These conceptions which markedly characterized his writings (most emphatically in *The Forgotten Man and Other Essays*) were carried over into his own political activities: as an alderman he opposed labor legislation, and he often addressed public audiences, always upholding laissez faire. In one instance, at least, Yale gained financially through his views when a contributor to the college funds doubled his check because Sumner's speeches had convinced him "that Yale is a good and safe place for keeping and using of property and the sustaining of civilization when endangered by ignorance, rascality, dema-

gogues, repudiationists, rebels, copperheads, communists, But-
lers, strikers, protectionists and fanatics of sundry roots and
sizes."

There is no question as to Sumner's laissez faire bias. Ward,
in speaking of Sumner and his followers, said that "*laissez-faire*
has with them become a creed and they feel as do religious
devotees when they see their faith breaking down and their
creed superseded by a more liberal and progressive one." Ward
actually welcomed Sumner's volume on *Social Classes*, as he
believed it would inadvertently illustrate the absurdity of the
laissez faire position. Dr. H. E. Barnes echoes Ward: "his views
regarding social initiative . . . were exceedingly biased and
archaic, being almost a *reductio ad absurdum* of the laissez faire
individualistic position."

Such extreme comments, however, fail to encompass an important quality of Sumner's laissez faire. While it is true that
he was extending the evolutionism of Spencer and Lippert to
the whole social field,[3] he had little faith in "systems" of complex theory, relying rather upon common sense. Sumner was
convinced that his individualism was the only practical approach to social life. He had little patience with high-spun
arguments, especially those of the spokesmen of labor; indeed,
his training had not equipped him to entertain theoretical ab-
stractions of any kind. This faith in "common sense" hardly
allowed Sumner to disregard completely the influence of man's
own effort upon social change. It has been stated frequently
that he disclaimed that man can arbitrarily intervene in the
natural processes of society. Sumner himself denied the validity
of such interpretation in his essay on "Laissez-Faire": "*Laissez-
faire* is so far from meaning the unrestrained action of nature
without any intelligent interference by man, that it really means
the only rational application of human intelligence to the assistance of natural development." The emphasis upon the "prac-

[3] Stern states: "Believing that the mores functioned through individuals without coordination by any formal authority, Sumner found his theories of the
origin and nature of social institutions consistent with his advocacy of laissez
faire."

tical," the disregard for "theory," the belief in the efficacy of "commonsense," are qualities which throw some light upon Sumner's treatment of class phenomena.

Concern with the topic of class marked Sumner's thinking from his undergraduate days until old age. While a student at Yale, he wrote a paper on "The Laboring Classes," and later, in his religious sermons, his favorite subjects included "Ill-gotten Wealth," "The Ordeal of Prosperity," "The Relation between Public and Private Morality," and the like. Class emphasis is revealed when one reads his several volumes of essays, the title essay of one volume being "The Forgotten Man," to Sumner a "class" in itself. His historical writings, such as "Politics in America, 1776-1876," "The Administration of Andrew Jackson," and "Advancing Social and Political Organization in America," stress the role of class divisions (or "classless" situations) in historical development. Although only one small volume (*What Social Classes Owe to Each Other*) carries the specific label, "class," his preoccupation with the subject is borne out in the majority of his essays in economics, politics, and sociology. One of the most interesting and significant examples of the class point of view is to be found in "Bequests of the Nineteenth Century to the Twentieth," in which appear several surprisingly accurate predictions.

This same emphasis is present in his sociological writings. Class conflict and class hatreds indicate the need of a "science of sociology," claimed Sumner. Lacking the objectivity characteristic of his treatment of other subjects, *Folkways* nevertheless devotes a number of pages to the analysis of class; an analysis, incidentally, which clearly reveals Sumner's laissez faire position. *The Science of Society*, completed posthumously by Professor Keller, gives much more weight to the topic, the first volume stressing class phenomena in relation to social origins, property, fertility, civilizational development, liberty, and the state. Professor Park includes, as among the important contributions of Sumner, the distinction between the masses and the classes, and the role of each in the formation of custom.

Though he did place great emphasis upon class, Sumner apparently devoted little time acquainting himself with the theoretical literature of his opponents, the socialists. His conceptions of "socialistic" doctrine were sometimes as naive as those of the "forgotten man" he eulogized. This ignorance of Marxian writing was emphatically brought to his attention, but there is no reason to believe he ever filled this intellectual gap. In this respect he stands with Ward. Perhaps his mistrust of theory and his reliance upon "commonsense" explain in part his refusal to read Marxian theory. The point is particularly interesting when one considers Sumner's own "economic determinism," which becomes an essential part of his class doctrines.

2. CLASS DIVISIONS AND SOCIAL CHANGE

"We have been whirled along . . . at the sport of forces which we set loose but cannot control, and loaded with consequences which we find it hard to bear." Sumner's evolutionism, natural, spontaneous, unconscious, automatic, with its emphasis upon the conditions of the struggle for survival, is the pattern of process into which he worked his theory of the role of class in social change. The general process is essentially "natural"; therefore any power or privilege that a group possesses is a natural phenomenon and consistent with the evolutionary forces. "Nothing but might has ever made right": the role of force is dominant in all social change.

Ever present also, and likewise natural, is "monopoly." The latter is not a special product of capitalism, or an invention of the bourgeoisie, so often claimed. Thus, anyone who condemns monopoly condemns no special human agency, but the very nature of the universe itself. Monopoly, inevitable and natural, necessarily leads to class divisions marked by the same qualities. Competition is the dynamic handmaiden of monopoly, and these two operating together produce class-stratified societies, economic conflict, and war. These latter, war and conflict, moreover, are not only a result, but a cause of class divisions.

A dominant factor in this natural evolutionary process is population pressure. If the pressure is great, the class order will be rigid and highly disciplined; if it is low, freedom and equality (class mobility) will result. An under-populated country, therefore, offers advantages to those of the occupations of lower status, and "liberty" has the greatest chance for expression. The major significance of the discovery of America was the role it provided the working class. The "earth hunger" that forces man to seek new lands is class-motivated and has important class results. Sumner, like Durkheim, viewed the man-land ratio as a constant dynamic in social change.

The emphasis throughout Sumner's evolutionism is on the "natural": monopoly, war, and classes are produced by forces outside human control. Attempts to hinder such forces are "retrogressive elements"; slavery of some kind must always be present, and those who interfere by instituting "controls" are attempting the impossible.[4] His doctrine, consistently applied to all social phenomena, including efforts to change or control human destinies, demands that they too be regarded as "natural" products. Such consistency was lacking in Sumner's application. This was well voiced by Ward: "In his severe condemnation of the 'friends of humanity' . . . he seems to forget that these very troublesome persons are merely products of society and *natural*."

The reader who regards sociology as a very special science is apt to ask—Do not such broad questions lie outside the range of our field? Sumner answered strictly in the negative and claimed that "conflicts about capital" are the most important subject of sociology.

Thus Sumner's conception of class was usually economic, related directly to his "economic determinism." "Moral forces" play a role in social change, but "the economic forces are far more primitive, original, and universal." "Self maintenance" is the prime motive and interest: "it gives shape to everything

[4] The "impossible" becomes in Sumner's thinking, the "wrong" or "wicked." See Division 5 of this chapter on Sumner's ethics.

else." The historians were criticized for their failure to understand the basic economic conditions which shape political developments, and even the socialists were accused of not realizing that the industrial organization determines the nature of social relations, value symbols, philosophy, political institutions, and customs.

The weight given the economic factor is most vividly illustrated in his discussion of the family. Sumner claimed agreement with the socialists as to the factual situation: property and the family are "inextricably interwoven," the former being the basic prop of the latter. The existence of any society depends upon the presence of both. It follows that an attempt to abolish property relations also demands the elimination of the family; thus, family sentiment is the most conservative force in society. "The reason why I defend the millions of the millionaire is not that I love the millionaire, but that I love my own wife and children, and that I know no way in which to get the defence of society for my hundreds except to give my help, as a member of society, to protect his millions." In *Folkways*, Sumner described marriage as an insurmountable barrier against socialism.

This apparently monistic economic interpretation was qualified by his recognition of the interaction among various forces. The family, Sumner went on to point out, greatly influences property relations. But it is not a case of one way causation, for social, economic, and ethical forces interact. Environment and ideas constantly affect each other. Nor did he agree that technological factors have any particular primacy. Like Marx and Engels, Sumner was chiefly interested in the underlying economic forces, but, as in their case also, this main interest did not become the all-sufficient explanation of history.

Before considering specifically Sumner's conception of the functions of capital, property, and class in the formation of history, attention should be given his theory of class origins. In *Folkways*, the "plutocratic effects of money" were cited as present in all societies, from Melanesia to New York. Labor has always existed, consequently wealth; there have always been men who have monopolized the latter, who are always "admired and envied." Capital is "social power"; thus classes constantly take shape and change as new social groups gain control of capital.

This economic explanation was repeated in *The Science of Society*, but the latter offers a more elaborate description in terms of the conquest theory of class origins.[5] Military conquest and enslavement, utilizing force for organizational purposes, initiate the class order. Slavery, the original class form, had its basis in the need of a labor force. Victims of capture could be made to perform tasks which, if forced upon the original members, would endanger the in-group. Like Ward, Sumner relied upon the theory of the Gumplowicz-Ratzenhofer school, concluding similarly that, after conquest, some degree of class amalgamation takes place through intermarriage and common economic enterprise. War and resulting conquest were especially important in creating new and more advanced social organizations marked by complex systems of stratification.

Sumner refused to conceive of any pre-class society or "primitive communism." Such a conception is "fanciful": the notion of a free and voluntary community is unhistorical. On the other hand, "communalism," the corporate ownership of certain types of property, is typical of all societies. True, it varies in degree according to the difficulty of the struggle for existence, but no people has ever possessed "any primitive communism or socialism." The class-order, then, is inherent in the fundamental social force: the struggle for existence, which demands organization, conquest, and war.—The "tooth and claw" philosophy on a grand scale.

It is only in terms of Sumner's understanding of the historical role of *capital*, however, that his conception of class conflict becomes clear. He viewed capital as no less than the major instrument in the progressive evolution of society. Wealth is

---

[5] The remainder of this discussion of origins is taken largely from this work. We are unaware of the extent to which Professor Keller contributed to the contents, though he has attributed the bulk of it to Sumner.

not simply the product of labor; in fact, monopoly of capital indicates the presence of "talent." The competition which is indigenous to all living demands monopoly, demands economic cleavage. Monopoly of capital has allowed the change from the simple, primitive man to the intelligent man. "Capital is labor raised to a higher power by being constantly multiplied into itself"; concentration of wealth represents a finer integration of society. This theme is elaborately developed in *The Science of Society:* "foresight" is named the key to economic success; capital and civilization grow together; capital "is a societal adjustment of the first order."

Though capital is pictured as the first essential to social development, there is no need for its equitable distribution. Its "beneficent function" operates regardless of how it is shared: it aids everyone by defeating poverty, ignorance, and vice, while any diminishing of capital is detrimental to the social whole. This argument was reiterated throughout Sumner's writings. *Social Classes* insists that capital turned over to the worker or the poor is not put to productive use. Productive use depends, apparently, upon the capitalist using it: state-controlled railroads in Germany were condemned. By far the greatest share of accumulated capital is used so as to benefit all: "No man can acquire a million without helping a million men to increase their little fortunes all the way down through all the social grades." The presence of accumulated wealth in one economic class has stimulated the "appetite for enjoyment" in all classes: concentration of capital is a "good thing" and must not be disturbed. To denounce capital is "utmost folly," is to "undermine civilization." The theme is repeated in *Folkways*, where, in addition, emphasis is given to the role of the upper class as the bearer of the standards of elegance, refinement, and good manners.

Sumner sometimes substituted "property" for capital as man's most fundamental interest and the basis of all social struggle. The "power of the dinner" is greater than any set of principles: it is the key to the understanding of all social conflict. The "institutions of societal self-maintenance," the socializing forces of love, vanity, desire for recognition, even religious fear and concern for the after life, have their roots in the interest of man to acquire property. The property mores, therefore, are the strongest and most important of all; they resist change forcefully because, in the last analysis, they are a requisite of life itself. To criticize them is "like complaining of the force of gravitation"; tampering with them means the promotion of social disintegration.

The interest in property, furthermore, is shared by all: capitalist and worker, rich and poor, propertied and propertyless. But Sumner saw no *common* sharing of this interest; rather, he emphasized the conflict between employer and employed. To say that the latter "are partners in an enterprise is only a delusive figure of speech." The employers have organized, have developed associations throughout history to promote their own property interests; employees also find it necessary to combine forces for their own gain. Sumner's theory of class conflict was essentially economic: the struggle of interest groups for the possession of property.

"I have sought diligently in history for the time when no class hatreds existed. . . . I cannot find any such period. . . ." Conflict, class versus class, has marked all historical development: this insistence runs through Sumner's essays. It is a conflict that entails the use of force whether it be the direct form of slave-capture of ancient Rome, or the forceful control and manipulation of finance and industry of the modern era. Though we may speak in terms of other abstract political theories, the foundation of political conflict is economic class struggle. We err in attributing great reforms or revolutions to individual leaders because such historical movements have their real roots in underlying class changes.

The heaviest historical weight in social change lies with the "masses." For they carry the folkways and mores, and thus constitute the most conservative force in history. Whatever class action the masses engage in is directly related to the standard of living; a higher standard tends to promote economic action of the masses for self-betterment, which may take the form of a class movement. But the differential between their standard of living and that of the upper class is not in itself a sufficient stimulus for lower class activity. There must be disciplined organization, which entails inequality; these factors plus leadership are indispensable requirements in any successful mass action.

In the advanced civilizations, class conflict sometimes assumes revolutionary form. Such social convulsions are to be explained in terms of class mores: the old mores are "persistent," while great changes occur in the class distribution of economic power. During the revolutionary period "there are no mores," and after, the traditional mores reassert themselves: the former scheme of control is reintroduced. Rational invention of new mores, concluded Sumner, is impossible. The classes which have won new economic power model their lives "on the old aristocratic models": the essential class nature of social structure remains the same.

Contemporary class conflict was one of Sumner's foremost interests. He believed modern democracy must be understood in terms of the historical struggle among the monarchs, the nobles, the peasants, and the bourgeoisie. Out of this conflict there has developed in modern democracies a class of wealth and luxury, the "high bourgeoisie," on the one hand, and on the other, a great "middle-class" of independent farmers (not peasants) and workers. The third large group is the "hungry proletariat" which stands in direct conflict with the first, a powerful plutocracy. Democracy, with its accompanying liberty, has provided impetus for class conflict, and has not, as some believe, curtailed it.[6] Similarly, one of the effects of general education has been to spur on the economic struggle. Particularly, industrial strife, trade wars, unionization and strikes, become a necessary part of an economic order operating within a democratic framework: conflict is essential to the integration of the system.

---

[6] This line of thinking concerning the role of democracy is in direct contrast to the notions of Cooley and Ross. See Chapters VI and VII.

Industrial war, an inconvenience to be sure, but hardly an evil, is in part a product of liberty. It offers a solution of problems for which there are no other solutions. The traditional class lines have been broken down by the introduction of liberty, but as liberty is promoted, as traditional privilege is eliminated, class inequalities increase. At this point, Sumner agreed with the Marxists: new classes form, the bourgeoisie and proletariat. But here we find Sumner's extreme conservatism typically expressed: "Poverty and misery will exist in society just so long as vice exists in human nature." In the last resort, "human nature," a sorry "explanation" at best, is the cause of society's ills.

Sumner viewed the contemporary conflict between industry and labor as resolving itself into a struggle between democracy and plutocracy. For industry must become plutocratic if it is to survive in the struggle. "That is the conflict which stands before civilized society today ... it is big with fate to mankind and to civilization." [7] But a more detailed analysis of Sumner's "plutocracy" becomes a necessary part of the following section.

3. CLASS AND STATE

It has been noted that Sumner's political ideas represent a mixture of a Hamiltonian advocacy of rule by a talented aristocracy, Jeffersonian individualistic libertarianism, and the conservative Republican plea for "hard money." While this curious combination is manifest in his writings, Sumner generally maintained a stubborn opposition to state activity which interfered in any way with the free operation of economic forces. Dr. H. E. Barnes suggests that any individual who was under the influence of Spencer's *Study of Sociology*, and who had several years' experience in American city politics, would necessarily feel that government machinery is the poorest agency for social reform. However, Sumner did place considerable stress upon

[7] Here again we find Sumner sharing common ground with his socialist opponents; the latter could indeed welcome this forecast which was also made by their own theorists.

the relationship between economic class and the political state.

As noted above, most of Sumner's theory was economically oriented. Thus, the strength of democracy today, he declared, rests upon fundamental economic conditions. This emphasis upon the economic basis of political phenomena was not confined to the present time: the primitive political chief was the "economic representative of his people"; the rulers of both the Greeks and Romans were primarily motivated by economic interests. This is not to say that a state is simply the instrument of a class, but class conflict is always of vital concern to government. There must be "a true peace-group" to overcome such conflict. Consequently, politics and economics are firmly intertwined: the industrialist can not neglect political forces, nor can the politician remain independent against capitalistic interest. Industry becomes increasingly dependent upon political action, and thus it is necessary that the economic powers insist upon the strict maintenance of laissez faire principles by the state.

The institutional forms of the state,[8] in the last analysis, are the result of growth and expansion of early customs: government is a "development of the mores." The state itself belongs to a relatively well-developed stage of social evolution. When attention is centered upon the early period of stage-emergence, the role played by economic classes assumes significance for Sumner.

The Science of Society pictures a parallel development: state and economic class grow together, the formation process being one of interdependence. Numerous illustrations lend weight to the principle that property forms and political chieftainship emerge simultaneously and support each other. Order must be maintained, the "peace-group" with strong political control must be instituted so that wealth may establish itself. The control of economic class activity in earliest society, therefore, necessitates the operation of a state. Professor Keller followed

[8] A large part of the material on state origins is taken from The Science of Society. In Sumner's own writings discussion of this topic is scanty.

Sumner when he emphasized wealth as "a factor of great significance . . . in the formation of social classes and in the distribution of political power and influence."

Intrinsically related to the need of class control is the factor of conquest in early society. Gumplowicz's writings were liberally cited to establish the sequential development of conquest, class stratification, and, finally, the "amalgamation" that gives rise to the state forms. Sumner's appraisal of the Gumplowicz-Ratzenhofer theory, however, did not equal the laudation of Ward's. In fact, Sumner's other writings reveal a picture of class and state forming *within* a given society; the conquest theory appears in *The Science of Society* as "tacked on."

A more consistent approach, though not specifically class-oriented, appears in *Folkways* in the discussion of the relationship between "in-group" and "out-group." The internal discipline (political and economic) and cohesion of the former are a reflection of external conflict with the latter. Or, more exactly, internal peace and external war are dynamically interactive, are reflections of each other. The specific relation between state and class within the "in-group" is our principal concern.

Sumner repeated Ratzenhofer's assertion that "the state is an organization of coercion." To control the state, and thereby the chief coercive power in society, is to the interest of all groups or classes. Consequently, history is always characterized by the struggle of classes for state domination. In contemporary society, both the capitalists and the masses desire and attempt to monopolize the state for their own interests. It becomes a function of the state to regulate the class-struggle: the "peace-group" must be maintained in the interests of the whole.[9]

The "neutral" position which the state assumes, coupled with the force it must employ, leads to the development of "rights": the state becomes "partly ethical." But civil rights and liberties themselves are class products, promoted by certain groups for class interests. The property-owning middle class, for example,

[9] Note the inconsistency between this idea and Sumner's strict "laissez faire."

"flattered the masses and obtained their help" in forcing the state to guarantee civil liberties. The latter are largely safeguards for the freedom of capital, and no one is "free" except those who have amassed capital. This narrow economic interpretation of civil liberty is consistent with Sumner's notion that private capital is basic to all civilizational advancement, though this part of his discussion is surprisingly similar to the views of some of his collectivist opponents.

"I cannot find an example of a state which has not been, in a great measure, subject to the power of capital." At the present time in the United States, the democratic institutions are greatly weakened: a small ruling "oligarchy" has been established which is very susceptible to capitalistic control. The political party boss is represented as the financially supported and controlled tool of the vested interests, whose aid is responsible for the strength and growth of the political machine. In fact, the state is now essentially a party in control, a party which represents the specific interests of a class.

Such examples could serve as support for the Marxian theory of the state, but Sumner, of course, would deny this. Actually, this class emphasis conflicts with many of his own statements. In *Social Classes*, he criticized the Hegelian notion of an ideal state and claimed that, "as an abstraction, the State is . . . only All-of-us," while, in practice, the state is a small group chosen in careless fashion to perform certain services for the whole community. The state, in other words, is an associational agency of the community. Such institutions as universal suffrage actually weaken the state by demanding the enforcement of "equal rights and equal chances." The two essential functions of all states are the protection of property and of "the honor of Women." [10] The first of these is the more important, for it is property and capital, and their safeguarding, that guarantee civilization and advance.

---

[10] This seemingly incongruous coupling of property protection and women's honor is an excellent example of Sumner's strongly felt ethics imposing themselves on his "scientific" analysis.

True, the state is to a considerable extent controlled by the dominant economic class. But the interests of this class, the protection of private wealth and the guarantees of independent economic action, are, in Sumner's thinking, the true interests of all society. Consequently, the workers' attempts to employ the state in curtailing capitalist enterprise are misdirected, suicidal for societal well-being, and utterly condemned by Sumner. He so obviously imposed his own values upon an "objective" analysis of class and government as to make of it an extreme and somewhat absurd defense of an unsophisticated laissez faire philosophy.

The criticism voiced above cannot be directed towards Sumner's realistic conception of "plutocracy," the governmental form which he considered to be the result of contemporary class-struggle. He described plutocracy as the political methods sometimes used by the capitalists to insure and protect their economic position. It is not "the power of capital" as such, but "the most sordid and debasing" ways which capital may utilize. Its chief principle is that money will buy anything, particularly political power. Not all wealthy men are plutocrats, but modern times have produced the most powerful controllers of capital, many of whom resort to plutocratic practices. Never before has wealth been as powerful and absorbing as today, when modern states display a rapidly increasing advance of plutocracy. This phenomenon is "really new and really threatening."

Democracy, at the same time, has tended to place political power in the hands of the largest class, the non-capitalists. Capitalists, therefore, must cater to the masses, must use their "wealth to protect themselves." Democracy breeds plutocracy when wealth becomes the actual power by using undercover and corrupt devices. These methods are forced upon the wealthy by the anti-capitalist actions of democratic states; the extent of such actions will mark the extent of plutocratic growth. There are inherent in all democracies plutocratic tendencies, and the United States, having the most extensive democracy, is threatened by the most extreme plutocracy. The lobby most obviously, the caucus, convention, legislative committee, and the desire for an elected judiciary subject to political machine control, are indices of plutocratic development. These, together with devices of illegitimate character, were named by Sumner "jobbery": the "vice of plutocracy."

Not only did Sumner distinguish between ideal democracy and the plutocracy which exists in fact, but he indulged considerably in political forecast. "The social war of the twentieth century," he claimed, was to be the antagonism between democracy and plutocracy. Expansion and imperialism were viewed as signals of plutocratic growth. "Democracy, as the power of the day, threatens capital which, on the defensive, reaches out toward plutocracy." The twentieth century faces the alternative of either succumbing to an attack on property interests or resorting to a defense of the latter which must thoroughly corrupt the state. The straws in the wind include the movement for pension laws, anti-trust legislation, and the demands of organized labor.

Sumner stressed the class nature of the conflict he believed would characterize the history of the coming century. The middle class, representing a "wide distribution of comfort and well-being," is bound to disappear. The conflict will shape itself into one between capitalists and proletariat in which the former will continue to gain more political and social power. (Possible, indeed, is the change of the economic rulers to a nobility caste.) The defense of capital against further demands of the proletariat will institute the vicious techniques of plutocracy. Sumner anticipated the future with considerable accuracy: "Jacobinism, communism, and social democracy on one side, . . . plutocracy on the other." [11]

Throughout this section emphasis has been given Sumner's

[11] Contemporary writers, such as John Strachey and Lewis Corey, have produced analyses of the present that are surprisingly close to Sumner's predictions offered before the turn of the century. While he violently opposed "socialistic" doctrines of any kind, Sumner's prophecies were strikingly similar to those of the Marxists.

treatment of the relationship between state and *class*. Although the relationship was important in his thinking, his general sociological theory stressed the role played by that numerically large section of population he called "the masses." In the long view, all governments are "democratic" because "the masses, carrying the mores, have their way. . . ." Ultimate power always rests with the people, and with their public opinion. Like many writers of the past century, Sumner proposed a kind of Rousseaunian general will: the people may be mistaken but they cannot be "wrong." But, paradoxically, he devoted a large amount of his work to the attempt to show that the "people's" efforts to hamper capitalistic enterprise were not only in error but morally corrupt. Before developing this statement we must consider in some detail Sumner's conception of the class structure of his day.

4. Class Structure and Class Consciousness

A number of English and Continental scholars, including Alfred Marshall and Herbert Spencer, hailed Sumner's *What Social Classes Owe to Each Other* (1883) as an excellent contribution to the class literature of the day. But it is only as one reads through the larger volumes of essays and *Folkways* that a clear-cut picture of class-stratified society emerges. *Folkways*, especially, presents a specific treatment of class criteria and class function.

Apparently inspired by the works of Galton and Ammon on the "natural" distribution of talent in society, Sumner proposed that the criterion of social class is the "societal value" rendered to the whole by each of society's segments. Intellectual, moral, economic, and physical elements combine to produce societal value, the highest degree occurring when there is a "harmonious combination" of these elements. Sumner was obscure concerning the nature of the forces which produce these various elements, though he did suggest that societal value almost conforms with "mental power." "Practical sense," health, and luck also aid in its determination.

With this criterion Sumner described the class structure of society in terms of the statistical curve of normal distribution. Following Ammon's work, a graph is reproduced revealing that the greatest number of persons belongs to the "mediocrity" group, with the curve tapering off to "genius" above, and to the "defective," "delinquent," and "dependent" below. According to this graph, the large mediocrity group is identical with the "masses," who are distributed just above and below the midpoint of the curve. Below the masses is found the "proletariat," which is described as serving society "only by its children." [12]

The conception of the great middle group, the masses, led to Sumner's famous distinction between the *masses* and the *classes*. The respective historical functions of these two groups are basic to all of Sumner's sociology. The first group is conservative, it carries the folkways and mores, it is led and never leads. The second, the classes, promotes change, struggles for political and economic power, and leads the masses in terms of *class* interests. The masses are "the core of society," the "inertia" group of society. The classes are the innovators, but, in the last analysis, their success depends upon acceptance or rejection by the masses. The illustrations in *Folkways* of "class" activity are largely confined to the upper groups, but Sumner's other writings indicate his interest in the innovations proposed by the lower classes as well.

It is significant that the criterion of societal value and the functional distinction between classes and masses are not of a specific economic nature. Both of these points were developed

---

[12] The utility of such a structural scheme of social classes is questionable. A social class, according to this plan, is simply an aggregate of individuals who possess similar economic and "mental" qualities which permit them to be grouped together for statistical or descriptive purposes. A social class thus defined is not a *social* group, but a statistical aggregate or logical class. Interest in the mores and group values prevented Sumner from adhering to this scheme in his many discussions of social class in *Folkways* and his other writings.

only in his sociological writings (*Folkways* and *The Science of Society*), but his more detailed discussion of class appears throughout his essays. In the latter, his approach is often more economically oriented. Thus, certain inconsistencies are revealed which should be understood as a reflection of the distinction between his extreme laissez faire economics and Sumnerian "sociology," with its emphasis upon the role of the mores in social change. His essays, for the most part, exemplify his economic, as distinct from his sociological, views.

To Sumner, inequalities of wealth, power, and prestige are essential to societal development. Communities must have classes if they are to advance. Early forms of communalism are only adequate for very undeveloped groups, attempts to return to such forms being "maladjustments." The equality aspect of modern democracy is inconsistent with evolution: if we are to be realistic, we must recognize the need for social inequalities, for social classes. The upper classes have throughout history held, and sometimes abused, "social power." Class possession of social power is consistent with human evolution and with the larger social welfare.

It is in terms of the necessity for and the ever-presence of social classes that Sumner turned to the study of contemporary class conditions. The "aristocratic system" out of which our society grew consisted of the three classes, landlords, tenants, and laborers. Under the condition of dense population these classes were widely separated as to power, living standards, and "earthly happiness." This system of "privilege and caste" was revolutionized by the growth of capitalism, the rise of the bourgeoisie, and the development of political democracy. The American Civil War serves as an example of the conflict between the old and the new class system.

The old system was "militaristic": it emphasized classes and rank. The present class order supplants rank by wealth: here is the historical distinction between status and contract. In America, particularly, the new "contract" system dominates the social scene, wealth being the chief determinant of class position: hence the impossibility in this country of tolerating the feudal vestige of slavery. Wealth is a mobile factor under capitalism and its acquisition is an individual, not a class, problem. Thus there is no class mobility *qua* class, but only the vertical movement of persons. The "laboring classes" are consequently really a fiction because actually there are only laboring individuals. As long as wealth is mobile economic class lines tend to disappear, for the individual's status is measured by his changing amount of wealth. But Sumner was aware of the tendency of wealth to become concentrated, making for the development of a new status quo. The possession of capital leads to conservative views, their possessors staunchly defending "the system." [13] Social and political power becomes identified with capital regardless of democratic forms and principles. Sumner ridiculed those socialists who advocated revolution by pointing out that the capitalists have control of the arms, leadership, and the army, by virtue of their ownership of wealth.

The power of capital, however, Sumner believed to be matched by the gains of individual laborers. For many do accumulate wealth by industry; the spirit of the contemporary mores is "progressive" and "optimistic." Industrial conflict and the growth of trade-unionism are conclusive evidence that the workers are generally prosperous, and are winning substantial gains and considerable power. He was describing the America of his day, an expanding capitalistic society marked by vertical class mobility, by geographical growth, by "progress." He found its antithesis in Russia, with its stability of class lines and control in the hands of a small traditional group. But he was not so immersed in this "American dream" as were many of his contemporaries. In fact, he stressed the idea that competition demands great inequality: it injects into society a wide dispersion of conditions. He condemned those "stump orators" who claimed that society could exist without poverty classes. He was even more insistent upon stressing the presence and im-

[13] Sumner's conception of a growing "plutocracy," noted above, is an excellent illustration of the developing rigidity of contemporary class lines.

portance of the wealthy *as a class*. The term, "people," is in itself an indication of the distinction between the general populace and the owning and ruling group. Sumner believed that a society which had only two classes, rich and poor, is in an "unsound" condition, but he claimed, nevertheless, that our own society was tending in the two-class direction. *"It is the tendency of all social burdens to crush out the middle class and force society into an organization of only two classes, one at each social extreme."* Thus he stated the theme of one of his best-known essays, referring to conditions in the United States. Two industrial classes, social groups based upon economic relations, were forming, and the conflict between them constitutes "the social question."

The thesis of a two-class trend was abandoned when Sumner (in only one early lecture) stressed the complex nature of our class structure and claimed that even a three-way division in this country would be meaningless. Again, an implicit shift from the two-class thesis is contained in the notion that the largest social group, the masses, is gaining more political and economic power: "comparative equality" has been brought about. These qualifications are somewhat clarified by a more specific consideration of Sumner's treatment of the middle class and proletariat.

As noted above, Sumner emphasized the "contract" nature of contemporary society, which offers strong contrast with the older rigid "status" system. The rationalistic procedure which is the basis of our present social order, together with the freedom and guarantees of property and the development of science and liberty, have resulted in the growth of a great middle class. Sumner was more in sympathy with this section of the population than any other: within it was to be found his eulogized "forgotten man." The presence of the middle class has produced the "elementary contradiction, that there are classes and there are not classes." The paradox is explained by the fact that the middle class possesses little or no class consciousness. In America, particularly, this group is of the greatest importance in the social structure: it makes absurd the distinction between "bourgeoisie" and "proletariat." For all in the middle rank possess an equality that renders the old status distinctions meaningless.

Within the middle class exists a dominant economic mobility that robs it of its status-class nature. This mobility, plus the independence of the American worker, gives him such strength in the labor market that trade-unionism is unnecessary.[14] The farmer, an important part of the middle class, is likewise "independent" because of the great availability of land.[15] Not only is the middle class economically emancipated, but ideologically unique. It is a class disciplined in terms of a sense of morality, of public feeling, and of responsibility. Politically too, it displays the virtues of self-criticism, equality, and rational procedure. Nobles and peasants have created only autocracies; the proletariat has developed nothing but revolution; but the glorious middle class has given us the stability of democracy. Sumner, like Professor A. N. Holcombe today,[16] found in the middle class the positive ethical quality of the Aristotelian mean.

Though Sumner lauded this middle group, he emphatically predicted its passing. The financial and technological advances of modern capitalism weed out the small independent person. Likewise, all taxation, and especially protective and "social" taxation, operates against the large middle class, and gives more and more control to a few capitalists. The economic disappearance of this class is encouraged by its political inefficiency, for the middle class is never organized as an associational group promoting its own political interests. On the contrary, it is the section of the population most susceptible to political manipulation by the class above. True, the bourgeoisie invented the safeguards of civil rights, which theoretically work for the benefit of all classes, but modern democracies reveal that they are

[14] Sumner's views on trade-unionism were anything but consistent.

[15] It is the farmer's position that gives orientation to Sumner's book on *Social Classes: "Social Classes* is the outcome of the study of a population predominantly rural. . . ."

[16] See *The New Party Politics* (New York 1933).

manipulated and abused. Both the economic and political trends illustrate the gradual elimination of the group in which Sumner found the basic social virtues.

Not only is the middle class threatened by the activities of the capitalists from above, but it faces as serious a menace from below, from the proletariat. The proletariat includes the dependent and delinquent groups which have maintained their political privileges. Actually, a proletariat which has no chance for advancement does not exist in modern society. But the term proletariat is becoming a political weapon wielded by certain "have-nots" to appeal to "the hot-headed, the ill-behaved, the ambitious, those who have nothing to lose, the flatterers of rising power, and other such persons who naturally gravitate toward a revolutionary party." [17] Sumner claimed that "proletariat" "should be a term of reproach," but indicated that its function is to render a section of the population "a fighting faction." He found it difficult to discover exactly what groups comprise the proletariat. There is no lowest limit, but the upper limits are vague. Certainly not all wage-earners (he mentions as wage-earners the President of the United States and "high officials") are to be included, and particularly not the workman who has small savings. The radicals' antipathy for the small bourgeoisie, the "forgotten man," convinced Sumner that only the lowest, most degraded persons belong in the proletariat. Neither the European peasants nor American farmers can be included: the proletariat is essentially an urban class. Because of the dominance of farmer, artisan, the worker with savings,— in other words, the middle class *minded* group in America— the "exotic" foreign distinction between bourgeoisie and proletariat has no legitimate local application.[18] It is the middle class

[17] This conglomerate of types represents an odd assortment of Sumner's values. We find the "ambitious" mixed with the pathological. It would be interesting to know exactly what he meant by those "who naturally gravitate" in a revolutionary direction. According to his own evolutionary theory all of these types should be "natural" products.

[18] Sumner's own application of such a distinction has already been noted. This is another illustration of the contradictions within Sumner's writings.

psychology of this group that is significant; and that raises the question of Sumner's views on class consciousness.

There is no specific analysis of class consciousness in any of Sumner's writings, but his interest in folkways and mores led to a considerable amount of material directly involving the psychology of class groups. Early in *Folkways*, he declared that there are not only mores common to a society, but that each class possesses its own mores. However, the lines that distinguish the mores of one class from those of another are blurred by the existence of a group of symbols surrounding the "people." These symbols or "tokens" are mythological, and they seem to represent a "superhuman energy." They are the collective representations that provoke common interest in a great community, weakening the consciousness of class lines. Especially in modern democracies which have driven out the old static castes the "common man" becomes the symbolic model for group emulation. A general levelling takes place in the thinking of the community, giving highest value to this essentially fictitious common denominator, "common man." Reinforcing the "classless" type of thinking are the empire-minded politicians and journalists who manipulate the symbols of patriotism for their own interests: the manifest destiny of a nation outranks the interests of any of its segments.

In the United States, there is a strong body of classless folkways, the result of our historic development. The notion of class is itself distasteful and misunderstood: "There is a superstitious yearning for equality." American ideology is of a competitive nature: the old status distinctions are not part of the mind of the masses. An economic system which has allowed great numbers of people to accumulate wealth, coupled with an increasing general standard of living, provides the basis for this competitive feeling: the "American dream" is produced by the economic order. The "cult of success" is in full swing to the detriment of class consciousness of the "corporate" type.[19] The

---

[19] Compare with the very precise distinction between corporate and competitive class feeling made by R. M. MacIver, *Society* (New York 1937), pp. 174, ff.

socialist, in attempting to impose corporate class consciousness upon modern society, mistakenly applies feudal conceptions to a situation relatively free of status.

This competitive ideology is linked with the concepts of competition and emulation which Thorstein Veblen so brilliantly analyzed and which found a place in Sumner's writing. Characteristic of the mores of the professional and semi-professional groups are the canons of style, display, envy, and "mean social ambition." In all classes the "social standard of comfort" is upheld by the fear of social disapproval, the latter being a powerful sanction of class mores. The standard "acts like honor," resulting in extravagance and detestible ostentation. This competitive feeling dominates the attitudes of most young men who see themselves as wealthy in the future. Wealth becomes the chief determinate of status, and with it, "leisure" develops as the symbol of prestige: "Leisure, not labor, is dignified." The non-manual pursuits, professional and white-collar, carry higher status because they are considered "easier" and more "genteel." Those who possess wealth and leisure in abundance set the patterns of conduct for all other groups. Modern society, particularly, shows a constant emulation of the upper class by the others, who compete among themselves to most closely duplicate their superior models.

However, in this modern world marked by individual competition and imitation, certain groups of the lower economic ranks manifest a growing feeling of solidarity which often leads to class action. Two factors operate in this direction. First, the economic situation, which actually raises the material standards of the working class, gives that class hope and expectancy of even better conditions, and leads it to organize for the purpose of attaining economic goals. Thus, where there have been the greatest gains there exists the greatest discontent. And second, there is an ideology which assures the worker that he has a chance to rise which doesn't correspond to the actual economic conditions. Indeed, revolutions have been caused by unfulfilled hopes and expectations. Democracy "has been lavish with its promises," and, consequently, faces a situation replete with potential trouble. Sumner failed to develop these ideas, nor did he specifically apply them to an analysis of the contemporary class system. But, obviously, he was aware of the problems involved in class psychology and its dynamics.

He noted several illustrations of strong corporate consciousness existing in specific groups. Each class, for example, develops to some extent powerful mores governing the actions of its own members: the epithet of "scab" used by class conscious workers is a case in point. Again, trade-unions often increase the *esprit de corps* of workers. Sumner condemned those who patronize the working class because they increase the class consciousness of labor; the "self-respect" of the worker is identical with the competitive feeling. On the other hand, there are examples of corporate feeling which Sumner recognized and did not condemn. The slum-dwellers enjoy their life, feeling strongly attached to their extremely low material surroundings. He saw no particular reason to attempt to change this feeling of complacency. In the same vein: it is impossible to bridge the social chasm which exists between Negro and White in the southern states. In general, Sumner's values called for a community devoid of class conscious groups, with noted exceptions which usually represented the extreme "low" of the social hierarchy.

5. SUMNER'S REFORMISM

Most sociologists in their scientific work strive to be "objective" about their own values; nevertheless, the influence of such values is usually discernible. Regardless of his claims of absolute neutrality, Sumner was no exception in this respect. His "science of society" was to arrive at "true conceptions . . . without prejudice or bias of any sort." The neutral, other-world attitude did dominate his general treatment of the mores in *Folkways*, but when he turned to "class" topics in this same work his own values forced themselves into the treatment. Henry Baldwin once remarked that Sumner "could see no difference between the poor plundering the rich and the rich plundering the poor." This is the essence of the "unbiased" position that marks *What Social Classes Owe to Each Other:* "we all owe to each other good-will, mutual respect, and mutual guarantees of liberty and security. Beyond this nothing can be affirmed as a duty of one group to another in a free state."

Such verbal neutrality stems partly from Sumner's conviction that the natural evolutionary forces work themselves out to man's best advantage, and that his efforts to change the social world are immoral because they are unnatural. He believed, in general, that whatever position an individual occupies in society reflects his abilities. Ward, referring specifically to the *Social Class* volume, stated that Sumner committed the serious error of assuming that privilege and security are distributed on the basis of merit.[20] Sumner's oft-repeated anti-reform position provides further illustration of this assumption. All reformers, he held, are essentially "mischief-makers" because they fail to realize that the mores demand a slow, gradual type of change. Any effort to direct social change is a "vain fancy"; the most we can do is to observe. It is our *duty* to "support the existing institutions": we are not to criticize them or attempt to change them.

Such a position makes of the social *status quo*, whatever it entails, an object of moralistic praise, and Sumner, though he found certain contemporary situations deserving of his bitter criticism, spoke and wrote as a moralist. His biographer describes him as being motivated chiefly by humanitarian values, indicating correctly that Sumner's anti-reform position possessed a strong "reform" quality. It is impossible to read much of Sumner without feeling in the presence of "sermons," and, though one may disagree violently with many of his conclusions, they cannot be assigned to the cold, non-human "science" of the academic cloister. It has been said that "Sumner was

[20] On more than one occasion, Sumner asserted that the working classes held the most advantageous position of any group in the United States. He denied that there was any reason for "sympathy" or aid in view of their strength.

primarily a preacher in the true sense of that term," and that this element "is not entirely absent even in *Folkways*." [21]

Max Weber, in analyzing the relationship between the ideologies of Protestantism and capitalism,[22] might have found in Sumner an interesting blend of those two patterns of values. Earlier were noted the strong religious influence in Sumner's early life that accompanied his gradual and hard-gained rise in the economic and social world, and his own conviction of the worth of the individualistic virtues. Throughout his writings, the values symbolized by "work," "temperance," "thrift," "small savings" form the nexus of the pattern of life he would have us all live. "Industry, self-denial, and temperance are the laws of prosperity for men and state; without them advance in the arts and in wealth means only corruption and decay through luxury and vice." These factors, the basis of the welfare of society, should be coupled with the rearing of children, who, in turn, should be impressed by the same values. Nature provides no "boon": our blessings are the "fruits of labor, toil, self-denial, and study." Sumner was distressed by the fact that young men were reading so-called literature that fails to stress hard work and conservative, respectable family life.

The key to the "good life," in fact, moral "happiness," is economic gain. Not the rich man, but the man who is growing richer, is the happy man; "this great happiness is possible to all." The power of capital not only maintains "civilization," but it "sustains the happiness of the individual." This doctrine, Sumner believed, is especially applicable to the lower classes. The only intelligent procedure for the wage-earner is to work industriously, to save part of his earnings, and to raise a family. If he does these things he is bound to realize the beneficence of capital and the folly of anti-capitalists. Sumner predicted that in the twentieth century "the chances for those who inherit nothing

[21] John Chamberlain presents an interesting analysis of Sumner's reformism, which he describes as "libertarian." See his *Farewell to Reform* (New York 1932), pp. 9-17.

[22] In *The Protestant Ethic and the Spirit of Capitalism* (London 1930), translated by Talcott Parsons.

will be good *provided* they are *industrious, prudent,* and *temperate.*" (Author's italics.)

Sumner, like Benjamin Franklin before him, identified the "good," the moral, with individualistic economic enterprise. Franklin, one of Max Weber's principal examples of the operation of the Protestant ethic, was, according to Sumner, among the "three men to whom we are most indebted." Of course it is impossible to say exactly to what extent the Protestant values influenced Sumner's economics and sociology. But that they carried some weight seems valid in the light of the above illustrations.[23] Their influence is also perceptible in his attack on socialism.

A "prominent American" once evaluated Sumner's critique of socialist theory: "I have for many years publicly and privately urged socialists to read—really read—Sumner as the most doughty and competent foe with whom they have to reckon." However, there is very little evidence in his writings that Sumner was familiar with the theory of his principal opponents, with the possible exception of Rodbertus.[24] In fact, he conceived of socialism in the broadest terms possible: "*Socialism is any device or doctrine whose aim is to save individuals from any of the difficulties or hardships of the struggle for existence and the competition of life by the intervention of 'the State.'*" Thus "protectionism" and state interference in economic activities of any kind are "socialistic and semi-socialistic absurdities." Socialism, in this broad sense, is an imported "bequeath" of the nineteenth century to the twentieth; democracy is yielding to it, and it in turn will lead to complete capitalistic control or "plutocracy."

Sumner ridiculed the socialistic doctrines because they were antagonistic to natural, evolutionary development. "The law of the survival of the fittest was not made by man and cannot be abrogated by man": one who is familiar with the laws of

---

[23] Some of the material in *Folkways* suggests a rather irreligious "objectivism," but this objective quality is lost in Sumner's treatment of class topics.

[24] So far as can be discovered, Marx is only once briefly quoted by Sumner.

evolution "is armed at once against socialism. . . ." Without considering the possibility of revolution itself being a manifestation of evolutionary developments, he claimed that only the latter could produce "good for society." In the final analysis, the socialists make the manifestly false assumption that the system can be changed: this "is as idle as anything which words can express." Sumner, to be sure, deserted his own evolutionary "determinism" by his energetic refutation of socialism. For him the "good way" was his conception of the "natural way," and all must be made to see that it is "good." He belied himself when he stated that the social scientist "who discusses socialism is like a physicist who discusses Jules Verne's novels"; he found socialism over-imaginative, over-simple, and mystical, but he took considerable care to guard people against it.

The description of society as two extremes of rich and poor gained Sumner's approval, but this great economic cleavage appeared to him a necessary one. The rights of private property and the individual accumulation of capital must be retained, not only for the economic and technological advance of humanity, but also because they are "right," "moral," sacred. "Socialism denouncing property is only trying to get property. . . ." And this attempt can produce only drastic results, including "despotism, favoritism, inequality, and universal misery." The laws which govern the social order "are precisely analogous to those of the physical order"; to attempt to change them, the socialists try to "destroy belief in an Almighty God." Socialism tends to revise and utilize the barbaric "witchcraft" of the more primitive cultures: it stimulates mob violence; it calls for societal retrogression—back to communism; it shuts its eyes to the future in its "blind speculation on the vicissitudes of classes and forms of property in the future."

Apparently for self-amusement, Sumner wrote an elaborate description of "The Cooperative Commonwealth" of the future. The antithesis of Bellamy's famous utopia, it is characterized by dictatorship, ridiculous stupidity, complete economic disintegration, military breakdown, and extreme brutality. Socialism, according to this speculation, would make no attempt to alter the economic structure, but would merely increase the degree of economic exploitation, and carry society back to a primitive stage.

Especially significant in Sumner's attack on socialism is his insistence that the greatest support of capitalism is the family "instinct." The condemnation of capitalism must lead to the condemnation of family life: "it is plain that liberty, . . . individualism, monogamy, and private property all hold together as consistent parts of the same structure of society. . . ." Thus, socialism must demand the abolition of "the tie of parentage." The family molds the individual whose "character" is the source "of all good in men or the state." This is one of the important reasons "why all socialism is profoundly immoral."

Sumner's well-known defense of the rights of private property was related not only to material, economic well-being, but as importantly to certain ethical considerations. The property interest "is the condition of civilization"; it is basic to state, religious, and educational activities; it is the bulwark of the family and the "good life." Any attack on property or capital privileges is a movement aimed at the moralistic structure of society, a threat to "societal welfare at its very basis": "property is sacred as marriage is sacred."

Sumner, moreover, interpreted the "pursuit of happiness" phrase as the pursuit of property and the accumulation of capital. The social guarantee of the latter is the only sure way of preserving the chief means of happiness. The general welfare of a great community depends upon the right to accumulate fortunes, and the process of fortune-building, rather than creating misery for some, is beneficial to all. Therefore, the devices that are used in financial practice, the joint-stock company, "market cornering," etc., though they may be abused at times, should not be denounced, but protected. We must always remember, reminded Sumner, that the accumulation of capital stems from the virtues of "industry, temperance, prudence, frugality. . . ." Historically, property has been the basis of liberty: "liberty and property go together, and sustain each other in glorious accord." The guarantees of freedom crumble with the removal of property rights, and conversely, those who are struggling to gain property are promoting the cause of freedom. The property ethics of the ascending economic class were Sumner's ethics, were also the ethics of the middle class-minded "masses," and were the ethics he would assign to all civilization.[25]

Sumner's conception of property rights was directly related to his opposition to state activity in the economic sphere. In general, the state should have the single economic function of property protection. Many of his best-known essays were powerful expositions, elaborating the theme of non-interference of government. He argued that the ends to be gained from a strict laissez faire include more than economic progress. If capital were rigidly confined to the laws of the market and protected from state action, the possibility of the development of a capitalistic plutocracy would be negated. Such separation is beneficial to all economic groups and classes, while state activity in the economic sphere aids only one class. For this reason charity in any form must be relegated to the sphere of private activity, where personal acquaintance and estimate largely direct philanthropy. In fact, Sumner would rule out "objective" study and treatment of charity as involved in (some) legislation, and place it in the realm of "sympathy and sentiment." Furthermore, he believed the attempt to fix working hours by law to be opposed to the individual's material and ethical interests because such legislation prevents the exercise of the industrial virtues which are indispensable for the accumulation of capital, the "means to happiness."

Sumner seemed to forget that the need for and the existence of hours and wages laws, relief statutes, and the like were as much a product of a "natural" social and economic order as

[25] In only one short passage did Sumner qualify this "sacredness of property" position. In some distant future, he admitted, the property institution may give way to some other system, but he believed such speculation lay outside the proper province of sociology.

his own ideal conception of a laissez faire world. The trend in social science marked by the "objective" study of social legislation and "social problems," which was well established during Sumner's lifetime, was a trend which his position on these problems would have condemned.

At times, Sumner has been identified with a rigid anti-union policy, while, for the most part, he was only opposed to certain trade-union practices. In fact, he was careful to point out that labor organizations were inevitable developments of the same industrial forces that created their capitalistic counterparts, trusts. Conflict between capital and labor, entailing organization of both groups, signifies a dynamic society and cannot be regarded as an "evil," for actually it is "an incident of liberty." Voluntary cooperation for economic interests is a necessity in democracies; trade-unions not only must form, but their formation must not be hampered. In one passage, Sumner suggests that labor unions may even "maintain the *esprit de corps*" of the working class. However, he gives no *carte blanche* to union groups. Strikes are legitimate in so far as they "test the market," and if they are conducted rationally without appeal to "sentiment." But employees should never prevent others from filling their positions by taking possession of a plant, or otherwise hinder the operations of the free labor market. Sumner condemned all industrial violence, but the only type of violence he mentioned was that instigated by employees.

While admitting the inevitability of trade-unions, he did not agree that these "necessary" and "natural" associations always promote working class interests. They interfere with the free competition of the labor market, restrict the supply of skilled labor by imposing apprentice standards, thereby keeping more workers in the unskilled class, and they raise consumers' costs by adding union and strike risks to the employers' costs. Unionization, in the long run, is a burden on the working class and the public at large. This is especially true of large-scale national or international unions, which are "irrational and at war with economic forces." These large organizations only "court calamity" and for them to strike "is simply suicide." Sumner's approval of large-scale organization for employers, on the basis of his own reasoning elsewhere, should have been extended to employees' associations. But he would restrict the workers to the decentralized forms of unionization.

The apparent lack of consistency in Sumner's discussion of trade-unionism is directly related to his strong ethical values. In the *Social Class* volume, several pages describe the ideals which motivate most employers. They are again the ethics of thrift, industry, private charity, and the like: the Protestant virtues. While Sumner's evolutionary thesis allowed the natural inevitability of unions, he was led to condemn labor activities which were not consistent with his values. Thus unions were found to be natural products and perverse, legitimate and illegitimate, both "good" and "bad."

Sumner's descriptions of contemporary society and his prediction of the future indicate that he was keenly aware of the nature of the social structure and its dynamics. He, like Veblen, perceived a coming plutocracy, increasing economic class conflict, and the destruction of his own values. Yet his writings are dominated by a plea that we should adhere to the "common sense" of the traditional middle classes.

His laissez faire meant simply "minding one's own business." The variously labeled social philosophers, with their schemes for social reconstruction, are "meddlers" who hamper the everyday job of making a living and conducting respectable lives. Their programs give rise to large groups of "amateur" reformers who threaten the foundations of twentieth century society. They do not realize, claimed Sumner, that the "masses," though they are the court of final social appeal, cannot absorb much "true knowledge," nor can mere numbers solve the vital problems of social policy. Even popular education is mistakenly considered an instrument of social betterment: "our faith in the power of book learning is excessive and unfounded." Actually, the masses could "get on very well" with a minimum of education. Not the amount or the specific content of imparted knowledge, but the ethical ends which are stressed were the important issue to Sumner. Those final values are summed up in the common sense "minding one's own business" policy of his ideal "forgotten man."

"Now who is the Forgotten Man? He is the simple, honest laborer, ready to earn his living by productive work. We pass him by because he is independent, self-supporting, and *asks no favors*." (Author's italics.) If he is unhampered by paternalistic government, by "reformers," by humanitarian-minded meddlers, he will prosper materially and spiritually. He is the one who suffers most by the "quack" programs of the socialists, protectionists, and the advocates of social legislation, for he is the one who follows the rules of an ideal laissez faire economic world. When we would aid him through some reform scheme, we really hinder him: we should "mind our own business" and let him mind his. The rules of social living he follows are the proper rules; we should not try to change them, but rather adopt them. He is "forgotten" simply because he is omitted from consideration when we plan to make over the world with the aid of some utopian fantasy. And he is not only abused by programs of the left, but by the jobbery practices of a small number of capitalists of the right.

Sumner's "commonsense" further demanded that we entertain no foolish notions about human equality. All societies of all ages have contained the weak and powerful, the poor and wealthy, and it is only reasonable that the same phenomena will be found in societies of the future. The doctrine of inherent natural rights or equalities is obviously a fiction that only confuses our thinking in the social field. Natural rights, correctly interpreted, pertain only to the guarantee of "chances," never to the guarantee of results. The only possible institutional device which will assure everyone chance for success is "constitutional liberty," which to Sumner meant strict laissez faire. But poverty is part of the struggle for existence and is therefore natural, necessary, and beneficial. The plea for the correctness of inequality, stemming from Sumner's "commonsense," finally became sermonized: "I regard the passion for equality as a vice of our age."

No other early American sociologists, except Veblen, have so concerned themselves with the subject of class as William Graham Sumner and his contemporary, Lester Frank Ward. Both of these writers looked upon class phenomena as basic material for social science. Both emphasized the class nature of the social structure and the class dynamic in social change. Their descriptions of society were close to Marxian descriptions, but the solutions they offered were radically un-Marxian. Ward's program conceived of a classless order to be gained essentially through melioristic education. But Sumner tolerated no such "visions." His awareness of class lines did not lead him to demand their abolition. Rather, he would have us move within the ambit of an ideal laissez faire set of rules: he would call into the present and future a kind of past that never actually existed.

Both scholars were "realists" in their observations and predictions of a class-stratified world. They both became "idealists" in their respective programs of social reform: Ward seeking a semi-utopia to be gained by the enlargement of the intellect, while Sumner desired a neat, tidy, respectable, hard-working society to be won by a correct application of his conception of Adam Smith.

CHAPTER FOUR: ALBION WOODBURY SMALL

(1854-1926)

ALBION WOODBURY SMALL

1. INTRODUCTION

WARD and Sumner were, so to say, the prophets of American sociology. A. W. Small, F. H. Giddings, C. H. Cooley, and E. A. Ross, together with Sumner, gave the science a "professional" status, and endowed it with an academic vested interest. Especially is this true of Small: he founded and directed the first large university department of sociology, he wrote texts for student use, established the first important journal in the field and edited it for many years. Sociology owes part of its "respectability" to Small, who has been described by one of his students as "the ideal of a gentleman" having the "quiet elegance of an ambassador."

Small's biography was the success pattern of academic life. The son of a clergyman, he studied for that profession in this country, and in Europe during the early 'eighties. His interest in religion was sustained throughout his career: he consistently denied agnostic leanings, demonstrating his faith by serving as trustee and deacon of the Baptist Church all his years in Chicago. He won scholarly distinctions at Johns Hopkins and, still a young man, was president of Colby College from 1889 to 1892.[1] In the latter year, Small was called to the newly organ-

---

[1] During these years Small's major interest was history. He believed this subject lacked an adequate causal explanation of social change, and thus turned to the new science of sociology.

ized University of Chicago as head of the sociology department. In 1905 he became Dean of Liberal Arts. Unlike Ward and Sumner, he enjoyed a generous salary and professional prestige from the beginning. This successful career was marked by prolific writings and energetic, conscientious teaching.

Examination of the records of Small's activities and study of his works reveal a dominant central note: his strong ethical sense supported by the Christian faith. His many professional and social functions, no less than his voluminous papers, were marked by emphasis upon the moral fibre of man. The quiet dignity and considerable erudition which Small brought to the great new university of the Middle West—set in a general social atmosphere relatively free of these qualities—failed to conceal the results of earlier religious training. He was chiefly interested in the ethical ends which men seek and the appropriate means for their attainment.

His ethics took the form of the Christian conception of the brotherhood of man. The latter, indeed, was wedded to the new "exact" science of sociology in what appears at times a strange combination.[2] It was this combination, the synthesis of Ward's and Ratzenhofer's theories and Christian ethics, that stamped the character of Small himself. Urbanity of manner, prepossessing physical appearance, contact with the world-wide prominent of many fields were blended with Small's concern for man's achievement of true community based upon an ethical foundation. Love of science and moral stress were joined in his pedagogy, his administration, his "social" life, and, most importantly, his sociology.

Small's "ethics" was essentially classless.[3] Its religious origins were revealed in an early volume which lauded the Christian

[2] Small's reconciliation of the drastic, "pessimistic" theories of Ratzenhofer with his own moderate ethical-reformism was accomplished by pointing up the *cooperative* aspect of the "social process." See Division 2 of this chapter.

[3] Small guarded against condemning any social class as "wicked," although *Between Eras: From Capitalism to Democracy* portrays in one chapter a degenerate scion of the wealthy seducing and causing the death of a working class girl.

Socialists for "maintaining the position that ultimate sociology must be essentially Christian." Later, this proposition was reversed by the insistence that "social science . . . is the only rational body for religion." Principles of moral philosophy were given first place in his studies of Adam Smith and the Cameralists. Small well described his own position in stating that Smith's works rested "upon a general conception of the subordinate relationship of all specific activities within an inclusive moral system to which, in effect though not in detail, all students of society must ultimately return." (Original italicized.)

Possessed of this ethical orientation, Small could not but be seriously concerned with social improvement. The rapid urbanization of Chicago, its commercial and industrial growth accompanied by economic exploitation, labor conflict and political corruption, were striking aspects of his surroundings. The reformism of the late nineteenth and early twentieth centuries, which influenced many American social scientists, had been part of his training.[4] Although his fortunate financial situation protected him from the kind of economic struggle that was part of Ward's and Sumner's family background, Small's humanitarian sympathies, his observations of the world around him, and his familiarity with the social literature of his day resulted in his allegiance to the cause of social reform.

There is no question but Small maintained a "Christian-reform" point of view throughout his life, yet he occasionally denied a place for reformism in social science. For example, his first book in sociology stated that the teacher should not be a reformer, claimed that sociology provides no short cut to the solution of social problems, and praised Ward for his emphasis upon the psychic forces rather than for his social remedies. In another volume, he chided the "sentimental species of sociologists" whose "emotional reactions were more in evidence than their analytical processes." But these are exceptional

---

[4] Professor F. N. House names the reform movement as the most important element in turning Small's interests towards class.

examples. He charged pedagogy with the task of social amelioration; he placed himself in the same reform camp as Ward and
Ross; he stated that he regarded planning for an improved
society one of the most important concerns of sociology. More
than this, he considered all social theories and every social
science as a "function of practical problems which contemporary men are attempting to solve."

To Dr. Bernhard Stern's statement that "Small's orientation
in sociology was fundamentally ethical" can be added the fact
that he considered an ethical orientation methodologically correct. "Sociology, in its largest scope, and on its methodological
side, is merely a moral philosophy conscious of its task, and
systematically pursuing knowledge of cause and effect within
this process of moral evolution." Modern sociology, he claimed,
should analyze society in terms of the implications of Adam
Smith's moral philosophy. Ethical considerations had produced
both socialism and sociology, the latter being a protest against
the amoral classical economics on the one side, and the morally-
mistaken Marxism on the other. "Men's experience is the evolution of human values" was the starting point from which Small
worked; he was fairly certain which contemporary values
should be dominant.

An article appearing in the early years of the *American
Journal of Sociology* began: "The fact which has begotten
sociology is a dawning social consciousness"; and concluded by
stating that "there can be no very stable theories of social
action until there are convincing standards of social aim." In
discussing "The Significance of Sociology for Ethics," Small
insisted that science must provide an ethical philosophy of
life: its essential task is the creation of normative standards. For
no science is itself an end, but rather a method of organizing
knowledge, the ultimate function of which is the promotion of
more intelligent *social action*. His last volume reiterated that
the task of science "is to interpret the meaning of human experience" and to establish ways of directing human experience
"toward a larger output of life-values." Social science, par-

ticularly sociology, must furnish the criteria for social action if it is to be more than esoteric exercise: the theme dominated Small's writings.

Like most ameliorative-minded writers of his time, Small opposed the natural evolutionism of the Spencer-Sumner school and the individualism of the orthodox economists. The latter's "economic man," he suggested, is often a "bar to knowledge." The strength of his anti-individualism feeling [5] was indicated in a letter written to Professor E. C. Hayes: "If my name is anywhere extant . . . I hope it will have a tag attached with the memorandum, 'he had something to do with laying the individualistic superstition.' " His anti-individualism received its most definite expression in Small's desire to reform capitalism. Little critical analyses of the *economic* tenets of capitalistic theory appear in his writings.[6] But he damned "old-fashioned 'cupidity' getting in its work all along the line from lowest paid employee to biggest operator under the special conditions of our capitalistic system." [7] He likewise decried the situation that gave end value to the gaining of wealth: this was an unwarranted warping of the motivations of human behavior. At the same time, he condemned an order that permitted extreme poverty, slums, and sweated labor conditions. The goals of "civilization" include the guarantee of material welfare for all; a society which fails in this respect does not fulfill its civilizational ends.[8]

Occupying an important place among the objects for reformation in modern society are the inequalities and injustices of the class system. Small warned sociologists not to "agitate" for

[5] On this point he shared the views of Ward, Cooley and Ross, and, to some slight extent, Giddings.

[6] With the exception of *Between Eras: From Capitalism to Democracy*.

[7] It is interesting that Small, the moralist, in his own criticism of capitalistic society accused both "conservatives" and "radicals" of making a moral issue of their quarrel. He insisted that the real conflict was between "assumption" and "knowledge"; no solution would be possible until the issues were thoroughly intellectualized and the sociologists devised a "scientific" reform program.

[8] Small identified "civilization" with *ends*, "culture" with *means*. This distinction reverses the use of these terms by R. M. MacIver and others.

any one social class. At the same time, he conceived of "the social problem" as the subordination of special interest groups: *general* interests must become the goal of all group activities. Sociology itself, in fact, developed from the recognition of the phenomenon of class-domination, and contemporary sociology must keep this problem the main object of its study. Sociology's goal is the problem's solution.

Small's concern with the class order was shaped in part by his contact with European, especially German, scholarship.[9] His thorough knowledge of the works of Schmoller and Wagner was partly responsible for his interest in class phenomena; probably Sombart's teachings stimulated his severe criticism of capitalistic society. The conflict theory of the Gumplowicz-Ratzenhofer school became the basis of Small's *General Sociology*, and the writings of Marx, uncommonly enough, were part of his intellectual equipment. Of the Europeans, Ratzenhofer was the most influential in the shaping of Small's own theories.

"The theme of class conflict occupied a central place in Small's system . . . as developed in his *General Sociology. . . .*" Professor House could have applied the statement to most of Small's work. Beginning with the publication of the text, *An Introduction to the Study of Society* (1894), the class emphasis remained.[10] At Chicago, Small conducted seminars on Marxism and class conflict. Dr. H. E. Barnes comments somewhat eulogistically: "If he had seen fit to put into print the well-organized material from which he gave his famous course on 'The Conflict of Classes' he would have produced a work which would have made him a rival of Veblen as an original and courageous economist." One does not require the experience of Small's seminar to be aware of his constant concern with its subject matter. It is indicated by his discussions in the *Journal* of such

[9] Among Small's contributions to American sociology the diffusion of European social theory ranks very high.

[10] His earlier historical study, *The Beginnings of American Nationality,* contains no explicitly stated interest in class. And his later *Origins of Sociology* fails to emphasize the subject. These are exceptions.

matters as the "Schmoller-Treitzchke controversy," by his reluctance to accept Sumner as a sociologist because of the latter's
biased position in his volume on classes, by his praise of Le Play
for his interest in the working classes. Even in his more specialized volumes, *The Cameralists* and *Adam Smith and Modern Sociology*, Small emphasized class phenomena: the former
stressed the Cameralists' assumption of a static, stratified society,
an assumption which contradicted the actual dynamic class
situation of the period; the Adam Smith volume, as suggested
above, was in part a plea for a return to Smith's "moral sentiments." Small praised Smith's concern for the laboring classes,
as well as the later economists, like John Stuart Mill, who were
conscious of the "humanitarian" basis of economics. Again, the
class nature of many "social problems" is borne out in his general works. For example, he named economic class conflict as
basic to the anti-Semitic movement in France and Germany;
in another place, he cited employers' use of detective agencies
in labor disputes as a manifestation of a "pathological" class
situation.

In the development of general sociological theory, Small's
name is identified with the classification of "social forces" in
terms of "interests," and with the concept of "social process."
His *magnum opus* is usually held to be *General Sociology*
(1905) which elaborated in detail the forces and processes of
society. In this volume he named the "great problem" which
faced science and the public:

The production of wealth in prodigious quantities, the machine-
like integration of the industries, the syndicated control of capital
and the syndicated organization of labor, the conjunction of interests in production and the collision of interests in distribution, the
widening chasm between luxury and poverty, the security of the
economically strong and the insecurity of the economically weak,
the domination of politics by pecuniary interests, the growth of
capitalistic world-politics, the absence of commanding moral authority, the well-nigh universal instinct that there is something
wrong in our social machinery and that society is gravitating
toward a crisis, the thousand and one demands for reform, the

futility or fractionality of most ameliorative programs—all these are making men wonder how long we can go on in a fashion that no one quite understands and that everyone feels at liberty to condemn.

This situation, marked by class struggle, exploitation, injustice, this confusion "that no one quite understands," demands the attention of sociology. The sociologist, Small cautioned, must not champion the rights of any one class, but must work for a scheme providing justice for the "social whole." Class conflict had set for him his problem, science was to provide the means of its solution.

2. The Social Dynamic: Conflict of Interests

In a letter written to Ward in 1899 Small remarked: "at the present moment I am inclined to think that Ratzenhofer is the biggest find in Sociology for some time." His interest in Ratzenhofer was centered in the latter's concept of interests and his theory of social conflict. Together, these two ideas became the backbone of Small's own sociological theory, though he considerably altered the notions set forth in *Wesen und Zweck* and *Sociologische Erkenntnis*. Conflict of interests and resulting social structures consistently held his attention, illustrated by his numerous *Journal* articles, including a translation of Simmel's *Ueberordnung und Unterordnung* (Superordination and Subordination).

This focus necessarily led Small to consider class interests and conflicts and to an examination of the structure and dynamics of capitalistic society. On one occasion, he maintained that "there is an irrepressible conflict in modern society between the presuppositions of capital and the paramount values of humanity," and on another, he ridiculed the "free competition" assumptions of the more orthodox economists. Statements like these must be understood in terms of his general theoretical system.

Small's interest in economic and class phenomena did not

result in his allegiance to an "economic determinism." The view of historical causation he endorsed was not far from Ward's, but remote from the kind of economic emphasis shown by Sumner. Economic relations, Small maintained, are but a part of the whole complex of social relations that form the pattern of the social process. The concern of the sociologist is the whole process, not any single aspect; he will fail in his analytical task if he places the burden of explanation upon any single factor. This theme, a favorite, appeared in all of Small's books and in a good share of his shorter articles. Thus, sociologically viewed, economic functions are merely one aspect of the total social process. For example, the attempts to reduce "social stages" to a common economic factor are "foreordained falsifications." Nor is the explanation of the totality of social life in terms of the conflict between capital and labor likely to lead to correct results. On occasion, Small interpreted Marxism as economic determinism, thus rejecting it as a reduction of the social process to a single force. And, remaining consistent with his own views, but inconsistent in his evaluations, his discussion of "Socialism in the Light of Social Science" praised Marx's economic interpretation of history as non-deterministic. Again, Simon Patten drew Small's condemnation for presenting the thesis that a nation's "thinking" is a product of its economic activities without admitting the validity of the converse of that proposition.

Small sought the explanation of change in the complex of factors—economic, political, ideological—that is marked by constant interaction. Both the tools with which a man works and the ideas he has gained aid in determining his behavior. He refused to credit "volition" or "free will" with causative force; at the same time, he denied priority to economic phenomena.

But, while voicing the total-causation principle, Small arrived at an almost deterministic position of his own: a "moral determinism." [11] He argued that economic action, in the final

[11] For a somewhat different interpretation see E. C. Hayes' chapter on Small in *American Masters of Social Science*, ed. by H. W. Odum (New York 1927), pp. 151-153.

analysis, follows group standards of rightness. All behavior is finally subject to the socially created "aesthetic standards"; again, "the real explanation must be found in the spiritual initiative which is superior to mechanical causation." The emphasis upon the force of social morals, the values that men possess, is illustrated by Small's insistence that capital is a moral category, not simply economic. Adam Smith, as has been shown, was regarded by Small as essentially a sociologist by virtue of his conception of moral sentiments. And in the field of economic class conflict, the issue is pictured as basically a conflict of opposing sets of ethics, resolution being difficult because there are no common ethical standards.

The several "interests" which determine behavior, and around which social structures develop and change, were named by Small: health, wealth, sociability, knowledge, beauty, and rightness. "The conspicuous element in the history of the race . . . is *universal conflict of interests*." The social process is nothing more than the eternal struggle of groups forming around these interests or combinations of them.

He refused to admit that the wealth interest was a rephrasing of the economic man concept. The first is "a simple social element," while the economic man is but one of the many complex social products of the more basic interest. Sociological research could well employ the wealth interest concept as a methodological tool for the analysis of the various groupings and conflicts that grow up around this interest.[12] If we are eager to study class structures and changes, for example, the most fruitful procedure would be, first, to analyze the several interests "actually operative" in the class situation; and second, "to calculate the relative force of the many interest-factors in reaction with each other in given concrete situations." By merely studying economic changes or political turnovers as such, claimed

---

[12] Veblen's theory of "the instinct of workmanship" was cited as a possible example of such research. What Small found in Veblen's analysis comparable with his "wealth interest" is a mystery.

Small, we would be overlooking the essential *interest* nature of the social process.

Small's program for research on the basis of his "interest" scheme calls for at least three obvious criticisms. First, its very vagueness: we are asked to seek "interests" and their inter-relationships without knowing exactly their nature. Whatever we find in human behavior can apparently be grouped around the concepts of health, wealth, sociability, knowledge, beauty, and rightness. Second, the acceptance of these six interests is an *a priori* device that is very likely to predetermine our results. This criticism (which can also be extended to Ward's "forces," or Thomas' "wishes," or Pareto's "residues") should always be qualified by the realization that such a set of ideal concepts is at best a methodological device necessary in social research. Third, it may be questioned that the "interest" concept was an innovation, or in any way added to our knowledge of "the social process," or aided in its further analysis. Some answers to these criticisms are revealed in Small's own analysis of class interests and conflicts.

In *General Sociology*, Small's discussion of class follows closely the outline provided by Ratzenhofer. Class conflict is looked upon as struggle within and about the state. The latter is "both the product and condition" of the social process; the state continually strives for emancipation from special interest groups warring with each other. Any stage of national development exhibits a conflict between the recognized common interests and the several special interest blocs. The various interest groups, including classes, are continually conducting programs of "opportunism," and the concessions that these groups make to one another provide a ground of "common cause" which gives the state the function of integrating interests "by compromise." Ideally, the state is independent of the specific interest groups, but the latter, particularly the economic classes, struggle for the control of the state. But the essential compromise nature of the state remains: "the State is a union of disunions, a conciliation of conflicts, a harmony of discords." It is the agency through which warring forces are channelled into some degree of common action.

Intra-state class conflict must be considered, Small claimed, in terms of the distinction between class interests *per se*, and the interests of individuals within classes. For example, a piece of legislation may threaten the landowning interest of a large group while, at the same time, the "subsistence interest" of individuals within the group may not be seriously endangered. The poorer the class, however, the greater this kind of threat: "the class interest and the subsistence interest approach identity as the class remains in its standards of life close to the margin of subsistence." This ratio determines, to a great extent, the violence of the class struggle, as illustrated historically by the peasant and artisan revolts, by groups whose very livelihood was threatened. Small's further illustrations threaten the validity of his generalization. He named the capitalists, the wage-workers, the manufacturers, and the producers of raw materials the principal conflicting classes. Both the capitalists and manufacturers, remote from the subsistence level, were described as being at least as well organized for conflict and as active in the conflict as the other two groups of lower economic status.

In discussing the "partnership of economic classes," which had appeared as an important section in the table of contents of Ratzenhofer's *Wesen und Zweck*, Small insisted that economic class conflict deserved more reconsideration by sociologists than any other aspect of the social process. His own treatment is prefaced by the idea that the state's interests demand a "harmony of the parts cooperating in the industrial process." But the state is not a mechanism; the assignment of people to various functions in the industrial system is only the beginning. There is no harmony, for example, between the production functions or assignments and the desires of people as consumers. The primary interest of the various economic classes is to influence the determination of the distribution of wealth. Largely unformulated and unconscious, the modern struggle aims for "constitutionalism" in economic life, just as an earlier movement fought for constitutionalism in politics. This is why "politics at bottom is very largely a manoeuvering to control the means of controlling wealth." Democracies are beginning to realize that the ballot, unless it becomes an instrument for the enforcement of class interests, is useless. The farmers, the wage-earners, economic groups of every type, are becoming conscious of their class interests and are making attempts to change the balance of political power.

To Small, the most significant features of this "modern social struggle" were, first, the fact that capital has been assigned end value in itself. Secondly, the incorporation of capital has given it the legal status of a person: "Capital thus becomes a titanic superman, incomparably superior to the natural persons who find their interests challenged by this artificial being." The struggle between capital and labor is the struggle between "a fictitious person" and "all natural persons" for dominance as a social force. This conflict phenomenon is the one to which the sociologist must turn in order to understand the true nature of the contemporary social process: it is the side of society requiring most study.

The solidification and conscious recognition of class interests were, for Small, an important clue in the analysis of history. Thus, he attributed the "characterless" nature of American politics during the second half of the nineteenth century to the fact that both major parties were controlled by "virtually the same type of interests," and to the lack of clear articulation of class interests. He claimed that no writer had studied the French Revolution from the "sociological" viewpoint. Such a study would include an interpretation in terms of the class interests of the French social hierarchy and the ways in which the interests conflicted within the social process. Unquestionably, such interpretations had been made, though not stated in the Ratzenhofer-Small language. But here the essential point is Small's insistence that the "great combinations" of class interests must be regarded as a major object of social investigation.

Many of Small's shorter articles gave even greater weight to class conflict than *General Sociology*. His article on socialism describes class struggle as an "axiom" of social science: "No one gets through a primer of social science today without learning that class conflict is to the social process what friction is to mechanics." Small condemned those members of the upper classes who had "fought their way into the security of our property system" when they blame the lower classes for becoming militant in the same manner. Nor did he believe that America is isolated from the dynamic force of class struggle. Irrespective of our private opinions, we must realize, he cautioned, that class war is increasing and will continue throughout the world, including the United States. The *Between Eras* volume is an extensive illustration of the force of class conflict in America: its theme is that "the bias of the capitalistic interest needs watching more than any other single factor in present social problems." The book portrays a family being disrupted by the all-pervading class conflict, and a romance being fulfilled by the same force. In another place, Small emphasized the "social moral" nature of class conflict: the warring classes all resort to "natural rights" arguments, each claiming vested interest in a set of common privileges. Thus, economic class conflict is much more than part of the subject matter of economics: it is a social force, a major dynamic of social change.

However, Small did not stop by presenting the social process as simply the conflict of interests. Conflict must resolve itself into some kind of a solution or adjustment. In his conception of the latter he passes from theoretical analysis of social change to a plea for its proper direction. Traditional individualism and modern socialism had offered contrasting resolutions of the conflict process: the one finding the solution in a semi-anarchistic conception of society, the other in a firm collectivism which negates the role of the individual, so Small thought. He sought a middle course which he termed "socialization."

"The Transition from Struggle to Cooperation," a chapter

title in *General Sociology*, is the clue to the synthesis of conflict. Following in part Simmel and Durkheim, Small pointed out that "struggle itself deposits elements of civilization." This, in spite of the "primarily centrifugal" character of conflict as contrasted with the "centripetal" nature of civilization: "Civilization, considered as the accumulating product of the social process, is centripetal, i.e., it integrates interests, and the groups that represent them, so that they settle themselves into types of association." The conflict process contains the seed of its solution, cooperation. For conflict always takes place within a larger framework than that of any of the conflicting individuals or groups. There is a common element, like "community," in terms of which solutions of the conflict are evolved. Consequently, the social process tends more and more to be influenced by increasingly conscious, collective purpose. Or, in personal terms, the individual's conception of his own interests is tending to shape itself in terms of general interests.

Small's illustrations of the socialization principle were for the most part taken from the field of economic class conflict. "Professor Edgerly," one of the characters in *Between Eras*, probably expressed the author's viewpoint when he sought for the cooperation of capital and labor, with each making concessions in terms of common "community welfare" interests. In the same volume, "Randall, the Sociologist," offers an ardent plea for the revision of old laissez faire notions along the line of active cooperation of the owning and working classes. In *General Sociology*, Small suggested that labor's demand "to be treated like men" was an appeal that could be legitimately answered only by an increase of socialization: the common sharing of values.

The purpose of cooperation, the aim of socialization, in fact the goal towards which the social process is leading, is "more and better life by more and better people." The perfection of social cooperation is directed to the end that each person may share, and increasingly so, in the totality of material and non-material culture. Small's ethical humanitarianism was provided with a "scientific" rationalization in the form of the cooperative aspect of the social process. His half-dialectic, conflict of interests followed by the synthesis of socialization, is, in the last analysis, a theory of linear progress. The next stage in human development demonstrating this principle, to follow capitalism, he termed "democracy." [13]

3. CLASS STRUCTURE AND CLASS CONSCIOUSNESS

There has always been a more or less evident division of men into those who looked upon life with the eyes of those who had reached secure standing ground, and those who regarded things from the situation of those who were struggling for place. The former have always been the minority. Their presumption has always been that things were about as well settled as could be, and that all good citizens should be content with the established order. The latter have always been the vast majority, and as a rule the social influence of the two strata at a given moment has been, let us say, at a venture, something like the inverse of the cube of their numbers.

Class structure, it follows, is basically dichotomous: the rulers and ruled, the haves and have-nots, conservatives and radicals. The traditional two-way division is occasionally illustrated in Small's writings. For example, he stated that capital and labor are antithetical *social* categories in the modern world. Similarly, the quotation above was applied to the growing separation of the workers and owners in the United States; he stressed the ownership or non-ownership of property as indices of class position. His analysis of the development of rural regions, villages, towns, and cities portrayed the growth of stratification, again in terms of ownership. However, in Small's earlier work, where this tendency is most manifest, he termed the lowest economic groups "pathologies" of society, implying that a normal community, regardless of the nature of its economic system, would be free of the poverty-stricken.

But Small's later theory, especially *General Sociology*,

[13] See Division 4 of this chapter.

elaborated the simple economic conception of a two-class structure into a basic system of three classes.[14] In all societies, he
held, there are always developed or developing three major
groups: "The privileged," the "middle class," and "Those without property, rights or influence." This stratification stems originally from the industrial development of a community and
later becomes officially sanctioned by the political order. Not
until the nineteenth century did these strata gain recognized
political standing. The three classes of modern Europe and
America are the historical successors of the rulers, freemen, and
slaves of an earlier period. Operating in the stratification
process, at first, was the conquest factor which provided the
earlier communities with the lowest stratum, the slaves. But the
abolition of chattel slavery failed to eliminate this group: they
"remained relatively strangers to property, rights, or influence."

In presenting his schema of three-way stratification, Small
introduced a qualification which led back to the simpler
dichotomous conception of classes. He distinguished between
ranks, those who have successfully established their position at
or near the top of the social order, and the *masses*, those who
are still concerned only with the necessities of life. The privileges of the former group allow it to pursue a variety of activities of a "cultural" nature; while "the masses are necessarily
devoted to . . . fundamentals, because daily labor alone will
secure them their daily bread." The ranks, so long as they remain firmly entrenched as a leisure class, can and often do provide society with valuable contributions. Small occasionally
praised them for this function.

The difficulty of establishing criteria for the "middle class,"
a problem still facing social science, led Small into certain inconsistencies. Following Ratzenhofer, he stated that the ruling
or upper classes of the ancient "conquest" states and of modern
Europe and America opposed with all their power the growth

[14] Earlier he had assigned three classes (aristocracy, middle class, working
class) to Europe, and four (wealthy, well to do, daily wage-earners, unskilled)
to the United States.

of a middle class. The upper class resistance to franchise extension and trade-unionism is cited as an example, suggesting that trade-union groups are actually or potentially "middle class." [15] Later, in distinguishing between rank and the masses, he declared that "rank interests" are of "little concern to Americans," implying, it seems, that this country is dominantly middle class regardless of the weakness of trade-unionism (1905). Small undoubtedly considered other criteria of class position, though he specifically voiced the unsolved problem of "locating" the middle class: "The line between the rich and the middle classes is of course not a line at all, but a ratio, and the measuring term in the ratio is a matter of judgment." [16]

The scheme of a three-class structure was derived, in part, from Ratzenhofer's conflict theory with respect to the growth of the state, in which subjugation by rulers is described as the beginning of social and political organization. The transition from a simple to a more complex, stratified society, with its three classes, is dependent upon the rise of a "culture-state" through which conquering groups rule. The original conquerors-conquered dual class formation gives way to the more complex system through either the internal rise of a middle section struggling for place, or the addition of new elements from without who usually become the lowest stratum.

It was in this process of societal development that Small discerned the significant relationship between class and state. "The culture-state comes into the foreground in consequence of the greater density of the society, and, by the side of violent subjugation, industrial exploitation by means of capital gains in-

[15] Small's notion that trade-unionism strengthens middle class *mindedness* is essentially correct with respect to the less stratified countries, especially America. Witness the traditional official "ideology" of the ¡American Federation of Labor.

[16] In one of his later articles (1914) Small suggested a possible breakdown of class categories, particularly that of "capital." He named three types of capital: "tool," "management," and "finance," each possessing a *social* nature; they were not, in his mind, simply "economic" classifications. The analysis of "finance" capital followed clues offered by Veblen—absentee ownership and the lack of the "instinct of workmanship." Small's thesis, however, was that "management" capital must be given social force through cooperation with labor.

fluence." The extreme examples of upper class control of the state are found in the "despotic" systems of Egypt and India in which the subjugated classes cannot express their "natural play of interests." But the framework of caste structure is the model which all societies tend to follow, for everywhere the ruling classes fight the attempts of others to gain power. The struggle of the third estate in the French Revolution, the contemporary (1905) developments in Russia, the campaigns of the last century for the extension of suffrage in England, all illustrate the general principle of class control of the state. In the United States, "with approximate abolition of political classes," the economic strata are engaged in the same conflict. American political campaigns are becoming more and more an attempt of the lower economic sections to oust from political control the vested interest class. The nature of this conflict in all societies leads the ruling class to consider its control of the state as an end to be sought and perpetuated at all times. Such control takes on ethical connotations: the upper class which rules becomes the only class "fit" to rule.

Small, discussing capitalist society, refused to simplify the class control conception to the point of accepting the simple formula, "as x is to y, so is administrative favoritism to the bulk of capital concerned." True, large capital is a dominant interest exercising considerable political power: all are aware that capital stands behind much legislation. But exaggeration and distortion of the role which capital interests play is rather common. Without naming specific distortions, Small described outstanding characteristics of capitalistic groups. The capitalist always feels that the promotion of his own interests is "honorable," and thus demands support by the state; he always strives to have the state financially indebted to him; he uses the state as an ally in the promotion of "vast undertakings far ahead of effective demand," and in the promotion of excessive commerce, over-production, and over-population; in allocating his losses to "small capital" and labor, he seeks the aid of the state. Certain highly developed single industries, such as South American cattle interests and British textile and iron interests, sometimes practically run the government. "The life of the State is a series of rapes of the law by the interest or interests within the State temporarily able to control the civic power." A most urgent problem in all modern nations is the determination of the extent to which state policies are the reflection of unwarranted subservience to vested powers.

Though ruling class interests are often dominant in determining state activity, the "class-instrument" theory of the state never gained Small's approval. His early text described the state as a mechanism for determining the common will, and *General Sociology* offered a modification of the same thesis. States always become "moral institutions" within which the conflict of interests is resolved in compromise fashion in response to the general interests of the society. These common interests are the "spiritual substance of the state." The state is always striving to maintain its own independent existence, is always struggling against becoming the instrument of any single class. The advancement of civilization is marked by increasing freedom of the state from control by any special interest groups.

A good portion of Small's description of class and state phenomena is not unlike similar treatments in socialist literature. Concerning class theory Professor P. Sorokin has stated: "It is rather surprising that A. W. Small found this part of Marx's theory especially valuable. I cannot style his statements in this respect as otherwise than a blunder." This comment probably refers to Small's laudatory remarks: "Marx was one of the few really great thinkers in the history of social science. . . . [His] is still a voice in the wilderness, but for one I have no more doubt that he was essentially right, and that conventionality was essentially wrong, than I have that Galileo will hold his place to the end of time as one of the world's great discoverers." But such appraisals are in no sense an indication of Small's adherence to Marxism.

In his first sociological work Small criticized socialism on several different grounds. The followers of Marx place undue importance on the economic factor; their materialism is blind to the true dual nature of "volitional determinism", they err in attributing the blame for our "pathologies" to the institution of private property; they overlook the "altruistic" incentives that are developed within such social groups as the family; and, in one place, Small admitted the possibility of poverty being a necessary incentive to further individual development. The only similarities to socialism appearing in this early work are Small's statement that wealth is a social product and his insistence that the transmission of wealth from generation to generation should be resolved not merely within the family, but partly, at least, through "society in its corporate capacity."

On the economic side of socialist theory, Small's ideas changed considerably during his writing career. The *Adam Smith* volume praised the father of classical economics for his belief that labor was the source of all wealth, and, in one place, Smith is interpreted as closer to the fundamental theories of Marx than to the leading premises of modern economic theory. In an article written a few years later, Marx's theory of surplus-value was criticized as being much too one-sided; in fact, one of Small's last papers (1925) was a strong attack on the "fallacious theory of profits" advocated by the socialists.

Small's major objections to Marxian theory, however, had little to do with its economic conceptions. In the first place, he highly valued individual initiative, describing Marxism as a "socialistic foreordination of mediocrity." He believed that the realm of science, especially, would be threatened by a completely collective social order. Secondly, and more significantly, Marxian thought was inconsistent with his own sociological theory. He pointed out, for example, that Marx *assumed* a sharp division between the laboring and capitalist classes. This "fatal mistake" was due to Marx's failure to consider the cooperative aspect of the social process. "We find the center of conflict which is the life of society, not in perpetual trial of strength between permanently defined classes, but we see the merging of these earlier alignments into incessant reassortment of classes in perpetual conflict for moral control of the terms of cooperation."

There is a further break with the theory and practice of socialism in his portrayal of the ideological aspect of class structure. True, Small continually emphasized the growing class consciousness of economic groups. In one of his earliest articles he stressed the increasing awareness of the "masses" of their economic position. He stated that "in future litigation of class interests, labor is bound to be better represented than in the past." He singled out, among others, the "professional" occupations of art, teaching, medicine, clergy, and journalism as those coming to align themselves on one or the other side of the class struggle. He recognized that the growing consciousness of workers demanded solutions outside the framework of "old-time philanthropy." At the close of the World War, Small stressed the effect of an international struggle on class feeling. Class conflict increases, revolutionary doctrines spread: "the revolutionary anticapitalist doctrines are likely in a short time to be as familiar in every trade-union local in this country as they have become in Europe." Socialism is bound to grow, and that "bizarre version of an idea," Bolshevist theory, will become a recognized part of class thinking. The upper classes are deemed "shortsighted" for not seriously considering this growing class consciousness which may well lead to overt class action.

But the ethical aspect of class consciousness occupied a good share of Small's attention. It has already been shown how he conceived of different classes as possessing different ethical codes, and how he decried the lack of an inter-class ethic. He emphasized the responsibility which the upper classes should feel by virtue of their controlling position, and, at the same time, condemned the extreme form of class consciousness manifested by "Russian nihilism, German socialism, French and Italian anarchism, and English and American trade-unionism." These movements are the "symptoms of dawning mass-consciousness"; their demands are "senseless extremes." Yet elsewhere, Small pled for the increase of trade-unions and approved their role of stimulating class feeling. He never established criteria for the distinction, but he insisted at one point that class consciousness can be either "good" or "evil."

Perhaps of most importance in Small's discussion of class feeling was his concern with the factors which create "middle class consciousness." The middle rank, he noted, is continually striving for place at the top of the social order, while the members of the lowest stratum compete for middle class status. Small cited Ratzenhofer and Veblen in explaining the class role of fashion: an incident and a method of social competition. The attitudes of the middle class are competitive, and are bound by no dominant common values. Its numbers "are likely . . . to be constant traitors to their own class." There is a distinct contrast between the competitive ideology of the middle group and the more corporate feeling of those above and below. This competitive feeling, however, invades a large section of the working class which Small named the "no-man's land" of class structure.

Several forces are at work creating the competitive attitudes. Small pointed out, in the first place, that the historical development from status to contract in no way eliminated the felt need of status in men. He believed that the social process was working toward the end that would eventually guarantee both security and mobility of status. *Between Eras* provided several vivid illustrations of the competition for status among workers and middle class groups. In the second place, the imitation by the lower classes of the leisure class promotes competitive feeling. This is especially true in the sphere of money interests, where each man feels he is a potential capitalist. A third factor is the political and functional divisions that develop within any community. Political leaders often spur the competitive feeling between such groups as Christian and Jewish artisans, or union and non-union labor; the result may be a strong group loyalty, but not class loyalty. The functional divisions— teachers, clerics, skilled workers in specific fields, the military, lawyers, and the like—tend to mould the members' interests around their occupations rather than along broad class lines. A further factor in the creation of competitive attitudes is the extent of physical contact with others of the same economic class. The greater solidarity of feeling among factory and mine workers is due in part to their physical proximity: they consciously "share a common lot." The opposite is true of agricultural wage-earners, who are usually the weakest groups in social conflict; their attitudes are often closer to those of the capitalist than the "workers."

Small's treatment of class consciousness assumed no such order as the above. The materials are scattered throughout his writings, yet his concern with the ideological aspect of class is apparent. What has been said suggests that his own "ideology" was "middle class"; his description of the goal of the social process would bear this out. However, a more complete picture of Small's values, hopes, and prophecies follows in the concluding section.

4. Social Reform: From Capitalism to Democracy

"He was a critical and sympathetic student of Marx but advocated gradual, orderly and constitutional reform to bring private property and capitalism in harmony with a functional order based on service, justice and Christian ethics." Professor L. Wirth's summary of Small's general reform position can be taken as the theme of these concluding remarks.

The volume, the title of which contains the heading of this section, is a vivid portrayal of the conflict between capital and labor, and an ardent plea for industrial democracy. It is the "case history" of a Chicago strike. The workers demand a share in the *control* of the business, an unusual picture of labor becoming militant for the sake of a principle, not for improvement of wages, hours, or working conditions. Rather than the "academic" treatment one might expect, Small gives the book the form and sometimes the style of a labor novel. It is crammed with dialogue taken from workers' meetings, Sunday sermons, the discussions of interested academicians, and, most importantly, the intimacies of the family circles of the owners and managers. The story is interwoven with a love affair of a labor leader and the daughter of the factory owner; in rather naive fashion it ends with the successful culmination of both love-match and strike.

The thesis of this "romance" is indicated by the dedication: "To the fertile fellowship of men and women who rate the interests of the whole above the claims of their special kind." The plea throughout is summarized by one of the characters: "unless it is coupled with economic democracy, the political democracy which men a century ago regarded as the sufficient guarantee of equal freedom is little more than a toy to pacify children." One reviewer, though decrying the lack of definite conclusions, stated that "this book is the cleverest, the most incisive, and the best-equipped analysis of the capitalistic system of industrial production which has appeared within our time." Dr. H. E. Barnes stated that only Veblen, Tawney, and the Webbs have produced "as relentless a criticism of our conventional unmitigated capitalism." The same author, in criticizing Small for de-emphasizing class factors in America, reminded him of his own work: "If one is . . . unconvinced he can turn to Dean Small's own work on *Between Eras: From Capitalism to Democracy*, and if he is not then converted we may leave him as unregenerate."

It would be incorrect to judge Small's program of amelioration on the basis of this single volume. Throughout his writings, there appears the demand for the overhauling of the capitalist system, with considerable emphasis upon its class features. In discussing the present status of social science, Small stated that "the most vital task of our period is confirmation or removal of the suspicion that the capitalism of our era is a social fallacy as patent and as fatal as the Roman *latifundia*." The major task facing the contemporary world is to determine "whether the civilized nations can restore themselves to sanity after their nineteenth-century aberrations of individualism and capitalism."

The lines Small set down for the problem's solution follow in general the pattern of "the middle road" and gradualism. In his first volume, he had insisted that reforms must come about slowly, that sudden amelioration is impossible. Later, he suggested that the "direct line of truth" lies some place between the respective positions of Adam Smith and Karl Marx [17]: that we must seek a valid generalization which avoids either of these polarities. Small's middle-of-the-road reformism was an outstanding theme of his writings until his very last years when (1925), in a less optimistic vein, he declared that no theories have been created which provide adequate substitutes for capitalism, either with respect to its psychology of acquisitiveness, or its economic technology.

The belief that capitalism was evolving into "democracy" stemmed partly from Small's conception of the social process. In an early article he interpreted the aggressiveness and growing organization of the working classes as the modern form of the same vital forces which have always been the spur of human progress. The struggle of the lower ranks for economic security, status, and cultural opportunities *is* the social movement: it is "inevitable, though not yet wholly intelligent. . . . It deserves the sympathy and the wise cooperation of all who love their kind." An important part of the social process is the growing recognition that the powers and privileges which traditionally have been monopolized by the upper classes must become the possession of all groups. The factors in social organization which guarantee to large capital undue privilege must inevitably give way to a control system which shall transform capital into a consistent agency of human welfare. Bulking large in this process is the reorganization of our whole scheme of economic distribution.

As noted earlier, Small considered cooperation as the means of resolution of the conflict of interests. Thus, we must dissipate

[17] Small, in surprisingly simple fashion, epitomized Smith's doctrines as: "Every capitalist deserves profits"; and Marx's doctrines as: "No capitalist deserves profits."

the illusion that life is an endless conflict of interests; we must add our force to the process that has as its goal a community of functional cooperation. It is especially necessary for the capitalist class to realize the need of cooperation with the workers: " 'Capital' and 'labor' in their present status are as impossible in perpetuity as the ancient social division into free-man and slave." Small apparently looked upon Henry Ford's distribution of profit scheme as a manifestation of the desirable kind of cooperative economic trend. At the same time, he consistently approved of trade-unionism. In 1925 he stated: "Thirty years ago . . . I believed ardently in trade-unionism, both as a means of self-expression by the many and as a curb upon the capitalism of the few. I believed, and I still believe, that the practice of collective bargaining is among the most constructive of modern inventions."

Extremely important among the methods of gaining more cooperation between capital and labor is the creation of "social consciousness." In his text, Small praised the socialists and other "agitators of social reform" for their role in developing public opinion and a common body of information which are primary requisites to constructive, cooperative reform. Later, in elaborating his own theory, he adopted (with emphatic acknowledgment) Ward's line of reasoning. The correct statement of the problem of class stratification is not to be made in terms of institutional structure; rather in terms "of the spirit which we shall show in working the institutions we have." If class alignments are to be altered, if class cooperation is to be achieved, the subjective environment must be changed. This is a direct appeal to general education, Ward's social dynamic factor: it is the factor which embodies that attitude toward society's problems indispensable to true social progress.

"Our program toward the central problems of our time will amount to nothing but impotent and irritating tinkering with details, until the leaders of our thought and action consent to a policy of candid and thorough inquiry as to whether there is something radically mistaken in the capitalistic system itself."

Such a statement seems to give Small's reformism an extremely "radical" tone. He did name four specific fallacies of capitalism: treating capital as though it were an active agent in the social process; excluding workers from representation in the control of business; uncontrolled incorporation; the inheritance system. He stated that the most questionable social regulations today are those pertaining to property. He insisted that the unrest of the lower classes is justified, that it could not be "sneered out of court" as the envy of the unsuccessful. And he strongly condemned those who spoke of "the red scare." In one place, he wrote a scathing article attacking the reactionary editorials of the *New York Evening Post*, and, in another, he appealed to the churches to unite in active participation in labor conflict.

But these items, which have at times been interpreted as an indication of a socialist or semi-socialist position, are negated by his criticisms of Marxian doctrine. "Marx's ideal of economic society has never appealed to me as plausible, probable, desirable, or possible." Far too often those who are working for the abolition of classes are interested in "avoiding labor." Socialistic and anarchistic dogma mistakenly assign a "radical vice" to the social system itself; furthermore, they are foreign importations having little application to the American scene. On more than one occasion, Small expressed a strong fear of revolutionary doctrines, denouncing the agitator who used the devices of "crowd psychology" to arouse class feeling. In one place, "peaceful picketing" was interpreted as a manifestation of "terrorism"; in another, Small emphatically denied that the University of Chicago was controlled by Standard Oil or any other capitalistic interests. In fact, in his most important work, he avoided attacking the "capitalistic system" as such. He questioned whether an unemployed class was a sign of institutional weakness of our social order, though he pointed out that if proof could be obtained of an actual decrease of economic *opportunity* such would indicate an "institutional disarrangement." The presence of defective, dependent, and delinquent classes "neither proves, nor fairly tends to prove, that the evil points to structural defects in the social order." The reorganization of our institutions would in no way guarantee the removal of our social problems.

Small's own principles of social amelioration, to be sure, were pointed directly toward certain institutions. "Not until we thoroughly understand that our social order now rests on the basis of property, and that it will not be a thoroughly moral order until it is transferred to the basis of function, shall we be in a position intelligently to reflect on social reconstruction." Small's desire for a "thoroughly moral order" has been made apparent; its achievement depends, it seems, upon the transition from a property to a functional basis of organization. The functional emphasis is one Small shared with the various schools of socialism; in fact, the article of which the above quotation is a part was prefaced by an elaboration of the point that "there are innumerable socialisms. There is no SOCIALISM." One variety of socialism is, possibly, his own vaguely formed conception of a moral, Christian, functional society. This statement might draw a strong denial from Small. He could cite his own words: "It is conceivable that the time may come when some of the postulates of socialism may be accepted as valid generalizations. Meanwhile, upon present social consciousness they have only the effect of more or less irritating distractions."

However Small felt about the socialist label, he was outspoken in forecasting the fate of capitalism. In 1914: "I predict that before long the statisticians and accountants will begin to show that capitalism is not solvently efficient in raising the funds to pay its own bills. Then the judgment day of capitalism will be due." And in the same article: "In another fifty years it may have been discovered that capitalism is a merger of famine and lottery. The majority pay for the cakes they do not get, and the surplus provides prizes for the minority." A decade later, shortly before his death, Small was less extreme in his predictions. He looked forward to a controlled capitalism in which the state would enforce rules for limiting profits, and regulations calling for profit-sharing.

From Capitalism to Democracy was Small's "middle road." It allowed him to attack the property basis of the class order which permitted extreme poverty and unmitigated exploitation. At the same time, it prevented him from deviating too far from a system of values which was an important part of that class order. He continually conceived of and worked for a new era: he lived, in his own words, "between eras."

While he was greatly interested in class, his contribution to the understanding of the subject was limited: by the imposition of his strongly-felt ethics on his sociological analysis; and by his acceptance of traditional usages of the term "class" with little reexamination of the realities of the phenomenon. His emphasis of "interests" could have been an important clue to the meaning of class as a *social* group; unfortunately, his work stopped short of this point. On the other hand, Small has pointed up the role of class in the social process, and has set down numerous keen insights into the social structure and its changes. Moreover, he has provided a "scientific" rationale for ethically-minded "liberals."

CHAPTER FIVE: FRANKLIN HENRY GIDDINGS

(1855-1931)

FRANKLIN HENRY GIDDINGS

1. Introduction

OF THE six American sociologists whose works are being examined, Franklin H. Giddings offers the most difficult analytical problem. Born shortly after the middle of the last century, he was surrounded during his younger years by what Prof. J. L. Gillin terms the "uncanny unreality" of a severely "strict Puritan atmosphere." As a boy, Giddings rebelled against the religious domination of his family by devoting himself to the practical problems of farming and mechanics. Fortunate contact with stimulating teaching and an early introduction to the writings of Spencer, Huxley, and Darwin gave him a taste for science; a college career interrupted by newspaper work trained him in the techniques of journalism. These two qualities, the exactness of scientific procedure and the popular appeal of journalistic jargon, were to characterize his contributions to sociology: the huge list of volumes and articles, and the years of lectures at Columbia University.

On this work, however, was stamped the effects of Giddings' boyhood intimacy with New England's Calvinistic traditions. The individualism that is a counterpart of this branch of Protestant thought was partially responsible for the strong individualistic quality which marked his writings throughout his life: as late as 1915, Giddings named Jonathan Edwards and Benjamin Franklin the "greatest of Americans."

During the ten years he spent in active newspaper work,

Giddings gained the attention of university leaders by his contributions to the *Political Science Quarterly*. In 1888, he began to lecture in politics at Bryn Mawr; in 1891, in sociology at Columbia. Contact with students at the latter institution was largely responsible for the influence he exercised in American sociology. Urbanity of manner, vigorous attack of subject matter, clever phrase-making, impressive appearance: these qualities marked his teaching. The stimulation and erudition he brought to the classroom were of more significance, perhaps, in placing Giddings' name among the Fathers of sociology than the impressive array of his books and articles.

Giddings had no one special interest. Like Sumner's, his activities spread over several areas of social science and into the non-academic fields of journalism and public life. He was an editor of the *New York Independent* for more than twenty years, trustee of two colleges, a leading participant in several professional associations, member of Citizens' Committees and a Board of Education, strong advocate of American participation in the World War, and, later, as powerful a supporter of a League to Enforce Peace. One of his commentators claims that these many activities of Giddings are "a splendid illustration of the usefulness of the sociological theorist in practical life."

True, as an observer remarked, "Giddings has convictions on all subjects of public weal." But both his "systematic" scientific writings and more popular articles omit the kind of consistency of interpretation that is expected of a scholar who purports to utilize a logically constructed body of theory. His changes in position on numerous topics, including class phenomena, are very noticeable. Dr. Bernhard Stern states that "he was inclined to base his own judgments . . . on immediate impressionistic reflections," while others attribute such shifts to Giddings' developing maturity as a great thinker.[1]

---

[1] Prof. A. A. Tenney, one of Giddings' closest associates, claimed that the latter was not influenced by Ward or Sumner, while Giddings himself named Sumner as perhaps the foremost sociologist.

The most striking instance of an "about-face" on a major topic is found in his interpretations of and comments upon war. As late as 1914 Giddings strongly denounced military activity, attributing war to basic economic factors. Within a very few years he became the author of a series of ultra-patriotic, anti-pacifist articles and speeches.

A similar shift of viewpoint is revealed in his treatment of "the social problem": the economic class phenomenon. His admiration for the status quo is best illustrated in the numerous editorials he wrote for the *Independent* in the early 'twenties. Here his attack was levelled at socialism in particular, with occasional thrusts at social legislation, trade-unionism, and government spending. These articles are an interesting contrast with his earlier newspaper work which disclosed a liberal, questioning approach, the application of Spencerian sociology, and the economic theory of John Bates Clark and, in some cases, Simon Patten.

The influence of these economists, especially of Clark, led Giddings into technical economic theory. Between 1887 and 1890, the economic journals contained several of his articles in which appeared some consideration of class factors in social life. Special emphasis was given to Ricardian principles of competition, and to Clark's four-class system which Giddings described as a "broad psychological gradation." In these articles, the role of psychological forces in the economic process took equal rank with such "material" items as competition; consideration was given to certain aspects of Marxian economics; trade-unionism was recognized as necessary and beneficial (though criticized for "refusing to allow to the best workmen the wages they could command as individuals"); stress was placed upon the "intellectual and moral qualities of the people" in shaping the pattern of economic life.

Giddings believed that the answers to the questions he confronted in his early economic studies were to be found in sociology. In 1891, he named the problems of this discipline as those of social structure and growth, of "volitional association," and, finally, problems of progress. Five years later he expanded his system of sociology in his *Principles*. The core around which his theories developed was Spencerian evolutionism; he consistently named Darwin and Spencer as the most important contributors to sociology. Evolution, its conflict and resulting structures were the central data of sociology: "Every social group, animal or human, since time began, has been in ceaseless struggle with its material environment and with other social groups." This struggle was interpreted as a *natural* evolution in Giddings' earlier works: the pattern of explanation was essentially Spencer's. Such "raw evolutionism" was tempered, however, in his first two sociological volumes, which assigned considerable weight to psychological factors. In *Principles*, Kropotkin's "mutual aid" was used in the explanation of general evolutionary development; in *Elements*, stress was given to superstition and emotionalism and their diminution in accordance with the "law of mental emancipation." But the basic framework remained the same: a physical evolution involving the principles of integration, differentiation, and segregation.

While the evolutionary emphasis persisted, Giddings' outstanding contribution to sociological literature was rather his treatment of psychological factors in social life. "The sociologist deals with phenomena of volition at every step." To develop a theory of social organization and social change one must, Giddings argued, first create a theory of social-psychological development. The foremost task of the general sociologist is to create a basic social psychology. This task occupied a good share of Giddings' volumes: the extensive discussion of "anthropogenic association" is an elaboration of the *mental* factors in evolutionary change; the "social composition" of society was said to be due largely to man's "passion for homogeneity," the "social constitution" to the "desire" to combine variety with homogeneity; again, the "standard of living" must be interpreted in psychological terms.

In the unequal response of different persons to the same stimulus and the subjection of similar persons to a variety of stimuli, Giddings found the key to the complexity of social organization and the processes of conflict and cooperation. This line of thinking resulted in the concept of "consciousness of kind," the original and elementary "fact" in society; and the similar concept of "like-mindedness," which he described as the basis of all social organization. His treatment of class phenomena was considerably influenced by this emphasis upon the sociopsychological aspect of society.[2]

Giddings believed sociology to be the most general social science. This view, together with his early intensive work in economics, brought to his attention the relationship between the two types of phenomena, economic and "social." In an early article, he wrote: "Economic activities transform the energies of physical nature into social force, of which there is no other source whatever, since artistic, religious, educational and political activities are but a further transformation of the results of economic effort." However, this economic "determinism" was short-lived: within a few years Giddings was insisting that a scientific economics must be based on sociology. In discussing social conflict, he denied that economic conditions are its basis; rather, conflict and adjustment are rooted in "aesthetic" factors. Late in his career, he suggested a definite distinction between the two disciplines: "In the same large sense in which economics is the science of the production and distribution of wealth, *for* man, sociology is the science of the production and distribution of adequacy, *of* man and *in* man. Economics tells us how, as far as it is possible, we can *get* the things that we desire to *have;* sociology tells us how, as far as it is possible, we can *become* what we desire to *be.*" Thus, the ends which men seek in social action are required material for sociology.

In his first sociological volume, Giddings agreed with Comte that science must be divorced from political or revolutionary

<hr>

[2] Dr. Stern states that Giddings' "idealization of the social stability arising from likemindedness led him to oppose mass immigration, to regard large cities with their heterogeneity of population with distrust, and to condemn radicalism as disruptive."

purpose. But, like Comte, he was concerned from the beginning with amelioration and progress.[3] He claimed that the study and promotion of a "rational telesis" rank with any inquiries into a "mechanistic evolution." His meliorism sometimes touched extremes: "It will be discovered one day that the chief value of social science, so far from being academic, is moral." Professor J. P. Lichtenberger declares that Giddings always regarded sociology as essentially pragmatic.

Giddings' conception of progress, nonetheless, was almost Sumnerian: more than once he named the goal of social evolution liberal individualism. The strong influence of Darwinian and Spencerian evolutionary doctrine no doubt accounts, in part, for his opposition to collectivism and his promotion of individualistic ideals.

An important part of the general setting within which his theory of social classes took form is Giddings' philosophy of history and historical causation, his major interest according to one of his colleagues. Here is revealed his principal modification of the natural evolutionary doctrine: by the emphasis upon "psychic" factors in history. In *Principles*, for example, Kropotkin was praised for his mutual aid thesis, an attack on "rigid evolutionism." Giddings' criticism of strict evolutionism was coupled with his rejection of a "materialistic" explanation of history because the latter overlooked the role of ideas, beliefs, and feelings. Thus, the conflict theories of Gumplowicz, Novicow, and Marx incorrectly ignore the causal force of psychological phenomena. His first textbook named economic activities as "most fundamental" in social development, but within a short time this position was abandoned in favor of one giving equal weight to psychic forces. The economic interpretation of history is inadequate: social change must be explained in terms of "mental evolution."

Throughout Giddings' studies there are many examples of

---

[3] Giddings' "popular" articles and many of his public lectures utilized "scientific sociology" for political and social causes of various kinds.

the application of a "psychological causation." The economic explanation of war is misleading because it omits psychic factors;[4] Protestant ideology was important in the development of the "liberty" of the present social order; modern socialism resulted from the force of the *theoretical* systems of Marx and others; in fact, the latter's theory of history is materialistic only in a "moral sense." Political developments are largely shaped by the social ideas and ideals of outstanding individuals; in a larger sense, the "social mind" is a significant causal factor. In one place, Giddings set down the thesis that "the urge to adventure is the cause of history"; in another, he named "mental and moral evolution" the key to historical progress.

Giddings' preoccupation with "non-materialistic" factors provoked the doctrine of a multiple causation, explicitly presented in his last volume. But, essentially, he believed causation must be conceived as an interaction between two kinds of phenomena, physical and psychical: "social causation is a process of psychical activity conditioned by physical processes and cosmic law." Occasionally, the "psychic" phenomena were named "ethical," and sometimes "volitional." Professor Gillin states that Giddings reconciled more consistently than any of his predecessors the respective evolutionary roles of physical or material phenomena and subjective or volitional factors.[5]

Giddings often couched his theories of social change in Spencerian language, stressing the idea that history is psychological "equilibration." He even used the notion of equilibration to explain collectivism and individualism: "Since the tendencies toward both cohesion and dispersion are persistent, the social system simultaneously exhibits phenomena of combination and of competition, of communism and of individualism." Ascendancy of one or the other is possible, but the historical process is

---

[4] The Spanish-American War was "caused" by the restless, adventurous American "spirit."

[5] This double emphasis is reflected in Giddings' treatment of class: the latter is neither an economic or "materialistic" group, nor is it simply a group "conscious" of its own psychic unity. See Divisions 2 and 3 of this chapter.

always marked by both, and the historical goal is their equilibration.[6]

The evolutionary process, progressively working towards equilibration, manifests itself in the phenomenon of class. The point was made in an early article (1891): progressive change means that groups fall behind "in different degrees," which explains the social class gradations of a population, and the well-marked differences of biological, economic, and, indeed, "moral" conditions. A few years later, after Giddings had evolved his "psychological" system of sociology, the "processes of internal equilibration" were explained in detail, and were directly related to class structure and conflict. The processes include the differentiation of population into like-minded classes, the evolution of consciousness of kind, and conflict between strong and weak classes. Equilibration takes one of three forms: the subjugation of the weak by the strong, economic exploitation, or "the uplifting of the weak by the strong through education, justice, and economic aid." The emphasis given to class data and their relation to evolutionary forces is illustrated by his conception of progress: "The moral advance of society is a progress from equilibration through subjugation and exploitation to equilibration through uplifting, and it depends upon the broadening and deepening of the consciousness of kind."

This line of thinking did not prevent Giddings from occasionally discounting the significance of the subject of class for sociology. In one of his later volumes, for example, he set down a "classification of societal facts," insisting upon its thoroughness, which omitted class altogether. Several of his "sociological" analyses of important historical movements, including the Reformation and the American Civil War, did not consider class factors. But, in his general approach to sociology, the subject was stressed: among the tasks and problems that sociology faces are questions relating to the different "ability" groups in

[6] Giddings definitely preferred the "ascendancy" of individualism. See Division 5 of this chapter.

society, types of social conflict, labor activity, class attachments versus community bonds, communism and individualism. Among the "descriptive problems" of sociology are the phenomena of cooperation and class divisions. Sociology, as the "science of natural groupings," must study hierarchies and classes; "class ways," a major example of pluralistic behavior, are part of its data.

Class conflict, an important specimen of the societal conflict basic to evolutionary change, demands sociological analysis. Our "interest . . . in general is most acutely in the class struggle . . ." and national struggle. These conflicts are basic to the historical process. He named the two wedded movements of *"group struggle* for dominion and subsistence" and *"class struggle* for ascendancy and revenue" as the starting point and the action of history. Conflict is basic, but not the materialistic class conflict of Marx. Correct understanding of the process must give equal weight to consciousness of class: with the creation of a capitalist class, "modern history arrives at noon," the proletariat becomes in its turn class conscious, "and Karl Marx makes the epochal discovery that class struggle impends—in history!"

Scientific sociology must concern itself not only with class structure, class consciousness, and conflict, but it must also consider the theories of all forms of socialism and anarchism. Not as advocates of ameliorative schemes, but as social scientists. Giddings believed this task important and extremely complex: the term "social class" has so many uses that it is "difficult to translate into coherent thought." As early as 1895 he abandoned indices of occupation and of economic status, and condemned sociology for allowing "class" a myriad of meanings. Whether he succeeded in clarifying the problem can be judged on the basis of the following pages.

2. Society's Natural Classes

"The conception of evolution has given to the natural sciences a true principle of classification. . . . That is a true class in which objects or individuals are grouped with reference to some characteristic that has been produced by evolutionary differentiation." This statement appeared in 1895; the following thirty years witnessed Giddings' attempts to classify society in keeping with its principle.

The commonly used distinctions between wealth and poverty, employer and employee, wage-earners, landlords, and capitalists, he believed, are secondary classifications, not true social classes. The latter must be sought in the evolutionary process which "perpetually generates inequality from equality, the heterogeneous from the homogeneous." Social classes are different from and basic to all political, industrial, and economic classes. They are the "natural" products of evolution, and all societies are arranged in social hierarchies which are "classes." They can not be eliminated while division of labor remains essential to social life; they are a counterpart of the "natural" inequalities of all societies, primitive and contemporary.[7]

Underlying Giddings' "social classes" were certain *types* of classes in society. An article appearing in 1895 outlined two basic classes: the "most fundamental population classes" or "personality" classes (such as those groups described by Galton and Lombroso); and the groups resulting from the "differentiation of the population not to personality as such . . . but to society itself, to social life as distinguished from non-social or unsocial life"—the real social classes. This original two-way scheme became a three-class system in *Principles* and *The Elements of Sociology*. Evolutionary "association" produces physical, mental, and moral inequalities which are socially manifested in population classes of three fundamental types, namely: vitality classes, personality classes, and social classes. The first, vitality classes, are produced by inheritance and "circumstances," as governed by association, and their criteria are the

---

[7] Giddings believed there were many types of natural classes, and suggested several schema which were never elaborated. For example, society could be divided into natural "types of disposition," or into "types of character." He also conceived of "inherently" progressive and "sluggish" groups as social classes.

ratios of birth-rates to death-rates.[8] The second type, person-ality classes, is created by the same circumstances and is repre-sented by the "talented and geniuses," the "normally endowed," and the "defective." Social classes, the last group, are distin-guished by differences of "social nature," the result of inherit-ance and education; the criterion is the degree of adjustment to social life.

The most detailed statement of these types of classes appears in *Inductive Sociology*, in which there is a further break-down into four major categories: vitality, mentality, morality, social-ity. (The original "personality" division is split into "mental" and "moral" classes.) Giddings' psychological emphasis is illus-trated by the general chapter heading under which these types of classes are outlined: "The Social Personality." Evolution works towards a "harmonious social nature," which, to Gid-dings, meant a balancing of the four elements of vitality, men-tality, morality, and sociality. But, as importantly, these four represent the major kinds of societal groupings: they are the categories with which the sociologist must pursue his "induc-tive" studies of social structure, the ideal constructs research must use in studying the phenomenon of class.

Here, the most significant of these "natural" types of class is the *social*. The "four true social classes," as originally stated by Giddings, are the social, the non-social, the pseudo-social, and the anti-social. The first is Harrington's "natural aristocracy among men," the true élite; the non-social class includes "those individuals who are sticklers for a narrow individualism," the "primordial" ultra-selfish groups; the dependent "pauper" is pseudo-social; and the anti-social class is composed of the "crim-inals." "The social classes . . . are created by the reactions of society upon its individual members in their capacity as socii." Their "social nature" is developed by association, a process involving unequal results—thus the variety of social classes.

---

[8] In modern communities the "high vitality" classes are roughly approximated with rural landowners, the "medium" with business and professional groups, the "low" with the urban proletariat.

The social class has a highly developed consciousness of kind, is a "positive and constructive element in society"; while the non-social class possesses an "imperfect" development of consciousness of kind, and is the class from which all other classes are differentiated. The consciousness of kind has become "degenerate" in the pseudo-social, or pauper, groups; it approaches "extinction" among the criminals, or anti-social. These gradations are all a part of the natural "constitution" of society: they represent evolution's basic social "division of labor."

In several of Giddings' later writings, the social classes appear as gradations of "socialization," essentially a phenomenon of discipline and education. Reversing the original order: the criminals are the "predatory"; the paupers (pseudo-social) are "intentionally or willingly dependent," and sometimes selfish and irresponsible; the original non-social class becomes the conventional, uninventing group, usually dependable, helpful, and considerate; the highest sociality group is independent, courageous, and cautiously experimental. (These gradations omit the "class" label employed in the earlier studies, and the descriptive terms tend to move the whole scheme to the right. For example, the original "non-social" class becomes "helpful" and "considerate"; the earlier "social" class becomes "cautious" in its innovations.) Giddings managed to fit these "classes" into the framework of the "normal curve" in a study of 1,888 individuals. The sample, the representative qualities of which were not mentioned, contained 52 "predatory" cases, 317 selfish and dependent, 1,044 conventional and "good," and 475 experimental and courageous (but also "conventional").[9] This, we are to suppose, is an example of Giddings' "inductive" sociology!

The classification in terms of degrees of socialization was accompanied in his work by a system of classes of "individualization." The latter corresponded, in general, to the mentality and morality groups described above. They are of no major

[9] This picture was presented to a group at Teachers College, whose educational function was conceived as creating more of the "social class."

importance in Giddings' theory of social class except that they offer further illustration of the *natural* group emphasis.

His interest in psychological phenomena resulted in an outline of further "natural" classes which reflected degrees of social "ability." Thus, the three personality classes (talented, normal, defective) develop into three psychical ranks. The first is identical with the first personality class, the talented; the second includes those who maintain their "business undertakings" independently; the third consists of the lower half of the normal personality class and the entire defective group. These ability differences, he noted, parallel differences of social function, and roughly correspond to differences of economic status. The first psychical rank "directs" the political, economic, and cultural activities of society; the middle, independent rank is critical but not creative; the lowest group is led in most activities, is completely dependent. This scheme (which appears to reflect an extreme social "laissez faire") includes "some of the poor" and many "merely comfortable" in the first rank, but, in general, is a hierarchy correlating economic and "psychical" factors. Similarly, these ability ranks are considered the natural products of "demogenic evolution."

In his later writings, Giddings renamed the psychical ranks the "natural superiors," "natural mediocres," and "natural inferiors." He suggested that the combination of intelligence scores and fecundity rates allows a further break-down into five grades or classes. Thus, there are natural superiors having high birthrates, natural superiors with few or no children, natural mediocres with either high or low birth-rates, infecund natural inferiors, and natural inferiors with high birth-rates. The first two groups "carry the entire load of constructive societal work" except "supervised toil": "all progress is their achievement." The last group is a "vast anti-social power."

It is a short step from these notions to the conception of an élite, a "natural aristocracy," or, to use Giddings' original phrase, a "preëminent social class." "Try . . . to imagine that comparatively small part of a population which is found in the social class and, at the same time, in that highest personality class . . . and is found also in the first and second vitality classes." This is the "most efficient class in the community"; it alone deserves to be called an élite or aristocracy. Though we do not know its exact extent, we can be sure that it is always a very small part of the population: Galton's estimate of 250 in each million was probably accurate. This is the class which nations have at times destroyed and yet it is the group most highly endowed with "intellectual power" and knowledge. The preëminent class "sets most of the examples and standards for mankind," it performs most of the original thinking, it leads, directs, and organizes society, and it contributes the greatest share of culture. This superior sociality class includes "wise philanthropists," "true reformers whose zeal is tempered by common sense and sober patience." In short, it includes all persons whom Giddings approved.

Closely allied with the idea of a preëminent social class, but described in more political terms, was Giddings' notion of a natural "protocracy." The small group which reacts "systematically and persistently" to changing conditions forms the nucleus of a ruling class. Every type of political system begins as a protocracy whose essential elements remain in all communities. The first principle of political science is: "the few always dominate." Democracy, even in its most radical form, merely places certain responsibilities upon the ruling protocracy. The latter consists of the "alert and effective." "Protocracy is always with us. We let George do it, and George to a greater or less extent 'does' us." Thus, the explanation of protocracy lies in the sphere of pluralistic behavior: those whose reactions to new social situations are quick and systematic become society's ruling groups. Their place of power in the social order is justified by their natural ability to respond most adequately to the changing social scene.

This doctrine of natural inequality received its most important application with reference to contemporary democracies. At an early date (1898), in *Elements*, Giddings stated the principle: "the success of democracy depends upon the existence in society of [the] preëminent social class . . . and upon its domination or successful leadership." Too many persons persist in the belief that humans are naturally equal: such an idea endangers the very existence of democracy. To succeed, democracies must be ruled by their natural aristocrats possessing the "good equipment" of birth and education. As Don Marquis phrased it: "Justice to the weak, but not mastery. Love and service to the weak, but do not let them rule you." The proletariat is the least competent part of the people; we should guard against its domination. All groups and classes should be represented in democratic governments, but the ruling power must remain in the hands of the natural élite.

In this connection, Giddings' distinction between "radical" and "conservative" democracies is important. The first assumes that all are competent to rule and is typified by Jacksonian ideology: the I.W.W. is a perfect modern example. (However, all radical organizations contradict their principles of democracy in their intra-control systems.) Conservative democracy, on the other hand, recognizes a natural aristocracy; the best examples are found in large business enterprises and educational organizations.

The idea of a "conservative democracy" was evolved into what Giddings named an important item of his own "wishful thinking": the combination of democracy and aristocracy. Aristocracy provides standards of honesty and of ethical behavior, the standard of individualistic independence, "canons of taste," and norms of etiquette. From democracy are gained the notion of the respectability of labor and the propriety of earning money. One great fault of the capitalistic classes is their lack of a *noblesse oblige* standard: they must be made to realize their obligation to maintain a decent standard of living. The wage-earners, on the other hand, must learn that the business leaders alone are competent to control and organize industry. Both groups must recognize that the natural aristocracy is a small group; our colleges must choose only the most able; we must work for the selection and the election to power of "the aristocracy of worth."

Giddings' dream pictured a "philosopher's utopia" within the economic framework of the status quo. Typically middle class, it joined the niceties of aristocracy with the thrift and industry of the class of which he was a member. Later we shall examine the specific recommendations which Giddings believed would lead to the goal: a society combining aristocracy and democracy.[10]

The natural classes, explained largely by the ability of people to react to new situations, afforded Giddings a clue for the explanation of economic classes. The people with "initiative" become employers, the others are left with the "leavings of the situation." There is a direct relationship between the creation of large amounts of surplus wealth and the growth of a large inferior class of paupers and criminals: the genesis of the latter is an essential part of the process of social differentiation, requiring the attention of the sociological theorist. In discussing the stages of natural class development, Giddings insisted that the world is entering a class "equalizing" period: an equilibrium among classes. And here his examples of class are often economic divisions: "there has been, in the last 150 years particularly, an amazing equalizing of power and political opportunity and economic opportunity in the masses of the population of the western world. . . ." His discussion of the economic and political aspects of class deserves special treatment.

3. Economic Classes and the State

Before Giddings expanded his theory of natural classes, he conceived of class largely in economic terms. He also used the concept in the traditional economic sense in many places in his writings, stressing such "class" phenomena as differential birthrates, economic exploitation, and trade-unionism.

He insisted that economic classes, including "the poor," are

[10] See Division 5 of this chapter.

a necessary part of any social structure. The personnel of the working class may change, but given progressive change, the class itself continues. Reformers deceive themselves when they believe otherwise: "The conditions that would eliminate poverty from the earth would infallibly terminate the life that is more than meat, in society first, and afterwards in individuals." This principle holds, if for no other reason than the necessity of a functional differentiation as a basis of social control. Likewise in primitive society: there is always some kind of class order based on property ownership, as R. H. Lowie has stated. We cannot dispense with economic classes, nor can we dispense with the accompanying factor of exploitation. We can abolish hereditary rank, but not industrial rank.

The emphasis given to economic classes is well illustrated in Giddings' discussions of the history of class struggle. Marxian history "naively" assumes *a* class struggle, as if the modern capitalist-proletarian conflict were a unique event. Known history, however, is marked by three great periods of class conflict: between the military and priestly groups, as in ancient Egypt and Babylonia; between landowning interests and the rising commercial group during the breakup of feudalism; today, between capitalistic "adventurers" and the proletariat. In these conflicts the economic factors bulk large: the modern struggle was launched by the growth of the factory system; the wealth-gaining middle class established the institutions of civil liberty largely for economic reasons.

The economic class factor was stressed once more in one of Giddings' favorite classifications of social structures, which names four "class" types: *Aristocracy* allows a sharing but not equalization of economic opportunity, and control is exercised by a "fit" privileged class. *Plutocracy* displays the same "opportunity" factors, but control is retained by a capitalist class. In a *kakistocracy* opportunity, though theoretically possessed by all, control is held, in fact, by an undisciplined, ignorant, dictating minority that has taken power by violent revolution. *Democracy* equalizes opportunity and shares control.

Democracies are "communistic" if property is equalized and occupation prescribed; they are "socialistic" if the major part of property is collectively owned and occupation prescribed; they are "individualistic" if most property is individually owned with "prescribed obligations and limitations," and occupation is freely chosen. Giddings, of course, favored the latter form of democracy, which he described as "socialized individualism."

Both the significance and the complexity of economic class phenomena, Giddings argued, are complicated by the tremendous growth of wealth and population in contemporary society. As the composition of society becomes more complex, with increased vitality and ability differences, a tendency appears to identify each element of heterogeneous society as an economic class. The density of population stimulates class differentiation and class conflict. And the problem of differentiating economic classes is further complicated by the important differences between urban and rural groups.

In the face of these difficulties Giddings, in *Inductive Sociology*, managed to set down a scheme for sociologists who wished to study economic classes. He pointed out that the traditional "social-economic" classes in Europe "were known as Gentlemen, Tradesmen, Farmers and Labourers." Notwithstanding the reluctance of many Americans to admit the presence of such divisions in this country, these groups do exist. Successful politicians and state officials, ranking professionals, and the leaders of capitalistic enterprise are the "gentlemen." This group is sharply set off from the other three.[11] For purposes of analysis, Giddings suggested six class categories which were derived from the four basic social-economic classes. He named them: 1. Professional Men and Women. 2. Wealthy Business Men. 3. Not Wealthy Tradesmen. 4. Farmers. 5. Mechanics. 6. Labourers. There is no

---

[11] Giddings decried these differences as "inimical to that perfect fraternity upon which the highest social evolution and resulting social welfare depend." He suggested that the "one way" to cure this "evil" is to diffuse the "gracious manners" of the "gentle born" throughout the other three classes: to establish an "equality of courtesy."

indication that he ever employed these groupings in research, though similar "occupational" classifications have been rather extensively used by subsequent investigators.[12]

One aspect of the economic class structure which Giddings pointed up was the social power wielded by capital. The latter has at times "become the sovereign back of and controlling the constitutional polity of the United States." The "shibboleths" of equality before the law and equality of educational opportunity are refuted by the facts of the case: wealth means privilege in both fields. And in industrial life the workman is oftentimes faced with the necessity of buying at company stores, and, in general, must yield to the strength of the employer.

This concentration of power in one economic class stimulates the organization of workers and the solidification of lower economic class groups. The two opposing classes form associations, restricted to the members of the respective strata. But not all of the members of the working class are organized; the result is a serious split in the ranks of labor. Giddings described this important relationship between organization and class solidarity, though he looked with considerable disfavor upon the methods of organized labor in its treatment of the non-organized. His description never reached the point of penetrating economic analysis. Rather, Giddings turned to the political and psychological aspects of class.

In approaching these latter phenomena, economic stratification was discounted in favor of more inclusive groupings. A long chapter in one volume on the history of social theory does not mention economic forces. (Marx does not appear.) The emphasis is placed upon "the people": a "psychological middle class." In other works, Giddings stated that there is more allegiance today to national community than to any sub-groups. Furthermore, economic class divisions are blurred by the presence of consciousness of kind in various groups, an extreme example being negro workers versus white workers. Before considering

[12] See, for example, A. M. Edwards, *Journal of the American Statistical Association*, 1933.

consciousness of kind, which is closely tied with his ideas of class ideology,[13] something must be said of Giddings' analysis of the state.

Though he devoted a good part of his work to political phenomena, particularly the state, his treatment of the relationship between political and economic factors is not well developed, and at times is inconsistent. For example, in one place he insisted that primitive societies always display a correlation between possession of wealth and political power. In others, he acclaimed the conquest theory for its explanation of state and class origins. The more important stress, however, in these writings and his later works which deal specifically with political problems, is his conception of "community" interests. The latter came to dominate class interests with the historical development of states. The Greeks, for example, broke down traditional class and kinship lines and instituted the "patriotism" essential for a state's existence. But states, in turn, develop new class divisions, such as various forms of "aristocracy." These divisions always effect changes in the state: witness the revolutionary results of the growth of the merchant class.

The economic "basis" of politics is illustrated throughout Giddings' volumes. In *Principles* and *Elements*, he described the effects on the state of economic class demands in English history, and illustrated the operation of the same forces, though less successfully, in America. His later works emphasized the workers' attempts to control industry through political means; Lassalle's workingmen's program was cited with cautious approval. In America, Giddings believed, the working class had won most political rights, and was exercising its power by curtailing corporation growth and extending the state's taxing power. Economic classes are always "would-be states"; a truly representative government must recognize economic class lines as the proper basis of representation. So far, class demands have played an important part in directing taxation, but other fields are open

[13] A detailed discussion of class and consciousness of kind appears in Division 4 of this chapter.

to invasion. In an article, Giddings generalized the theme: "In every sovereign state there are would-be states" or classes. "Every would-be state strives actively to become sovereign. It initiates and foments class struggle."

The most striking illustration of the role of economic classes in political life appeared in his discussion of political parties. Giddings briefly traced the history of these groups in the United States, stressing their fundamental economic antagonism. This cleavage accounts for the existence of only two great political parties; there can never be more, he claimed. Republican strength is essentially the solid class-feeling of the capitalistic and commercial sections of the population. The major political parties are "controlled more by class feeling than by political philosophy." The wide-spread belief that parties represent specific "policies" is mistaken. Thus we have the situation:

The natural nucleus of one great political party in every country is the middle class of business men engaged in manufacture and commerce. The interests of commercialism and capitalism always dictate the policy of the party to which the business classes belong. The opposing party is quite as naturally constituted by an alliance of the land-owning, professional, and wage-earning classes.

Here is the "natural" line-up of economic classes reflected in the party structure of the nation.

This emphasis upon economic class factors in the political sphere, however, produced no theory of a class controlled state. Furthermore, like most Madisonian exponents of democracy, Giddings severely condemned the German political and juristic philosophy which viewed the state as the creator of moral right. He spoke of the "monstrous contention that the state is morally absolute and can do no wrong," and insisted that this authoritarian conception was responsible for the "militarism" of the "dynastic family" and "privileged class" control in Germany.

Giddings believed the state to be essentially an agency of social "integration." In this capacity, the primary concern of government is the harmonizing of social classes and group interests. The function of integration necessarily carries the state into economic and cultural activities. He was never explicit as to how far a state could or should extend its control over the economic and cultural spheres; some such extension, however, is "inevitable." In one place he stated: "The functions of the state are coextensive with human interests." This extreme view was inconsistent with many of his own arguments.

The state's function of social integration is rooted in certain common interests of the whole public: "The state . . . is the entire natural society responding in like ways to the same stimuli and cooperating in the achievement of useful tasks of common interest. . . ." This is true whether the public displays direct, active cooperation, or passive acceptance. This notion of a "general will" is typical of the democratic school of state theory. Giddings, in support of the thesis, argued that the "consent of the many" is the real basis of *all* sovereignty. Sovereignty itself may be expressed through a plutocracy, aristocracy, or any other state form, but its sanction lies in the general will. In sociological language, he reiterated the point by assigning the determination of "stateways" to the fundamental folkways of the community. The state, "noblest expression of human purpose," is always sanctioned by the dominant common interests of the people.

Giddings rejected any rigid conception of the proper role of the state; he preferred a middle road between "socialist" and "individualist." The socialists are correct in maintaining that the state *could* "carry on all social undertakings." The individualists are equally correct in insisting that society *could* "achieve its ends without authoritative governments." But under normal social conditions neither occurs: the actual distribution of functions varies with the needs of the moment. The extremes of state rule are "absolutism" and "anarchy," the "mean" which Giddings advocated being "democratic republicanism." He discarded the arguments of the extremists in favor of "experiment and an experimental policy." During the war, he predicted that both individualistic and socialistic policies would resolve themselves into more intelligent experimentation. A more equal distribution of labor-produced wealth was the specific "class" aspect of state function upon which he insisted.

This "middle of the road" policy was tempered in Giddings' writing by the fear he expressed of lower class rule. It is a "false notion of democracy" that conceives of government run by the "masses." This would mean intolerable class domination by the "ignorant," which would extinguish liberty. The masses can be trusted only when "the better instincts of human nature are appealed to." Unfortunately, Giddings never was explicit regarding the makeup of the "masses." Whether he feared their ignorant stifling of the "natural aristocracy," or their economic demands, is not clear.

4. CONSCIOUSNESS OF KIND AND CLASS

"The social composition is a psychological rather than a physical fact . . . it may be described as a mutual toleration and alliance among the unlike individual elements of a society, supplemented by an alliance of the like, and non-toleration of the unlike, among its component groups." The "psychological" nature of society's composition took shape in Giddings' formulation of consciousness of kind, a conception similar to the "sympathy" of Adam Smith's *Theory of Moral Sentiments*. Consciousness of kind became a part of the general doctrine of pluralistic behavior. Pluralistic reactions to common stimuli rule out a strictly individualistic interpretation of social life, for pluralistic behavior has its own laws, conditions, and forms. Thus, the "ethical motive" of human conduct must be examined in the light of psychological factors; the presence or absence of class consciousness demands analysis; toleration and other group feelings must be understood in terms of sociopsychological elements.

Professor Theodore Abel has recently indicated the utility of Giddings' consciousness of kind, interpreting the "social distance" research of Bogardus and others as "unconsciously" using the concept. Giddings himself considered the consciousness factor of great importance in the study of class phenomena. In his earliest article on class, he stated that "interchange of thought and feeling" must receive as much attention as "material" elements. He stressed the role of economic forces in creating like-mindedness; he advocated intensive study of conflict and toleration between economic classes and other groups with a view to the location of consciousness of kind. Consciousness of kind is both perception and feeling. Its reality is established, indeed, by the existence of such important facts as race and class prejudices. Consciousness of kind is an "ever-changing" phenomenon: it cannot always be identified with class consciousness or race consciousness, but it is often identical with one of them. This ever-changing phenomenon, in its relation to class, requires examination: first, as an element *of* class, and later, as a factor militating *against* the formation of social classes.

Any idea or group of ideas, any belief or group of beliefs, may happen to be, or may become, a common interest, shared by a small or large number of like-minded or potentially like-minded individuals. It may draw and hold them together in bonds of acquaintance, of association, even of cooperation. So it may play a group-making role. Contradictory ideas or beliefs, therefore, may play a group-making role in a double sense. Each draws into association the individual minds that entertain it or find it attractive. Each also repels those minds to whom it is repugnant, and drives them toward the group which is being formed about the contradictory idea or belief. Contradictions among ideas and beliefs, then, it may be assumed, tend on the whole to sharpen the lines of demarcation between group and group.

And so with classes. There are created "hostile camps on questions of theory and belief," because men have been differently informed and, as significantly, because of the different positions they occupy in the social structure. The shifts in the latter account, in part, for the shifts in consciousness of group membership, for the realignment of class conscious groups. Giddings found this "mobility of consciousness" desirable, but he believed that "relatively stable" groups possessing consciousness of kind were also present in society. Aiding ideas and beliefs in the creation of class consciousness is "spatial association." The physical segregation of groups, workers in the slums, farmers in rural regions, develops the "mental intimacy" necessary for consciousness of kind.

Classes are often marked by a strong consciousness of kind or like-mindedness. Class consciousness exists when each individual feels that he is a member of a class group, and is aware of similar feelings in others. A class must display "like attitude and interest" of the kind often observed in gangs. This consciousness of kind is reflected in class symbols, the manifestations of common interest. It is partly produced under conditions of modern economy by similar habits of consumption, the "psychological" standard of living being a possible index of class position.

Psychological solidarity, class *esprit de corps*, is increased by threats and various forms of conflict. "Under circumstantial pressure gangs of like kind tend to consolidate, and thereby to become a class." Crises, such as wars or drastic economic conflict, intensify like-mindedness and often lead to collective action; at times crises cause "open" classes to become "closed." [14] Intra-class cooperation, essential for success in conflict, depends upon "the extension of like-mindedness and the expansion of the consciousness of kind," as well as forceful leadership. Thus, every effective class contains a "dominating protocracy."

It is not to be understood from the above that Giddings advocated the intensification of class consciousness. Quite the contrary.[15] In fact, he was more interested in consciousness of kind as an important factor hindering the formation of strong social classes. The point is well brought out in a chapter he suggestively labeled "The Mind of the Many." The latter, sometimes dominated by common religious or community

[14] C. H. Cooley elaborated the distinction between "open" and "closed" classes. See Chapter VI.
[15] See Division 5 of this chapter.

interests, cuts across the class divisions of many societies. Like-mindedness is often found among the youth: a contrast to the conscious solidarity of the older members of a community, and a force operating against the development of class consciousness. The same theme was expressed in Giddings' discussion of the relation of like-mindedness to class control: concentrated control in society is an incidence of "behavioristic solidarity." Homogeneity and like-mindedness broaden the basis of proto-cratic rule, diminishing authoritarianism. The less class consciousness, therefore, the greater the chances of national democracy.

Giddings' foremost concern was this last factor, national community feeling. Nations always struggle to maintain social cohesion by attacking such disruptive psychological divisions as class conscious groups. *The Responsible State* contains a detailed analysis of the development of patriotism, "the soul of politically organized society." Here Giddings tended to confuse state and community, but the emphasis is the same: national values supersede all factional feelings within modern communities.

It is .with reference to national community that Giddings' numerous discussions of societal "heterogeneity" are important. Populations possessing a high degree of heterogeneity, whether divided along "cultural" or class lines, tend to be either anarchic or dictatorial in their systems of political control. Democracy demands common values which will allow "unlike responses to the same stimulus." Normally heterogeneity and differentiation decrease collective action, for under such conditions there is apt to be a strong race or class consciousness. But in a psychologically homogeneous group there will be no sharp class divisions. Unity, liberty, and equality stem from a community consciousness of kind. Given this latter force, "the transformation of the weak by the strong necessarily becomes to some extent an uplifting, instead of an exploitation." Such "uplifting" means a greater chance for successful liberal democracy.

Giddings believed that absence of class feeling was particularly marked in the United States. On the other hand, America has a very powerful community spirit. "Group struggle" has played a role in our history, but class struggle is "practically unknown." He argued that the Protestant movement, essentially middle class, and the strong Puritan tradition abetted the "classless" democratic development of this country. In one of his earlier articles he even spoke of the classless nature of local political parties, a contradiction of his more extensive writings on the same subject. American traditions and population mixture have led us to "distrust the highbrow, to love the average." We are a community with a consciousness of kind distinctly "middle class." It is for this reason that the conflicts that do arise between class and class must be resolved by *cooperation*.

5. The Middle Way and Societal Engineering

Spencer's influence, especially in Giddings' earlier writings, prompted the latter's statement that evolution works for the betterment of all society, including the "masses"; he once branded poor-laws "maudlin sentimentalism." It is a mistake, however, to interpret the bulk of Giddings' work as "raw evolutionism," for he was seriously concerned not only with the direction of social change, but with the extent to which it could be most advantageously directed by man.

Of first importance to Giddings, social change must be gradual, especially political and economic reform. He mistrusted attempts to throw the balance of favor to any one class; he strongly condemned revolutionary activity and believed that democracy offered a safeguard against class revolution. He was suspicious of social legislation that did not have its basis in the more permanent folkways of the community; at the beginning of the century, he looked upon the woman suffrage movement as progressing too rapidly. Giddings' fear of class revolt is apparent at many points: impulsive social action is harmful; propertyless workers endanger the welfare of society; eventual industrial democracy depends upon the "patience" of labor; democracy in general is dangerous because of the emotionalism of the lower classes; the "direct action" of general strikes and overt class movements is "primitive" and "uncivilized."

In one place, Giddings attributed progress to the process involving the rise to power of new classes. But, paradoxically, he insisted that this process contains a grave danger of new class alignments: the newly formed proletariat is particularly "dangerous." In fact, Giddings viewed the growing class differences in America as a threat to liberalism, and feared that the "masses" might curtail civil liberty. He condemned class separation and conflict for creating in the lower class an "inferiority complex" which could become inimical to the social whole.

Such views could only mean strong denunciation of socialist theory. Giddings did praise Marx and Engels as historians, and sent his students to the works of the English Fabians and to the research of Charles Booth. But he named socialism "nonsense," spoke of its "tremendous fallacy," and criticized it for being ultra-normative: those who attribute economic exploitation "to the wickedness and greed of a capital-owning class" commit a "tissue of economic and sociological fallacies." [16] Both the economic and class analyses of socialism are manifestly incorrect, opined Giddings. It is claimed that unskilled labor creates a great share of the wealth: "it would be nearer the truth to say that large classes of unskilled labor hardly create their own subsistence." Marxian economics is guilty of complete misunderstanding of the nature of historical change in which all "social gains" mean the exploitation of a class. Nor does Marxism begin to comprehend the "complex sets of folkways" involved in class behavior. A thorough knowledge of human psychology and pluralistic behavior is "damnatory against all programs of communism and communistic socialism." Socialism also fails to recognize natural inequalities: it is a "paradox" because it assumes human equality.

[16] Giddings apparently overlooked the objective, "materialistic" basis of Marxian theory.

In 1927, Giddings prophesied a future unmarked by social-ism. Its threat, however, was strong enough to inspire a thorough description of its effects. Socialism, declared Giddings, is distinctly anti-evolutionary. It would reduce the "kinetic" development of industry to a "static" level. "Decentralized" socialism would merely continue competition, while "centralized" socialism would establish an anti-progressive dictatorship, or carry as heavy a poverty burden as capitalism. People must be convinced "of the fallacy of a cardinal socialistic notion,— namely, that industrial derangements can be prevented in a progressive world." A socialist regime would deal a death blow to individualism: it would mean extreme standardization and inefficient adaptability. Furthermore, the socialistic organization of the proletariat is a sign of "decay and danger," with dire consequences for the future of society. (The anarchists and pacifists would lead the world back to chaos.) Socialism is contrary to the ethics of most "conscientious men" who deny the right of the majority to dictate to the minority. Most leftists are really "anti-social": in one place, criminals and socialist revolutionaries are coupled as secret conspirators against society.

Socialism must be rejected, therefore, in favor of "socialized individualism" and "societarianism." Giddings described societarianism as a qualification of Sumner's extreme laissez faire. Thus, he distinguished between governmental action that, at once, adds "social burdens" and decreases the burden-absorption power of the people, and the state behavior that diminishes the burdens and increases energies. The latter is societarian, not socialistic. Social cohesion should be maintained, but with minimum restriction of individual liberty.

Giddings' positive reform program included adherence to "progressivism," which was distinguished from "radicalism" or "conservatism." His discussion of natural selection attacked the continental "conservative" policies and approved the progressive and liberal English program. The exact content of such policies was not made clear, though he criticized certain "social laws of tradition," and stated that a variety and harmony of interests are necessary for "progressive choice" in a community. He also characterized progressive communities as possessing a rising standard of living and a high inter-class mobility.

Protection of progressivism and liberalism requires the dominance of an "ethical consciousness." The latter does not permit class institutions to be viewed as ends in themselves. Work for life, not life for work, is the proper view: economic activity viewed as an end aids unethical class exploitation and bolsters the "plutocratic spirit." The drive for "money grabbing" and the over-evaluation of competition must be abolished. Giddings suggested that certain "evils" were perpetuated by the upper classes (especially in England), and advocated further extension of public education to combat class privilege.

These factors—the emphasis upon evolutionary gradualism, the contempt for socialism, the belief in individualistic liberalism and progressivism, the desire for an ethical consciousness directed towards social ends—together constitute Giddings' "middle way." Dr. Stern suggestively states: "He defended what he designated a creed of socialized individualism, advocating that the successful, who were to him synonymous with the superior, should refrain from abusing their power to exploit the unsuccessful."

In the more complex world of the future, with its greater degree of social amelioration, individualism and socialism "will not be the mutually exclusive things that they now seem to be." Giddings would have society steer a middle course between them. Certain economic reforms are desirable, but business enterprise must not be discouraged. There are no set rules for government interference: more state control in the economic sphere is laudable, but not state ownership. Democratic republicanism can achieve some degree of economic equality, but must retain society's "natural aristocracy." *The Western Hemisphere* proclaimed that America's "responsible state" is working out the correct balance between individualism and "organized societary power." In an article in the *Independent*, Giddings stated that the sociologist stands midway between laissez faire and socialism: "the economist who is true to form is too often an uncompromising individualist or a baptized Socialist; the sociologist frankly wonders how the Socialist 'gets that way. . . .' "

In keeping with Giddings' compromise view was his praise of the middle class. He stated (in a long review of John Corbin's *The Return of the Middle Class*, 1922) that "the middle class has been conspicuous throughout history until now. Twilight has fallen upon it, but it will stand forth again in full day." When the middle class "gives up the ghost the structure of human society will fall in ruins. . . ." This class, moreover, represents a concentration of intellectuality. Giddings pleads: "Brain Workers of the World, Unite!"

This middle position often led Giddings into self-contradictions. In *Principles*, it is stated that "the worst mistake that political philosophers have made has been their unqualified approval or condemnation of the rule of *laissez-faire*." In the same volume, and elsewhere, Giddings argues both for and against laissez faire. Of the former: the struggle to rise in the world produces many of the best human traits; "progress" is identical with "individualistic freedom"; legal restraints impose a "status of legal villeinage"; "liberty" demands "individualism"; "individual efficiency" is the clue to better social organization; monopolies negate individualistic attainment; proportional taxation is anti-social; the attempt of the modern world to reconstruct society upon a "hypothetical equality," if successful, would "destroy historic achievement from the beginning, and . . . send mankind to perdition." On the other hand: the "public good" must be the supreme end (civil service reform, for example, is advocated); pro-labor legislation is constructive; laissez faire's "unmitigated competition" runs counter to social morals; trusts are necessary today, and proportional taxation is demanded; dangerous is an "outmoded" laissez faire which "piles up in the community a frightful wreckage of physical and moral degeneration"; the United States has enjoyed unlimited individual, but little "collective" achievement.

In line with his attack on unrestricted laissez faire, Giddings pled for a more equitable distribution of wealth. This is essential for the proper mental and moral homogeneity of a community. If democracy is to succeed, it must increasingly provide to the working class a greater share of the economic and cultural products of society. The concentration of economic power is a problem demanding solution. Greater sharing of wealth will promote peace and international cooperation. Specifically, "profit-sharing" should be thoroughly extended. On occasion, Giddings deserted altogether the individualistic position in his demand for economic security and some degree of equality for all people. Especially, society must provide for the "burdensome" and aid the lowest economic classes.

Illustrative of his middle view are Giddings' comments on unionism. An early article stated: "It is conceivable, though not probable, that the industrial organization of society . . . may become democratic." His first two books in sociology spoke somewhat favorably of the American Federation of Labor. But soon after and in the following years, Giddings was hesitant about the advisability of allowing labor to organize: certain moral considerations were involved, not simply economic factors. Whether the rights to organize, picket, and strike "are expedient is a controversial question." And in several places he severely criticized trade-unionism: it is the best example of "untrammeled majority rule"; labor organization hampers the "fit," and has harmed society more than capitalist practices; it stupidly sabotages machinery instead of following the "true line" of educating workers in the technical skills. On this question, Giddings moved to the right with advancing years, his bitterest attacks on organized labor appearing during the immediate post-war period.

It has already been noted that Giddings desired a combination of democracy and aristocracy, again the compromise emphasis. He praised the traditional democratic institutions: all men are equal in some respects, and democracy must be maintained. Though it means rule by the majority, civil liberties must be protected except during war. Democracy must include all classes; it "does not and cannot exclude those relatively successful persons who constitute the so-called classes." At the same time, democracy keeps the intelligence level low: "the percentage number of individuals participating in a collective decision diminishes as the intellectual quality of the decision rises." Of course, the "intellectuals" and "masses" can arrive at common agreement by compromise.

Giddings' middle way was aimed at furthering progress. Progress, he claimed, involves material, mental, and moral elements. Objectively, progress means more intercourse, higher material standards, a larger population, and an increase of rational conduct. Subjectively, it is the extension of the consciousness of kind. Christianity has provided the pattern: we must unite "the classes and races of men in a spiritual humanity." Thus, permanent class separation is unthinkable: the "American Dream" is the goal. Progressive "liberty" results from "mental and moral equality," and contemporary society places too great a stress on material values. A good share of social ills is due to lack of "character"; therefore social consciousness must be inculcated. In fact, social personality is the "ultimate end" of social organization.

In his earlier work, Giddings recommended three specific policies which he believed would maintain progress. The program included regulation of international migration, compulsory education for the lower classes, and finally, the enslavement, "not figuratively, but literally," of the vagabond group: it should be forced into constructive labor. These reforms, if carried out, he argued, would bring about a vastly improved world.

From the early 'twenties on, Giddings forwarded as the solution for social problems the notion of "societal engineering." The methods of engineering, he suggested, have been followed rarely "in social reform, class struggle, public policy, or legislation." Borrowing clues from Lester F. Ward, and expressing some approval of the latter's *Dynamic Sociology*, Giddings stressed the need of a special brand of "organized endeavor."

He conceived of two "telic" patterns, "form" and "action." The latter, the telic action pattern, contains three main features: first, "rude impulsive struggle which often becomes violent and revolutionary, by individuals, groups, blocs, and classes"; second, orderly and systematic work of individuals and small groups; third, "scientifically planned and systematically executed societal engineering." The pattern of action which prevails at a given time and place determines the nature of the telic process: its selection is governed by mentality, knowledge, and circumstance. Giddings believed that the general trend of the telic process is "normally from rude struggle towards societal engineering."

Societal engineering is not to be identified with class or political movements. It is rather the "scientific" laboratory pushed into the forefront of social action, a kind of sociological technocracy. Giddings prided himself on this "radicalism," but was careful to distinguish it from the common variety: "The trouble . . . with modern radicalism is that it is never radicalism. The revolutionist is never a radical." He never gets to the "roots" of the situation. But societal engineering is valid radicalism: "a radicalism that is many-sided," characterized by intellectual sincerity and courage, and the substitution of "the engineering way of doing things for the merely smashing and destructive way. . . ." The societal engineer is primarily interested in "projects of amelioration." The "uplifters" give these projects very little attention, and they receive "none whatever from our phosphorescent ignorati of revolt and revolutionism."

What precisely does societal engineering involve? Giddings' answer occupied five pages of *The Scientific Study of Human Society*. He named Herbert Spencer's "Our Need of It" (from his *Study of Sociology*) an excellent statement of "the need of societal engineering." Societal engineering is simply the acceptance of principles worked out by sociology as the basis for social action.[17] The procedure is "hard and expensive," but

[17] Giddings implied that there is a set of generally accepted principles in sociology.

necessary; it involves imagination, but not "wishful thinking."

The present situation in need of ameliorative engineering is one of "bad heredity and bad environment," which have created the array of contemporary social problems. Just as the engineer is aware of the limits of energy and speed of his materials, so must the human engineer be conscious of human and social limitations. "Not a few of our self-constituted advisors . . . to mankind are preaching the delusion that backward races and slum populations can be speeded up to any velocity if they are given a few turns in the educational lathe. . . ." In the same vein, many conceive of a limitless "social surplus," forgetting that the social "expenditure of energy" is limited.

At the disposal of societal engineering are religious (energy releasing), educational, economic, and governmental functions. They are all based upon an "ultimate procedure": "equilibration, a balancing of resources and energies, processes and forms." Thus, societal engineering and natural evolution are identical, there can be no conflict between them. They are identical with respect to both method and "causes and effects." [18]

Giddings placed his final scheme for reform within the Spencerian evolutionary framework, which had been his starting point in sociology:

The visualized ends of telic activity in human society . . . are: Amelioration of the human lot, by security and material abundance; the survival (which security and abundance make possible) of variates from a standardized human type in whom lie our hope of discovery, of invention and of experimentation; the socialization of entire populations with elimination of the antisocial; and that individuation which is an evolution of intelligent, responsible, self-determining personality—of adequate man. And these ends, for which we strive, we have perceived and found desirable, because a societal evolution which we did not plan produced us, produced them, and enabled us to see them! [19]

[18] At this point, Giddings failed to mention the similarity between his program and that of Ward's, or even of Comte's.

[19] We wonder whether Giddings ever read William James' "translation" of Herbert Spencer's definition of evolution: "Evolution is an integration of matter

Spencerian terminology and naturalistic emphasis, brought even into his ameliorative program, beclouded Giddings' work. His foremost contribution, the analysis of consciousness of kind and like-mindedness, might have paved the way to a more exact understanding of group life: of community, of class, of association, of their interrelations. The stress upon *natural* class, the imposition of personal values upon social materials, the inconsistencies of his "middle way," were hindrances to a more positive analysis of social class. Giddings emphasizes the significance of class for social science. His theory, however, sheds little light upon the details of class phenomena.

---

and concomitant dissipation of motion; during which the matter passes from an indefinite, incoherent homogeneity to a definite, coherent heterogeneity; and during which the retained motion undergoes a parallel transformation." (Spencer) "Evolution is a change from a no-howish untalkaboutable all-alikeness to a somehowish and in general talkaboutable not-all-alikeness by continuous sticktogetherations and somethingelseifications." (James)

CHAPTER SIX: CHARLES HORTON COOLEY

(1864-1929)

CHARLES HORTON COOLEY

1. COOLEY'S SOCIOLOGY

THE contrast between Giddings and Charles Horton Cooley is striking: the former a dynamic figure plunging into journalism and public affairs, while Cooley's activities were those of a quiet, academic life. His father, Thomas M. Cooley, had migrated as a young New York farmer to Michigan, where he became a foremost leader in the field of law. Most of Charles' years were spent in this mid-western state, as a student and as a teacher of sociology at the University of Michigan. Almost from the beginning, young Cooley's intellectual predisposition was pronounced, marked by an "idealism" of which he was keenly aware. "My intenser life was always a dream-life. I did a little, read a great deal and fancied infinitely." Cooley's "dream-life" became partially reflected in his sociology.

Like Giddings, Cooley began as an economist, but soon found in sociology a more adequate means for the expression of his conception of social life. He wrote much less than Giddings, and yet his theory has probably been at least equally as influential in American social science. His influence lay not so much in his "system" of sociology as in the provocation he afforded students and readers. "He was more concerned with questions than with answers, with the starting point than with the march of the argument." Walton Hamilton has emphasized his intellectual radicalism: "Cooley was one of the great intel-

lectual radicals of his generation." Professor A. E. Wood states
that "to adopt his ideas in the America of today would be,
indeed, to create a social upheaval." Certainly an account of
the class thought of early American sociology must encompass
Cooley's work, a large portion of which was devoted to that
topic.

Cooley's name is associated with the analysis of primary
groups, with the conception of the interdependence and in-
separability of individual and society, with the study of communication as a basic aspect of the social process, and with the
broad understanding of and almost limitless faith in democracy.
These emphases and his views on social class form an "organic
unity" of the kind he ascribed to society itself. His theory fills
three major volumes, *Human Nature and the Social Order*
(1902), *Social Organization* (1909), *Social Process* (1918),
and several short articles, the most important of which appear
in the posthumous volume, *Sociological Theory and Social
Research*.

Though one may disagree with many of his generalizations,
Cooley's efforts to remain unbiased in the discussion of social
phenomena are impressive. Interest in social class led him to
"counteract a possible conservative bias" due to his "conservative antecedents," by living at times among the poverty groups
and "otherwise undergoing influences supposed to be radical."
Interestingly enough, Cooley manifested a decided personal
preference for working class folk, the "handworking classes."
He felt that they possessed the qualities best suited for a better
social order; he claimed that "we ought . . . to stand by them
not from pity but as comrades." Students of humble origins received his highest praise, while he objected to the social complacency of the more well-to-do. The degree to which these
preferences influenced Cooley's theory of social classes, however, appears negligible. On the other hand, his program of
social reform, hardly separable from his entire system of sociology, strongly reflects his personal values.[1]

[1] See Division 3 of this chapter.

Cooley assigned the topic of class major position. Indeed, it is questionable whether his system would hold together without the class materials. He stated, for example, "that anyone who studies the theory of social classes . . . using what has been written upon the subject to stimulate his own observation and reflection, will find that the contemporary situation is illumined for him and his grasp of the trend of events enhanced." Professors Angell and Carr, as Cooley's collaborators, have emphasized the significance of class in two unusually extensive chapters of their text. Certain aspects of Cooley's general theory must be noted before analysing his specific treatment of social classes.

Like most of his contemporaries in sociology, Cooley was influenced by the evolutionary doctrines of Darwin and the organicism of the Spencerian school.[2] But he preferred on the whole to use the writings of the nineteenth century *literati* as "source" material. It was perhaps in keeping with his conception of sociology as an "artistic" science that he valued the works of, say, Emerson above those theorists such as Spencer and Marx. Just as he found the most useful clues in the thoughts of the literary giants, so he discovered that men's thoughts, beliefs, and ideas were the most important aspect of society. That these psychological factors are the central data of society is the major principle of most of his writings. He believed that the "immediate social reality" is the "personal idea": society is fundamentally "a relation among personal ideas." He rejected a materialism which regarded the person as a "shadowy material body, a lump of flesh, and not as an ideal thing at all." [3] The notion of the priority of psychical factors in social life he shared with Ward, though the latter's theories did not come within his view until his mature years, at which time Ward gained his strong approval.

This emphasis upon "subjective" data was responsible, in

[2] As noted below, however, Cooley's own "organic" position is not Spencerian.
[3] Thus, to Cooley, the *basic* relationship between classes is *psychical:* "The relation between the employing and hand-laboring classes is first of all a matter of personal attitudes. . . ."

part, for Cooley's well-known methodological axioms. A society basically psychical must be studied with "sympathetic introspection," with "imagination," with artistic insight. Space does not permit a discussion of Cooley's methodology, but it should be noted that many of his conclusions, including certain generalizations concerning social classes, coincided with those of other investigators who employed far different methods.

Cooley conceived of sociology as pragmatic: "practical guidance is what we have a right to ask of every social science. . . ." And he believed that it should afford the basis for a proper social ethics. Any social science, he stressed, which is not rooted in the desire for progress forsakes its deepest responsibility. He severely criticized traditional economics for not seriously considering social problems, and for its unconcerned laissez faire.

His sociology, pragmatic and ethical, continually stressed inter-relationships, the organic unity of the aspects and segments of society. Thus, the relation of individual to society is one of interdependence: "A separate individual is an abstraction unknown to experience, and so likewise is society when regarded as something apart from individuals." "Progress" means a further development of both: one cannot move ahead at the expense of the other. In the same vein, heredity and environment must be conceived as parts of a process of reciprocation, not two separate forces of different weight in the determination of social or psychological phenomena.

Strengthening the organic unity of society and playing a fundamental role in the social process is communication. Communication allows the development of "social consciousness" and, most importantly, extends democracy into every part of the social whole by multiplying contacts. Communication breaks down the barriers of caste (though it allows self-identification with class), it promotes community feeling and lessens class conflict, it leads to the formation of an intelligent, progressive public opinion, and encourages the growth of intra-national justice and international harmony. Even sympathy for members of other classes is derived largely from the writings of scholars and journalists: again communication. For Cooley, communication was the means by which society was to attain the better life, in the same sense that Ward's education was to provide the path to the same goal.

Though the role of communication was stressed in all of his works, Cooley denied that priority in social change could be assigned to any one set of factors.[4] His conception of social causation was "organic," which he contrasted with "materialism" on the one hand and "idealism" on the other. Society is of a piece, there is no basic starting point, there are no prior factors. Of economic determinism: "I cannot see that the getting of food, or whatever else the economic activities may be defined to be, is any more the logical basis of existence than the ideal activities." Of materialism: "Why should the stimulus or spur of progress be ascribed to things more than to the mind itself?" Cooley objected to the various "particularisms," including Marxian socialism, as possessing the "illusion of centrality." Social change is a process of "universal interaction" within which even the individual is a "cause."

One might ask: very well for social causation, but what of the "progress" of which Cooley spoke so often? The answer lies in the fact that Cooley's conceptions of historical change and progress are inseparable.[5] His disciples, Angell and Carr, have italicized the statement that "the central fact of history, from a psychological point of view, may be said to be the gradual enlargement of social consciousness and rational co-operation." Historical change *is* progress: "life as a whole is . . . an eternal growth, an onward and upward development. . . ." Ideals which are first developed in the primary groups "become the motive and test of social progress." "We-feeling," the growing consciousness of "moral unity" in society, these are the

[4] The first chapter of *Social Process,* however, could be fairly termed a statement of "psychological causation."

[5] In one place, Cooley stated that "progress is a matter of faith, not of demonstration." His own writings are an illustration of his claim that such faith is necessary.

marks of historical change. An increasingly *free* intermingling of thought, the breakdown of caste and class barriers, the extension of communication and sympathy characteristic of the intimate face-to-face groups are the marks of progress. "His sociology was in a sense an account of the American community to which he belonged, and pre-supposed its normal healthful process." Although Professor Mead's comment requires some qualification, Cooley's sociology was partly a reflection of the less urbanized, "free," primary community life of the Middle West. Like the writings of those other westerners, Ward and Ross, it emphasized the democracy, the castelessness, and the "progressive" social idealism of that area.

Thus, he rejected "raw evolutionism" and the rigid individualism that often accompanied it. Cooley's theory, states G. H. Mead, "discards as outworn individualism and presents an adequate intellectual basis for a program of social control." His analysis of social change emphasized the *social*, and condemned the attempts of those who applied the "survival of the fittest" notion to human history. He pointed out that its loose application to class structure was fostered by the upper classes. Finally, he criticized the conception of the "economic man" and the hedonism of individualistic economics.

But Cooley's criticism of rigid individualism never reached the point of adopting any form of "rigid" collectivism. He desired a society in which the individual would have a real opportunity to find his "natural place": this to be accomplished scientifically. His faith in democracy demanded the protection of individuality and the condemnation of "isms" of right or left. Rivalry was, on the whole, he believed, a progressive force; the "equality" notions of the spokesmen of the proletariat were antithetical to his (once-stated) preference for a natural aristocracy.

Although populism, revolutionary socialism, and other "radical" movements sometimes entail "waves of unreason," Cooley believed them to be socially healthful. They are sincere attempts to institute order in a somewhat chaotic world, and could hardly destroy a democracy he believed inherent in the social process. Radicalism's chief danger is that it affords opportunity for reactionary movements.

Cooley refused to condemn or fear the socialist, but he disagreed fundamentally with the Marxian analysis of class. The idea of two basic classes in constant opposition could not be reconciled with his conception of society becoming more and more an organic unity through the operation of advancing communication. The very fact that suggestion and discussion are a constant part of social life disallows a total separation of classes. Class "parties" may have a "permanent function" in a democracy, but an ever-present class struggle, resolving itself in revolution, he pronounced contrary to the obvious facts. Furthermore, the common culture necessary for "group devotion and militant ardor" is lacking in classes as such: "Social classes, make what you will of them, have not separate cultures, traditions, or currents of daily thought, and are not likely to have." Men think and feel, and increasingly so, in terms of the larger group: today the nation, tomorrow society itself.

2. CLASS IN SOCIETY

"We may call any persistent social group, other than the family, existing within a larger group, a class." All societies, save possibly the most primitive, have such groups: all are class-divided. Cooley maintained that the presence of classes, thus defined, was a manifestation of the degree to which "cooperating" groups are distinct from one another in a given community. In general, class differentiation is useful and necessary, and though there may be at times "useless and harmful" classes, society cannot dispense with its internal divisions. Class, defined in this broad way, is a concept as basic to Cooley's understanding of society as the social division of labor was to Durkheim's. He contended that there are always great differences of "opportunity" because all societies are stratified along lines of wealth, occupation, and education; such class divisions tend to become hereditary. In *Life and the Student,* he emphasized that, though it may be somewhat controlled in its activities, there always has been and always shall be an "upper class." Its presence necessarily implies the existence of a class or classes "lower" in the social scale.

Believing social class essential in any type of society, Cooley refused to attach moral stigma or special inherent qualities to any specific stratum. "Brains" and the attributes of successful leadership are found in the membership of all. The capitalist class, in ascendancy at the present, reflects the inevitable concentration of wealth in society. (Equality of wealth or power "is inconsistent with the free working of human forces. . . .") Capitalists do not have the attitudes of an aristocratic caste; they represent freedom of social mobility; they are the result of the "survival of the fittest, not necessarily of the best." Their moral qualities run from positive "aggressiveness" and organizing ability to negative "opportunism" and methods of wealth-getting "by something akin to piracy." The poor, on the other hand, contrary to the mistaken views of Malthus and Darwin, are "unfit" only in a social sense: "The truth is that poverty is unfitness, but in a social and not a biological sense." They are not inherently poor stock. The "masses," of which the poor form a large part, contribute "sentiment" [6] to society. Radical movements, such as early Christianity, have been sponsored by the common people. The poor are likely to be the "initiators" of higher ideals for the better world of the future; they are notable for "primary faith and kindness." So with every group that can be looked upon as a class: each has a necessary social function and deserves no especial praise or condemnation.

Cooley was somewhat interested in the vital statistics of different classes, and was emphatic in refuting the views of Galton and his followers. The eugenicists, he believed, were confused in their conclusions concerning class birth-rates and

---

[6] Cooley defined sentiment as "socialized feeling, feeling which has been raised by thought and intercourse out of its merely instinctive state and become properly human."

in their proposed remedial program. A well-known article, "Genius, Fame and the Comparison of Races" (originally published in 1897), attacked that part of Galton's *Hereditary Genius* which failed to assign proper influence to social factors in the rise to fame of men of genius. There is no class basis, he claimed, for this phenomenon: the *discovery* of genius is largely determined by the nature of the social system. His critique of Galtonism was continued in *Social Process*, in which was examined the vital figures of three economic classes: "successful," "intermediate," and poor. From the eugenic point of view he found that the intermediate group—"those who maintain themselves in tolerable comfort" by continual work and strict economy—is marked by conditions "favorable to the increase of good types." It is in this group that the excess of births over deaths is greatest. In discussing "poverty and propagation," he rejected the extreme biological view on the one hand and the extreme "social" view on the other, and advocated a moderate program of birth control. In connection with this analysis, Cooley claimed that poverty, though not "misery," is somewhat necessary in social life: "we need a struggle . . . to shut out incompetence. . . ."

In the passages cited above, and elsewhere, Cooley utilized income differentiation as the criterion of class. But in *Social Organization* (a major division of which is entitled "Social Classes"), he named inheritance and competition as the two principles determining class membership. These are "very much intermingled in their working": hereditary distinctions have their origins in competition; competition, in turn, is greatly influenced by inherited advantages. In addition, class divisions are partly determined by the operation of the unprincipled factors of chance. Using these criteria, heredity and competition, Cooley distinguished two basic types of class system: "closed" caste and "open" class.

A *closed class*, or caste, is "somewhat strictly hereditary." It is a phenomenon found in all societies, for its "perennial source" is the desire of families to provide for children: thus caste is rooted in "human nature and the moral unity of the family." The endeavor to establish security for the young is by no means confined to the wealthy. It is present in the regulations of certain trade-unions and in the institutional behavior of all economic groups. "The most obvious and tangible source of caste" is wealth, easily transmissible and, as significantly, transferable into the educational and cultural advantages favorable to the retention of caste position. Caste is never absolutely rigid: its mold is often broken by very strong or very weak individuals. But it is always to be found. Even democratic communities are roughly divided into hereditary strata, binding upon the majority.

When social function tends to be transferred within the family, a "caste spirit" or sentiment often develops which supports the transmission and opposes inter-class mobility. This is true of all ranks of the social hierarchy: "the caste thus becomes a psychical organism consolidated by community of sentiment and tradition." [7] Caste sentiment gives rise to social, political, and economic institutions, such as the European medieval system, which reinforce and perpetuate hereditary distinctions.

Cooley named three major sets of factors which strengthen and weaken the growth of caste: the homogeneity or heterogeneity of a population, the tempo of social change, the condition of communication and enlightenment. Heterogeneity, slow change, and poor development of communication bolster caste; their opposites mean its diminution. Heterogeneity provides natural cleavages which facilitate the creation of hereditary groups; static conditions permit consolidation of hereditary power; while little communication negates the possibility of erasing caste consciousness. Race, immigration and conquest, and functional differentiation provide the materials for unlikeness, which favors caste. Especially so with race: Cooley spoke of "race caste," illustrated most significantly by the Negro-

---

[7] Cooley's "caste sentiment" is comparable to Professor R. M. MacIver's "corporate class consciousness," which the latter contrasts with "competitive class feeling." See his *Society* (New York 1937), pp. 174 ff.

White chasm in America.[8] The degree to which immigration adds to heterogeneity depends upon the cultural and racial background of the immigrant groups and the nature of the social system into which they come. "Conquest has been one of the main sources of caste the world over": it usually leads to a "consciousness of superiority," restricts intermarriage between castes, and, in general, tends to solidify the community into a strict hierarchy. There also develop within originally homogeneous populations important "functional" differences. The increasing complexity of the social division of labor along political, religious, military, and industrial lines "may have a caste tendency." This is observed in European medieval society ("the whole institution of chivalry . . . was a thing of caste . . ."); and in India, aided by original factors of conquest, is found the same phenomenon. Writing of the Indian caste structure, Cooley emphasized the role of ideology by stressing that the prevalent *idea* that caste is natural and sanctified tends to further caste where it might not otherwise occur.

A community in a "settled state" favors a closed system which tends to disappear during periods of rapid social change. The principle of inheritance depends upon the maintenance of certain functions through several generations. Any forces operating to destroy custom destroy caste, tend to "open" the closed structure. With respect to America, Cooley remarked that "the openness of classes . . . *may* be due as much to confusion as to a permanent decline in the caste principle."

When Cooley's analysis turned from the factors of homogeneity and social change to the extension of communication, it sounded the keynote of his favorite theme. The growth of communication must be recognized as antagonistic to caste if the "psychological" nature of caste is realized. For caste "is an organization of the social mind on a biological principle." Such a principle "means the subordination of reason to convenience,

---

[8] Cooley suggested: "The practical question here is not that of abolishing castes but of securing just and kindly relations between them, of reconciling the fact of caste with ideals of freedom and right."

of freedom to order." The "ideal principle" of social organization, on the other hand, is not biological, but "moral": it disregards faulty conceptions of biological descent and points up the "spiritual gifts of individuals," whatever their caste position. The debunking of biological notions through the diffusion of education and wealth will erase caste sentiment and keep class lines open. Such mobility has not yet been achieved, but to Cooley it seemed as inevitable as the march of progress; indeed it was progress.

In America, however, Cooley found a "conflict of tendencies," militating against and lending support to caste, the outcome of which is a matter of speculation. Aiding the principle of inheritance is the decreasing rate of social change. The development of a new community and especially commercial and industrial innovations have produced "a somewhat confused and disorderly sort of competition." He believed that the next half-century (from 1909) would witness a diminution of technological invention and population movement resulting in a "maturity" favoring caste solidification. The concentration of the control of wealth would seriously challenge democracy, which would be put to the test of preventing the growth of an "aristocratic spirit." An additional prop to the "sentiment of regard for ancestry" is America's great rural population. The growing functional differentiation of the population also favors caste: specialization means the rise of groups which may conceivably adopt a system of inheritance of function.

Counteracting these forces and the growth of caste are the role of "ambitious young men" and the "general current of democratic sentiment." The former will naturally oppose the restriction of opportunity inherent in a caste order. The latter was, to Cooley, the most obvious factor in our history. American community feeling is essentially "classless," containing little to support a rigid hierarchy: [9] "all the people feel sub-

[9] A more precise, though in some respects similar, analysis of the contrast between community feeling and class sentiment is found in the sociology of R. M. MacIver. See *Society* (New York 1937), pp. 173-174.

stantially alike." Behind this democratic feeling is the belief that "equal opportunity," in which there is competition for place, leads to the general welfare. Yet Cooley foresaw no complete abolition of caste and inheritance. On the contrary, he expressed the belief that the inheritance of both fortune and function would permanently mark our society, and the hope that a working adjustment be established between them. "These things are not inconsistent, and both will make for order and contentment." However, he insisted upon the necessity of providing in the future a far greater degree of material and spiritual aid to the underprivileged.

In a sense, the conception of caste or hereditary class was a reflection of the more pronounced social hierarchies of the older communities. Cooley's other major principle, *open class*, was derived from his own relatively mobile, casteless society. The development of open classes accompanied the "growth of freedom," being rooted in the play of competition which assigns persons to status positions according to individual merit, not inherited rank. "The theory of a free order is that everyone is born to serve mankind in a certain way"; in so far as classes are based upon this theory they are simply cooperative groups furthering general social efficiency. This ideal, of course, is never wholly attained: there is no "pure" system of open classes, some degree of caste always being present. Social organization is always a compromise between the struggle for liberty and the rigidity of status.

For the most part, the open class gradations of society are based upon wealth. Wealth is an obvious symbol not subject to the uncertainties of the "more intrinsic" but less determinable differences of character or culture. The different standards of living based upon income determine, to a great extent, site and type of habitation, dress, education, "culture," personal acquaintance, and the like. In a word, wealth today is the chief means of attaining the attributes of status position. Nor will it cease being so: "The ascendency of wealth is too natural to disappear." However, the emphasis placed upon wealth as an index to class did not prompt Cooley to assign it a basic causative role. It is "not that this distinction really dominates life, but that it is a focus of the more definite and urgent class controversies." Competition for wealth means active conflict, while other aims are pursued peacefully.

Cooley carefully indicated that an open system is, in fact, composed of many *kinds* of classes: thus different investigators name different class divisions in society. There are occupational, income, and cultural groups which shade off into each other. An individual may belong to more than one and pass from one to another. The income criterion is the most useful simply because of its direct relation to class conflict.

The maintenance of open classes Cooley found desirable on several specific counts. It means the extension of opportunity, which results from the abolition of the privileges of inheritance. The naturally competent may rise to positions in keeping with their talents and thus promote society's larger interests. He believed this kind of mobility quite prevalent in American life. It is the actuality of an open system that leads the poor but "ambitious young men" to support the existence and privileges of the upper classes: "Their aim is *not to raise the lower class, but to get out of it.*" Furthermore, so long as classes remain open they promote "democratic high aims" through education and the competition of "functional" classes. For the proper basis of privilege to Cooley, as to many of the "socialists," was function. He dismissed the "total-cleavage theory of economic classes" of certain European writers, who were influenced by the caste traditions of their own countries, as inconsistent with a social process working towards an open functional system. The classes of the future will be mostly functional ranks, open to the many through a democratic extension of education.[10]

Although Cooley attempted no systematic or extensive analy-

---

[10] Professors Angell and Carr deviate somewhat from Cooley's general position by defining social class in terms of economic position and function: "In every society complex enough to have division of labor, association tends to stratify on levels determined by economic power and function. The groups thus formed are called social classes."

sis of class consciousness, his study of the socio-psychological aspects of communication included consideration of the problem. Communication is basic to all group life: in so far as a group is "social" it rests upon a foundation of interchange of thought and feeling. The "sympathies" of an individual are a reflection of group membership, including class, and "self" can be understood only in relation to the organizational makeup of the society of which it is a part. And so with group consciousness: its analysis involves the study of the self-consciousness of individuals *and* the groups or classes to which they belong.[11] "Conscience," as well as consciousness, is always a group phenomenon. Our "moral sentiment" depends upon group affiliation: opposing standards exist between employer and employee, as between slaveholder and slave or Norman conqueror and Saxon conquered. Cooley commented upon the marked difference between the consciousness of the working class and that of other ranks. He spoke of an "upper-class atmosphere" which surrounds most of us to the extent "that it is not easy for us to understand or fairly judge the sentiment of the hand-working classes." He recommended that people read working class literature and participate in the life of workers in order to "become aware of being in a new medium of thought and feeling."

Capitalists, professionals, a large section of the hand-workers, are social classes *because* they possess group consciousness. This is implicit in Cooley's entire treatment of class, and was explicitly expressed in his analysis of poverty. Thus, the poor, with no common psychological bonds, are not a class. In fact, it is this "lack of common consciousness" that explains most of their exploitation by the class conscious groups above.[12]

Where classes are open, inter-class mobility exists; conse-

[11] This emphasis of Cooley's is illustrated, we believe, in the recent work of Professor Dollard. He employs semi-psychiatric techniques in the study of class and caste structure. See J. Dollard, *Caste and Class in a Southern Town* (New Haven 1937).

[12] The identification of the fact of class with its consciousness is basic to the recent work of Alfred Bingham. See his *Insurgent America* (New York 1935).

quently, they cannot be distinct "mental wholes" such as castes. Thus Cooley emphasized the relationship between the type of class system obtaining in a society and the resulting ideological factors. Castes involve "separation" of consciousness, while open classes, though conscious of their hierarchical position, indicate "specialization." The latter, furthermore, "share the general spirit of the whole in which they are rooted." In the United States, for example, there exists strong community feeling, as well as a class consciousness which will probably increase.

Cooley approved such development: American classes have "too little corporate ideality and pride." Nor is there any real danger of class war. The American system is open: the community spirit, the sense of the whole, is strong. Only in terms of caste conditions could a class revolution, as predicted by some, actually occur. Cooley insisted upon the need of stronger class consciousness in all groups, especially the manual workers. He suggested that our newness as a going community is the principal reason for the meager development of such group feeling: "there is a lack of those snug nests of special tradition and association in which more settled civilizations are rich." A more corporate consciousness, he believed, would bring contentment to the worker by providing psychic allegiance to his fellows, and would "foster that spirit of art in work" lacking in this country. Every effort should be made to promote the "we-feeling" of social classes.

It is clear that Cooley's analysis of class represents no strict economic approach. He was greatly concerned, however, with the effects of "commercialism" in the modern world. The spirit of commercialism "is largely mechanical, unhuman, seeking to use mankind as an agent of material production. . . ." It disregards the plight of the lower classes and promotes vice for selfish gain. Commercialism has brought about the institutionalization of the upper classes, accompanied by retrogression of social feeling and sense of responsibility; has separated the rulers from the rest of humanity, and stimulated selfishness. Self-interest takes precedence over service to the social whole.

Academic life has not escaped: "In spite of much sound theory and honest effort on the part of teachers, the stifling gasses of commercialism have passed from the general atmosphere into academic halls and devitalized almost everything having no obvious economic purpose."

The "evils of commercialism" are particularly manifest in our system of "pecuniary valuation," which, conservative on account of its institutional development, requires serious over-hauling. It must be rationally controlled by the aid of more comprehensive social sciences. Cooley believed that pecuniary values could be raised to a higher plane, could be socialized and humanized. The non-recognition of the ethical aspect of the economic sphere is fatal: the dollar, like any other element of social life, must become a recognized part of the progressive social process. It is not that the membership of certain economic groups is "immoral," but the rules of the economic game in which capitalists and those who emulate them participate are "outworn." These rules derived from the older caste societies: contemporary life contains "pecuniary self-assertion and display," "ideals of a superficial refinement," "crude human-nature values." Their change into "something higher" will result from the development of "group disciplines."

Cooley singled out the "economic" process of competition for special, and, on the whole, non-condemnatory, treatment. As a part of the social scheme, personal competition assigns to each individual a role. This process is necessary for the very life of society. The only alternative to a competitive system is one of "status," necessitating an undesirable caste order. These two principles, competition and status, have vied for domination throughout history. Neither is ever completely eliminated, but the predominance of competition means the greater rapidity of progressive change. For competition is accompanied by greater "personal liberty," and its diminution by the solidification of closed classes. Nor need competition be of the tooth and claw variety: there is no reason why it should "generate personal hostility." It always involves some degree of "mutual comprehension," and, if carefully controlled, can be a force promoting "broader social feeling." This is true of the competition of the market-place. And the life-struggle of great leaders (Lincoln is the foremost example) illustrates how competition can indeed be a "moral" force: "To be a man is to compete." True, competition today increases in unprecedented degree "restlessness, insecurity and strain," but with the rise of broader social ideals it can and will become a positive moral force, freeing the channels for personal development and working towards a casteless society.

In *Life and the Student*, Cooley strongly attacked the "stagnant" and "futile" contemporary situation of a society largely dominated by a small class. He elsewhere argued that control by the upper class "lies in the nature of organization" and spreads throughout most phases of social life. In the economic sphere capitalists exercise considerable power, even in the manipulation of "demand." They hold sway over "goods and services" and, to a greater extent, over political institutions: "Wealth can generally have its way in our politics if it makes an effort to do so." Legal, medical, religious organizations, professional groups of every kind, are at least indirectly influenced by capitalist interests. So with newspapers and other organs of public opinion. Where direct control is lacking, the canon of "prestige" compensates. "Culture," which Cooley conceived as that pertaining to the "human and social," is dictated by the upper class: our traditional culture, scarcely democratic, consists overwhelmingly of inherited conceptions of an older, decayed society.

It is obvious that such control exists in communities dominated by caste. But Cooley insisted that open class systems display the same phenomenon. The open class order may be more subtle in its mechanisms of authority, and yet almost as rigid. Note the operation of class emulation, a potent factor, as Veblen (cited by Cooley) took pains to indicate. Nor do competitive societies maintain equality of opportunity or other sure safeguards against rigid capitalist control, especially found in the sphere of "pecuniary evaluation." The capitalist class "sets fashions . . . which permeate society and control the market." Cooley found this situation in America: "there is in effect if not intention a dominant upper class which controls our system in its own image." This holds notably with the press,[13] which hides the true nature of class conflict, and even with the schools and universities.

One important part of social life, however, remains relatively free from invasion by upper class interests. Cooley believed that the "materialism" of the capitalist and his imitators carries little weight in the "spiritual" life of contemporary society. Most men, after all,—witness the "ordinary farmer, mechanic or sober tradesman"—are "idealists," valuing a simple, modest existence above the attainment of riches. Democracy, he often stressed, increases such feeling.

As the capitalist meets defeat in the spiritual sphere, so does he eventually in his attempt to control public opinion. As has been pointed out, he may and usually does dictate to press and school, but the "democratic judgments" of posterity will in time assign him his proper place. Indeed, Cooley held that the "unchristian," unfair separation of rich and poor, and the rigid, selfish control exercised by the rich, must succumb to the demands of "common man."

3. CLASS CONFLICT AND ITS RESOLUTION

From what has been said it is clear that Cooley's entire system of sociology, and especially his theory of social classes, cannot be disassociated from the topic of social reform. The social process pictures social change moving in the direction of a better world. Classes, in their origin, development, and evolution into new types of social organization, play an important role in this progressive historical movement.

[13] In *Life and the Student* Cooley observed: "The upper class is narrow-minded because the press gives it only one kind of social ideas; and the press does this because it knows that the upper class, being narrow-minded, doesn't want any other kind of ideas."

Any review of his program of social amelioration must take into account Cooley's "idealism." [14] He believed that we are occupied far too much with the problems of "material production and physical science," that we neglect the more important issues of the "spiritual and aesthetic sides of humanity." The leadership of the future must be a "leadership of idealism." Prof. A. E. Wood notes that "no one more than Cooley stressed the spiritual confusion of our contemporary life." The cure for extreme individualism and excessive materialism lies in the "broadening of the spirit," and in the shaping of higher social ideals and moral standards.

There is a fairly strong religious note in Cooley's work, with the emphasis upon Christian values. The democratic movement itself is of the same nature as the development of Christianity, for ideal democracy is essentially religious, its "true sovereign" being "the higher nature, or God," which it attempts to inculcate in its institutions. The imperative values of social action must be molded in the form of the religious spirit. Thus socialism, for example, is becoming a creed of "social salvation" and imposing itself as a rival to the truer creed, democracy.[15]

However, Cooley adhered to conventional sociological tradition in assigning "social causes" to those phenomena in need of adjustment. Crime, much insanity, pauperism—the "social problems"—are rooted in a social environment subject to man's control. Especially the economic aspect of the environment is in a condition of "disorder" marked by periodic and technological unemployment, "lack of standards of economic justice," political corruption: almost an anarchical situation. This state of affairs, intensified by the rapidity of industrial change, produces serious maladjustments for both rich and poor: the families of the wealthy are characterized by a "lack of reverence and love," by an "ill-regulated life"; and the poverty classes suffer from "premature and stunting labor." The economic sys-

[14] "Idealism" is not used to indicate the basis of Cooley's philosophical system, but rather his *emphasis* upon ideals, values, etc.

[15] G. H. Mead states that the "essence" of Cooley's sociology is "the gospel of Jesus and democracy."

tem is also largely responsible for friction between classes and the many correlated problems.[16]

The "organic" approach provided Cooley the key to the understanding of all social ills. With no single process nor single feature of social life lies determining weight in the creation of social phenomena of any kind: they are all the product of the web of processes we call society. Hence, those problems that demand amelioration can be fruitfully attacked only by the application of an organic or general program. There are no valid particularistic panaceas, say the socialization of the means of production. Reform must take the shape of a "common organic ideal."

Though Cooley was not an active participant in reform movements, he advocated many specific social remedies.[17] He was particularly concerned with special aspects of the economic order, speaking strongly in favor of better educational facilities for the poor, child-labor legislation, slum clearance and housing projects, and, most importantly, the raising of the general standard of living by means of more "scientific management" of economic life. The trade-union movement also gained Cooley's praise. He considered the organization of labor not only socially healthful but a part of the inevitable growth of democracy, thrusting itself into the economic system. Some kind of industrial democracy is needed to "give the individual a human share in the industrial whole of which he is a member"; the organization of workers is necessary to inject "morality" into competition.[18]

Cooley regarded the political process as an instrument for social reform. But he considered the state a limited agency: "government is merely one way of doing things." Nor did he

---

[16] In *Life and the Student,* Cooley placed most of the responsibility for social problems with the upper classes.

[17] W. H. Hamilton states somewhat misleadingly: "Cooley concerned himself little . . . with passing causes or current reform."

[18] In *Social Process,* Cooley stated that "socialism" might be the means of extending democracy into economic life; but elsewhere he looked upon the institution of private ownership as inevitably a part of the economic system.

believe that the state could or should ever become an all-powerful organization as some theorists viewed it. He decried the "mechanical" and "unhuman" qualities that seemed an essential part of the elaborate government. At the same time, he welcomed the extension of state activities into the fields of public works, education, monopoly control, and the like. And he condemned those laws which were "practically class legislation." Typically, he preferred the expansion of government functions by local, not central, agencies, and especially praised "municipal socialism." The latter is unmarked by "deadening uniformity and obliteration of alternatives" characteristic of centralized state socialism. Within the limits of local areas true "communal" spirit can direct the efforts of the government.[19] "State extension," however, must grow both centrally and locally because of the necessity for controlling the activities of the economic rulers and the need of meeting the new problems of urban life. Socialistic experiments, inevitable to be sure, will doubtless be instructive and beneficial. In the last analysis, the enlargement of public control is a "natural" phenomenon, part of the social process itself. Furthermore, the state should become more a part of the ingrained consciousness of the people: should be an object of respect and loyalty, as in Germany. Cooley desired the extension of democratic institutions, combined with a state-oriented *Volkgeist* possessing the humane and communal qualities of primary groups.

Cooley's many arguments for social reform, at the same time, were marked by caution and distrust of the "agitator." The social process reveals no indication of revolution: the fears of the upper class are "an elephant trembling at a mouse." The economic system must be changed, but slowly. Any devices involving danger of violence, such as the general strike, are "childish expedients." They are directly contrary to the central

---

[19] Cooley may have had in mind as "municipal socialism" the contemporary activities of the "Henry George mayors," such as Jones and Whitlock of Toledo, Johnson of Cleveland, and Seth Low of New York. See J. Chamberlain, *Farewell to Reform* (New York 1933), pp. 56-64.

principle of progress: the combination of stability and improvement. The opponents of gradual, orderly change, however, are found more among the wealthy than in the ranks of
labor: "If we have at one extreme anarchists who would like
to despoil other people, we have, at the other, monopolists and
financiers who actually do so." Cooley's advocacy of gradualism
in social reform was in keeping with his conception of the
ameliorative nature of the evolutionary social process. Progress
rests in the order of nature.

Certain elements of the social process likewise afford the
clues to his understanding of class conflict and its resolution.
Social conflict is essential to the very existence of society. But
it is resolved, and increasingly so, in the process of cooperation.
Competing groups never *simply* compete: synthesis or combination always develop. Like Ward, Cooley viewed conflict
and cooperation as part of a single organic process. "The function of struggle is to work out new forms of cooperation"; the
extent to which this is not achieved represents "mere waste."
Conflict cannot be eliminated, but it can be controlled in the
channels of "service" and "sympathy." The "competitive spirit,"
not harmful in itself, is gradually being directed to the betterment of the whole. This is the true nature of the "modern
integration" of group conflict, and it is this general movement
that is creating the demand for a "discipline" based upon
service and community sentiment.

Cooley's explanation of economic class conflict was shaped,
for the most part, in this same general pattern. Like all conflict,
class struggle has its positive corrolary, cooperation. It, too, is
an essential element of changing society, its solution resting in
the creation of more potent common interests, the enlargement
of the "human spirit," and the advance of "rational democracy."
Open discussion of class problems in "the white light of the
public square" must supplant the raw struggle found in the
"dimness of a class environment."

Cooley's appraisals of economic class conflict were not consistent. On occasion he approved the concerted effort of the

working class to organize for struggle with the vested groups. Elsewhere he argued that class conflict should end (though he probably meant that it should be channeled into more workable social grooves), and that it is on the whole a "waste." More importantly, he condemned the lack of "standards" in industrial conflict and stressed the "confusion" in class struggle. Particularly in America, the lack of sharp class lines and the "poor sportsmanship" and "lawlessness" of the capitalists result in unnecessary disorder and waste. In *Social Process* (1918), Cooley ventured to predict that class conflict in this country, rather than becoming "class war," would continue along the lines of "mild reconnoissances and skirmishes" in both political and industrial spheres. Any methods involving violence or reaction will fail. Progress will continue, slowly to be sure, but towards the goal of increased social justice.

The core around which grew Cooley's conception of the solution of conflict of all kinds was his fundamental interest in the values and social consciousness generated within the small primary groups. He was convinced that the "we-feeling" and the sense of interdependence and integration characteristic of the family, the old-fashioned neighborhood, and the small rural community, must be extended on a scale great enough to encompass the nation. Cooley displayed decided personal preference for the primary relations typical of rural life; he regretted the growing associational character of traditional primary groups, and pled for the restoration of their communal qualities; he attributed the weakening of "primary ideals" to the faulty organization of society; he felt that "humanism" was the chief sentiment of primary groups; he believed that "occupational" organizations could and should re-create the primary group qualities.

Once Cooley stated that all people require "something" in which to "believe." Hence, workers tend toward socialism or unionism because these provide common values. The comprehensive extension of primary group feeling introduces the common values necessary for the proper solution of class conflict. This is the "trend of sentiment" in which "classes seek to understand each other," which leads to "a larger organization of moral unity," and which means the true development of "freedom." Kropotkin sensed the nature of this process in his *Mutual Aid*, but it is only within the open-class framework of democracy that the primary values can be completely realized. This growth of sentiment is illustrated by the change of philanthropy "from alms to justice and from condescension to fellowship"; and even by the display and publicity-seeking of the upper classes, who by these means seek the good will of all. The classlessness of our dress, speech, and manners indicates the growing spirit of unity, the primary feeling. Socialism, "even anarchism," and the labor movement are tinged by the same sentiment. Indeed, there is a growing belief on the part of all groups that service to the whole of society is a necessary function for every class and individual.

The sense of emotional and material security, the "social emotion," and the standards for action of the primary groups are being diffused throughout the larger and more diverse sphere of the national community. "We need . . . a system of social groups, corresponding to the system of functions in society, each group having *esprit de corps*, emulation and standards within itself, and all animated with a spirit of loyalty and service to the whole." The governing of individuals' and intra-national groups' consciousness by the sense of the whole marks the useful aspect of extreme forms of national spirit, even the Hegelian ideal of the state. (The latter, unfortunately, is a perversion of the primary ideals.) A national community sentiment which is the outgrowth of primary values carries with it proper concern for poverty and other social problems, diminution of the "hostile feeling between classes," furthering of the "democratic spirit" with its ideals of service, and, ultimately, a "functional" society. Community feeling of this kind is the answer to our need of a "more conscious," better directed "public will." To Cooley it represented the very essence of progress.[20]

Inseparable from progress also, and functioning hand in hand with the expansion of primary community feeling in the social process, is democracy. It has been said that Cooley considered democracy "a system of social organization, based upon free choice, open classes, and opportunity for self-development." More than this, democracy to Cooley was a progressive growth as important in social life as the survival of the fittest in natural evolution. "Democracy is rooted in human nature, and against that no distorted social system can prevail: so Cooley thought." For him, democracy was as much an object of faith as principle of scientific explanation or type of social order.

As an element of his system of sociology, democracy is an outgrowth of the central facts of history: the "enlargement of consciousness" and cooperation. The individual becomes more intimately a member of the larger group: he passes from the stage of attachment to caste or class to identification with the democratic community. This is the inevitability of social evolution. A democracy is non-stratified in so far as it rejects the older forms of closed caste; thus America is in the vanguard of progressive evolution. But the open classes which are a part of the democratic structure must win their freedom *as classes*, and so must strive for organization and conscious unity. Especially so with the laboring groups. Cooley saw no inconsistency between the powerful organization of open classes and the further development of democratic community feeling. The heterogeneity of society demands the former, the organic unity and progressive march of social consciousness the latter.

The presentation of Cooley's views on class and social re-

[20] Cooley's frequent pleas for the extension of "culture" were of the same order as his conception of an expanding sentiment rooted in primary ideals. He construed culture as the "human and social," as distinct from the "technical." Thus, culture must be diffused throughout society, particularly among the "masses"; it must be rigidly separated from wealth in the public consciousness; it will lead to "sympathy" between classes, and to community sentiment.

form has involved the discussion of his entire sociological system, which can not be evaluated here. But, in the treatment of class, his contribution (apart from the useful distinction between open and closed classes, and the multiplicity of shrewd observations of class phenomena) is highly colored by the application of his sympathies, preferences, and optimism to the society of his day. Those who are similarly "humanitarian" in their outlook will find solace in his class ideas. The rigorous demands of a modern, more exacting social science will send many of us elsewhere.

CHAPTER SEVEN: EDWARD ALSWORTH ROSS

(1866-⸺)

EDWARD ALSWORTH ROSS

1. INTRODUCTION

PROFESSOR EMERITUS at the University of Wisconsin where he has served for many years, Edward Alsworth Ross can look back over a notable career. Together with the other scholars whose views have been discussed in this study, Ross is considered a "father" of American sociology. His life, unlike Cooley's, has been that of a crusader, not only in the development of a new science, but in "progressive" movements, in political and social activities. The energy with which he championed the silver movement years ago is matched by his later efforts in behalf of prohibition, trade-unionism, and academic freedom. Naturally, the phenomenon of class arrested his attention from the beginning.

In reading through the long list of Ross's sociological works, one is struck by the vivid portrayal of the man conjured by his words. It is unnecessary to refer to the autobiographical *Seventy Years of It* to sense his "largeness." The impressive dimensions of Ross's physique are equalled in scope by the extensive range of his interests and activities, by the intensive and sensitive qualities of his feelings. A good share of his writing typifies the early "scientific muck-rakers": fact-finding, fearlessness, demand for reform. *Sin and Society* (1907) and *Changing America* (1908) belong essentially, in American literature, with the works of the same period of Tarbell, Steffens, and Phillips, at least in sympathy and tone. His "sociology proper" carries on the struggle against chicane and exploitation: it symbolizes in the language of a scientific discipline the spirit of American progressivism.[1] And more than any other American sociologist, save Sumner, Ross has never "pulled a punch"; he has given the truth as he conceives it with a vigorous, moral self-confidence not too common in academic circles.

Ross's academic training included graduate work here and abroad, largely in the field of economics. A member of the now famous group under Ely at Johns Hopkins, he absorbed the theories of Karl Marx and Henry George and became acquainted with Lester F. Ward. Ward and, according to his own testimony, his concern for "human values," convinced Ross that he should devote himself to the development of sociology. Under Ward's influence,[2] he adhered in his earlier writings to a qualified version of the doctrine of social forces.

Ross's sociology also bears a resemblance to Small's in its elaboration of "interests" and the basic role they play in social action. The theories of Small and Ratzenhofer were, however, rather severely criticized by Ross in *Foundations of Sociology*. In *Social Control*, Ross stated that underlying interests were far more important in determining the "direction" of social control than the "cross-currents of sentiment" that mark the "surface of society." [3] In *Principles*, he set up a scheme of interests simpler than Small's, naming them wealth, government, religion, and knowledge. The conception of basic interests has some bearing on Ross's class theory for, as he pointed out, all

---

[1] B. J. Stern has stated that both Ross and Ward "may be considered part of the intellectual fringe of the populist movement."

[2] *Social Control,* Ross's first major work, and often considered his most important, is dedicated, "To My Master, Lester F. Ward."

[3] Somewhat inconsistently, Ross stated in the same volume that sentiment and belief hold society together, regardless of the "ultimate" associational role played by interests.

social groups, including classes, are united or divided in terms of one or more underlying interests.

Ross's theory of social process, similar to Ward's and Small's, and almost identical with Cooley's, is of major importance in his analysis of social class. He pictures society stratified by conflict "into non-fraternizing classes or castes." But stratification is "limited by certain processes of *socialization* which tend to assimilate the members of different classes. . . ." Thus the social process is dual: conflict always tempered by cooperation. This socializing process is of the same nature as Cooley's expanding primary consciousness; in *Principles*, Ross speaks of the accelerated process of mankind growing "into something like one big family." Common interests are multiplied and intensified, forming larger social unions of men and decreasing group struggle; collective ideals are playing a more significant role in social action.[4] This growth of social consciousness is due in large part to modern methods of communication which, in the words of Cooley, have " 'spread like morning light over the world, awakening, enlightening, enlarging, and filling with expectation.' "

Ross's discussion of "public opinion" is in the same vein: the belief that the rationalization and modernization of public knowledge will lead to the solution of the major social problems. The "era of jangling classes" can be ended by the reshaping of the popular will. A truly enlightened public opinion is the product of modern casteless society, which is coming to be classless. The importance of opinion in shaping the trend of events and in eliminating social conflict is illustrated, opines Ross, by the "muck-raking" era in American history: muck-raking, indeed, prevented a period of social violence in this country, followed by military dictatorship.[5]

[4] Thus, Ross declared in *Sin and Society* that the best of modern law stems from the growing "common conscience," not from a ruling class.

[5] In *Social Control*, Ross expressed great faith in the social intelligence of the public, opposing the views of Carlyle and others. But, in the same volume and elsewhere, his conception of an *"élite"* (to be discussed later) somewhat contradicts such a belief.

Ross is even more extreme than Cooley in his condemnation of uncontrolled laissez faire. The use of this doctrine to rationalize the ruthlessness of the business class in the exploitation of human and natural resources meets his sharp criticism: "In such matters a *laissez-faire* attitude on the part of society is suicidal." He speaks of the complete "discrediting of do-nothing" resulting from the efforts of writers like Ward, and, more importantly, from the success of such "interventionist" policies as universal public education, social insurance, control of child and female labor, and public works.

But Ross does not oppose all forms of conflict. "Competition," for example, is a necessary part of the social process: it "stimulates but does not destroy." (Original italicized.) Stimulation, "the good side of opposition," is tempered by "antagonistic effort," the "bad side." Competition is reconcilable with "sympathy," as demonstrated by the "spirit of sportsmanship" noticeable among Americans and British.

Nor is the competitive process to be condemned in terms of social organization. For competition performs the function of assigning to each a niche in the social order. The principal alternative to this method is the rigid institutional structure of "hereditary status." [6] "Under *inherited status* institutions make the character of their people; under *competition* the people make the character of their institutions." Competition is carrying the greater weight in the social process, and is producing the liberation of contemporary life on many fronts, including the economic, political, familial, religious, and intellectual. Thus, class control is giving way to social democracy, and in the United States where, it is true, class conflict has been somewhat sharpened in recent years by the growing class consciousness of capitalists,[7] the inevitable cooperative democratic

[6] Note the parallel between Ross's and Cooley's arguments all along here. Ross's, however, are expressed more forcefully.

[7] Ross cites the Lynds' studies of "Middletown" as major evidence of increasing class conflict. This kind of evidence, however, has had little effect on Ross's main contention that social democracy is increasing.

trend is leading to the diminution of rigid classes and the negation of class revolution.

Like his fellow middle westerner, Cooley, Ross has reluctantly admitted that America is marked by classes. In *Sin and Society*, he claimed that "public scorn" has had an effectiveness here impossible in a community "already split into classes." In accounting for the "classless" ideology and social democracy of the United States, he has emphasized the frontier traditions and liberal movements which have been most pronounced in the Midwest. It is this same "classless" ideology, typical of his home region, that has produced, in part at least, Ross's strong condemnation of the obvious class features of American society. The parallel between his sympathies and Cooley's is further borne out by his positive appraisal of the "brotherhood of man" aspect of Christianity, and his self-styled "prejudice" favoring the industrial and farming classes. The lower classes, he argues, speed the process of cooperation, for among them is the greatest amount of "mutual aid" and social consciousness.

There is perhaps no better illustration in Ross's work of the combination of individualistic competition and social collectivism than his "canons" of social control. He states that each item of "social interference" should bring more aid to "persons as members of society than it entails inconvenience to persons as individuals"; that social interference should not antagonize "the passion for liberty" and should "respect the sentiments that are the support of natural order"; nor should social interference hamper the "selective process" so as "to check the self-extinction of the morally ill-constituted." In short, the contemporary struggle between "moral individualism" and "moral socialism" must be canalized into a system providing the maximum welfare for the least loss of freedom.

To Ross, no single factor explains the nature or direction of the social process. He has generally supported the notion of multiple causation and has severely criticized the monists. He has emphatically denounced strict economic determinism, stating that Loria's simple philosophy "masks the real complexity of social phenomena." At times, Ross stresses specific factors in explaining social change. In *Foundations of Sociology*, he named the chief causal forces "religio-scientific innovations" and "industrial military inventions"; and in *Principles*, he suggests that technological factors are the most important in contemporary movements. *The Social Trend* develops the theme that war is a causal factor in history as important as the economic: "Karl Marx's doctrine of *economic determinism* . . . needs to be rounded out by the doctrine of *martial determinism*. . . ." Ross has styled himself a "pluralist": his *World Drift* (1928) names as the "keys" to the understanding of contemporary social change the diffusion of culture, the "suspension of the survival of the fittest," the intensification of capitalism, and the development of the "military mind."

2. THE MATERIAL AND PSYCHOLOGICAL STRUCTURE OF CLASS [8]

In the chapter on "Domination" in *Principles*, Ross suggests that militaristic and commercial periods of history must be understood in terms of the class structure of society. The class emphasis continues throughout the volume, a large division of which is entitled "Class and Caste." Together with "population" the subject of class occupies, in fact, a central position in most of Ross's studies.

Apart from conquest, strata develop within communities as a result of social processes. This phenomenon of "stratification," as Ross puts it, is typical of most societies, including sections of contemporary America, and is usually the product of forces operating within society. "All about us we see men rising or sinking in influence, responsibility, or power on account of their personal traits, but this does not result in distinct layers."

[8] A very large part of Ross's systematized materials on class structure appears in *Principles of Sociology*. Most of the class data directly related to "social control" are in the volume thus entitled, and are discussed in Division 4 of this chapter.

For stratification is based upon *inheritance* of property, status, occupation, or authority, or combinations of these.

There are several methods used to maintain systems of hereditary stratification. These methods, which lead to "the rise of gross inequalities," include: the primitive system of male dominance founded on fighting ability; the institution of "God-descended families"; [9] the inheritance of wealth—"the root cause of the rank differences among families"—which often originates in "booty," "priority," or "landgrabbing"; the granting of tracts of land, so characteristic of American history; the practices of undemocratic class-controlled states such as the earlier French and English monarchies; and systems of primogeniture and entail that enter the institutional structure and which, when found in modern society, are "embryos of feudalism." These methods must be understood in relation to the rapidity of social change that marks a given period. Thus, stratification during dynamic epochs is much less rigid, and both the "channels" and "sources" of social power may be greatly altered.

Hierarchies originating in "force, fraud or corruption" usually become legitimatized by the circulation of untruths or the cloaking of the actual sources of wealth. "In order that the dungheap fortunes may be deodorized they undergo a process of *legitimation*, whereby ill-gotten wealth is made to smell precisely like well-gotten wealth." Legitimation devices are employed by officials, teachers, and press in a " 'conspiracy of silence' " which blinds most people to the actualities of the social order. Supporting legitimation are "secondary" differences of personality and attitudes which are the result of traditional hierarchies. Members of the upper rank learn to be "proud, free-handed, and high-spirited," and consequently the "myth" is circulated that "the nobility had its origin in the deliberate recognition and promotion of the best." On the

[9] Ross cites the modern craze for genealogical distinction, typical of "successful Americans," as a vestige of this system.

other hand, the lower orders accept the stigma of "disgraceful-ness"—of the work that permits their very existence. Ross con-cludes that "it is thus that enduring distinctions in rank are set up, and made to appear wise, sound, and inevitable." [10]

In his analysis of "gradation," Ross names status as the basic criterion of class hierarchy. Wealth and power are essentially means of attaining prestige, and status differences, in the final instance, rest upon function, possession, living standards, or power. The "honorific" occupations include soldiery, typical of primitive communities, though still an important mark of pres-tige, "government" that is closely related to military pursuits, professional religion, and agriculture. Agriculture has generally outranked trades just as wholesale trade has enjoyed higher status than retail. Ross stresses the odious reputation of manual labor, due in part to its association with dirt, neglect of appear-ance, and the like.[11] Particularly striking is the "ignominious-ness of menial service" so wide-spread in this country.

In the "barbarian stage," function carried more prestige than possession. But, since very ancient times, wealth has been the most important index of status, as it is today. Distinctions of wealth are often supported by occupational differences: witness the expenditures necessary for preparation for many of the professions. Wealth *per se* has less honorific quality than wealth supported by inheritance, the ownership of rural land, and traditional customs. There are a number of "derivative criteria of superiority" such as scale of living,[12] number of personal servants, "ceremonial cleanliness," ability to refrain from gain-ful work, genteel breeding, ornamentation, and learning. These indices of status should not be confused with "ability" or "char-

[10] This analysis of "legitimation" and "secondary differentiation" is consistent with Ross's severe criticism of the idea of "natural class differences" and hereditary class distinctions in *Changing America*.

[11] Thus, Ross states that "the diffusion of bathtub, shower-bath, underclothing, tooth brush, nail scissors, safety razor, and leather shoe, along with the short-ening of the working week, is sapping the very foundations of the traditional class distinctions."

[12] Ross refers to Veblen's *The Theory of the Leisure Class* as a major treatise on "conspicuous lavishness."

acter," the *personal* ratings. Seldom does the individual of unusual ability enjoy automatic *entrée* to the ranking class, and
though character may at times have some influence in one's
social status, the fact remains "that definite and inheritable
social gradings *never* rest on personal worth differences, but
always on differences in respect to employment, function,
wealth, and the conventional signs of wealth."

Status gradation, Ross continues, has a number of results. Inferiors must maintain an unemotional "front" in their contacts
with superiors; creation of "personality" is very unequal in the
different classes; contacts between the classes are regulated
in terms of rank; "the inferior comes to be regarded as existing
for the sake of the superior." These attributes of status hierarchy are obviously opposed to Ross's system of values.

When consciousness of status becomes so keen as to induce
in the upper ranks a feeling that the lower are of a different
"species," society is patterned by "closed hereditary classes."
Ross's description of this hereditary phenomenon (under the
heading "Segregation and Subordination") parallels Cooley's
"closed class." When otherwise "eligible commoners" are ex-
cluded from the upper ranks class becomes caste, and birth the
major mark of status. It is a "spiritual necessity" for the members of caste societies to look "down on somebody"; the sense
of hierarchical social distance is diffused throughout the class
order. Segregation and subordination are greatly intensified by
the economic dependence of the lower classes on the upper, and
by the usurpation of the state by the superior rank. It is not
necessary to retrace history for examples of closed classes: they
are found in contemporary nations.[13] Subordination carried with
it the lessening of "self-respect and self-assertiveness" of the
lower groups. This "crippled spirit" is most manifest in the
very lowest classes, and with solidification of a closed system
develops a perpetuation of "social inferiority." Furthermore,
subordination and dependence produce class-controlled "char-

[13] The "company collar" in sections of the United States illustrates the "half-
feudal dependence of the wage-earner."

ity," a device offensive to members of democratic communities. In *World Drift*, Ross argues that caste is a foe of patriotism and community feeling, and discusses with approval the forces undermining the caste order in contemporary India.

An upper class, which rigidly closes its ranks to newcomers, pushes slowly but inevitably toward its own destruction. Its efforts to maintain itself at the top of the hierarchy are illustrated by its attempts to excel in such honorific activities as war, sport, exploration, and letters. But these activities cannot prevent the collapse of an aristocracy unless the social system is modified so as to broaden competition.

In contrast to subordination and segregation, or closed class, is the conception of open class. *Social Control* describes the successive stages by which a society evolves from caste to competitive class: first, the "ennobling of new fortunes"; second, allowing "talent" to pursue professional careers; third, the equalization of opportunity; fourth, the intermingling of traditional classes; and finally, the large-scale development of channels of inter-class mobility. In the same volume, Ross carefully distinguishes between "a parasitic society and a society that is truly competitive." The position of the poor in the former is the result of the class-controlled institutions, while under a competitive system the social sieve has assorted all groups according to merit; control is *social*, not class. Unfortunately, Ross cited no examples of "truly competitive" societies.[14]

Principles expands the idea of "equalization of opportunity" and open class. The transition from a frozen hierarchy to a more mobile system is largely due to the efforts of the middle class. The "unlettered masses" lack the foresight to engage in effective conflict for anything but immediate gains, while the middle ranks can both anticipate general results and fill the positions won in the class struggle. When they are successful in introducing the principle of competition the "class state"

[14] Later, in *Sin and Society*, Ross described the United States as possessing very low class barriers, but very high "race" barriers.

gives way to the "civic state," personal freedom is extended, inalienable rights supplant the doctrine of hereditary privilege, and the right to organize is guaranteed. Economic opportunity is widely diffused, aided by the exposure of craft and professional "mysteries," the abolition of primogeniture and entail, and the restriction of testation. Such were the effects of the settlement of the western regions of the United States, but today technological advance and the necessity for large capital in most economic enterprises have greatly decreased the laborer's opportunities. In fact, the present trends place more and more power with capital and management.

However, Ross cites several movements that guard against capitalist aristocracy and extend opportunity: the "downward percolation of culture" that decreases class feeling, the diffusion of leisure and education, political democratization which lessens class influence in public affairs, and the improvement of the social sciences.[15] But he insists: "the diffusion of opportunity is not enough." If an open class order is to be maintained against the inroads of monopoly and big-scale capitalism, "radical, invasive and stringent" measures must be adopted. Ross doesn't reveal the exact nature of these measures, but he suggests that "the future holds in store a socially controlled capitalism" like Sweden's, and the continuous increase of income taxation.

In *Foundations* (1905), Ross stated that the "process of economic differentiation" stimulates class mobility; in his more recent *Principles*, he has devoted a chapter of the "class" division to "the social circulation of individuals." Admittedly influenced by Sorokin's *Social Mobility*, Ross utilizes the latter's concepts of "horizontal" and "vertical" mobility. Horizontal movement, involving no change in class status, includes migrancy, the "circulation of ideas," industrial turnover, divorce, and movements within such groups as political and religious bodies. This type of mobility has increased tremendously in recent times, the result of advancing communication and

[15] Ross, at this point, takes it for granted that the "social sciences" are and will be directed towards social improvement.

transportation, the enlargement of political units, and the lowering prestige of tradition.

Vertical mobility, or movement from class to class, is found in all societies, to some extent even among stratified castes. Ross cites Sorokin's figures and the work of Taussig and Joslyn,[16] among others, in his discussion of "vertical occupational ascent," in which he concludes that hereditary position still plays a significant role in determining ascent. The army, church, government, school, and professions are mentioned as "channels" of vertical mobility, but historically the most common channel has been wealth accumulation. Vertical mobility has a selective quality indicated by "occupational descent" which, though slow in operation on account of the persistence of hereditary influence, somewhat balances movement up the social scale. Revolutionary periods completely upset the selective quality of vertical mobility, while wars and reform movements merely increase the tempo of mobility up and down.

Ross points out that America is marked by high mobility, endorsing Professor R. E. Park's statement that " 'no man, it seems, is so far down that he cannot hope to rise.' " He insists, however, that even a very high degree of vertical mobility is no indication of the equalitarian nature of democracy. On the contrary, American democracy is opportunistic: "In the degree that social classes become true ability grades you get 'looking down' and 'looking up'; so in the long run democracy as *opportunity* says 'no' to democracy as *equality*."

In closing his chapter on social mobility, Ross outlines a number of its typical effects. Fluid societies stimulate individual "versatility" and extend the "breadth" and open-mindedness of their members. At the same time, nervous strain and social isolation ("detachment and loneliness") increase, and traditional morals disintegrate. On the other hand, extensive social mobility tends to shift "the right person in the right place," and thus guarantees greater social stability. The danger of revolution is

[16] *American Business Leaders, A Study in Social Origins and Social Stratification,* (New York 1932).

lessened because in a mobile society there is little accumulation of potentially dangerous frustration from unfulfilled hopes and expectations.

The subject of class consciousness is not systematically presented in Ross's major works, but in all of them appear materials directly related to the sociopsychological aspect of class. *Social Control* states that systems of "morality" reflect the hierarchical structures of societies; sect and class feeling constitutes an important barrier against the formation of united public opinion. At the same time, Ross claimed that "classless" thinking was somewhat typical of "the people." Especially so in democracies: "It is to the masses, and not to the classes, that one must protest against national wrong-doing." [17]

In *Foundations*, Ross named classes "held together by . . . consciousness of kind" as important subject matter of sociology. This volume and *Principles* contribute an analysis of class psychology within a pattern largely Veblenian.[18] Veblen has set down the significant principle that the degree to which a leisure class is influential is reflected in the *"reigning standards of right, of decency, of beauty, and of ritualistic fitness,"* which conform to the canon of conspicuous waste. Ross has also employed Veblen's concept of emulation, explaining that the stigma attached to manual labor is the result of imitation of leisure class values, and is constantly reflourished through *invidious comparison*. Societies marked by great inequalities of wealth are characterized by the notions that the acceptance of money for labor is disgraceful, that work itself lacks respectability, and that ostentatious consumption is the criterion of "human worth." Democratic institutions encourage emulation of these canons: "all classes are inflamed with new desires from the example of the classes above them. . . ."

[17] This distinction between "the masses" and "the classes," which Ross first employed before the turn of the century, is identical with Sumner's use of the same terms, which appeared several years later in *Folkways*.

[18] In *Seventy Years of It,* Ross has expressed great admiration for Veblen's theories, particularly the concept of "conspicuous waste."

Ross especially admires the Veblenian distinction between "pecuniary" and "industrial" employments as a clue to ideological differentiation in the class structure. He explains that business men operate within and are dominated by the institution of ownership. Their concern with competition, bargaining, and the acquisition and protection of property produces conservatism, faith in competition, and destroys "any artistic interest in industrial operations." Industrial workers, on the other hand, are "attentive to natural law," and heed less conventions of "truth and validity": thus they are often thriftless and unwise in the ways of economy. Laborers' susceptibility to socialism, with its emphasis on the abolition of private ownership, is likewise the product of convention-releasing occupations. The roots of class consciousness, as "Veblen's remarkable book" indicated, lie in the occupational and economic structure of society.

The concepts of pecuniary evaluation, emulation, conspicuous waste, and conspicuous leisure receive less thorough treatment in *Principles* than the foregoing. But in this more recent study, Ross's discussion of "leisure class ascendancy" has a bitter quality absent in the earlier *Foundations*. "Foppish standards . . . spread through society and corrupt homebred notions of what is fit. . . . People come to scorn the joys at their elbows and pine for luxuries out of their reach . . . greed is whetted till even the decent turn to monopoly, extortion, chicane, and acquisitive crime." Veblen's "canons" remain, but this description of class domination is much more a reflection of Ross's "democratic" values than application of *The Theory of the Leisure Class*.

There is very little original material on class psychology in Ross's writings. He does devote a few pages to the "social rating of occupations" in which he refers to recent research studies as indicating rather alarming degrees of social distance between occupations in America. And he has shown how pecuniary evaluation and class emulation tend to lower the birth-rates, particularly in those groups most affected by competitive ideology.[19]

3. CLASS CONFLICT AND REVOLUTION

"The diametrical oppositions worthiest to figure in sociology are such unlikenesses as conflict and compromise, competition and combination, class struggle and social solidarity. . . ." Thus in *Foundations*, Ross named a number of constantly recurring antitheses which he placed among the central data of social science. His treatment of various aspects of social change in the same volume stresses the role of class in history and the effects of change on class. The exposition of the group-conflict school of sociology lists the types of groups that engage in social struggle: "functional," "regional," "likeness," "interests." The last includes "guilds, corporations, sects, and classes"; the conflict between them impairs social cohesion "just in proportion" as it perfects their internal solidarity.

Ross's first volume presented the class conflict theme as one of the "vicissitudes of social control." When there appear in society sects, each possessing unique standards, beliefs, and "fascinating personalities," strain is placed upon the social structure. And when these sects cannot "secede" from their native communities, when they become interdependent *social classes*, conflicting economically, the threat to the social whole is greatly intensified. For "the sect ethos saps the life of the social ethos" and social control takes the form of ruthless military rule.

Ross argues that the possibility of such intense class conflict depends upon certain conditions. First, there must be a *"sharp conflict of interest"* between classes. Secondly, the "means"

[19] Ross's well-known writings on population problems have emphasized class differentials in vital statistics. Lack of class mobility in society means very high birth-rates among the lower ranks. The decline of caste in western society, in fact, is of major importance in the growth of an "adaptive fertility." However, in contemporary times, Ross continues, birth control regulations favor the upper classes, the poverty groups remaining the chief victims of overpopulation.

used by the different interest groups must differ, on account of the "extremes of misery and luxury." And, most importantly, there must be a striking *"inequality of opportunity,"* correlated with differences in material possession. In other words, social mobility is a safeguard against violent class struggle. Ross suggests that there is a rhythmic "see-saw between static and dynamic epochs." Older societies which have been economically developed are usually marked by strong class lines, though they often enter new dynamic periods: witness the case of England. Italy and Spain, on the other hand, are "seats of class strife." Class struggle and "class spirit," which saps "social spirit," tend toward anarchy, which, however, is avoided by the introduction of centralized autocratic control. It is indeed probable that when capitalistic production has reached its climax, he prophesied, the static nations will become autocratic, or collectivist, or both; only dynamic communities will remain "individualistic, property-respecting, and free."

The foregoing analysis of class conflict hardly follows the pattern of *Klassenkampf* of Europeans like Gumplowicz or Loria. Ross stated that their ideas were uncongenial to the scholars of the more democratic nations, and in *Foundations*, evolved a qualified version of the conflict theme "shorn of certain East-European exaggerations, and coordinated with established sociological principles."

In the first place, contends Ross, the idea that interest groups are "absolute unities" with no limit to selfish aggression, "contradicts the law that *sympathy is strong in proportion to the degree of resemblance recognized."* Consequently, community membership and common culture always moderate class struggle. Secondly, the notion that classes always exert maximum effort is qualified by "the principle that *the will to resist is greater than the will to aggress."* And thirdly, the "universal law" that the cohesion of a group increases with danger and decreases with security means the weakening of class conflict when nations are threatened by war or other international crises. On the other hand, a community involved in its own affairs tends to divide into conflict groups. Finally, conflict between strata is tempered by intra class conflict: a "thoroughly competitive society" contains little jangling of classes. In addition to these four major principles which qualify the conflict thesis, are traditional religious, moral, or political ideals, the continuous growth of competitive ideology, the extension of education, the "ebb and flow of prosperity," and the democratization of the state: all of these serve as brakes upon class war. These qualifications notwithstanding, Ross concludes that "it would be rash" to predict the end of class conflict until men "cease to have closer relations or greater community of interests with *some* of their fellow-citizens than with *all*." *Community*, not class, must become superordinate.

In more recent years, Ross has considerably enlarged his analysis of class conflict, although most of his earlier ideas remain intact. The chapter on the subject in *Principles* opens with the statement that class struggle "is precipitated by some economic or technological change which throws up a new class or depresses an old one." *World Drift* is even more explicit in grounding the basis of contemporary class conflict in the strains created by the warring interests of capitalistic production. Modern capitalism, which separates the worker from his tools and eliminates his share in the control of production, "is the root of that vast issue which has grown up in modern society and threatens to destroy it by internecine conflict."

Ross's broad conception of the nature of social class is illustrated by his outline of types of class conflict. Laity versus clergy, military versus non-military, leisure class versus the "active" class, nobility versus commoners, agrarian workers versus landlords, and finally strife between labor and capital, are all examples of conflict between *social classes*. However, he carefully distinguishes the last type, capitalist against laborer, from "industrial conflict." The latter takes place between employer and worker with the object of settling "specific grievances . . . *within the existing social system*," while class conflict is the result of labor's demands that "cannot be met without fundamental change in the relative status of labor and capital. . . ." [20]

Members of economic classes are motivated by forces of a compulsive nature. The extreme measures used by opposing classes today are due largely, claims Ross in *World Drift*, to the tremendous invested capital per worker. And elsewhere he states that classes cloak their "selfish" interests in the garb of "high-sounding" principles. Threatened upper classes use the infrequent semi-violent demonstrations of populist movements "to strike the fetching pose of 'champion of law and order.'" Each class, in order to arouse militant feeling in its members, circulates "shameless lies" about the others, claims that "its very existence is at stake," and, if possible, ruthlessly utilizes economic weapons in attacking its opponents.

But conflict between classes, as Ross had noted much earlier, is confused by intra-group strife. "Not only is class arrayed against class but the elements which make up a class may quarrel among themselves": this states the theme of a vivid chapter in *Principles*. The oppositions other than class which mark any community are reflected within classes: competition for employment, antagonism between natives and newcomers, urban versus rural, religious bickerings. The interference of race feeling with class conflict is particularly noticeable in the southern United States where working class consciousness has not bridged the color line. The split between skilled and unskilled labor and the development of "craft" rather than class consciousness in the former are a great barrier to class organization; so with the rampant factionalism in the labor movement.[21] The capitalist class, too, is disrupted by internal rifts; however, the conflicts within this class are so well concealed that it seems impossible to clarify them.

Class struggle, then, cannot be considered in isolation, but

[20] Ross devotes a chapter of *Principles* to "Industrial Conflict," in which he makes a strong appeal for its arbitration by publicly controlled agencies, and offers most of his sympathy to the side of labor.

[21] Ross adheres to the "general principle that *opposition is sharpest when it arises between those who have been united.*"

only within a complex of many forms of conflict. Other types of conflict both strengthen and weaken opposition between classes: every form of conflict confuses every other form, except when the divisions are strictly parallel, and consequently bolster one another. Ross illustrates, for example, that much so-called "race-conflict" is essentially competition between economic classes, and that the " 'natural antipathy' " between races is often a device which hides the true economic situation. But ethnic differences sometimes aggravate conflicts between capital and labor, demonstrated in certain regions of this country.

Similar to the earlier analysis in *Social Control*, *Principles* contains the conception of cyclical class conflict: the "alternation of social strife with social peace." Economic or technological change is the basic factor in this rhythmic process, which often includes "alternating revolutions."

Revolution is defined in class terms: *"A revolution is an abrupt shift of the center of dominance in society,* a wresting of power from the dominant element by an emergent element." The control of the state is the major object of revolutionary action, which is brought about through stupid repressions by the dominant class. Ross ridicules the idea that revolutions can be "engineered" by a few agitators, or the "even sillier" notion that they are the product of "mob mind." Though it is often eased prior to the revolutionary movement, oppression is the root of class overthrow, which is apt to occur when the oppressed class is already on the rise. The precipitating factor is usually war, economic collapse, or some other national disaster which exposes the weaknesses of the ruling group. An important warning that a revolutionary period is impending is the shift of the "intellectuals'" support to the oppressed class. And the revolutionary movement is accelerated by the spread of "social myths," as Sorel had claimed. The revolution is a *fait accompli* when those in revolt have stripped the ruling class of "all means of regaining power."

Ross refers to his personal experiences with social revolts in

China, Mexico, and Russia in evaluating revolution. They always *"cost more than their leaders anticipate."* Likewise, they wipe out conventional inhibitions and release primitive behavior. But the "good from revolutions" tempers the evil, as the American War of Independence so clearly illustrates. This fact, however, does not justify a force "so terribly costly and demoralizing that we ought to dread it as we dread smallpox." Society can protect itself from this menace, Ross believes, only if it eliminates class exploitation.[22]

4. SOCIAL CONTROL AND CLASS

Ross's first claim to sociological fame was a series of articles appearing in the *American Journal of Sociology* on "Social Control," published as a volume in 1901. The book was partly the result of the author's sensitive reaction to the phenomena of social hierarchy, the rigidity of property institutions, and the growing power of the capitalist class. He carefully distinguished "social control," which "has behind it practically the whole weight of society," from "class control," which "always entails a rupture of social consciousness." Often enough minorities hold the reins of social dominance, but almost as often their position is sanctioned by the willingness and trust of the masses of men; this is control by society, not class. The thesis of the volume is the idea that "a kind of collective mind" results from social interaction, which, through its conventions, ideals, and institutions, has the "task of safeguarding the collective welfare from the ravages of egoism." Social control is directed primarily toward group, not individual, welfare.

The *forms* or "radiant points" of social control, as Ross terms them, have class implications. "Clericalism," "militarism," "officialism," "capitalism," "liberalism," and "individualism" indi-

---

[22] The advocate of class struggle could cite Ross's own analysis to reply that the elimination of class exploitation is precisely the aim of revolution. Of course, Ross's objection to class revolt is directed to means more than to ends of accomplishment. Unfortunately, Ross failed to discuss at this point the important relationship between means and ends in social movements.

cate the official and dominant guides of the community. They locate the centers of "social power"—much more important than and usually the determinant of "political power." Ross's "laws" of social control, too, have class bearing. "The volume of social requirement will be greater when social power is concentrated than when it is diffused. . . . The greater ascendancy of the few, the more possible is it for social control to affect the course of the social movement. . . . The character of social requirement changes with every shifting of social power. . . . The more distinct, knit together, and self-conscious the influential minority, the more likely is social control to be colored with class selfishness." (Original italicized.)

The detailed and systematic analysis in this same work defines class control as that exercised by a "parasitic" group, a burden to the remainder of the community. Historically, the institutions of slavery, serfdom, political absolutism, and private property have been utilized by ruling classes to exploit others. The evolution from ancient slavery to modern capitalism has been marked by the growth of greater liberties; class control has become less harsh. The chief blows at class domination have been delivered by the masses whose efforts to introduce true social control are largely the product of their response to changing economic and technological conditions.

"It is by studying the *constitution* of a society that we learn if there is a parasitic relation . . .": the institutional makeup of communities locates class control. Parasitic groups cannot effectively employ the devices of "suggestion" or "public opinion," which rest upon the sharing of a "common life" not found between exploiter and exploited. Nor are the "stimuli" associated with "religion, art, personality and personal ideas" suitable for class domination, for their "source" is not centralized or determinate. The most important parasitic "tools" are: "*law, belief in the supernatural, custom, ceremony, and illusion*"; and their "degenerate forms" of "*force, superstition, fraud, pomp, and prescription.*" These devices often resemble the institutions of social control, but actually have a quality of their own rooted in their origin in "selfish policy." The "socializing" methods spring from "disinterested ethical sentiment" and "shrewd social policy," unlike the instruments of class domination "shaped by cunning and achieving a control that is crude and repulsive." Ross describes each type of ruling class as having its peculiar methods. A "military caste" employs brutal force; a theocratic group uses hypocritical and crafty "superstition and fraud"; a nobility impresses with "pomp and show," its rule marked by "pride" and "rapacity." Continuation of control consecrates the methods, and in time the ruling class becomes "conservative."

But seldom does one type of group have complete power. Parasitic classes combine into a "great exploiting trust," possessing a distinct social "anatomy." The exploiters are at first a small governing segment which expends effort for its spoils. Later, the anatomy reveals an idle group surrounded by lesser and busier "retainers, mercenaries, police, priests, teachers, or publicists" who are the active exploiters. The "art" of exploitation (and also of social control) has been developed historically by ruling classes which have superimposed themselves upon others through conquest, as Gumplowicz, Ratzenhofer, and others have shown.[23] Even today it is difficult to keep the state from retrogressing into its traditional role as the instrument of the parasitic class.

Ross evolves the theme that the *"technique of coercion"* used by the exploiting class ushers in, in dialectical fashion, the *"counter technique of freedom."* Law thus evolves from force, and right from might. "Superstition," especially valuable for class rule because it provides the masses a "protector against the Unseen," and "fraud," always a major tool of the dominators, are combated by the *"technique of enlightenment,"* predicated upon freedom of speech, press, assembly, teaching, and the like. Declining aristocracies utilize "pomp and circumstance" to separate themselves as far as possible from the masses

---

[23] This appears to be the only major utilization of the "conquest school" made by Ross in his analysis of class.

in order to appear as "beings apart"; these techniques give way to democratic "simplicity." And finally, controlling classes are supported by "prescription," the institutional resistance of the social structure based upon the forces of precedent and suggestion. "With the aid of a little narcotizing teaching and preaching" prescription cements the *status quo*. Prescription is defeated by basic social changes, particularly by revolution.

The conception of prescription as a bulwark of class domination is directly related to several comparable notions in *Social Control*. Ross describes society moralizing its system of order into a value scheme—often an "illusion"—which sometimes supports vested interests. In the same way: "belief," more than any other form of social control, is apt to become a class instrument; and "custom," usually the creation of upper classes, regulates through suggestion and resists class change.[24]

In a somewhat similar vein, Ross's description of "social types," created by tradition, stresses their function of social regulation. Confirmation of caste and opposition to mobility invariably result from the pressure of class-bound values, imposed on most individuals. Upper class ideals have more appeal for the masses than those "of the prophet or reformer." The higher orders develop a unique "morality," its origins residing in "pride." But with the arrival of modern economy the "sense of worth," formerly restricted to the privileged, spreads through the classes. Honor, once a "caste badge," becomes the property of all ranks of men. Unfortunately, however, as Ross points out, capitalism brings with it slums and new class restrictions which prevent the complete diffusion of common ideals.

"Ceremony," with its honorific symbols and etiquette, and the "personality" of ruling class members, the result of special privileges, aid class control. Ross argues that personal domination is passing, that in the future the superordination of single

---

[24] A brief but systematic treatment of the idea of institutional resistance and its relation to class control appears in Ross's later *Principles of Sociology* in the chapter, "Ossification."

men will be a greatly limited phenomenon.[25] For individual rule is likely to bring with it the rigidity of a caste order.

But Ross would not eliminate the influence of the exceptional individual. The *élite* has the function of creating ideas and ideals which determine the progress of man; the "true *élite*" provides the proper "ethical" guides for social action. And so with the "great man," whose "superior social insight" is indispensable for human advance.[26] Ross's understanding of the nature of a true *élite* is indicated in the closing passages of *Social Control*: the "wise sociologist" will reveal the secrets of social control *only* to "teachers, clergymen, editors, law-makers . . . judges . . . poets, artists, thinkers, and educators." The "official hierarchy" frequently degenerates into class control, which can only be corrected by the rise of this "genuine *élite*."

A brief chapter in *Principles* summarizes Ross's earlier *Social Control*, including the emphasis upon class factors. How "class control masquerades as social control" is illustrated with materials from the Lynds' "Middletown" studies. In addition, the more recent volume contains a thorough discussion of "domination," directly bearing on class control. The several means of domination include physical force and the resulting "political inequalities," "corruption" and "patronage" typical of modern political machines, the use of religious power by the controlling class, the maintenance of ignorance among the dominated, and the control of propaganda which is the favorite device employed in democracies. Often the major support of domination is the conviction of the masses of the correctness of the status quo relations. Domination results in the "weakening of character" of the oppressed and the development of "emotional depression," "oppression psychosis," and compensating aggressiveness. The opposition to domination comes first from those less severely dominated: labor history illustrates that the

[25] This statement (1901) is hardly reconcilable with the modern rise of dictatorships.

[26] In *Seventy Years of It,* Ross states: "A social order should be rated according to its success in getting superior human beings into positions where they can wield power or influence." (Original italicized.)

better paid workers are in the vanguard of the struggle against capital.

Also of class significance are Ross's recent materials on "exploitation." Exploitation is of many types, the most important being sexual, religious, "egotic," and economic. The last, which overshadows all other forms, consists of *"making others work for you or taking for your use the fruits of their unrequited toil."* This appears in the exploitation of the young by adults, females by males, and the poor by the wealthy. Economic power can be transformed into political, social, or religious power, which in turn are converted into money power. Placing the burden of taxation upon the poorer classes, squeezing out the small business man, various forms of debt slavery, and unreasonable loan charges, permit the wealthy to continue their exploitation.

Ross's "general truths about exploitation" [27] are an elaboration of the similar analysis in *Social Control*. "1. *The social elements differ in original disposition to exploit.*" The leisure class, for example, uses the most ruthless means, while "hand workers" have little desire to exploit. "2. *Exploitation is more open, ruthless and stubborn between the unlike than between the like.*" Where community sense is strong, exploitation is weak; it is most extreme following conquest. Exploiting classes further their own interests by emphasizing, or even inventing, intracommunal differences. "3. *An element is ready and wholehearted in exploitation in the degree that it constitutes a self-conscious group.*" Group solidarity bolsters the subjugation of others. Ross exemplified this "law" from past history. Modern-day Germany serves as a striking example. "4. *Exploiters never relinquish exploitation.*" Parasitic classes never consent to give up their stake, but must be coerced. "5. *Foreign domination is likely to suppress intra-social exploitations.*" Imperialism thus subdues native exploiters in favor of those of the mother-country. "6. *Outside control menaces the maintenance of an exploitation.*" "Home rule" is sometimes dangerous because it throws

[27] Termed "Laws" in an earlier edition of *Principles*.

control back into the hands of native predatory groups. "7. *Masked exploitation outlasts open exploitation.*" Clandestine control is rampant today; the resistance of capitalists to publicity concerning their activities is suspicious. "8. *The favorite mask of an exploitation is a counter-service or return which falls far short of being an equivalent.*" Witness the notorious examples in southern lumber and turpentine industries in this country. "9. *Opportunities for masked exploitation multiply as social relations become involved and social interdependence more extended.*" Hidden control becomes simpler to attain with the growing complexity of society. "10. *Whatever lessens inequalities among social elements in respect to intelligence, courage, organization, discipline or situation narrows the power of the one to exploit the other.*" Here Ross pleads for mass education and class organization as barriers against domination. (All Ross's italics.)

It is apparent that Ross considers class an important factor in the control of society. However, his conception of class control is much less rigid than that, say, of socialist theory. His analysis of control, too, reveals a number of partial contradictions. He has described how business interests, press, and government work hand-in-hand in certain countries, and how the upper class manipulates foreign policy. But he rejects the notion of the state as a class instrument, pointing out that the state, theoretically a "channel" of social control, often becomes an independent "source" of control. The state, in fact, notwithstanding a certain amount of class domination, is society's best collective agent. In the creation of legislation, Ross argues, the influence of the capitalists overshadows that of the other segments of society. The legal profession, he claims, is controlled by the vested interests, resulting in the exploitation of the poorer classes. But the analysis in *Social Control* interprets law as the product and "force" of the *community*, not class.

In several places, Ross observes with displeasure the growing power of the capitalist class in the control of public opinion. In *Changing America*, he strongly favors endowed newspapers.

His autobiographical study, on the other hand, points with pride to the author's role in exposing capitalist domination of public information, and expresses the belief that such control will never gain a stronghold in this country. The same volume bitterly denounces the attempts of business to dictate to sociology: "the demand of the heel-grinders of the business corps that sociology shall say only what they are willing to have it say is tantamount to raping a modest and gifted maiden of fifteen." Ross claims that the extension of business class domination in college life has produced a "university sneak." But in his earlier studies he had shown that class-controlled education, typical of earlier historical periods, is eliminated by modern democracy. His remarks on religion follow the same general pattern. In the past, religion has been "a prop to the authority of the dominating class"; and in backward countries today it remains the "opiate of the people." This function of religion, however, can't compare with the "skinning of labor" by industry in our own nation.

In *Social Control*, Ross had stated that the business class most vigorously supports the *status quo*, and that that class was rapidly gaining more social power. The most recent edition of *Principles* takes stock on the present position of capitalist power. The anti-capitalist events include: exposure of leisure class standards; the public awakening to the fact that vertical mobility is diminishing; the recognition by economists of the acquisitive nature of the economic system, absentee ownership, and the consequent development of a "hereditary leisure class" susceptible to "demoralization and corruption"; the growing realization of the antagonism between democratic principles and the anti-democratic pressure exerted by capitalists. But arrayed against these: "pro-capitalist developments" involving the "mental testing" experiments which reveal great natural inequalities in the population; the movement of the most talented out of the ranks of labor which robs the latter of its leadership; the increasing complexity of the economic order which tends to prevent working class leaders from seizing it; the successful efforts of the business class in enlisting the aid of scientists in solving technological problems; the continual bombardment of the public by the press with the prejudices and ideas of business leaders.

Also in this recent volume, Ross utilizes the analysis of business class control made by the Lynds in their "Middletown" surveys. He optimistically predicts, however, that such internal domination of society will probably decrease.[28] In like manner, he speculates on the "outlook for exploitation." Ross believes that some kind of exploitation will continue indefinitely. Today the "encroachments of production-for-sale on production-for-use" enhance the possibilities for exploiting, and the complexity of modern society makes the problem of curbing it equally complex. The outlook is not hopeless, however, for sentiment against exploitation is increasingly widespread. But successful elimination of the bulk of it demands an "intellectual and moral *élite*," and the extension of educational facilities. Persons competent for the administration of restrictive legislation and the direction of controlling boards are plentiful; it remains for the government to safeguard all of its groups against exploitation. Such a government "need have no dread of a revolutionary uprising." The "employer-employee relation" does not necessitate exploitation: exploitation derives from inequality of bargaining power. Ross offers a final warning: the "foes of exploitation" must not attempt to eliminate all inequalities of income, for such a system would be quickly doomed. Opportunity, not pay, must be equalized. The "primitive capitalism" of the muckrakers, and of the elder LaFollette of Wisconsin, typifies an important element in Ross's sociology.

5. CAPITALISM AND SOCIAL REFORM

In an early work, Ross labeled the concept of progress "vague and dubious." For the most part, however, his own sociology

---

[28] "On the other hand, alien *domination* may actually increase in the near future."

is ameliorative: the "over-mastering purpose" of sociology is "*to better human relations.*" He regards social reform itself as a scientific problem, as borne out by the generalizations set forth in his "canons of social reconstruction." Primary concern with improvement is, in fact, one of the foremost features of his writings, illustrated by the analysis of the "criminaloid" in *Sin and Society*, and by the typical argument that all businesses and professions, being affected with broad social interests, must be geared to community welfare.

Such reforms as Ross advocated are in part a reflection of his antagonism toward certain aspects of capitalist society. He states that the role of capital is the most significant feature of "the modern social question," and insists that the enormous social power wielded by the capitalist class intensifies the untouchability of property legally and morally, glorifies "frugality and thrift," and enhances the property protection function of the state. Capitalism endangers democracy to the point of threatening its existence, unless democracy enforces a redistribution of wealth. And it has many anti-social characteristics: the business class becomes narrow in point of view, in contrast with the broadening "social view" of the general public; the success of capitalist enterprise has convinced the business man of his "God-given right to run this country"; the consumer, laborer, and farmer "are gouged, and gyped in a great variety of ways"; those who combat the "brutalities and knaveries of capitalism" deserve praise. Furthermore, the dominant economic motive leads to international conflict; and the "repressions" imposed upon the masses by industrial capitalism warp the natural impulses and stimulate revolutionary fervor.

Nor does Ross approve of the effects of "commercialization," defined as the domination of the profit motive in occupational life. The superordination of the profit motive over pride of workmanship and creative bent is the result of the growing separation of producer and consumer, and of producer and owner. Professional and artistic standards are warped by the "corporation collar" and the desire for profit. Commercialization exploits and perverts the agencies of amusement and recreation, and corrupts a large part of the press. Ross names the "business man the most indulged and spoiled element in American society," but points out that his commercialized practices have been largely "vanquished" in the fields of marriage, religion, and government. Still, "the master iniquities of our time are connected with moneymaking." (Original italicized.) Commercialism is particularly rampant in the United States due partly, Ross suggests, to the absence of aristocratic standards. He would not dispense with the desire to possess, which is indeed a part of human nature, nor eliminate economic conflict. But the "plane of competition," he argues, must be raised.

Notwithstanding these denunciations of the economic system, Ross remains critical of capitalism's severest opponents, the socialists. He has occasionally lauded Marx's contributions, but his evaluation of Marxian theory is double-edged: Marxism correctly demands that all people must be socially useful, but contains the "dangerous idea" that all capitalists are parasites. Though socialism is a manifestation of the universal spread of democracy, revolutionary socialists err in assigning guilt to "the competitive system" rather than monopoly, and in assuming corporation growth to be a natural part of capitalistic development; [29] and they deserve condemnation because they are "revolutionary," because they conceive of a "chimera" which is contrary to human nature, because their "wild proposals excite apprehensions which hinder the progress of genuine constructive work." In Mexico, for example, Marxists have overlooked the country's backward economic development; their program consequently is harmful to the community.

The progressive process, argues Ross, need involve no drastic "socialistic" transition from private capitalism to public ownership. True, if the present type of capitalism is continued the result will be a "sham" of democracy, or "capitalistic feudalism." He suggests the solution: a system of "industrial dual-

[29] Note, once more, the anti-monopoly stress. Ross continues the tradition of the earlier American "progressives."

ism," dividing the economic field between public and private ownership, with the former gradually extended in the larger industries. By this method, democracy may be saved from either the decadence of "capitalistic feudalism" or the "bogs and thickets of socialism."

Ross's critical evaluation of socialist theory is directly related to his belief that population pressure acts as a significant and independent factor in social change. "Over population and class exploitation are independent causes of mass poverty." He contends that "population tendency" and the economic system, regardless of their interaction, must be conceived and studied as closed systems. Such economic reforms as agrarianism or Marxism offer no solution of population pressure, the only existing corrective for the latter being the spread of birth control. Such conditions as class-oriented customs, tradition-bound masses, little vertical mobility, and lack of popular education cause over-population; while standards of comfort and decency for all classes, inter-class diffusion of culture, class mobility, opportunity for property accumulation, and political democracy prevent population pressure. The imperialists, clergy, capitalists, and socialists are "population boosters," "exposed" by scientists, feminists, social workers, anti-militarists, and humanitarians. Crowded population serves as a useful "stage property" for capitalistic imperialists with which to arouse the masses. Furthermore, the working classes are always hardest hit by over-population.

Ross's sociology not only points up weaknesses of the present social order, but, though less explicitly, contains a general scheme for its reform. Of first importance as an ameliorative instrument is the state. As noted earlier, Ross believes that modern democracy greatly modifies the class role of the state; the latter, indeed, is becoming the community's principal collective agent. The state should not be viewed as an instrument of exploitation; on the contrary, it must be molded into a powerful agency. For weak government breeds class struggle, which, in turn, ushers in the "man-on-horseback."

In the future, when all class influence is erased, the state will greatly expand its range of activities. Specifically, Ross would have government further invade the economic sphere by assuming such functions as the control of a "legal dismissal wage" through publicly formed boards in each important community. It is particularly important that the government curb the devastation of natural resources, brought about by large-scale private ownership. And it should institute extensive social services, which, up to the present, have been inadequately rendered by capitalistic "philanthropy with strings." Ross urges, too, that more and better education be provided all classes, a program consistent with democratic principles. "A democracy . . . will use its schools to counteract the anti-social spirit that too often radiates from the big masterful figures of commercial life."

In *Seventy Years of It*, Ross praises the militant action of the working class, and elsewhere he strongly advocates organization of both laborers and farmers for the advancement of their economic interests. The modern labor movement should not be viewed as "anarchistic," but rather as the struggle of the exploited for minimum economic and social necessities. Economic organization of classes is necessary and desirable, so long as the solidified classes do *not* function as political units.

Promotion of class consciousness, too, is essential for the advance of the working classes. In struggle between classes, the lower group can make no gains as long as it is imbued with the official viewpoint of its rival. Labor must throw off "bourgeois" ideology, but it is questionable, Ross warns, whether workers should adopt strict "formulations of their own" or "universally valid standards of human achievement and worth." For modern capitalism stimulates class conflict and intensifies class feeling and class loyalty, to the detriment of those common social bonds which are rooted in the "sense of right and justice." The development of broad social consciousness which will outweigh any intra-societal group allegiance is so important to Ross (as it was to Cooley) that he occasionally condemns efforts to intensify class consciousness. Uncontrolled immigration, for example, is dangerous to the social whole for it heightens class feeling, tends to further separate classes, and decreases the socially necessary like-mindedness of the community.[30]

In common with most of the other writers whose class notions have been discussed, Ross finds in the middle class those elements necessary for "social health." A large middle class guarantees vertical mobility, and serves as mediator in the clash between the extreme social divisions. It prevents the state from becoming a class instrument, "and social institutions from becoming mere props of injustice." And most significantly, the middle class is motivated by and tends to diffuse an ideology that is essentially classless: inclusive community feeling. Indeed, the ideological pattern of the middle rank of our society is reflected, in some part, in Ross's stand on social reform; as it is in Ward's melioristic "sociocracy," Sumner's "forgotten man," Small's cooperative society, Giddings' community "consciousness of kind," and Cooley's "open class" democracy.

In closing this chapter, it seems appropriate to mention Professor Ross's views on contemporary world developments. The author of three earlier volumes on Soviet Russia,[31] he has recently commented favorably on certain features of the Soviet Union, especially praising its stand on race differences. On the other hand, in the most recent edition of *Principles* (1938) he argues that fascism and national socialism are "the logical reply to the tactics followed by the Communists in Russia and intended for use elsewhere. The dictatorship of the middle class is a natural reply to the Marxian doctrine of 'the dictatorship of the proletariat.' "[32] Both communist and fascist threats, continues Ross, can be withstood in this country by the preservation of the traditional rights of speech, press, and organization.

---

[30] Ross argues in the same vein in the analysis of "art" in *Social Control:* the essential service of art is the cementing of community feeling and the bringing together of different classes.

[31] *Russia in Upheaval,* 1919, *The Russian Bolshevik Revolution,* 1921, *The Russian Soviet Republic,* 1923.

[32] Ross does not explain the meaning of "middle class" in this connection. We assume that he merely uses a popular phrase; and that he does not imply that control under fascism resides in the middle class.

These privileges are attacked, unfortunately, "not so much by honest patriots to hamper the propagation of revolutionary ideas as by unprincipled schemers to persecute the more trenchant critics of the class that is in the saddle."

This capitalist control of society is no longer tolerable: it must give way to a more humanitarian pattern. But the socialist vision of a proletarian dictatorship is unthinkable. The spread of education and the consequent loss to the proletariat of its most capable members remove from that class the power and ability to establish a " 'dictatorship' over society." The future, claims Ross, should witness the regulation of private enterprise of the kind that Sweden has already instituted, and an economy planned by trained experts in the employ of the state. Furthermore, sociology, the science of society, should greatly widen its functions: in providing guides for social betterment, in safeguarding the community from the "extremists" of right and left. Science assumes the social role of the middle class.

In the manner of Cooley, whose sympathies were identical with Ross's, and perhaps with the great majority of Americans, Ross closes his *Principles* with a final thrust at the revolutionary doctrines of Marxism and the counter-revolutionary practices of reactionary fascism. A better world can be constructed, he believes, only along the path of "representative democracy."

CHAPTER EIGHT: CONCLUSION

CONCLUSION

Is THIS study more than an additional item in the structure of organized knowledge? Surely an important question, its answer falls into the realm of interpretation and forecast. In the introduction it was stated that this volume was conceived as the first of a series on "Class and American Sociology"; in conclusion and on the basis of the preceding chapters this statement requires elaboration.

Ward, Sumner, Small, Giddings, Cooley, and Ross represent a distinct period in American sociology. This was a period marked, on the one hand, by broad social theorizing, by system-making, and by the general belief that theoretical sociology would somehow play a major constructive role in the progressive development of our society: sociology had the grandiose ambitions of youth. On the other hand, empirical research was largely neglected. An eye was given, of course, to the statistical facts collected by private and governmental agencies, but few of these major figures thought it necessary to dig intensively into the field of human relations.

With the emphasis upon the "larger" task of constructing theoretical systems of social structure and social change, great importance was assigned to class phenomena; in this respect sociology was in the vanguard of American social science. For it is only within recent years that the other social disciplines have begun to recognize in any real measure the significance of class. (There were exceptions, of course, like Veblen and Patten.) This emphasis, found largely in sociology and in the works of so few scholars of stature in this country, contrasts sharply with European social science where men like Gustav Schmoller, Georg Simmel, Arthur Bauer, Othmar Spann, Max Weber, Werner Sombart, Karl Bucher, Paul Mombert, Roberto Michels, and Vilfredo Pareto, naming only a few and omitting the orthodox Marxists, plunged into detailed analyses of class structure and change.

No doubt, in Europe, the traditional social hierarchies and stronger elements of class consciousness, as well as the rise of Marxism, stimulated such studies. Because these same conditions were lacking or relatively undeveloped in the United States, and because here existed the additional factors of frontier expansion and vertical mobility on a larger scale, the attention of our scholars was seldom drawn to the role of stratification in our society. Even the sociological Fathers, constituting an exception to this general situation, gave voice to class theories which were, in the final analysis, highly colored by the "classlessness" of the American scene.

The roots of the thinking of these men, regardless of the fact that several of them had extensive contact with European scholarship, were imbedded in the soil of native conditions—socioeconomic and sociopsychological. They were all, in one way or another, impressed by the anti-class elements of American democracy and by the social virtues of that "classless" segment of society—the middle class. For the outstanding qualities of the middle class, at least so they thought, were its emphasis upon the *common* elements of a society and its negation of all separating barriers. They desired, as most social philosophers desire, the superordination of *community* over all intra-communal groups. It is not strange that they found, in the established American tradition, the *modus operandi* for this desire in the middle class. This is borne out, in different degrees and in various interpretations to be sure, in Ward's plea for a true "sociocracy," in Sumner's analysis of the "Forgotten Man" who in one sense epitomizes the middle class, in Small's passionless prediction of a cooperative society, in Giddings' emphasis upon and demand for a stronger "consciousness of kind," in Cooley's faith in the development of a greater "open class" democracy, and, finally, in the progressivism of Ross's social reform program. In their general distrust of the "Lords of Creation" at the one extreme and the class-pointed proletarian leaders at the other, they stand truly in a stream of tradition which remains today a powerful, though somewhat shakier, force in American ideology.

The close of the World War signaled a period in the history of American sociology quite different from the years of the Fathers. Their work, with its broad systematizing, historical speculation, and concern with the role of class forces in American life, gave way to detailed empirical research in problem areas somewhat narrower in scope. Thus the sociological field was differentiated into research compartments: the family, population, crime and delinquency, and the like.

In the decade and a half following the war, monographs, periodicals, and filing cabinets were crammed with statistics and case records from these various areas. In this more "exact" and "scientific" treatment of social phenomena, the problems of class were largely neglected. American sociologists in the new "research" era of their science overlooked an important field—unlike their European colleagues who were influenced by similar methodological trends. The Europeans, especially in the Germanic countries, utilized their sharpened instruments of research in documenting and interpreting the shifting social hierarchies of their communities and in compiling an impressive body of class literature.

Only recently have American investigators begun to exploit intensively the class field. Using the research tools which have been developing for some twenty years, sociologists, anthropologists, and social psychologists are finding America's social stratification a subject worthy of scientific attention. Our "class-caste" phenomenon in the South, especially complex in its hierarchical interrelations, has prompted a good share of this research, illustrated in the studies of John Dollard, Lloyd Warner, Charles S. Johnson, and Hortense Powdermaker among others. The Lynds' intensive surveys of "Middletown," an American community typical of many, have brought into sharp focus the socioeconomic and sociopsychological class situation. Marxian interpretation applied to American history, past and present, has been provided by Lewis Corey in two ambitious volumes. In addition, European sociological concepts, with their greater degree of class orientation, are being diffused into American social science by virtue of our acquisition of many of Europe's best scholars—thanks to the activities of the dictatorships.

This growing emphasis on class as subject matter for social science research demands a sharper inquiry than has heretofore been made in this country into the *concept* of *class*. For surely one of the major tools upon which investigators depend is the conceptual framework, explicitly stated or implicitly assumed, in terms of which a research problem is conceived. Conceptual interpretation, in fact, partly defines the problem and limits the area of investigation. And it is by no means true that social scientists generally agree upon the meaning of class.

Nor did the Fathers. Throughout their writings appear, though not always clearly expressed, two quite distinct approaches. All of them, at one time or another, used "class" in the generally accepted sense as a group demarcated by *economic* factors: by income, economic function, or relation to a system of production. This conception pushes to a category of secondary importance questions of group cohesion, "consciousness of kind," or class consciousness. These latter phenomena, however, are of primary interest to sociologists, especially to those like Giddings and Cooley who found in the attitudinal relationships of society the very essence of their sociological material. And so a second conception of social class emerged, one based upon the "subjective" elements of group consciousness. Cooley epitomized this conception in declaring that "the relation between the employing and hand-laboring classes is *first of all* a matter of personal attitudes. . . ." (Author's italics.) Cooley's elaboration of closed class and "caste sentiment" is an analysis based upon the "subjective" approach. Variously expressed and with different marks of stress, the same can be said of Ward's extensive plea for the educational upward levelling of the social strata, of Sumner's treatment of the declining middle class and the cohering "proletariat," of Small's criticism of the rigid Marxian distinction and his description of "middle class consciousness," of Giddings' emphasis upon consciousness of kind as both a requirement of social class and a factor hindering class formation, and of Ross's stress of *status* as the criterion of class and his Cooley-like distinction between "open" and "closed" classes.

The writings of this group of scholars constitute a major illustration of the duality of the concept of class. Class, in one of its meanings, is a *socioeconomic* aggregate whose distinction is rooted in the economic cleavages of a community. Thus Marxism, with its materialistic basis and economic emphasis, defines class as a group standing in a specific relation to a system of economic production; in capitalistic society there are basically those who own productive means and those who do not. As an instrument in the analysis of historical change and social structure (as well as a group-molding *device* in the changing of history itself), this conception of class has proved to be of great value. It follows from this approach that the "subjective" elements of class, class attitudes and consciousness, are "superstructural" reflections of fundamental lines of economic division.

It is no simple matter, however, especially in our own society, to square the "fact" of class in this economic sense with the kind of stratification reflected by social attitudes. This attitudinal structure gives point to the second meaning of class: class as a *sociopsychological* phenomenon. Here the emphasis in the first instance lies with class consciousness; without it a group is not a class. Those in this country who speak of the "middle class" as our largest cohesive social group apparently have in mind this conception: they refer to those millions of Americans who share, in general, common values, attitudes, and aspirations. Such spokesmen reiterate a view presented "scientifically" by the sociological Fathers.

To stress this double meaning of class is not to claim that either the one or the other can be used exclusively, nor to maintain along with the Marxists that one is "basic" and the other "superstructural." Indeed, as working concepts in social research both can be effectively employed. The work of Lloyd Warner and John Dollard, cited above, in making the distinction between "caste" and "class," illustrates, essentially, the socioeconomic *and* sociopsychological usages. In very explicit terms, both meanings have been recently applied by Professor Goetz A. Briefs in his socio-historical analysis of the proletariat.

These recent studies, and many others directly bearing upon class structure and change in contemporary life, are significant material requiring systematic organization and evaluation. They represent the efforts of present-day scholars to bring into the light of scientific understanding the intricacies of our social stratification. In this effort they carry on the tradition established by much of the work of Ward, Sumner, Small, Giddings, Cooley, and Ross. In using the writings of these scholars as the basis of this volume, we hope to have gained a finer equipment for the analysis of class in contemporary research.

NOTES

CHAPTER ONE

P. 3, lines 15-22. J. L. Gillin, "The Development of Sociology in the United States," *Publications, American Sociological Society*, Vol. XXI (1926), p. 3; cf. A. W. Small, "Fifty Years of Sociology in the United States," *American Journal of Sociology*, Vol. XXI (1926), pp. 724-725.

P. 4, lines 4-13. cf. H. David, *History of the Haymarket Affair*, p. 4.

P. 4, line 14. See L. M. Hacker and B. B. Kendrick, *United States Since 1865*, pp. 183-221; L. Corey, *The Decline of American Capitalism*, pp. 24-27.

P. 4, lines 15-21. Corey, *op. cit.*, pp. 27-28.

P. 4, lines 22-23. F. A. Shannon, *Economic History of the People of the United States*, pp. 552-571.

P. 4, lines 25-26. See H. M. Kallen, *Individualism—An American Way of Life*, pp. 79-86.

P. 4, lines 27-28. See Shannon, *op. cit.*, pp. 533-552; A. M. Simons, *Social Forces in American History*, pp. 304-305.

P. 4, lines 31-34. L. Corey, *The Crisis of the Middle Class*, pp. 113-115.

P. 4, lines 34-37. Kallen, *op. cit.*, pp. 93-97.

P. 5, lines 3-8. *The Decline of American Capitalism, op. cit.*, pp. 28, 30-31.

P. 5, lines 8-13. Simons, *op. cit.*, pp. 309-310.

P. 5, lines 13-16. Shannon, *op. cit.*, pp. 488-512; see J. Chamberlain's interesting account in *Farewell to Reform*, pp. 119-123.

P. 5, lines 19-24. C. A. and M. R. Beard, *The Rise of American Civilization*, vol. ii, pp. 196-198; cf. *The Crisis of the Middle Class, op. cit.*, pp. 132-137.

P. 5, lines 24-28. V. L. Parrington, *Main Currents in American*

Thought, vol. iii, *The Beginnings of Critical Realism in America, 1860-1920*, pp. 7-47.

P. 5, lines 31-34. F. C. Palm, *The Middle Classes, Then and Now*, p. 224; see *ibid.*, pp. 222-225.

Pp. 5-6, lines 34-2. Beard and Beard, *op. cit.*, pp. 122-125; cf. *The Decline of American Capitalism, op. cit.*, pp. 28-29; *The Crisis of the Middle Class, op. cit.*, pp. 118-121.

P. 6, lines 2-4. See Beard and Beard, *op. cit.*, pp. 209-210.

P. 6, lines 7-12. Simons, *op. cit.*, p. 307.

P. 6, lines 13-18. Beard and Beard, *op. cit.*, pp. 204-207.

P. 6, lines 18-22. Cf. David, *op. cit.*, p. 24.

P. 6, lines 25-34. Beard and Beard, *op. cit.*, pp. 211-254; Hacker and Kendrick, *op. cit.*, pp. 222-237; Simons, *op. cit.*, pp. 312-318; David, *op. cit.*, pp. 3-24.

P. 7, lines 3-14. Cf. David, *op. cit.*, pp. 54-76.

P. 7, lines 14-19. Cf. Beard and Beard, *op. cit.*, p. 163.

P. 7, lines 20-25. Kallen, *op. cit.*, p. 103.

P. 7, lines 26-34. See Chamberlain, *op. cit.*, pp. 21-23; Simons, *op. cit.*, pp. 305-306, 311.

P. 8, lines 2-5. Cf. *The Crisis of the Middle Class, op. cit.*, p. 115.

P. 8, lines 6-12. Parrington, *op. cit.*, pp. 259-261.

P. 8, lines 12-16. Beard and Beard, *op. cit.*, pp. 125, 271-278; Hacker and Kendrick, *op. cit.*, pp. 164-182; Simons, *op. cit.*, pp. 306-307.

P. 8, lines 17-30. Beard and Beard, *op. cit.*, pp. 280-284; Hacker and Kendrick, *op. cit.*, pp. 295-320; Parrington, *op. cit.*, pp. 263-282; Chamberlain, *op. cit.*, pp. 25-30; Palm, *op. cit.*, pp. 302-303; *The Crisis of the Middle Class, op. cit.*, pp. 130-132.

P. 8, lines 32-34. Parrington, *op. cit.*, p. xxvii, Introduction.

P. 9, lines 1-3. Cf. Beard and Beard, *op. cit.*, pp. 394-395.

P. 9, lines 3-7. Chamberlain, *op. cit.*, p. 42.

P. 9, lines 9-11. Hacker and Kendrick, *op. cit.*, p. 241.

P. 9, lines 11-13. Beard and Beard, *op. cit.*, pp. 399-402.

P. 9, lines 14-18. Cf. Palm, *op. cit.*, pp. 294-296, 301-302.

Pp. 9-12, lines 23-3. Beard and Beard, *op. cit.*, pp. 285-343; cf. Hacker and Kendrick, *op. cit.*, pp. 262-320.

P. 12, lines 6-13. Beard and Beard, *op. cit.*, pp. 236-238, 383; Hacker and Kendrick, *op. cit.*, pp. 248-261.

P. 12, lines 14-34. Parrington, *op. cit.*, pp. 125-136; Chamberlain, *op. cit.*, pp. 43-48; J. Dombrowski, *The Early Days of Christian Socialism in America*, pp. 35-49; R. G. Tugwell, "George, Henry," *Encyclopaedia of the Social Sciences*; J. R. Commons, and others, *History of Labour in the United States*, pp. 446-461.

Pp. 12-13, lines 35 19. Dombrowski, *op. cit.*, pp. 121-131, Chamberlain, *op. cit.*, pp. 48-55; L. M. Hacker, "Lloyd, Henry Demarest," *Encyclopaedia of the Social Sciences*; C. Lloyd, *Henry Demarest Lloyd, 1847-1903: A Biography*, vol. ii, ch. xxv.

Pp. 13-14, lines 23-9. Parrington, *op. cit.*, pp. 302-315; Dombrowski, *op. cit.*, pp. 84-95; Chamberlain, *op. cit.*, pp. 55-56; J. O. Hertzler, "Bellamy, Edward," *Encyclopaedia of the Social Sciences*.

P. 14, lines 12-14. G. Hicks, *The Great Tradition*, p. 164.

P. 14, lines 17-27. Quoted in Parrington, *op. cit.*, p. 85; see *ibid.*, pp. 69-86; Beard and Beard, *op. cit.*, pp. 435-436.

Pp. 14-15, lines 28-6. Parrington, *op. cit.*, pp. 86-101.

P. 15, lines 7-21. *Ibid.*, pp. 137-168; Beard and Beard, *op. cit.*, pp. 434-437; Palm, *op. cit.*, pp. 385-387.

P. 15, lines 22-30. Parrington, *op. cit.*, pp. 169-186; cf. Beard and Beard, *op. cit.*, pp. 440-446.

Pp. 15-16, lines 31-8. Chamberlain, *op. cit.*, pp. 86-118; Parrington, *op. cit.*, pp. 186-188; David, *op. cit.*, p. 6; cf. Hicks, *op. cit.*, pp. 164-206.

P. 16, lines 9-18. Beard and Beard, *op. cit.*, pp. 437-440.

P. 16, lines 22-24. H. Kallen, "Reformism," *Encyclopaedia of the Social Sciences*.

P. 16, lines 26-27. Palm, *op. cit.*, p. 289.

P. 16, *footnote* 7. Dombrowski, *op. cit.*, pp. 14-30, 132-193.

Pp. 16-17, lines 30-4. Quoted in *Ibid.*, p. 9; see *Ibid.*, pp. 8-10; cf. Beard and Beard *op. cit.*, pp. 420-423.

P. 17, lines 5-19. Beard and Beard, *op. cit.*, pp. 460-467.

Pp. 17-18, lines 20-8. Chamberlain, *op. cit.*, pp. 119-143; information on S. S. McClure and the muckrakers has been obtained from Mr. McClure's children and grandchildren, one of the latter being the author's wife.

P. 18, lines 10-14. *Ibid.*, p. 199.

P. 18, lines 14-23. Small, *op. cit.*, pp. 723, 774-776.

P. 18, lines 23-25. Beard and Beard, *op. cit.*, p. 547.

P. 18, lines 26-35. Small, *op. cit.*, pp. 730-731; Dombrowski, *op. cit.*, pp. 50-59; H. E. Barnes and H. Becker, *Social Thought from Lore to Science* (Heath, New York 1938), vol. ii, pp. 974-975.

Pp. 18-19, lines 36-24. Cf. Chamberlain, *op. cit.*, pp. 199-233.

P. 19, lines 25-27. Beard and Beard, *op. cit.*, p. 418.

P. 19, lines 27-31. Parrington, *op. cit.*, p. 190.

P. 19, lines 31-35. *Ibid.*, pp. 102-125; Beard and Beard, *op. cit.*, pp. 469-477.

P. 20, lines 3-6. Beard and Beard, *op. cit.*, pp. 406-408, 415; Gillin, *op. cit.*, pp. 3-4; Palm, *op. cit.*, pp. 274-275.

P. 20, lines 6-8. Parrington, *op. cit.*, pp. 197-211.

P. 20, *footnote 8.* Barnes and Becker, *op. cit.*, p. 956.

P. 20, lines 10-12. Cf. H. W. Odum, ed., *American Masters of Social Science*, pp. 9-11.

P. 20, lines 15-17. Gillin, *op. cit.*, pp. 8-9.

P. 20, lines 24-25. Cf. *Ibid.*, p. 6.

P. 21, lines 7-10. Small, *op. cit.*, pp. 724, 774.

Pp. 21-22, lines 29-7. Cf. Odum, *op. cit.*, pp. 11-14; Gillin, *loc. cit.*

P. 22, lines 8-16. Cf. Barnes and Becker, *op. cit.*, p. 975.

P. 22, lines 16-24. Cf. Odum, *op. cit.*, p. 15.

P. 22, lines 30-31. Gillin, *op. cit.*, p. 16.

P. 23, lines 6-9. H. W. Odum and H. E. Moore, *American Regionalism* (Holt, New York 1938), pp. 508-511.

P. 23, lines 11-12. Palm, *op. cit.*, p. 384.

P. 23, lines 13-15. Beard and Beard, *op. cit.*, p. 429; cf. Chamberlain, *op. cit.*, pp. 9-16.

P. 23, lines 28-32. Odum and Moore, *op. cit.*, p. 490; cf. *Ibid.*, p. 473.

P. 24, lines 11-26. See J. Dorfman, *Thorstein Veblen and His America* (which contains Veblen's complete bibliography); P. T. Homan, *Contemporary Economic Thought*, pp. 105-192; A. Johnson, "Veblen, Thorstein Bunde," *Encyclopaedia of the Social Sciences;* W. Bradbury, unpublished manuscript on Veblen's class theory, Columbia University.

P. 25, lines 11-13. Dorfman, *op. cit.*, p. 311.

CHAPTER TWO

(Unless otherwise noted, the author in all cases is L. F. Ward.)

P. 30, line 5. B. J. Stern, "Ward, Lester Frank," *Encyclopaedia of the Social Sciences;* cf. J. Q. Dealy, "Lester Frank Ward," *American Masters of Social Science* (ed. by H. W. Odum), p. 62.

P. 30, lines 7-8. F. H. Hankins, *The History and Prospects of the Social Sciences* (ed. by H. E. Barnes), p. 302.

P. 30, lines 9-10. L. Gumplowicz, "An Austrian Appreciation of

Lester F. Ward," *American Journal of Sociology*, Vol. X, pp. 643-653.

P. 30, lines 27-31. *Ibid.*, p. 650.

P. 30, lines 31-33. U. G. Weatherly, "Lester F. Ward," *American Journal of Sociology*, Vol. XIX, p. 69.

P. 30, lines 33-36. Cf. Dealy, *op. cit.*, p. 67.

P. 31, lines 9-12. *Ibid.*, pp. 71-73; see the first two sections of *Young Ward's Diary* (ed. by B. J. Stern).

P. 31, lines 17-19. Stern, *loc. cit.*

P. 31, lines 19-23. Cf. B. J. Stern, ed., "Giddings, Ward and Small: An Interchange of Letters," *Social Forces*, Vol. X, No. 3, p. 306.

P. 31, lines 23-26. W. B. Bodenhafer, "The Comparative Role of the Group Concept in Ward's *Dynamic Sociology* and Contemporary American Sociology," *American Journal of Sociology*, Vol. XXVI, especially pp. 273-314.

Pp. 31-32, lines 13-5. E. A. Ross, "Lester F. Ward," *American Journal of Sociology*, Vol. XIX, p. 65; cf. Dealy, *op. cit.*, p. 89.

P. 32, lines 5-8. *Applied Sociology*, p. 377.

P. 32, lines 8-10. B. J. Stern, ed., "The Letters of Albion W. Small to Lester F. Ward," *Social Forces*, Vol. XII, p. 164.

Pp. 32-33, lines 30-1. Gumplowicz, *op. cit.*, p. 647.

P. 33, lines 3-12. *Pure Sociology*, pp. 203-204.

P. 33, lines 12-16. "Social Classes in the Light of Modern Sociological Theory," *American Journal of Sociology*, Vol. XIII, p. 617.

P. 33, lines 17-33. *Pure Sociology*, pp. 205-206.

P. 34, lines 1-7. See, e. g., "Social Classes in the Light of Modern Sociological Theory," *op. cit.*, pp. 617-622.

P. 34, lines 7-14. *Pure Sociology*, pp. 213, 238.

P. 34, lines 17-20. *Ibid.*, p. 202.

P. 34, lines 26-27. Cf. R. M. MacIver, *Society* (Farrar & Rinehart, New York 1937), p. 172.

P. 35, lines 1-22. *Pure Sociology*, pp. 206-208, 276; compare with Ward's earlier views in *Dynamic Sociology*, vol. i, p. 394; vol. ii, p. 217-223.

Pp. 35-36, lines 32-6. *Pure Sociology*, pp. 208-209.

P. 36, lines 6-14. *Ibid.*, pp. 208-212.

P. 36, lines 17-24. *Ibid.*, p. 261.

Pp. 36-37, lines 27-16. *Ibid.*, pp. 267, 271-272.

P. 37, lines 17-32. *Ibid.*, pp. 273-277.

Pp. 37-38, lines 33-6. *Ibid.*, pp. 277-278; cf. *Dynamic Sociology*, vol. i, pp. 494-496.

P. 38, lines 10-17. "Social Classes in the Light of Modern Sociological Theory," *op. cit.*, pp. 622-623.

P. 38, lines 19-22. *Ibid.*, p. 619.

P. 38, lines 23-26. *The Psychic Factors of Civilization*, p. 100.

P. 39, lines 1-5. "Social Classes in the Light of Modern Sociological Theory," *op. cit.*, pp. 617-618.

P. 39, lines 20-29. *Dynamic Sociology*, vol. i, pp. 13, 30; vol. ii, p. 163.

Pp. 39-40, lines 31-1. J. Q. Dealy and L. F. Ward, *A Text Book of Sociology*, p. 154.

P. 40, lines 1-6. *The Psychic Factors of Civilization*, pp. 109, 162-168.

P. 40, lines 6-10. *Pure Sociology*, p. 289.

P. 40, lines 11-19. *Applied Sociology*, p. 4.

P. 40, lines 19-25. *Ibid.*, pp. 14-16, 22.

P. 40, lines 25-31. *Ibid.*, pp. 26-27.

P. 40, lines 33-36. *Ibid.*, pp. 90-95.

P. 41, lines 8-11. *Outlines of Sociology*, ch. vi; cf. *American Journal of Sociology*, Vol. I, No. 6.

P. 41, lines 14-16. *Applied Sociology*, p. 46.

P. 41, lines 17-19. *Ibid.*, p. 47.

P. 41, lines 25-28. *Ibid.*, p. 49.

P. 41, lines 28-31. *Pure Sociology*, p. 289.

Pp. 41-42, lines 32-2. *American Journal of Sociology*, Vol. XIII, p. 646.

Pp. 42-43, lines 20-30. *Dynamic Sociology*, vol. i, pp. 492-525.

P. 43, lines 31-34. *Ibid.*, vol. i, p. 526.

P. 43, lines 35-36. *Ibid.*, vol. i, p. 581.

P. 44, *footnote 8*. "Giddings, Ward and Small: An Interchange of Letters," *op. cit.*, p. 316 (Letter to Mrs. Unger, 1903).

P. 44, lines 11-13. *Dynamic Sociology*, vol. ii, p. 598.

P. 44, lines 13-28. *Ibid.*, vol. ii, pp. 599-605.

Pp. 44-45, lines 29-15. *Applied Sociology*, pp. 90-95.

P. 45, lines 16-29. *Dynamic Sociology*, vol. ii, p. 475.

P. 45, lines 32-34. See *Psychic Factors of Civilization*, ch. xxxii; *Pure Sociology*, pp. 245-246.

Pp. 45-46, lines 35-10. *Applied Sociology*, pp. 95-110.

P. 46, lines 11-26. *Ibid.*, pp. 145-223, *passim*.

P. 47, lines 3-6. *Ibid.*, p. 214.

Pp. 47-48, lines 21-13. *Dynamic Sociology*, vol. ii, pp. 448, 452-457.

P. 48, lines 18-25. *Psychic Factors of Civilization*, pp. 165-167.

Pp. 48-49, lines 30-3. *Pure Sociology*, pp. 245, 278, 485, 513.

P. 49, lines 3-9. *Applied Sociology*, pp. 243-244.

P. 49, lines 13-20. See *Psychic Factors of Civilization*, pp. 281-331; *Pure Sociology*, ch. xiii.

Pp. 49-50, lines 21-1. *Pure Sociology*, p. 447; *Applied Sociology*, pp. 98-99; "The Sociology of Political Parties," *American Journal of Sociology*, Vol. XIII, pp. 439-454.

P. 50, lines 14-23. *Dynamic Sociology*, vol. ii, pp. 465-467.

P. 50, lines 23-32. *Applied Sociology*, pp. 321-328.

Pp. 50-52, lines 33-3. *Dynamic Sociology*, vol. i, pp. 526-596.

P. 52, lines 6-8. F. H. Giddings, "Lester F. Ward," *American Journal of Sociology*, Vol. XIX, p. 67.

P. 52, lines 10-17. *Pure Sociology*, pp. 445-447, 504.

P. 52, lines 17-22. *Applied Sociology*, pp. 233-234.

P. 52, *subtitle*. For a thorough discussion of Ward's political doctrines, see H. E. Barnes, "Two Representative Contributions of Sociology to Political Theory," *American Journal of Sociology*, Vol. XXV, p. 150 ff.

Pp. 52-53, lines 30-5. *Dynamic Sociology*, vol. i, pp. 61-64.

P. 53, lines 5-11. *Ibid.*, vol. ii, pp. 168-169, 214-216.

P. 53, lines 14-16. "The Letters of Albion W. Small to Lester F. Ward," *loc. cit.*

P. 53, lines 19-20. *Dynamic Sociology*, vol. i, pp. 585-587.

P. 53, lines 21-31. *Ibid.*, vol. ii, pp. 217-243.

Pp. 53-54, lines 31-1. *Psychic Factors of Civilization*, p. 321.

P. 54, lines 1-5. *Outlines of Sociology*, pp. 269-270.

P. 54, lines 11-15. Cf. Barnes, *op. cit.*, p. 163.

Pp. 54-55, lines 22-7. *Pure Sociology*, pp. 549-555.

P. 55, lines 7-15. "The Sociology of Political Parties," *op. cit.*, pp. 452-453.

P. 56, lines 4-7. Cf. Weatherly, *op. cit.*, p. 69.

P. 56, lines 7-10. "Letters of Albion W. Small to Lester F. Ward," *loc. cit.*

P. 56, lines 10-14. *Applied Sociology*, pp. 287, 318.

P. 56, lines 15-18. *Dynamic Sociology*, vol. i, p. 596.

P. 56, lines 18-29. *Outlines of Sociology*, p. 286.

Pp. 56-57, lines 29-4. *Pure Sociology*, pp. 49, 255, 283.

P. 57, lines 5-33. *Applied Sociology*, pp. iv, 7, 9-10, 19-21, 24-26, 29, 31, 35-36, 38, 83, 234, 287, 319-320, 321.

Pp. 57-58, lines 34-11. *Dynamic Sociology*, vol. ii, pp. 468-469.

P. 58, lines 12-24. *Psychic Factors of Civilization*, ch. xxxiv; cf. Dealy and Ward, *op. cit.*, pp. 74-75.

Pp. 58-59, lines 25-2. *Outlines of Sociology*, pp. 204, 207, 280; *Pure Sociology*, p. 548.

P. 59, lines 15-23. *Dynamic Sociology*, vol. ii, pp. 15, 72, 407, 425.

P. 59, lines 25-27. *Psychic Factors of Civilization*, p. 301.

P. 59, lines 27-30. *Pure Sociology*, pp. 574-575.

Pp. 59-60, lines 31-6. *Applied Sociology*, pp. 95-107, 229, 238-242, 246-250, 292.

P. 60, lines 7-14. *Ibid.*, pp. 115-128, 131, 137-140, 144.

P. 60, *footnote 18. Ibid.*, pp. 133-135.

P. 60, lines 15-17. *Dynamic Sociology*, vol. ii, p. 539.

Pp. 60-61, lines 17-6. *Applied Sociology*, pp. 230-236, *passim.*

Pp. 61-62, lines 7-4. *Dynamic Sociology*, vol. ii, pp. 541-633, *passim.*

P. 62, lines 8-11. *Applied Sociology*, pp. 308, 312-313.

P. 62, lines 12-16. Ross, *op. cit.*, p. 65.

Pp. 62-63, lines 31-1. *Dynamic Sociology*, vol. ii, p. 573.

P. 63, lines 3-6. Cf. "The Letters of Albion W. Small to Lester F. Ward," *loc. cit.*

P. 63, lines 7-13. G. Allen, *Mind*, vol. ix, p. 305.

P. 63, lines 17-20. *Outlines of Sociology*, p. 264.

P. 63, lines 21-24. Cf. Barnes, *loc. cit.*

Pp. 63-64, lines 26-4. *Dynamic Sociology*, vol. ii, pp. 394-395, 398-399.

P. 64, lines 8-11. Barnes, *op. cit.*, p. 167.

P. 64, lines 12-18. *Psychic Factors of Civilization*, pp. 303-304.

P. 64, lines 18-28. *Dynamic Sociology*, vol. ii, pp. 576-585.

P. 64, lines 30-32. *Pure Sociology*, p. 260.

Pp. 64-65, lines 34-9. *Ibid.*, pp. 558-568.

P. 65, lines 9-13. "Sociology of Political Parties," *op. cit.*, p. 454.

P. 65, lines 17-20. Cf. Barnes, *op. cit.*, p. 159.

P. 65, lines 20-27. See *Psychic Factors of Civilization*, ch. xxviii.

P. 65, lines 28-29. *Ibid.*, p. 330.

Pp. 65-66, lines 29-1. *Outlines of Sociology*, pp. 292-293.

P. 66, lines 4-9. *Applied Sociology*, pp. 10-11.

P. 66, lines 18-20. *Psychic Factors of Civilization*, pp. 328-329.

P. 66, lines 20-27. "The Sociology of Political Parties," *op. cit.*, pp. 446-447.

P. 66, lines 27-30. Cf. Barnes, *loc. cit.*

Pp. 66-67, lines 32-8. *Pure Sociology*, pp. 280-282, 568, 571.

P. 67, lines 8-13. *Applied Sociology*, pp. 294-295.
P. 67, lines 15-31. *Psychic Factors of Civilization*, pp. 263-272, 275, 278-279.
P. 68, lines 7-10. *Dynamic Sociology*, vol. i, p. 566.
P. 68, lines 11-14. *Ibid.*, vol. ii, p. 89.
P. 68, lines 16-19. *Pure Sociology*, p. 275.
P. 68, lines 20-23. "Sociology of Political Parties," *op. cit.*, p. 447.

CHAPTER THREE

(Unless otherwise noted, the author
in all cases is W. G. Sumner.)

P. 73, lines 1-5. H. E. Barnes describes the contrast in the political doctrines of Sumner and Ward, *American Journal of Sociology*, Vol. XXV, Nos. 1 and 2.
P. 73, *footnote 1.* H. Kallen, *Individualism, An American Way of Life* (New York 1933), p. 104.
P. 73, *footnote 1.* B. J. Stern, "Sumner, William Graham," *Encyclopaedia of the Social Sciences.*
Pp. 73-74, lines 8-8. H. E. Starr, *William Graham Sumner*, pp. 1-18.
P. 74, lines 11-14. *Ibid.*, p. 171.
P. 74, lines 16-19. Cf. *Ibid.*, p. 35.
P. 74, lines 23-24. *Ibid.*, p. 22.
P. 74, *footnote 2.* Letter written by Sumner in 1865, quoted by Starr, *Ibid.*, p. 65.
P. 75, lines 4-6. cf. *Ibid.*, p. 149.
P. 75, lines 8-11. H. W. Farnum, *Yale Review*, Vol. XIX (First Series), p. 2.
P. 75, lines 21-22. See C. H. Cooley's comments in *Sociological Theory and Social Research*, p. 325.
P. 75, lines 22-24. Cf. F. N. House, *Development of Sociology*, p. 275.
P. 75, lines 25-27. "Sketch of William Graham Sumner," in *Challenge of Facts and Other Essays*, p. 5.
P. 75, lines 27-30. Starr, *op. cit.*, pp. 182-183.
Pp. 75-76, lines 31-3. Quoted in *Ibid.*, pp. 300-301.
P. 76, lines 4-10. L. F. Ward, *Glimpses of the Cosmos*, vol. iii, p. 303.
P. 76, lines 11-14. Barnes, *op. cit.*, p. 7.
P. 76, *footnote 3.* Stern, *loc. cit.*

P. 76, lines 16-21. See Introduction, *War and Other Essays*, pp. xxiii-xxiv.

P. 76, lines 21-24. Cf. "Sketch of William Graham Sumner," *op. cit.*, pp. 3-4.

P. 76, lines 26-28. See *ibid.*, p. 11; cf. H. E. Barnes' similar statement in *Sociological Review*, Vol. XIV, p. 211.

P. 76, lines 29-33. *Essays of William Graham Sumner*, eds. Keller and Davie, p. 469.

P. 77, lines 4-9. Starr, *op. cit.*, pp. 41, 140-141.

P. 77, lines 20-22. "Bequests of the Nineteenth Century to the Twentieth," *Yale Review*, Vol. XXII (1933), pp. 732-754.

P. 77, lines 25-26. *The Forgotten Man and Other Essays*, pp. 402-403.

P. 77, lines 26-28. *Folkways*, pp. 39-53.

P. 77, lines 34-36. R. E. Park in *Methods in Social Science* (ed. by S. A. Rice), p. 161.

P. 78, lines 5-6. Starr, *op. cit.*, pp. 296-297.

P. 78, lines 13-15. "Bequests of the Nineteenth Century to the Twentieth," *op. cit.*, p. 749.

P. 78, lines 15-19. See W. G. Sumner and A. G. Keller, *The Science of Society*, vol. i, pp. 4-8, 20.

P. 78, lines 19-23. *Folkways*, pp. 65-66, 80, 85.

P. 78, lines 24-28. *Earth Hunger and Other Essays*, p. 248.

P. 78, lines 28-29. *Ibid.*, p. 219, 237-244; *What Social Classes Owe to Each Other*, p. 17.

P. 78, lines 30-33. *Challenge of Facts and Other Essays*, p. 25; *War and Other Essays*, p. 9.

P. 79, lines 1-4. Sumner and Keller, *op. cit.*, vol. i, p. 67.

P. 79, lines 4-6. *War and Other Essays*, pp. 183-184.

P. 79, lines 6-10. *Earth Hunger and Other Essays*, pp. 31-46.

P. 79, lines 12-17. Sumner and Keller, *op. cit.*, vol. i, p. 159; *Folkways*, pp. 78, 267.

P. 79, lines 21-24. L. P. Ward, *Glimpses of the Cosmos*, *op. cit.*, vol. iii, p. 305.

P. 79, lines 27-29. *The Challenge of Facts and Other Essays*, p. 409.

P. 79, lines 31-33. *Ibid.*, p. 30.

Pp. 79-80, lines 33-1. Sumner and Keller, *op. cit.*, vol. iii, pp. 22-39.

P. 80, lines 1-3. *Earth Hunger and Other Essays*, p. 162.

P. 80, lines 3-6. *War and Other Essays*, p. 197.

P. 80, lines 7-19. *Earth Hunger and Other Essays*, pp. 258-260, 266, 269.

P. 80, lines 19-20. *Folkways,* p. 377.

P. 80, lines 23-27. *Earth Hunger and Other Essays,* pp. 34, 193-198, 264; *The Challenge of Facts and Other Essays,* p. 304.

Pp. 80-81, lines 33-4. *Folkways,* pp. 151-157, 161-162.

P. 81, lines 5-7. Sumner and Keller, *op. cit.,* vol. i, pp. 96-98.

P. 81, lines 7-12. *Ibid.,* vol. i, pp. 143, 147-148, 221-223; cf. *Folkways,* pp. 262-263.

P. 81, lines 12-16. Sumner and Keller, *op. cit.,* vol. i, p. 450.

P. 81, lines 16-18. *Ibid.,* vol. i, pp. 400-401; cf. *Earth Hunger and Other Essays,* p. 138.

P. 81, lines 19-26. Sumner and Keller, *op. cit.,* vol. i, pp. 275, 317-319, 323-324, 327.

P. 81, lines 32-33. *Earth Hunger and Other Essays,* p. 341.

Pp. 81-82, lines 33-2. *Ibid.,* p. 134.

P. 82, lines 2-4. *Ibid.,* p. 236.

P. 82, lines 4-5. *What Social Classes Owe to Each Other,* pp. 80-86.

P. 82, lines 5-8. *The Challenge of Facts and Other Essays,* pp. 21, 82.

P. 82, lines 8-11. Sumner and Keller, *op. cit.,* vol. i, pp. 100-101, 107-109, 142-143, 163, 166-167.

P. 82, lines 12-17. *Ibid.,* vol. i, pp. 182, 231.

P. 82, lines 18-19. *What Social Classes Owe to Each Other,* p. 125.

P. 82, lines 19-22. *War and Other Essays,* pp. 201-203.

P. 82, lines 22-29. *The Challenge of Facts and Other Essays,* pp. 27, 36, 89, 423.

P. 82, lines 29-31. *Folkways,* pp. 94-95.

P. 82, lines 32-35. "Bequests of the Nineteenth Century to the Twentieth," *op. cit.,* p. 752.

Pp. 82-83, lines 35-3. Sumner and Keller, *op. cit.,* vol. i, pp. 89, 167-169.

P. 83, lines 3-8. *Ibid.,* vol. i, pp. 259-260, 338-341; *Folkways,* pp. 76-77.

P. 83, lines 9-17. *What Social Classes Owe to Each Other,* pp. 84-89.

P. 83, lines 20-21. *The Forgotten Man and Other Essays,* p. 253.

P. 83, lines 22-23. See *The Challenge of Facts and Other Essays,* pp. 49, 129; *Earth Hunger and Other Essays,* p. 132.

P. 83, lines 23-26. *War and Other Essays,* p. 199.

P. 83, lines 26-31. "Bequests of the Nineteenth Century to the Twentieth," *op. cit.,* p. 737; *Folkways,* p. 118.

P. 83, lines 32-34. *Folkways,* pp. 45-46.

Pp. 83-84, lines 34-2. Sumner and Keller, *op. cit.*, vol. i, pp. 71-75.

P. 84, lines 2-7. *Folkways*, p. 48.

P. 84, lines 8-18. *Ibid.*, pp. 86-87, 167-169.

P. 84, lines 20-30. *Earth Hunger and Other Essays*, pp. 312-316.

P. 84, lines 30-31. Sumner and Keller, *op. cit.*, vol. i, p. 77.

P. 84, lines 31-34. *The Forgotten Man and Other Essays*, p. 228.

P. 85, lines 1-3. *War and Other Essays*, pp. 234, 236, 239.

P. 85, lines 3-10. *The Challenge of Facts and Other Essays*, p. 31.

P. 85, lines 12-17. *War and Other Essays*, p. 204.

P. 85, *subtitle.* For a summary of Sumner's political doctrines, see H. E. Barnes, *American Journal of Sociology*, Vol. XXV, No. 1, pp. 1-23.

P. 85, lines 19-22. *Ibid.*, p. 13.

P. 85, lines 25-30. *Ibid.*, pp. 10-11.

P. 86, lines 3-4. "Bequests of the Nineteenth Century to the Twentieth," *op. cit.*, p. 742.

P. 86, lines 4-9. Sumner and Keller, *op. cit.*, vol. i, p. 481; *Folkways*, p. 106.

P. 86, lines 9-15. *War and Other Essays*, pp. 28, 160.

P. 86, lines 15-18. *Earth Hunger and Other Essays*, p. 320.

P. 86, lines 19-25. Sumner and Keller, *op. cit.*, vol. i, pp. 460, 701.

P. 86, lines 26-34. *Ibid.*, vol. i, pp. 500, 561-562, 701.

Pp. 86-87, lines 34-3. *Ibid.*, vol. i, p. 577.

P. 87, lines 5-8. *Ibid.*, vol. i, pp. 474-477, 592-599, 703.

P. 87, lines 13-19. *Folkways*, pp. 12-13, 498-500.

P. 87, lines 22-28. "Bequests of the Nineteenth Century to the Twentieth," *op. cit.*, pp. 734-737; cf. Sumner and Keller, *op. cit.*, vol. i, p. 707.

P. 87, lines 28-30. Sumner and Keller, *op. cit.*, vol. i, pp. 587, 597.

P. 87, lines 31-33. *Ibid.*, vol. i, p. 709.

Pp. 87-88, lines 33-2. *Ibid.*, vol. i, pp. 591-592.

P. 88, lines 2-4. *Earth Hunger and Other Essays*, pp. 144-145, 150.

P. 88, lines 9-13. *Ibid.*, pp. 306, 329-330.

P. 88, lines 13-16. "Bequests of the Nineteenth Century to the Twentieth," *op. cit.*, p. 743.

P. 88, lines 16-18. Sumner and Keller, *op. cit.*, vol. i, p. 710.

P. 88, lines 22-26. *What Social Classes Owe to Each Other*, p. 9.

P. 88, lines 27-33. *Ibid.*, pp. 41, 101.

P. 89, lines 1-7. *Ibid.*, p. 101.

P. 89, lines 15-26. *Earth Hunger and Other Essays*, pp. 293-297.

P. 89, lines 27-30. *War and Other Essays*, p. 159.

P. 89, lines 30-32. "Bequests of the Nineteenth Century to the Twentieth," *loc. cit.*

P. 89, lines 32-35. *War and Other Essays*, p. 207.

Pp. 89-90, lines 35-6. *What Social Classes Owe to Each Other*, pp. 104, 107, 141.

P. 90, lines 9-12. *War and Other Essays*, pp. 225-226.

P. 90, lines 12-14. Sumner and Keller, *op. cit.*, vol. i, p. 573.

P. 90, lines 14-19. "Bequests of the Nineteenth Century to the Twentieth," *op. cit.*, pp. 738, 753.

P. 90, lines 20-23. *The Challenge of Facts and Other Essays*, p. 75.

P. 90, lines 23-27. *Folkways*, p. 162.

P. 90, lines 27-28. *Earth Hunger and Other Essays*, p. 289.

P. 90, lines 29-31. *Ibid.*, p. 209.

P. 91, lines 4-7. Sumner and Keller, *op. cit.*, vol. i, pp. 724, 508.

P. 91, lines 16-19. Starr, *op. cit.*, pp. 502-505.

Pp. 91-92, lines 24-2. *Folkways*, pp. 40-41.

P. 92, lines 3-13. *Ibid.*, pp. 39-40, 42.

P. 92, lines 14-24. *Ibid.*, pp. 45-51.

P. 93, lines 10-14. Sumner and Keller, *op. cit.*, vol. i, pp. 328-329.

P. 93, lines 14-17. *Ibid.*, vol. i, p. 725.

P. 93, lines 17-20. *Folkways*, p. 99.

P. 93, lines 23-31. *The Challenge of Facts and Other Essays*, pp. 156, 349.

P. 93, lines 32-34. "Bequests of the Nineteenth Century to the Twentieth," *op. cit.*, p. 742; Sumner and Keller, *op. cit.*, vol. i, p. 405.

Pp. 93-94, lines 34-2. *The Challenge of Facts and Other Essays*, pp. 293-302.

P. 94, lines 2-7. Sumner and Keller, *op. cit.*, vol. i, pp. 173-176.

P. 94, lines 7-13. *Ibid.*, vol. i, pp. 171-172.

P. 94, lines 13-14. *Folkways*, p. 162.

P. 94, lines 15-17. *The Challenge of Facts and Other Essays*, p. 58.

P. 94, lines 17-21. *Folkways*, pp. 101, 163-165.

P. 94, lines 21-24. *The Challenge of Facts and Other Essays*, p. 139.

P. 94, lines 26-28. *Folkways*, pp. 88-90.

P. 94, lines 30-32. *The Challenge of Facts and Other Essays*, p. 150.

P. 94, lines 32-33. *The Forgotten Man and Other Essays*, p. 150.

Pp. 94-95, lines 34-3. *The Challenge of Facts and Other Essays*, p. 307; *Earth Hunger and Other Essays*, p. 291.

P. 95, lines 3-13. *The Challenge of Facts and Other Essays*, pp. 70, 130.

P. 95, lines 14-17. *Ibid.*, p. 392.

P. 95, lines 17-21. *War and Other Essays*, p. 241.

P. 95, lines 24-26. *What Social Classes Owe to Each Other*, pp. 29-35; *The Forgotten Man and Other Essays*, p. 474.

P. 95, lines 26-30. *Earth Hunger and Other Essays*, pp. 175-176.

P. 95, lines 30-32. *What Social Classes Owe to Each Other*, pp. 21-24.

P. 95, lines 32-36. *Ibid.*, p. 15.

Pp. 95-96, lines 36-4. *The Challenge of Facts and Other Essays*, pp. 157, 161.

P. 96, lines 5-8. *What Social Classes Owe to Each Other*, pp. 96-97.

P. 96, lines 8-10. *The Forgotten Man and Other Essays*, p. 71.

P. 96, *footnote 15*. A. G. Keller, Foreword, *What Social Classes Owe to Each Other*, pp. 4-5.

P. 96, lines 12-13. *Folkways*, p. 53.

P. 96, lines 13-17. *The Challenge of Facts and Other Essays*, pp. 76-77.

P. 96, lines 20-22. "Bequests of the Nineteenth Century to the Twentieth," *op. cit.*, p. 736

P. 96, lines 23-25. *The Challenge of Facts and Other Essays*, p. 74.

Pp. 96-97, lines 25-1. *Folkways*, pp. 51, 169-171.

P. 97, lines 6-8. *The Challenge of Facts and Other Essays*, p. 162.

P. 97, lines 8-9. *Ibid.*, p. 169.

P. 97, lines 9-14. *Ibid.*, p. 164.

P. 97, lines 14-30. *Ibid.*, pp. 161-163.

P. 98, lines 6-8. *Folkways*, p. 39.

P. 98, lines 8-14. *Ibid.*, pp. 176-177; cf. "Bequests of the Nineteenth Century to the Twentieth," *op. cit.*, p. 739; Sumner and Keller, *op. cit.*, vol. ii, pp. 1051-1052.

P. 98, lines 14-19. *Folkways*, pp. 205-207.

P. 98, lines 19-23. "Bequests of the Nineteenth Century to the Twentieth," *op. cit.*, p. 745.

P. 98, lines 24-25. *Folkways*, p. 63.

P. 98, lines 25-27. *War and Other Essays*, p. 151.

P. 98, lines 27-34. *Ibid.*, pp. 67, 163, 652; Sumner and Keller, *op. cit.*, vol. iii, pp. 2091-2093.

Pp. 98-99, lines 34-3. *Earth Hunger and Other Essays*, p. 191.

P. 99, lines 7-12. *Folkways*, pp. 164-165, 171-172.

P. 99, lines 13-14. *Earth Hunger and Other Essays*, pp. 230-231.

P. 99, lines 14-19. *The Forgotten Man and Other Essays*, p. 242; *Earth Hunger and Other Essays*, p. 189.

P. 99, lines 19-23. *Folkways*, pp. 94-95, 116, 184; Sumner and Keller, *op. cit.*, vol. i, p. 82.

P. 99, lines 24-32. "Bequests of the Nineteenth Century to the Twentieth," *op. cit.*, p. 746; cf. *Earth Hunger and Other Essays*, pp. 337-338.

Pp. 99-100, lines 32-2. *Earth Hunger and Other Essays*, pp. 180-181.

P. 100, lines 6-10. *Folkways*, pp. 95-96.

P. 100, lines 10-11. *What Social Classes Owe to Each Other*, p. 93.

P. 100, lines 11-14. *Ibid.*, pp. 127-128.

P. 100, lines 16-19. *War and Other Essays*, p. 156.

P. 100, lines 19-21. *Folkways*, pp. 77-78.

P. 100, lines 28-30. *Ibid.*, p. 192.

P. 100, lines 30-33. See *ibid.*, pp. 39-53.

Pp. 100-101, lines 33-1. In *The Challenge of Facts and Other Essays*, p. 432.

P. 101, lines 2-6. *What Social Classes Owe to Each Other*, pp. 168-169; cf. *ibid.*, pp. 21-24, 37, 39-42.

P. 101, lines 12-15. Ward, *op. cit.*, vol. iii, p. 303-304.

P. 101, *footnote 20*. *The Forgotten Man and Other Essays*, pp. 477-478; *War and Other Essays*, p. 196.

P. 101, lines 16-18. *Folkways*, p. 113.

P. 101, lines 19-20. *War and Other Essays*, p. 210.

P. 101, lines 20-22. *Ibid.*, p. 225; *The Challenge of Facts and Other Essays*, pp. 247-248.

P. 101, lines 26-29. Starr, *op. cit.*, pp. 390-392.

Pp. 101-102, lines 33-2. Barnes, *American Journal of Sociology*, *op. cit.*, p. 4.

P. 102, lines 12-15. *The Challenge of Facts and Other Essays*, p. 52.

P. 102, lines 15-21. *War and Other Essays*, p. 186; *Earth Hunger and Other Essays*, pp. 235, 368.

P. 102, lines 22-24. *The Challenge of Facts and Other Essays*, p. 147.

P. 102, lines 25-26. *Earth Hunger and Other Essays*, p. 353.

P. 102, lines 26-31. *Ibid.*, pp. 347-348.

Pp. 102-103, lines 31-2. "Bequests of the Nineteenth Century to the Twentieth," *op. cit.*, p. 733.

P. 103, lines 5-7. Statement to *The New York Times*, quoted in Starr, *op. cit.*, p. 312.

P. 103, lines 13-16. Quoted by Keller in *The Forgotten Man and Other Essays*, p. 462.

P. 103, lines 17-19. See *Earth Hunger and Other Essays*, pp. 48-49.

P. 103, lines 20-23. *The Forgotten Man and Other Essays*, p. 79.

P. 103, lines 24-26. *War and Other Essays*, p. 225.

P. 103, lines 26-29. "Bequests of the Nineteenth Century to the Twentieth," *op. cit.*, p. 747; *The Challenge of Facts and Other Essays*, p. 212.

Pp. 103-104, lines 30-1. *War and Other Essays*, pp. 172, 182.

P. 104, lines 1-4. *The Challenge of Facts and Other Essays*, p. 207.

P. 104, lines 4-7. *Ibid.*, p. 55; cf. Sumner and Keller, *op. cit.*, vol. i, p. 316.

P. 104, lines 7-14. *Earth Hunger and Other Essays*, p. 91; *War and Other Essays*, p. 169.

P. 104, lines 15-17. *The Challenge of Facts and Other Essays*, p. 65.

P. 104, lines 17-20. *What Social Classes Owe to Each Other*, p. 163; *The Challenge of Facts and Other Essays*, p. 41; Sumner and Keller, *op. cit.*, vol. i, p. 338.

P. 104, lines 20-21. "Bequests of the Nineteenth Century to the Twentieth," *op. cit.*, p. 742.

P. 104, lines 21-23. *The Forgotten Man and Other Essays*, p. 25.

P. 104, lines 23-26. *The Challenge of Facts and Other Essays*, pp. 36-39; cf. Sumner and Keller, *op. cit.*, vol. i, p. 334, vol. iii, p. 2235.

P. 104, lines 26-31. *War and Other Essays*, pp. 126, 190-191; *The Challenge of Facts and Other Essays*, pp. 47-48; *Folkways*, p. 165.

Pp. 104-105, lines 32-4. *The Forgotten Man and Other Essays*, pp. 441-462.

P. 105, lines 5-14. *The Challenge of Facts and Other Essays*, pp. 43-44, 46; *Earth Hunger and Other Essays*, p. 178.

P. 105, lines 17-20. *The Challenge of Facts and Other Essays*, pp. 60-61.

P. 105, lines 20-23. *Earth Hunger and Other Essays*, p. 252; Sumner and Keller, *op. cit.*, vol. i, pp. 348, 350.

P. 105, lines 24-33. *What Social Classes Owe to Each Other*, pp. 47, 54-57, 163.

P. 105, lines 33-36. *The Challenge of Facts and Other Essays*, p. 201.

Pp. 105-106, lines 36-5. *Earth Hunger and Other Essays*, pp. 174-175; Sumner and Keller, *op. cit.*, vol. i, p. 348.

P. 106, *footnote 25*. *War and Other Essays*, pp. 179-180.

P. 106, lines 10-14. See especially *Earth Hunger and Other Essays*, pp. 239-253, 270-279.

P. 106, lines 14-18. *Earth Hunger and Other Essays*, pp. 310-311.

P. 106, lines 18-25. *What Social Classes Owe to Each Other*, pp. 151-152, 157.

P. 106, lines 26-30. *The Challenge of Facts and Other Essays*, pp. 34-35.

P. 107, lines 8-11. *The Forgotten Man and Other Essays*, p. 262.

P. 107, lines 11-13. *War and Other Essays*, pp. 234, 242-243.

P. 107, lines 14-16. *What Social Classes Owe to Each Other*, p. 110.

P. 107, lines 16-18. *Ibid.*, p. 93.

P. 107, lines 19-23. *The Forgotten Man and Other Essays*, pp. 251-252; *The Challenge of Facts and Other Essays*, p. 99.

P. 107, lines 23-25. *What Social Classes Owe to Each Other*, p. 93.

P. 107, lines 26-34. *War and Other Essays*, pp. 250-251.

Pp. 107-108, lines 34-1. *The Challenge of Facts and Other Essays*, p. 102; *The Forgotten Man and Other Essays*, pp. 243, 246.

P. 108, lines 8-11. *What Social Classes Owe to Each Other*, pp. 98-100.

P. 108, lines 23-26. *Ibid.*, pp. 112-122.

P. 108, lines 27-32. "Bequests of the Nineteenth Century to the Twentieth," *op. cit.*, pp. 746, 748, 750.

P. 108, lines 32-34. *Folkways*, pp. 51-52, 628-629.

P. 108, lines 34-36. *War and Other Essays*, p. 159.

P. 109, lines 5-8. *The Forgotten Man and Other Essays*, p. 476.

P. 109, lines 8-22. See the two essays, "On the Case of a Certain Man Who Is Never Thought Of," pp. 247-268, in *War and Other Essays; What Social Classes Owe to Each Other*, pp. 21-24, 145.

P. 109, lines 23-27. *What Social Classes Owe to Each Other*, pp. 69-71.

P. 109, lines 27-31. *Ibid.*, pp. 134-137; *Earth Hunger and Other Essays*, p. 224.

P. 109, lines 31-33. *The Forgotten Man and Other Essays*, p. 258.

P. 109, lines 34-35. *The Challenge of Facts and Other Essays*, p. 57.

P. 110, lines 1-2. *Earth Hunger and Other Essays*, p. 332.

CHAPTER FOUR

(Unless otherwise noted, the author in
all cases is A. W. Small.)

P. 113, lines 10-11. E. C. Hayes, "Albion Woodbury Small,"
American Masters of Social Science (ed. by H. W. Odum),
p. 149.

P. 113, lines 15-16. See "The Significance of Sociology for
Ethics," *University of Chicago, Decennial Publications*, first
series, Vol. IV, p. 148.

P. 113, lines 16-18. T. W. Goodspeed, "Albion W. Small," *American Journal of Sociology*, Vol. XXXII, No. 1 (1926), p. 12.

Pp. 113-114, lines 18-5. Hayes, *op. cit.*, especially pp. 153-158.

P. 114, lines 6-16. *Ibid.*, especially pp. 149-150, 153, 166, 171-172,
184-187.

P. 114, *footnote 3*. *Between Eras: From Capitalism to Democracy*, pp. 391-404.

Pp. 114-115, lines 29-2. A. W. Small and G. E. Vincent, *An Introduction to the Study of Society*, p. 38.

P. 115, lines 2-4. *The Meaning of Social Science*, p. 275.

P. 115, lines 1-6. *Adam Smith and Modern Sociology*, see pp.
1-24; *The Cameralists*, see p. 596.

P. 115, lines 6-10. *Adam Smith and Modern Sociology*, p. 77.

P. 115, *footnote 4*. F. N. House, *The Development of Sociology*,
(McGraw-Hill, New York 1936), pp. 252-253.

P. 115, lines 25-26. See Goodspeed, *op. cit.*, pp. 1-14.

P. 115, lines 27-31. Small and Vincent, *op. cit.*, pp. 19, 75.

P. 115, lines 31-34. *The Meaning of Social Science*, p. 71.

P. 116, lines 1-2. "Some Demands of Sociology Upon Pedagogy,"
American Journal of Sociology, Vol. II, No. 6 (1897), pp. 839-851.

P. 116, lines 2-3. "The Significance of Sociology for Ethics," *op. cit.*, p. 137.

P. 116, lines 3-4. B. J. Stern, ed., "Letters of Albion W. Small to
Lester F. Ward," *Social Forces*, Vol. XIII, No. 3 (1934), p. 332.

P. 116, lines 4-7. "The Present Outlook of Social Science," *American Journal of Sociology*, Vol. XVIII, No. 4, p. 435.

P. 116, lines 8-9. "Letters of Albion W. Small to Lester F.
Ward," *op. cit.*, Vol. XII, No. 2 (1933), p. 164.

P. 116, lines 11-19. *Adam Smith and Modern Sociology*, pp. 22, 126, 130, 133, 137, 238.

P. 116, lines 19-22. *The Meaning of Social Science*, pp. 137-148.

P. 116, lines 23-27. "The Sociologists' Point of View," *American Journal of Sociology*, Vol. III, No. 2 (1897), pp. 145, 170.

P. 116, lines 27-30. "The Significance of Sociology for Ethics," *op. cit.*, pp. 141, 145; cf. *General Sociology*, chs. xli-xlvi.

P. 116, lines 30-33. "The Subject Matter of Sociology," *American Journal of Sociology*, Vol. X, No. 3 (1904), p. 298.

P. 116, lines 33-36. *Origins of Sociology*, p. 7.

Pp. 116-117, lines 36-3. See Small and Vincent, *op. cit.*, pp. 66-70; *General Sociology*, pp. 3-39, 691-727; *The Meaning of Social Science*, pp. 227-243 and ch. ix.

P. 117, lines 6-7. *General Sociology*, p. 42.

P. 117, lines 7-12. Hayes, *op. cit.*, p. 184.

P. 117, lines 15-18. "Letters of Albion W. Small to Lester F. Ward," *op. cit.*, Vol. XV, No. 2 (1936), p. 182.

P. 117, *footnote* 7. *General Sociology*, pp. 382-390.

P. 117, lines 18-20. *Ibid.*, p. 455; *The Meaning of Social Science*, pp. 279-281.

P. 117, lines 20-22. Small and Vincent, *op. cit.*, pp. 269-272.

P. 117, lines 22-25. *General Sociology*, p. 354.

Pp. 117-118, lines 28-1. *Ibid.*, p. 303.

P. 118, lines 1-3. *Ibid.*, p. 279.

P. 118, lines 4-7. Small and Vincent, *op. cit.*, pp. 34-38, 66.

P. 118, lines 8-9. See House, *loc. cit.*

P. 118, lines 10-13. H. E. Barnes, "The Place of Albion Woodbury Small in Modern Sociology," *American Journal of Sociology*, Vol. XXXII, No. 1 (1926), pp. 16, 18, 25.

P. 118, lines 19-20. House, *op. cit.*, p. 254.

P. 118, lines 22-24. See Small and Vincent, *op. cit.*, pp. 34-38, 40-42; "The Present Outlook of Social Science," *op. cit.*, pp. 436, 459-469.

P. 118, *footnote* 10. *Johns Hopkins University Studies*, Vol. VIII (1890).

P. 118, lines 24-30. Barnes, *op. cit.*, p. 43.

P. 119, lines 1-3. "Fifty Years of Sociology in the United States," *American Journal of Sociology*, Vol. XXI, No. 6 (1916), pp. 732-733.

P. 119, lines 3-4. Small and Vincent, *op. cit.*, p. 47.

P. 119, lines 6-9. *The Cameralists*, pp. 1-20, 590; cf. Hayes, *op. cit.*, p. 170.

P. 119, lines 9-13. *Adam Smith and Modern Sociology*, p. 11.

P. 119, lines 15-16. *General Sociology*, p. 573.

P. 119, lines 17-19. Small and Vincent, *op. cit.*, p. 356.

P. 119, lines 20-22. See Hayes, *op. cit.*, pp. 160-164.

Pp. 119-120, lines 27-4. *General Sociology*, p. 653.

P. 120, lines 5-11. See Small and Vincent, *op. cit.*, pp. 76-85.

P. 120, lines 12-14. "Letters of Albion W. Small to Lester F. Ward," *loc. cit.*

P. 120, lines 14-19. See Hayes, *op. cit.*, pp. 164-165; House, *op. cit.*, pp. 252-253.

P. 120, lines 26-29. "Socialism in the Light of Social Science," *American Journal of Sociology*, Vol. XVII, No. 6 (1912), p. 819.

P. 120, lines 29-30. "The Social Gradations of Capital," *American Journal of Sociology*, Vol. XIX, No. 6 (1914), pp. 732-734.

P. 121, lines 4-7. *General Sociology*, p. 20.

P. 121, lines 9-10. See, for example, Small and Vincent, *op. cit.*, pp. 43, 181; *The Meaning of Social Science*, pp. 45, 75, 124-125.

P. 121, lines 10-12. "The Subject Matter of Sociology," *op. cit.*, p. 297.

P. 121, lines 12-16. *General Sociology*, pp. 218-219, 374.

P. 121, lines 16-18. *Ibid.*, p. 238; cf. "Fifty Years of Sociology in the United States," *op. cit.*, p. 860.

P. 121, lines 18-21. "Socialism in the Light of Social Science," *op. cit.*, pp. 811-812.

P. 121, lines 21-25. *General Sociology*, p. 575.

P. 121, lines 26-28. "Fifty Years of Sociology in the United States," *op. cit.*, pp. 788-815.

P. 121, lines 29-30. *General Sociology*, pp. 412-413, 423-424.

Pp. 121-122, lines 34-4. *Ibid.*, pp. 579, 639.

P. 122, lines 4-7. "The Social Gradations of Capital," *op. cit.*, especially pp. 725-726.

P. 122, lines 7-12. *General Sociology*, pp. 658-660.

P. 122, lines 13-19. *Ibid.*, pp. 198, 203-205, 209.

P. 122, *footnote 12.* Ibid., pp. 450-451.

Pp. 122-123, lines 20-2. *Ibid.*, pp. 214, 282-283.

P. 123, lines 20-27. *Ibid.*, pp. 241, 247-248.

P. 123, lines 27-32. *Ibid.*, p. 305.

P. 123, lines 32-34. *Ibid.*, pp. 262-264.

Pp. 123-124, lines 34-3. *Ibid.*, pp. 252-253.

P. 124, lines 4-22. *Ibid.*, pp. 256-266.

Pp. 124-125, lines 23-9. *Ibid.*, pp. 299-302.

P. 125, lines 10-18. *Ibid.*, pp. 302-303.

P. 125, lines 18-21. *Ibid.*, p. 394.

P. 125, lines 24-28. *Ibid.*, p. 306.

P. 125, lines 28-32. *Ibid.*, pp. 515-516.

P. 125, lines 34-36. *Ibid.*, p. 330.

P. 126, lines 2-9. "Socialism in the Light of Social Science," *op. cit.*, pp. 812-813.

P. 126, lines 9-13. "The Church and Class Conflicts," *American Journal of Sociology*, Vol. XXIV, No. 5 (1919), p. 483.

P. 126, lines 13-17. *Between Eras: From Capitalism to Democracy*, p. 175.

P. 126, lines 17-19. *Ibid.*, pp. 227-235, 407-421.

P. 126, lines 19-22. *Adam Smith and Modern Sociology*, pp. 123-125.

P. 126, lines 32-34. *General Sociology*, pp. 476-477.

Pp. 126-127, lines 36-9. *Ibid.*, p. 361.

P. 127, lines 9-17. *Ibid.*, pp. 361-363, 370-371.

P. 127, lines 20-23. *Between Eras: From Capitalism to Democracy*, pp. 149-168, *passim*.

P. 127, lines 24-26. *Ibid.*, pp. 307-318, *passim*.

P. 127, lines 26-30. *General Sociology*, pp. 459-460.

P. 127, lines 31-36. *Ibid.*, pp. 522-523.

P. 128, lines 7-17. "Socialism in the Light of Social Science," *op. cit.*, p. 808.

P. 128, lines 21-22. *Adam Smith and Modern Sociology*, pp. 100, 112.

P. 128, lines 22-24. "The Church and Class Conflicts," *op. cit.*, pp. 482-483.

P. 128, lines 24-26. Small and Vincent, *op. cit.*, pp. 156-157.

P. 128, lines 26-28. *Ibid.*, pp. 112-165, *passim*.

P. 128, lines 28-32. *Ibid.*, pp. 289-299.

P. 129, *footnote 14*. *Ibid.*, p. 201.

P. 129, lines 2-15. *General Sociology*, pp. 275-276.

P. 129, lines 16-25. *Ibid.*, pp. 274-275.

P. 129, lines 25-28. See "The Bonds of Nationality," *American Journal of Sociology*, Vol. XX, No. 5 (1915), pp. 662-663.

Pp. 129-130, lines 31-4. *General Sociology*, p. 230.

P. 130, lines 4-8. *Ibid.*, p. 274.

P. 130, lines 10-12. "The Bonds of Nationality," *op. cit.*, p. 661.

P. 130, *footnote 16*. "The Social Gradations of Capital," *op. cit.*, pp. 726-751.

P. 130, lines 13-23. *General Sociology*, pp. 191, 193, 229-230.

Pp. 130-131, lines 25-1. *Ibid.*, p. 194.

P. 131, lines 1-19. *Ibid.*, pp. 231-234.

Pp. 131-132, lines 20-7. *Ibid.*, pp. 266-267, 270-274; cf. "The Significance of Sociology for Ethics," *op. cit.*, p. 140.

P. 132, lines 10-11. Small and Vincent, *op. cit.*, p. 352.

P. 132, lines 11-15. *General Sociology*, p. 239.

P. 132, lines 15-20. *Ibid.*, pp. 247-248.

P. 132, lines 23-26. P. Sorokin, *Contemporary Sociological Theories* (Harpers, New York 1928), p. 543.

P. 132, lines 27-32. "Socialism in the Light of Social Science," *op. cit.*, pp. 809-810.

Pp. 132-133, lines 35-7. Small and Vincent, *op. cit.*, pp. 249, 271, 283, 290, 361.

P. 133, lines 7-12. *Ibid.*, pp. 255, 260.

P. 133, lines 14-18. *Adam Smith and Modern Sociology*, pp. 7, 98-99.

P. 133, lines 19-20. "Socialism in the Light of Social Science," *op. cit.*, pp. 813-814.

P. 133, lines 20-22. "The Sociology of Profits," *American Journal of Sociology*, Vol. XXX, No. 4 (1925), pp. 439-461.

P. 133, lines 24-28. *The Meaning of Social Science*, p. 295.

Pp. 133-134, lines 30-2. "Socialism in the Light of Social Science," *op. cit.*, pp. 814-815.

P. 134, lines 6-8. "The Meaning of the Social Movement," *American Journal of Sociology*, Vol. III, No. 3 (1897), pp. 343-344.

P. 134, lines 8-10. *Adam Smith and Modern Sociology*, p. 153.

P. 134, lines 10-13. *General Sociology*, p. 302.

P. 134, lines 13-15. *Between Eras: From Capitalism to Democracy*, pp. 89-91.

P. 134, lines 15-22. "The Church and Class Conflicts," *op. cit.*, pp. 487-492, 495.

P. 134, lines 22-25. "Socialism in the Light of Social Science," *op. cit.*, pp. 818-819.

P. 134, lines 27-29. "The Significance of Sociology for Ethics," *op. cit.*, pp. 113, 116-117.

P. 134, lines 29-36. *General Sociology*, pp. 594, 599-600.

Pp. 134-135, lines 36-2. *Between Eras: From Capitalism to Democracy*, pp. 99-100.

P. 135, lines 2-4. "The Sociology of Profits," *op. cit.*, pp. 459-460.

P. 135, lines 7-14. *General Sociology*, p. 277.

P. 135, lines 14-16. "The Bonds of Nationality," *op. cit.*, pp. 655-656.

P. 135, lines 16-18. "The Church and Class Conflicts," *op. cit.*, p. 483; cf. *General Sociology*, pp. 268-270.

P. 135, lines 20-24. *General Sociology*, pp. 606-607.

P. 135, lines 24-26. *Between Eras: From Capitalism to Democracy, passim.*

P. 135, lines 26-29. "The Bonds of Nationality," *op. cit.*, pp. 664-666; *General Sociology*, pp. 268-270, 598.

Pp. 135-136, lines 29-1. *General Sociology*, pp. 260-261, 278.

P. 136, lines 2-9. *Ibid.*, p. 268.

P. 136, lines 18-21. L. Wirth, "Small, Albion Woodbury," *Encyclopaedia of the Social Sciences*, Vol. XIV.

P. 137, lines 11-14. *Between Eras: From Capitalism to Democracy*, p. 228.

P. 137, lines 14-18. W. Rauschenbusch, *American Journal of Sociology*, Vol. XIX (1914), pp. 853-854.

P. 137, lines 18-20. Barnes, *op. cit.*, p. 25.

P. 137, lines 20-25. H. E. Barnes, *Papers and Proceedings of the American Sociological Society*, Vol. XV (1920), p. 195.

P. 137, lines 29-33. "The Present Outlook of Social Science," *op. cit.*, p. 469.

P. 137, lines 33-36. "A Vision of Social Efficiency," *American Journal of Sociology*, Vol. XIX, No. 4 (1913), p. 440.

P. 138, lines 2-4. Small and Vincent, *op. cit.*, pp. 299, 334.

P. 138, lines 4-8. *Adam Smith and Modern Sociology*, pp. 113-114.

P. 138, lines 8-13. "The Sociology of Profits," *op. cit.*, p. 460.

P. 138, lines 16-26. "The Meaning of the Social Movement," *op. cit.*, pp. 345, 348, 350-354.

P. 138, lines 26-29. "The Social Gradations of Capital," *op. cit.*, p. 752.

P. 138, lines 29-31. *General Sociology*, p. 518.

Pp. 138-139, lines 33-3. "The Evolution of a Social Standard," *American Journal of Sociology*, Vol. XX, No. 1 (1914), p. 17.

P. 139, lines 3-7. "National Preparedness—American," *American Journal of Sociology*, Vol. XXI, No. 5 (1916), pp. 606-608.

P. 139, lines 7-9. "The Ford Motor Company Incident," *American Journal of Sociology*, Vol. XIX, No. 5 (1914), pp. 656-658.

P. 139, lines 11-15. "The Sociology of Profits," *op. cit.*, p. 459.

P. 139, lines 18-21. Small and Vincent, *op. cit.*, p. 318.

P. 139, lines 21-31. *General Sociology*, pp. 379-381.

P. 139, lines 32-36. "A Vision of Social Efficiency," *op. cit.*, p. 445.

P. 140, lines 2-5. *Ibid.*, pp. 440-441.

P. 140, lines 6-7. "The Evolution of a Social Standard," *op. cit.*, p. 16.

P. 140, lines 7-10. "The Social Gradations of Capital," *op. cit.*, p. 722.

P. 140, lines 10-12. "Shall Science Be Sterilized?" *American Journal of Sociology*, Vol. XIX, No. 5 (1914), pp. 651-653.

P. 140, lines 12-13. "The Church and Class Conflicts," *op. cit.*, pp. 496-501.

P. 140, lines 16-18. "Socialism in the Light of Social Science," *op. cit.*, p. 816.

P. 140, lines 18-19. "The Meaning of the Social Movement," *op. cit.*, p. 342.

P. 140, lines 20-22. *General Sociology*, p. 376.

P. 140, lines 23-25. "The Church and Class Conflicts," *op. cit.*, pp. 493-494; "The Significance of Sociology for Ethics," *op. cit.*, p. 196.

P. 140, lines 25-27. *General Sociology*, p. 315.

P. 140, lines 27-29. "Fifty Years of Sociology in the United States," *op. cit.*, pp. 764-765.

Pp. 140-141, lines 29-3. *General Sociology*, pp. 377-379.

P. 141, lines 5-9. "Socialism in the Light of Social Science," *loc. cit.*

P. 141, lines 14-16. *Ibid.*, pp. 804-808.

P. 141, lines 20-23. *General Sociology*, p. 316.

P. 141, lines 25-32. "A Vision of Social Efficiency," *op. cit.*, pp. 443, 444.

P. 141, lines 32-36. "The Sociology of Profits," *op. cit.*, pp. 460-461.

CHAPTER FIVE

(Unless otherwise noted, the author
in all cases is F. H. Giddings.)

P. 145, lines 3-12. J. L. Gillin, "Franklin Henry Giddings," *American Masters of Social Science* (ed. by H. W. Odum), pp. 196-198.

P. 145, lines 22-23. *The Western Hemisphere in the World of Tomorrow*, pp. 36-37.

P. 146, lines 6-8. Material on Giddings' "personality" has been provided through informal conversation with several of his former students and colleagues, including Professors A. A. Tenney, T. Abel and B. J. Stern of Columbia University, Professor Frank Ross of Syracuse University, Professors W. B. Guthrie and Samuel B. Joseph of The City College of New York, and Professor Lee Deets of the University of South Dakota.

P. 146, lines 8-9. See Gillin, *op. cit.*, pp. 198-199, 226.

P. 146, line 11. See *A Bibliography of the Faculty of Political Science of Columbia University 1880-1930*, pp. 63-76.

P. 146, lines 20-23. Gillin, *op. cit.*, pp. 226-228.

P. 146, lines 24-25. J. P. Lichtenberger, "Franklin H. Giddings: An Appreciation," *Journal of Applied Sociology*, Vol. IX, No. 5 (1925), p. 329.

P. 146, lines 30-32. B. J. Stern, "Giddings, Franklin Henry," *Encyclopaedia of the Social Sciences*.

P. 146, lines 32-33. See Gillin, *op. cit.*, p. 200.

P. 146, *footnote 1.* A. A. Tenney, "Franklin Henry Giddings," *Columbia University Quarterly*, Vol. XXIII, p. 321.

P. 146, *footnote 1.* *Studies in the Theory of Human Society*, p. 293.

P. 147, lines 3-4. "The Changing Attitude Toward War" (Introduction), *Special Bulletin of the American Association for International Conciliation*, September, 1914.

P. 147, lines 4-6. See "The Democracy of Universal Military Service," *Annals, American Academy of Political and Social Science*, Vol. LXVI (1916), pp. 2-3, 6; "Patriotism," *Teachers College Record*, Vol. XXVI, No. 6 (1925); *Americanism in War and Peace.*

P. 147, lines 8-13. See, for example, the following articles in the *Independent:* "The Bolsheviki Must Go," January 18, 1919; "What the Economic Crisis Calls For," August 16, 1919; "One Big Union Idea," May 1, 1920; "Absolutist Communism," July 3, 1920; "The Social Revolution Not Yet," April 30, 1921.

P. 147, lines 13-17. Gillin, *op. cit.*, pp. 198, 202; "The Theory of Capital," *Quarterly Journal of Economics*, Vol. IV (1890).

P. 147, lines 19-24. "The Persistence of Competition," *Political Science Quarterly*, Vol. II, No. 1 (1887), especially pp. 66, 69-71, 73.

P. 147, lines 24-28. "The Cost of Production of Capital," *Quarterly Journal of Economics*, Vol. III (1889), especially p. 506.

P. 147, lines 28-32. "The Natural Rate of Wages," *Political Science Quarterly*, Vol. II, No. 4 (1887), especially pp. 620-623, 625, 632-637.

Pp. 147-148, lines 35-1. "Sociology as a University Study," *Political Science Quarterly*, Vol. VI, No. 4 (1891), p. 645.

P. 148, lines 1-2. For an uncritical exposition of Giddings' system, see C. H. Northcott, "The Sociological Theories of Franklin H. Giddings," *American Journal of Sociology*, Vol. XXIV, No. 1 (1918); for a thorough critique, see L. F. Ward, "Principles of Sociology," *Annals, American Academy of Political and Social Science*, Vol. VIII (1896), pp. 1-31.

P. 148, lines 2-5. See, for example, "Sociology as a University Study," *op. cit.*, p. 637.

P. 148, lines 5-9. "The Concepts and Methods of Sociology," *American Journal of Sociology*, Vol. X, No. 2 (1904), p. 172.

P. 148, lines 9-11. See "The Province of Sociology," *Annals, American Academy of Political and Social Science*, Vol. I (1890), pp. 66-67; "The Laws of Evolution," *Science*, Vol. XXII (1905), pp. 206-208.

P. 148, lines 13-15. *Principles of Sociology*, pp. 199-207.

P. 148, lines 15-17. *Elements of Sociology*, p. 230.

P. 148, lines 17-19. *Ibid.*, pp. 336-339.

P. 148, lines 22-23. "The Province of Sociology," *op. cit.*, p. 74.

P. 148, lines 23-27. "Sociology as a University Study," *op. cit.*, pp. 647, 649.

P. 148, lines 28-30. *Principles of Sociology*, pp. 208-225.

P. 148, lines 30-34. *Inductive Sociology*, pp. 158, 198, 224.

Pp. 148-149, lines 35-2. See Gillin, *op. cit.*, pp. 218-219.

P. 149, lines 2-4. *Principles of Sociology*, pp. 17-20.

P. 149, lines 4-6. *Inductive Sociology*, p. 183.

P. 149, footnote 2. Stern, *loc. cit.*

P. 149, lines 9-10. "The Relation of Sociology to Other Scientific Studies," *Journal of Social Sciences*, No. 32 (1894), p. 5; cf. Gillin, *op. cit.*, p. 203.

P. 149, lines 12-17. "The Ethics of Social Progress," *International Journal of Ethics*, Vol. III (1893), p. 142; cf. *Studies in the Theory of Human Society*, ch. xiv *passim*.

P. 149, lines 18-19. "The Economic Ages," *Political Science Quarterly*, Vol. XVI, No. 2 (1901), p. 220; cf. *Studies in the Theory of Human Society*, ch. iii *passim*.

P. 149, lines 20-22. "The Basis of Social Conflict," *American Journal of Sociology*, Vol. XIII, No. 5 (1908), p. 645.

P. 149, lines 23-29. *Studies in the Theory of Human Society*, p. 291.

Pp. 149-150, lines 32-1. *Principles of Sociology*, p. 6.

P. 150, lines 1-2. See Gillin, *op. cit.*, pp. 205-207.

P. 150, lines 2-4. "Social Work and Societal Engineering," *Journal of Social Forces*, Vol. III, No. 1 (1924), p. 8.

P. 150, lines 4-6. "Societal Variables," *Journal of Social Forces*, Vol. I, No. 4 (1923), p. 345.

P. 150, lines 6-8. Lichtenberger, *op. cit.*, p. 330.

P. 150, lines 9-11. See "The Concepts and Methods of Sociology," *op. cit.*, p. 174.

P. 150, lines 11-14. See Stern, *loc. cit.*

P. 150, lines 16-18. Tenney, *loc. cit.*

P. 150, lines 18-20. See *Studies in the Theory of Human Society*, pp. 3-18.

P. 150, lines 20-22. *Principles of Sociology*, pp. 79-81.

P. 150, lines 22-27. "A Theory of Social Causation," *Publications, American Economic Association*, Third Series, Vol. V (1904), pp. 386-391; cf. *Studies in the Theory of Human Society*, ch. viii *passim*.

P. 150, lines 27-28. *Elements of Sociology*, p. 42.

P. 150, lines 28-32. "The Economic Ages," *op. cit.*, pp. 201, 219; cf. *Studies in the Theory of Human Society*, chs. ii, iii *passim*, especially p. 218; "Alternatives Seen as Basic Economic Facts," *Economic Essays in Honor of John Bates Clark* (New York 1927), pp. 196-197.

P. 151, lines 1-3. "Pluralistic Behavior," *American Journal of Sociology*, Vol. XXV, No. 4 (1920), p. 391; cf. *Studies in the Theory of Human Society*, ch. xv *passim; The Relation of Social Theory to Public Policy*, Pamphlet No. 58, of American Association for International Conciliation (1912), pp. 7-8.

P. 151, *footnote 4. Democracy and Empire*, pp. 269-279.

P. 151, lines 3-4. *Ibid.*, pp. 336-337.

P. 151, lines 4-6. *Civilization and Society*, pp. 203-204.

P. 151, lines 6-7. "A Theory of History," *Political Science Quarterly*, Vol. XXXV, No. 4 (1920), p. 494; cf. *Studies in the Theory of Human Society*, ch. v *passim*.

P. 151, lines 7-8. "The Nature and Conduct of Political Majorities," *Political Science Quarterly*, Vol. VII, No. 1 (1892), p. 132; cf. *Democracy and Empire*, ch. ix *passim; Principles of Sociology*, pp. 139-140.

P. 151, lines 8-9. *Inductive Sociology*, p. 67.

P. 151, lines 9-11. "A Theory of History," *op. cit.*, p. 520.

P. 151, lines 11-12. *The Responsible State*, p. 108.

P. 151, lines 13-15. *Civilization and Society*, p. 394.

P. 151, lines 15-19. *Elements of Sociology*, p. 353; cf. "A Theory of Social Causation," *op. cit.*, especially pp. 397-418; for a more extensive discussion, see *Principles of Sociology*, pp. 363, 400, 416-417.

P. 151, lines 19-20. *Principles of Sociology*, p. 308.

P. 151, line 20. "The Relation of Sociology to Other Scientific Studies," *op. cit.*, pp. 5-6.

P. 151, lines 20-23. Gillin, *op. cit.*, p. 212.

P. 151, lines 24-26. "A Theory of History," *op. cit.*, p. 495.

P. 151, lines 26-30. *Inductive Sociology*, p. 278.

P. 152, lines 4-9. "Sociology as a University Study," *op. cit.*, p. 651.

P. 152, lines 9-24. "The Concepts and Methods of Sociology," *op. cit.*, p. 173.

P. 152, lines 27-29. *The Scientific Study of Human Society*, pp. 59-79.

P. 152, lines 29-32. See *Principles of Sociology*, p. 310; *Americanism in War and Peace*, *op. cit.*, p. 9.

Pp. 152-153, lines 32-2. *Studies in the Theory of Human Society*, pp. 295-298.

P. 153, lines 3-7. *Principles of Sociology*, p. 71; *Studies in the Theory of Human Society*, pp. 101, 134; *The Scientific Study of Human Society*, pp. 50-57.

P. 153, lines 8-9. *Principles of Sociology*, p. 101.

P. 153, lines 10-12. *Civilization and Society*, pp. 187, 190, 193, 199; "Pluralistic Behavior," *op. cit.*, p. 547.

P. 153, lines 12-21. "A Theory of History," *op. cit.*, pp. 507-508, 511.

P. 153, lines 22-24. *Civilization and Society*, pp. 281-282.

P. 153, lines 24-25. "Sociological Questions," *The Forum*, October-December 1903, p. 245.

P. 153, lines 27-30. "Is the Term 'Social Classes' a Scientific Category?" *Proceedings, National Conference of Charities and Correction*, 1895, pp. 111-112.

Pp. 153-154, lines 33-3. *Ibid.*, p. 112.

P. 154, lines 6-13. *Ibid.*, p. 113.

P. 154, lines 13-17. *Principles of Sociology*, pp. 341, 373; *Elements of Sociology*, pp. 103-104; *Civilization and Society*, pp. 120-139.

P. 154, *footnote 7*. *Inductive Sociology*, pp. 78-79, 82-83. "The Ethics of Social Progress," *op. cit.*, p. 162; cf. *Studies in the Theory of Human Society*, ch. xiv *passim*.

P. 154, lines 19-25. "Is the Term 'Social Classes' a Scientific Category?" *op. cit.*, p. 114.

Pp. 154-155, lines 25-7. *Principles of Sociology*, pp. 124-128; *Elements of Sociology*, pp. 104-109; *The Theory of Socialization*, pp. 23-24.

P. 155, lines 8-21. *Inductive Sociology*, pp. 249-265.

P. 155, lines 23-30. "Is the Term 'Social Classes' a Scientific Category?" *op. cit.*, pp. 115-116.

P. 155, lines 30-32. *Elements of Sociology*, pp. 109-112.

P. 156, lines 1-9. *Principles of Sociology*, pp. 71-73.

P. 156, lines 10-18. "Pluralistic Behavior," *op. cit.*, pp. 558-559; *Studies in the Theory of Human Society*, pp. 287-288; *Civilization and Society*, pp. 254-255.

P. 156, lines 23-28. *Civilization and Society*, p. 256.

Pp. 156-157, lines 31-2. See "A Provisional Distribution of the Population of the United States into Psychological Classes," *Psychological Review*, Vol. VIII, No. 4; "Pluralistic Behavior," *op. cit.*, p. 559; *Studies in the Theory of Human Society*, pp. 288-290; *Civilization and Society*, pp. 256-259.

P. 157, lines 3-21. *Principles of Sociology*, pp. 341-344; *Elements of Sociology*, pp. 309-311.

P. 157, lines 22-31. *The Scientific Study of Human Society*, pp. 204-207; cf. "Is There a Class Psychology?" *Journal of Abnormal and Social Psychology*, Vol. XXI (1926), pp. 231-233.

Pp. 157-158, lines 35-13. *Elements of Sociology*, pp. 113-118.

P. 158, lines 13-15. *Inductive Sociology*, p. 262.

P. 158, lines 19-26. *The Responsible State*, pp. 17-20.

P. 158, lines 26-28. "Pluralistic Behavior," *op. cit.*, p. 539.

P. 158, lines 28-33. *The Responsible State*, pp. 17, 23; *Civilization and Society*, p. 210.

Pp. 158-159, lines 36-3. *Elements of Sociology*, p. 317.

P. 159, lines 3-13. *Civilization and Society*, pp. 216-221.

P. 159, lines 14-22. "Social Control in a Democracy," *Papers and Proceedings, American Sociological Society*, Vol. XII (1917), pp. 202-204.

Pp. 159-160, lines 23-2. *Civilization and Society*, pp. 327-336.

P. 160, lines 12-14. *Ibid.*, pp. 35-36.

P. 160, lines 14-16. *Principles of Sociology*, p. 128.

P. 160, lines 16-18. "Is the Term 'Social Classes' a Scientific Category?" *op. cit.*, p. 115.

P. 160, lines 18-25. *Civilization and Society*, pp. 210-213.

P. 160, lines 27-31. See "Sociology as a University Study," *op. cit.*, p. 653; *Democracy and Empire*, pp. 171-172; *The Scientific Study of Human Society*, pp. 200-201.

Pp. 160-161, lines 32-6. "The Ethics of Social Progress," *op. cit.*, pp. 148-149; *The Scientific Study of Human Society*, ch. xiv *passim*.

P. 161, lines 7-8. "Social Control in a Democracy," *op. cit.*, p. 202.

P. 161, lines 8-10. "A Theory of History," *op. cit.*, p. 514.

P. 161, lines 10-13. "Alternatives Seen as Basic Economic Facts," *op. cit.*, p. 197; *The Western Hemisphere in the World of Tomorrow*, pp. 41-45.

P. 161, lines 14-26. "Pluralistic Behavior," *op. cit.*, p. 547; *Civilization and Society*, pp. 199-201; "The Destinies of Democracy," *Political Science Quarterly*, Vol. XI, No. 4 (1896), p. 727.

Pp. 161-162, lines 27-8. "A Theory of History," *op. cit.*, pp. 515-516; cf. *Studies in the Theory of Human Society*, ch. v *passim*.

P. 162, lines 9-18. *Principles of Sociology*, pp. 318-319, 337-338; "A Theory of Social Causation," *op. cit.*, p. 412.

P. 162, lines 19-32. *Inductive Sociology*, pp. 242-243, 247-248.

P. 163, lines 4-12. *The Western Hemisphere in the World of Tomorrow*, p. 33; *Civilization and Society*, pp. 213-215; *Democracy and Empire*, p. 105.

P. 163, lines 13-21. *Inductive Sociology*, pp. 214-216; *Democracy and Empire*, pp. 106-108, 132.

P. 163, lines 26-29. *Studies in the Theory of Human Society*, pp. 94-124.

P. 163, lines 30-31. See "Pluralistic Behavior," *op. cit.*, p. 548.

P. 163, lines 31-34. *Principles of Sociology*, pp. 186; *ibid.* cf., p. 338.

P. 164, lines 7-9. *Ibid.*, pp. 293-296.

P. 164, lines 9-10. *Ibid.*, pp. 315-316; *Elements of Sociology*, pp. 272-276.

P. 164, lines 10-20. *The Responsible State*, pp. 8-18, 29; *Civilization and Society*, pp. 140-147; *Principles of Sociology*, pp. 319-320; *Elements of Sociology*, p. 280.

Pp. 164-165, lines 22-1. *Principles of Sociology*, pp. 345-346; *Elements of Sociology*, pp. 311-312, 315-316; *Democracy and Empire*, pp. 99-104, 108-110; *The Scientific Study of Human*

Society, pp. 88-90, 155-166; *Civilization and Society*, pp. 57, 221-225.

P. 165, lines 1-4. "Social Work and Societal Engineering," *op. cit.*, p. 11.

P. 165, lines 7-23. *Principles of Sociology*, pp. 182-184; *Elements of Sociology*, pp. 206-207; *Inductive Sociology*, pp. 218-219.

P. 165, lines 26-32. *The Responsible State*, pp. 6, 60-61, 86-87.

Pp. 165-166, lines 33-6. *Principles of Sociology*, pp. 177-179; *Elements of Sociology*, pp. 202-203; *Inductive Sociology*, pp. 210, 212.

P. 166, lines 8-13. *Inductive Sociology*, p. 119.

P. 166, lines 15-23. *The Responsible State*, pp. 47-48; *Civilization and Society*, pp. 61, 63.

P. 166, lines 24-31. *Principles of Sociology*, p. 195; *Elements of Sociology*, p. 213.

Pp. 166-167, lines 31-3. *The Responsible State*, pp. 26, 98-104, 106-107.

P. 167, lines 5-10. *Elements of Sociology*, pp. 312-313, 316-317.

P. 167, lines 14-18. *Principles of Sociology*, p. 170.

P. 167, lines 18-21. *Ibid.*, pp. x-xi, Preface to the Third Edition.

P. 167, lines 22-25. "Pluralistic Behavior," *op. cit.*, p. 388; cf. *Studies in the Theory of Human Society*, ch. xv *passim*.

P. 167, lines 26-30. *Democracy and Empire*, pp. 19, 26; *The Responsible State*, p. 66.

P. 167, lines 31-34. T. Abel, "The Significance of the Concept of Consciousness of Kind," *Social Forces*, Vol. IX, No. 1 (1930), pp. 1-10.

P. 168, lines 2-4. "Is the Term 'Social Classes' a Scientific Category?" *op. cit.*, p. 113.

P. 168, lines 4-7. "The Quality of Civilization," *Publications, American Sociological Society*, Vol. VI (1911), p. 5; *Studies in the Theory of Human Society*, ch. iv *passim; Inductive Sociology*, p. 107.

P. 168, lines 8-13. *Principles of Sociology*, pp. xiii-xiv, Preface to Third Edition.

P. 168, lines 17-29. *Studies in the Theory of Human Society*, p. 175.

Pp. 168-169, lines 30-2. *Ibid.*, pp. 178, 180, 183-184.

P. 169, lines 2-6. *Inductive Sociology*, pp. 274-275.

P. 169, lines 7-11. "Pluralistic Behavior," *op. cit.*, pp. 402, 541; cf. "Societal Variables," *op. cit.*, p. 348; *Elements of Sociology*, pp. 79-80.

P. 169, lines 11-13. *Elements of Sociology*, p. 123; *Inductive Sociology*, p. 143.

P. 169, lines 13-16. *Studies in the Theory of Human Society*, p. 62; *Principles of Sociology*, p. 145.

P. 169, lines 17-22. "Pluralistic Behavior," *op. cit.*, pp. 395-396, 545-547.

P. 169, lines 23-26. *Elements of Sociology*, pp. 86-87; "Pluralistic Behavior," *op. cit.*, p. 541.

Pp. 169-170, lines 31-1. *Democracy and Empire*, pp. 45-65.

P. 170, lines 1-4. "Pluralistic Behavior," *op. cit.*, p. 393.

P. 170, lines 5-9. *Ibid.*, p. 540.

P. 170, lines 13-15. *Principles of Sociology*, p. 148.

P. 170, lines 15-20. *The Responsible State*, pp. 13-16.

P. 170, lines 23-35. *Civilization and Society*, pp. 337-347; "Sociological Questions," *op. cit.*, p. 252; "A Theory of Social Causation," *op. cit.*, pp. 392, 404-418; *Studies in the Theory of Human Society*, ch. viii *passim*.

Pp. 170-171, lines 36-4. *Democracy and Empire*, pp. 339, 356.

P. 171, lines 4-6. "A Theory of History," *op. cit.*, p. 510; *The Western Hemisphere in the World of Tomorrow*, pp. 28-29.

P. 171, lines 6-8. "The Nature and Conduct of Political Majorities," *op. cit.*, pp. 122-131.

P. 171, lines 9-11. See *Americanism in War and Peace*, *op. cit.*, p. 6.

P. 171, lines 11-12. "Pluralistic Behavior," *op. cit.*, p. 543.

P. 171, lines 14-17. *Principles of Sociology*, pp. 129, 302.

P. 171, lines 22-30. "The Ethics of Social Progress," *op. cit.*, p. 164; *The Relation of Social Theory to Public Policy*, *op. cit.*, p. 7; "Sociological Questions," *op. cit.*, pp. 250-251; "Social Control in a Democracy," *op. cit.*, p. 201; "What the War Was Worth," *Independent*, July, 1919, pp. 16-17; *Civilization and Society*, p. 368; "The Destinies of Democracy," *op. cit.*, p. 781.

Pp. 171-172, lines 30-4. "The Democracy of Universal Military Service," *op. cit.*, pp. 3-4; *Inductive Sociology*, p. 222; *Studies in the Theory of Human Society*, p. 170; *Elements of Sociology*, pp. 137, 140; *Democracy and Empire*, pp. 130-131, 239-240; "Pluralistic Behavior," *op. cit.*, pp. 554-555.

P. 172, lines 5-13. "The Ethics of Social Progress," *op. cit.*, p. 143; *Elements of Sociology*, pp. 318-320; *Democracy and Empire*, pp. 77-82; "Sociological Questions," *op. cit.*, p. 254;

"The Destinies of Democracy," *op. cit.*, p. 728; *Civilization and Society*, pp. 204-207.

P. 172, lines 15-17. *Civilization and Society*, p. 201; see *Topics and Readings, Sociology*, Columbia University, 1912.

P. 172, lines 17-21. *Democracy and Empire*, p. 82; *Civilization and Society*, p. 204; "The Ethics of Socialism," *International Journal of Ethics*, Vol. I (1891), pp. 239-240; "The Ethics of Social Progress," *op. cit.*, p. 150.

P. 172, lines 21-30. "The Ethics of Social Progress," *op. cit.*, pp. 145-148, 151; "Alternatives Seen as Basic Economic Facts," *op. cit.*, pp. 198-199; "Unemployment—The Views of a Sociologist," *Independent*, October 8, 1921, p. 23.

P. 172, lines 30-32. *The Scientific Study of Human Society*, pp. 31-36.

P. 172, lines 32-34. *The Responsible State*, pp. 31-32; *Democracy and Empire*, pp. 118-121, 132-133.

P. 173, lines 1-2. "Sociology as a Science," *Scientific Monthly*, Vol. XXV (Oct., 1927), p. 344.

P. 173, lines 2-13. "Societal Variables," *op. cit.*, p. 350; *Principles of Sociology*, p. 336; "The Ethics of Social Progress," *op. cit.*, pp. 152-153, 161; *Democracy and Empire*, p. 255; "Pluralistic Behavior," *op. cit.*, p. 556.

P. 173, lines 13-20. *Principles of Sociology*, p. 351; *Democracy and Empire*, pp. 84, 85, 274; *The Responsible State*, p. 70; "The Ethics of Socialism," *op. cit.*, pp. 240-242; "Social Work and Societal Engineering," *op. cit.*, p. 15; *Elements of Sociology*, p. 205.

P. 173, lines 22-29. *Studies in the Theory of Human Society*, p. 12; *Democracy and Empire*, pp. 111-114.

Pp. 173-174, lines 30-3. *Inductive Sociology*, p. 181; *Principles of Sociology*, pp. 326-334; *Elements of Sociology*, pp. 154, 171, 304; "The Contradictions of Ideas and Beliefs," *American Journal of Sociology*, Vol. XIII, No. 6 (1908), p. 788.

P. 174, lines 4-5. *Principles of Sociology*, p. 352; *Elements of Sociology*, p. 321.

P. 174, lines 5-10. *Principles of Sociology*, pp. 150, 354-355; *Civilization and Society*, pp. 207-208; *Democracy and Empire*, p. 84.

P. 174, lines 10-13. *Civilization and Society*, p. 203; *The Western Hemisphere in the World of Tomorrow*, p. 31.

P. 174, lines 18-22. Stern, *loc. cit.*

P. 174, lines 23-35. "The Ethics of Social Progress," *op. cit.*, p. 155; *Democracy and Empire*, pp. 25, 87, 93, 115, 147-156, 302-303; *Inductive Sociology*, p. 222; *The Responsible State*, pp. 33-36, 79; *The Western Hemisphere in the World of To-morrow*, pp. 34, 47.

Pp. 174-175, lines 35-4. "Unemployment—The Views of a Sociologist," *loc. cit.*

P. 175, lines 6-13. "Resurgent Middle Class" (Book Review), *The New York Times*, December 31, 1922.

P. 175, lines 15-17. *Principles of Sociology*, p. 353.

P. 175, lines 17-28. *Ibid.*, p. 397; *Elements of Sociology*, pp. 290-293, 307; *The Scientific Study of Human Society*, pp. 162-163; "The Destinies of Democracy," *op. cit.*, p. 729; "The Laws of Evolution," *op. cit.*, p. 208; "The Relation of Recent Economic Theory of Profit Sharing," reprinted from *Employer and Employed*, 1893, p. 10; *Democracy and Empire*, pp. 159-163; "A Theory of History," *op. cit.*, p. 495.

P. 175, lines 28-36. *Inductive Sociology*, p. 230; "Social Work and Societal Engineering," *op. cit.*, pp. 11-12; *Democracy and Empire*, pp. 86, 116-117, 127, 137-143; "The Ethics of Social Progress," *op. cit.*, pp. 154, 158; "The Quality of Civilization," *op. cit.*, p. 4.

P. 176, lines 1-9. *Inductive Sociology*, p. 241; "Social Control in a Democracy," *op. cit.*, p. 205; "The Relation of Social Theory to Public Policy," *op. cit.*, pp. 3, 13; *Studies in the Theory of Human Society*, p. 223; "The Relation of Recent Economic Theory to Profit Sharing," *op. cit.*, *passim.*

P. 176, lines 9-13. *Inductive Sociology*, pp. 235-239; *Elements of Sociology*, p. 93; *Civilization and Society*, pp. 45, 253; "Pluralistic Behavior," *op. cit.*, p. 551.

P. 176, lines 15-17. "The Destinies of Democracy," *loc. cit.*

P. 176, lines 17-18. *Principles of Sociology*, p. 189; *Elements of Sociology*, pp. 209-210.

P. 176, lines 18-23. *Democracy and Empire*, pp. 122-125; *The Scientific Study of Human Society*, p. 161; "Social Work and Societal Engineering," *op. cit.*, p. 12.

P. 176, lines 23-28. *The Responsible State*, p. 43; *Civilization and Society*, pp. 47, 201-203.

Pp. 176-177, lines 34-8. *Elements of Sociology*, pp. 324-329; *The Responsible State*, pp. 75-77; "Social Control in a Democracy," *op. cit.*, p. 202; *Civilization and Society*, p. 69; "Pluralistic Behavior," *op. cit.*, p. 398.

P. 177, lines 10-17. *Principles of Sociology*, pp. 356-360.

P. 177, lines 17-22. *Inductive Sociology*, pp. 228, 233; *Civilization and Society*, p. 309; *Democracy and Empire*, p. 241.

P. 177, lines 23-28. "The Ethics of Social Progress," *op. cit.*, pp. 163-164; *Democracy and Empire*, p. 95.

P. 177, lines 30-34. "Social Work and Societal Engineering," *op. cit.*, p. 14.

P. 177, lines 34-36. "Pluralistic Behavior," *op. cit.*, pp. 556-557.

P. 178, lines 1-12. *The Scientific Study of Human Society*, pp. 144-148; "Social Work and Societal Engineering," *op. cit.*, p. 8.

P. 178, lines 13-27. *Civilization and Society*, pp. 382-384; *The Scientific Study of Human Society*, pp. 166-167; "Social Work and Societal Engineering," *op. cit.*, p. 14.

Pp. 178-179, lines 28-19. *The Scientific Study of Human Society*, pp. 165-170.

P. 179, lines 23-33. *Ibid.*, pp. 170-171.

P. 179, *footnote 19.* Quoted in K. Burke, *Attitudes Toward History*, Vol. i, pp. 11-12. (The New Republic Series, New York 1937).

Chapter Six

(Unless otherwise noted, the author in all cases is C. H. Cooley.)

P. 183, lines 11-12. Quoted by R. C. Angell in his "Introduction" to *Sociological Theory and Social Research*, p. ix. See pp. vii-viii for a general discussion of Cooley's life.

P. 183, lines 16-17. See *ibid.*, pp. 343-345, for a complete bibliography of Cooley's writings.

P. 183, lines 20-22. W. H. Hamilton, "Cooley, Charles Horton," *Encyclopaedia of the Social Sciences*.

Pp. 183-184, lines 23-1. W. H. Hamilton, "Charles Horton Cooley," *Social Forces*, Vol. VIII, No. 2 (1929), p. 187. This article contains a general appraisal of Cooley's influence in social science.

P. 184, lines 2-3. A. E. Wood, "Charles Horton Cooley: An Appreciation," *American Journal of Sociology*, Vol. XXXV, No. 5 (1930), p. 715.

P. 184, lines 21-24. "The Development of Sociology at Michigan," in *Sociological Theory and Social Research*, p. 10.

P. 184, lines 25-31. *Life and the Student*, pp. 46-48, 155, 179-180; cf. Wood, *op. cit.*, p. 714.

P. 185, lines 3-7. *Social Process*, p. 402.

P. 185, lines 7-10. C. H. Cooley, R. C. Angell, L. J. Carr, *Introductory Sociology*, pp. 287-341.

P. 185, lines 15-20. *Life and the Student*, p. 63; cf. Wood, *op. cit.*, pp. 707-708.

P. 185, lines 23-24. Cf. R. C. Angell, "Cooley's Heritage to Social Research," *Social Forces*, Vol. VIII, No. 3 (1929), p. 340.

P. 185, footnote 3. *Human Nature and the Social Order*, pp. 84-89, 101; cf. *Social Organization*, Preface.

P. 185, lines 24-32. "The Development of Sociology at Michigan," *op. cit.*, p. 5; "Personal Competition," in *Sociological Theory and Social Research*, pp. 179-180, 200.

P. 186, lines 1-3. *Social Organization*, p. 7; Cooley's methodological principles appear in five articles published in *Sociological Theory and Social Research*, pp. 289-339; R. C. Angell ably discusses Cooley's methodology in "Cooley's Heritage to Social Research," *op. cit.*, pp. 340-347.

P. 186, lines 8-15. "Political Economy and Social Process," in *Sociological Theory and Social Research*, pp. 251, 254-255, 258-259.

P. 186, lines 16-21. *Human Nature and the Social Order*, p. 1; see also, *ibid.*, pp. 1-13, 78-79, 92-93.

P. 186, lines 21-23. *Ibid.*, p. 11.

P. 186, lines 23-26. *Social Process*, pp. 197-208.

P. 186, lines 27-31. *Life and the Student*, p. 5.

P. 186, lines 31-36. *Social Organization*, pp. 64, 72-90; "The Process of Social Change," *Political Science Quarterly*, Vol. XII (1897), p. 73.

Pp. 186-187, lines 36-2. *Human Nature and the Social Order*, p. 361.

P. 187, lines 6-17. "Discussion of Giddings' Paper, 'A Theory of Social Causation,'" *American Economic Association, Publications*, Third Series, Vol. V, No. 2 (1904), pp. 183-184; cf. *Social Process*, p. 170.

P. 187, lines 17-20. *Social Organization*, p. 255; *Social Process*, pp. 43-51; *Human Nature and the Social Order*, p. 322.

P. 187, footnote 5. *Social Process*, p. 408.

P. 187, lines 24-28. Cooley, Angell, and Carr, *op. cit.*, pp. 195-196.

P. 187, lines 28-29. *Social Process*, p. 34.

Pp. 187-188, lines 30-1. *Social Organization*, pp. 32-50.

P. 188, lines 1-4. *Ibid.*, p. 131.

P. 188, lines 5-7. G. H. Mead, "Cooley's Contribution to American Social Thought," *American Journal of Sociology*, Vol. XXXV, No. 5 (1930), p. 705.

P. 188, lines 14-16. Hamilton, *Encyclopaedia of the Social Sciences, loc. cit.*

P. 188, lines 17-20. "The Process of Social Change," *op. cit.*, pp. 63-73.

P. 188, lines 21-22. *Human Nature and the Social Order*, pp. 8-9; *Social Organization*, p. 354; *Social Process*, pp. 29, 356; *Life and the Student*, pp. 49-50.

P. 188, lines 24-27. *Social Process*, pp. 57, 59.

P. 188, lines 27-32. *Life and the Student*, pp. 14, 23; *Human Nature and the Social Order*, pp. 4-6, 277; *Social Process*, pp. 364-365.

Pp. 188-189, lines 33-3. *Social Process*, pp. 368, 374-375; *Social Organization*, p. 323; *Life and the Student*, p. 15

P. 189, lines 4-19. *Social Process*, pp. 268-269, 271.

P. 189, lines 20-28. *Social Organization*, pp. 209-210.

Pp. 189-190, lines 31-1. *Social Process*, p. 78.

P. 190, lines 1-3. *Life and the Student*, p. 50.

P. 190, lines 8-9. *Ibid.*, p. 24; *Human Nature and the Social Order*, p. 295.

P. 190, lines 9-18. *Social Organization*, pp. 256-262.

P. 190, lines 18-22. *Ibid.*, pp. 294-296.

P. 190, *footnote 6. Ibid.*, p. 177.

P. 190, lines 22-27. *Ibid.*, pp. 135-138.

P. 190, lines 30-31. See, for example, *ibid.*, pp. 358-359.

Pp. 190-191, lines 32-1. *Life and the Student*, p. 31.

P. 191, lines 1-3. *Annals of the American Academy of Political and Social Science*, Vol. IX, No. 3, pp. 1-42.

P. 191, lines 3-7. The article appears in *Sociological Theory and Social Research*, pp. 121-159; see especially pp. 132-140.

P. 191, lines 7-21. *Social Process*, pp. 218-238.

P. 191, line 22. See, for example, *Social Organization*, p. 144.

P. 191, lines 23-31. *Ibid.*, pp. 210-211.

Pp. 191-192, lines 34-12. *Ibid.*, pp. 211-215

P. 192, lines 13-20. *Ibid.*, pp. 215-216.

Pp. 192-193, lines 21-18. *Ibid.*, pp. 217-225; further discussion of "race caste" appears in *Social Process*, p. 279.

P. 193, lines 19-26. *Social Organization*, pp. 225-226.

Pp. 193-194, lines 27-9. *Ibid.*, pp. 226-228.

P. 194, lines 10-26. *Ibid.*, pp. 230-233.

Pp. 194-195, lines 27-11. *Ibid.*, pp. 233-238.

P. 195, lines 16-26. *Ibid.*, pp. 239-240.

Pp. 195-196, lines 27-5. *Ibid.*, pp. 250-255.

P. 196, lines 6-11. *Ibid.*, pp. 248-250.

P. 196, lines 14-17. *Social Process*, pp. 79-85.

P. 196, lines 17-18. *Human Nature and the Social Order*, pp. 118-119.

P. 196, lines 18-22. *Social Organization*, pp. 273-274.

P. 196, lines 22-26. *Life and the Student*, p. 40; *Social Organization*, p. 147.

P. 196, lines 26-31. *Social Process*, pp. 273-274.

P. 196, *footnote 10.* Cooley, Angell and Carr, *op. cit.*, p. 287.

P. 197, line 3. *Social Organization*, p. 64.

P. 197, lines 3-8. *Human Nature and the Social Order*, pp. 111, 153.

P. 197, lines 8-11. *Social Organization*, p. 5.

P. 197, lines 11-15. *Human Nature and the Social Order*, p. 360.

P. 197, lines 15-23. *Social Organization*, p. 272.

P. 197, lines 27-30. *Ibid.*, p. 291.

Pp. 197-198, lines 31-25. *Ibid.*, pp. 240-245; *Life and the Student*, pp. 42-43.

P. 198, lines 28-32. *Social Process*, pp. 192-194.

P. 198, lines 32-36. *Social Organization*, pp. 138-141.

P. 199, lines 1-5. "A Primary Culture for Democracy," *Publications of the American Sociological Society*, Vol. XIII (1918), p. 9.

P. 199, lines 6-15. *Social Process*, pp. 316, 320, 326-328; "Personal Competition," *op. cit.*, p. 225.

P. 199, lines 15-22. *Social Process*, p. 342; "Personal Competition," *op. cit.*, pp. 200, 203.

Pp. 199-200, lines 23-10. "Personal Competition," *op. cit.*, pp. 164-169, 174, 208-219.

P. 200, lines 11-13. *Life and the Student*, p. 53.

P. 200, lines 13-14. *Social Process*, p. 336.

P. 200, lines 14-17. "Political Economy and Social Process," *op. cit.*, pp. 253-254.

P. 200, lines 17-24. *Social Organization*, pp. 267-272.

P. 200, lines 24-28. "A Primary Culture for Democracy," *op. cit.*, pp. 1, 3.

Pp. 200-201, lines 30-2. *Social Process*, pp. 302-308, 325, 334-335.

P. 201, *footnote 13.* *Life and the Student*, pp. 45-46.

P. 201, lines 3-7. *Ibid.*, pp. 41-42, 44-46, 186; "A Primary Culture for Democracy," *op. cit.*, p. 6.

P. 201, lines 9-15. *Social Organization*, pp. 279-281.

P. 201, lines 16-20. *Ibid.*, p. 125.

P. 201, lines 20-23. *Life and the Student*, pp. 266-267.

P. 202, lines 2-6. *Human Nature and the Social Order*, pp. 310-311, 402-403.

P. 202, lines 7-8. Wood, *op. cit.*, p. 713.

P. 202, lines 8-11. *Social Organization*, p. 350; *Social Process*, p. 344.

P. 202, lines 13-20. *Social Organization*, pp. 203-205, 379-380.

P. 202, *footnote 15.* Mead, *loc. cit.*

P. 202, lines 23-25. *Human Nature and the Social Order*, pp. 375-380.

P. 202, lines 25-28. *Social Organization*, pp. 383-386; cf. *Social Process*, pp. 184-186.

P. 202, lines 28-33. *Social Organization*, pp. 101, 158-159, 362.

Pp. 202-203, lines 33-2. *Ibid.*, p. 294.

P. 203, *footnote 16. Life and the Student*, p. 42.

P. 203, lines 3-12. *Social Process*, pp. 156-157, 160-168, 394.

P. 203, *footnote 17.* Hamilton, *Encyclopaedia of the Social Sciences, loc. cit.*

P. 203, lines 14-20. *Social Organization*, pp. 227, 293, 318; *Human Nature and the Social Order*, p. 401; *Social Process*, p. 347.

P. 203, lines 21-23. *Social Organization*, pp. 262-264.

P. 203, lines 23-25. *Social Process*, p. 324.

P. 203, lines 26-27. "Personal Competition," *op. cit.*, p. 198.

P. 203, *footnote 18. Social Process*, p. 324.

P. 203, *footnote 18. Social Organization*, p. 229.

Pp. 203-204, lines 28-18. *Ibid.*, pp. 402-410.

P. 204, lines 18-20. "Political Economy and Social Process," *op. cit.*, pp. 257-258.

P. 204, lines 20-25. *Social Process*, pp. 147-149, 257.

P. 204, lines 26-27. See Wood, *op. cit.*, p. 715.

P. 204, lines 28-29. *Life and the Student*, p. 49.

Pp. 204-205, lines 29-6. *Social Organization*, pp. 275-278; cf. *Social Process*, pp. 180-181.

P. 205, lines 11-17. *Social Process*, pp. 35-42; cf. "Personal Competition," *op. cit.*, pp. 175-187; "Political Economy and Social Process," *op. cit.*, pp. 255-257.

P. 205, lines 18-22. *Social Process*, pp. 125-136, 241-255.

P. 205, lines 22-24. *Ibid.*, pp. 144-147.

P. 205, lines 26-33. *Ibid.*, pp. 269-273, 348; *Social Organization*, p. 199.

Pp. 205-206, lines 35-1. See, for example, *Social Organization*, p. 200.

P. 206, lines 2-4. *Ibid.*, p. 89; *Life and the Student*, p. 50.

P. 206, lines 4-9. *Human Nature and the Social Order*, p. 275; *Life and the Student*, pp. 48-49.

P. 206, lines 9-15. *Social Process*, p. 273.

P. 206, lines 16-23. See "A Primary Culture for Democracy," *op. cit.*, pp. 1-10.

P. 206, lines 23-31. *Human Nature and the Social Order*, p. 112; *Social Organization*, pp. 27, 53, 178; *Life and the Student*, p. 10.

P. 206, lines 32-34. *Life and the Student*, p. 230.

Pp. 206-207, lines 34-17. *Social Organization*, pp. 180-199.

P. 207, lines 18-25. *Social Process*, pp. 137-143.

P. 207, lines 25-29. *Ibid.*, pp. 261, 418-422.

P. 207, lines 29-34. *Social Organization*, pp. 51, 297-309.

Pp. 207-208, lines 34-2. *Ibid.*, pp. 395-401, 411-419.

P. 208, *footnote 20*. "A Primary Culture for Democracy," *op. cit.*, pp. 1, 3; *Human Nature and the Social Order*, pp. 103, 107, 114-115; *Social Organization*, pp. 179-180; *Life and the Student*, pp. 17-18.

P. 208, lines 5-8. Wood, *op. cit.*, p. 714.

P. 208, lines 10-12. *Idem.*

P. 208, lines 15-23. *Social Organization*, pp. 113-120, 126, 168.

P. 208, lines 23-26. *Ibid.*, pp. 245-247, 284-289.

CHAPTER SEVEN

(Unless otherwise noted, the author in all cases is E. A. Ross.)

P. 213, lines 8-9. See *Seventy Years of It*, pp. 61-62.

P. 214, *footnote 1*. B. J. Stern, ed., "The Ward-Ross Correspondence," *American Sociological Review*, Vol. III, No. 3 (1938).

P. 214, lines 10-14. *Seventy Years of It*, pp. 11-20, 26-39, 40-52.

P. 214, lines 17-18. See *Foundations of Sociology*, pp. 149-181.

P. 214, lines 21-22. *Idem.*

P. 214, lines 23-26. *Social Control*, pp. 66-67.

P. 214, *footnote 3*. *Ibid.*, p. 215.

P. 214, lines 26-28. *Principles of Sociology*, pp. 95-102. This reference and all others (unless otherwise indicated) to this work refer to the Third Edition, published in 1938.

Pp. 214-215, lines 28-2. *Ibid.*, pp. 481-482, 492-500.

P. 215, lines 5-9. *Foundations of Sociology*, pp. 96, 285.

P. 215, lines 11-13. *Principles of Sociology*, pp. 486-489.

P. 215, lines 13-16. *Foundations of Sociology*, p. 275; *Social Control*, pp. 327-434.

P. 215, *footnote 4*. *Sin and Society*, pp. 81-82.

P. 215, lines 16-20. *Principles of Sociology*, pp. 138-140; cf. *Foundations of Sociology*, p. 135.

P. 215, lines 24-27. *Sin and Society*, Preface, p. viii; pp. 18, 85.

P. 215, lines 27-31. *Seventy Years of It*, p. 111.

P. 215, *footnote 5*. *Social Control*, p. 103.

P. 216, lines 2-6. *Principles of Sociology*, p. 554.

P. 216, lines 6-10. *Ibid.*, p. 644.

P. 216, lines 11-17. *Ibid.*, pp. 204-214, 222-223.

P. 216, lines 19-24. *Ibid.*, pp. 216-217, 237; cf. *Sin and Society*, p. 24.

P. 216, lines 24-27. *Principles of Sociology*, pp. 514-526.

Pp. 216-217, lines 27-2. *Ibid.*, pp. 282-287; cf. *Changing America*, p. 4.

P. 217, lines 4-6. *Sin and Society*, p. 76.

P. 217, lines 7-10. *Changing America*, pp. 163-186; *The Social Trend*, pp. 70-77.

P. 217, lines 13-15. *Social Control*, pp. 206-207, 213.

P. 217, lines 15-16. *Seventy Years of It*, p. 6; cf. *Sin and Society*, pp. 16-17.

P. 217, lines 16-18. *Principles of Sociology*, p. 349.

P. 217, lines 21-31. *Social Control*, pp. 417-427.

P. 217, lines 33-34. See *Foundations of Sociology*, pp. 9-10, 14, 78-80, 254; *Principles of Sociology*, pp. 101, 707-710.

Pp. 217-218, lines 34-1. *Foundations of Sociology*, pp. 25-27, 279-280.

P. 218, lines 2-4. *Ibid.*, p. 230.

P. 218, lines 4-6. *Principles of Sociology*, pp. 638-639.

P. 218, lines 6-10. *The Social Trend*, pp. 214-235.

P. 218, lines 10-14. *World Drift*, see especially the Preface.

P. 218, lines 15-17. *Principles of Sociology*, pp. 154-158.

Pp. 218-219, lines 22-2. *Ibid.*, pp. 401-407.

P. 219, lines 3-19. *Ibid.*, pp. 407-418.

Pp. 219-220, lines 20-4. *Ibid.*, pp. 419-421.

P. 220, *footnote 10*. *Changing America*, pp. 13-17.

P. 220, lines 5-17. *Principles of Sociology*, pp. 422-426.

Pp. 220-221, lines 18-7. *Ibid.*, pp. 426-432.

P. 221, lines 8-13. *Ibid.*, pp. 432-433.

Pp. 221-222, lines 15-1. *Ibid.*, pp. 434-442.

P. 222, lines 2-4. *World Drift*, pp. 120, 140-144.

P. 222, lines 5-11. *Principles of Sociology*, pp. 442-443.

P. 222, lines 13-19. *Social Control*, pp. 378-379.

P. 222, lines 19-24. *Ibid.*, pp. 393-394.

P. 222, *footnote 14*. *Sin and Society*, p. 86.

Pp. 222-223, lines 27-11. *Principles of Sociology*, pp. 444-451.

P. 223, lines 12-23. *Ibid.*, pp. 451-456.

P. 223, lines 24-25. *Foundations of Sociology*, p. 93.

P. 223, lines 25-28. *Principles of Sociology*, p. 457; also p. ix, Preface to First Revision, which appears in the 1938 edition.

Pp. 223-224, lines 28-2. *Ibid.*, pp. 457-460.

P. 224, lines 3-17. *Ibid.*, pp. 461-465.

P. 224, lines 18-26. *Ibid.*, pp. 465-466.

Pp. 224-225, lines 27-3. *Ibid.*, pp. 466-468.

P. 225, lines 7-13. *Social Control*, pp. 71, 75, 96.

P. 225, lines 14-15. *Foundations of Sociology*, p. 87.

P. 225, *footnote 18*. *Seventy Years of It*, p. 248.

P. 225, lines 17-21. *Foundations of Sociology*, pp. 66-67.

P. 225, lines 21-31. *Ibid.*, pp. 36, 93, 221, 334-335.

P. 226, lines 1-16. *Ibid.*, pp. 321-323.

P. 226, lines 21-26. *Principles of Sociology*, pp. 158-159.

P. 226, lines 31-34. *Ibid.*, pp. 555-558.

Pp. 226-227, lines 34-2. *Ibid.*, p. 60; *Changing America*, p. 39.

P. 227, *footnote 19*. *Principles of Sociology*, pp. 54-58; *Standing Room Only*, pp. 233-236, 147-148, 225, 240-242.

P. 227, lines 3-8. *Foundations of Sociology*, p. 78.

P. 227, lines 8-10. *Ibid.*, pp. 244-247, 250-253.

P. 227, lines 10-15. *Ibid.*, pp. 272-274.

P. 227, lines 16-24. *Social Control*, pp. 400-401.

Pp. 227-228, lines 25-17. *Ibid.*, pp. 401-404; cf. *ibid.*, p. 436.

P. 228, lines 20-21. *Foundations of Sociology*, pp. 276-277.

Pp. 228-229, lines 21-12. *Ibid.*, pp. 285-290.

P. 229, lines 13-14. See *Principles of Sociology*, pp. ix-x, Preface to First Revision, which appears in the 1938 edition.

P. 229, lines 15-18. *Ibid.*, p. 275.

P. 229, lines 18-24. *World Drift*, pp. 79-80.

P. 229, lines 25-30. *Principles of Sociology*, pp. 276-279.

Pp. 229-230, lines 30-2. *Ibid.*, p. 294.

P. 230, *footnote 20*. *Ibid.*, pp. 294-300.

P. 230, lines 4-6. *World Drift*, pp. 82-84.

P. 230, lines 6-14. *Principles of Sociology*, pp. 280-281.

P. 230, lines 15-31. *Ibid.*, pp. 288-293.

Pp. 230-231, lines 32-5. *Ibid.*, p. 201.

P. 231, lines 5-11. *Ibid.*, pp. 258-259; *Foundations of Sociology*, pp. 393-394.

P. 231, lines 12-16. *Principles of Sociology*, p. 276.

Pp. 231-232, lines 17-9. *Ibid.*, pp. 649-656.

P. 232, lines 12-15. *Social Control*, pp. 2, 52-56, 82.

P. 232, lines 15-21. *Ibid.*, pp. 77-78.

P. 232, lines 21-26. *Ibid.*, pp. 49, 293.

Pp. 232-233, lines 27-3. *Ibid.*, p. 79.

P. 233, lines 3-12. *Ibid.*, pp. 84-86.

P. 233, lines 13-23. *Ibid.*, pp. 376-378, 399-400.

Pp. 233-234, lines 24-11. *Ibid.*, pp. 379-384.

P. 234, lines 12-24. *Ibid.*, pp. 384-386.

Pp. 234-235, lines 25-7. *Ibid.*, pp. 386-393.

P. 235, lines 10-15. *Ibid.*, pp. 139, 151, 183, 190, 194, 316, 321.

P. 235, *footnote 24*. *Principles of Sociology*, pp. 585-593.

P. 235, lines 16-29. *Social Control*, pp. 221-233, 236-240.

Pp. 235-236, lines 30-2. *Ibid.*, pp. 250, 252, 282-283, 290.

P. 236, lines 4-8. *Ibid.*, pp. 328-329, 332, 355-357, 361.

P. 236, *footnote 26*. *Seventy Years of It*, p. 249.

P. 236, lines 8-12. *Social Control*, p. 441.

P. 236, lines 12-14. *Ibid.*, pp. 370-372.

P. 236, lines 16-18. *Principles of Sociology*, pp. 501-513.

Pp. 236-237, lines 18-2. *Ibid.*, pp. 159-169.

P. 237, lines 4-15. *Ibid.*, pp. 172-176.

Pp. 237-238, lines 16-15. *Ibid.*, pp. 185-190.

P. 238, lines 21-23. *Seventy Years of It*, pp. 204, 211; *Standing Room Only*, p. 166.

P. 238, lines 23-28. *Social Control*, pp. 74, 82; cf. *Sin and Society*, pp. 138-139, 143.

P. 238, lines 28-30. *Foundations of Sociology*, p. 241.

P. 238, lines 30-32. *The Social Trend*, pp. 162-164.

P. 238, lines 32-33. *Social Control*, pp. 106-125.

P. 238, lines 34-35. *Principles of Sociology*, p. 398; *Social Psychology*, p. 351; *World Drift*, pp. 17-18.

P. 238, line 36. *Changing America*, pp. 109-136.

P. 239, lines 1-4. *Seventy Years of It*, pp. 169-170.

P. 239, lines 4-10. *Ibid.*, pp. 181, 289.

P. 239, lines 10-13. *Social Control*, pp. 169-172.

P. 239, lines 14-18. *Changing America*, p. 9.

P. 239, lines 19-21. *Social Control*, pp. 87-88, 363.

Pp. 239-240, lines 21-4. *Principles of Sociology*, pp. 279-280.

P. 240, lines 5-8. *Ibid.*, pp. 169-171.

P. 240, lines 8-27. *Ibid.*, pp. 190-191.

P. 240, lines 30-31. *Foundations of Sociology*, p. 189.

P. 241, lines 1-2. *Principles of Sociology*, p. vii, Preface to First Revision, which appears in the 1938 edition.

P. 241, lines 2-4. *Ibid.*, pp. 646-648.

P. 241, lines 6-7. *Sin and Society*, pp. 45-71.

P. 241, lines 7-9. *The Social Trend*, p. 178.

P. 241, lines 11-13. *World Drift*, p. 78.

P. 241, lines 13-17. *Foundations of Sociology*, pp. 217-218.

P. 241, lines 17-19. *Changing America*, pp. 18-19.

P. 241, lines 19-21. *The Social Trend*, p. 175.

P. 241, lines 21-26. *Seventy Years of It*, pp. 94, 119, 319.

P. 241, lines 26-27. *Principles of Sociology*, pp. 318-319, 323; *Standing Room Only*, pp. 166-167; cf. *The Russian Soviet Republic*, p. 285.

P. 241, lines 27-29. *Principles of Sociology*, pp. 94-95.

Pp. 241-242, lines 30-6. *Ibid.*, pp. 559-569; cf. *Changing America*, pp. 83-108.

P. 242, lines 6-7. *Sin and Society*, p. 97.

P. 242, lines 8-9. *Changing America*, pp. 88-89.

P. 242, lines 10-12. *Principles of Sociology*, p. 92; *Sin and Society*, pp. 154-162.

P. 242, line 15. See *Foundations of Sociology*, p. 77.

P. 242, lines 16-18. *The Russian Soviet Republic*, pp. 108-109.

P. 242, lines 19-20. *Changing America*, pp. 30-31.

P. 242, lines 20-27. *Sin and Society*, pp. 148-149.

P. 242, lines 27-29. *Seventy Years of It*, p. 189.

P. 242, lines 30-32. *Ibid.*, p. 292.

Pp. 242-243, lines 32-5. *World Drift*, pp. 86-94.

P. 243, lines 8-14. *Standing Room Only*, pp. 123-126; cf. *Principles of Sociology*, pp. 38-47.

P. 243, lines 15-23. *Standing Room Only*, pp. 150-152, 202-206.

P. 243, lines 23-26. *Ibid.*, pp. 167-168, 314.

P. 243, lines 30-33. *Foundations of Sociology*, p. 22.

P. 243, lines 33-34. *Principles of Sociology*, pp. 176-177.

P. 243, lines 34-36. *Sin and Society*, pp. 144-145.

P. 244, lines 1-2. *Principles of Sociology*, pp. 703-704.

P. 244, lines 2-5. *The Social Trend*, pp. 183-194.

P. 244, lines 6-8. *Principles of Sociology*, pp. 87-88; cf. *Standing Room Only*, p. 186.

P. 244, lines 8-10. *The Social Trend*, pp. 121-136.

P. 244, lines 10-14. *Social Control*, pp. 167, 303; *The Social Trend*, p. 181.

P. 244, lines 15-16. *Seventy Years of It*, p. 269.

P. 244, lines 16-20. *The Social Trend*, pp. 66-68, 195-213.

P. 244, lines 20-22. *Sin and Society*, pp. 145-146.

P. 244, lines 23-24. *Principles of Sociology*, p. 203.

P. 244, lines 24-29. *Social Psychology*, p. 115.

P. 244, lines 29-36. See *Sin and Society*, pp. 110-117.

Pp. 244-245, lines 36-3. *Standing Room Only*, pp. 315, 326-331.

P. 245, *footnote 30*. *Social Control*, pp. 259-260, 416.

P. 245, lines 5-12. *Principles of Sociology*, p. 606.

P. 245, lines 20-22. *Ibid.*, pp. 264-265; *Seventy Years of It*, pp. 171-176.

Pp. 245-246, lines 23-4. *Principles of Sociology*, pp. 656-657.

P. 246, lines 5-6. *Ibid.*, p. xii, Preface to Third Edition (1938).

P. 246, lines 6-17. *Ibid.*, pp. 704-706.

P. 246, lines 20-23. *Ibid.*, pp. 712-713.

CHAPTER EIGHT

P. 250, lines 1-8. For a brief discussion of the views of some of the European scholars on class see Mombert, Paul, "Class," *Encyclopaedia of the Social Sciences*.

Pp. 250-251, lines 20-9. The emphasis upon the middle class as the group destined to work out the progressive development of America is illustrated today, in the social sciences, in the writings of many, including Holcombe, A. N. (see especially his *New Party Politics*, New York 1933) and Bingham, A. M. (see especially his *Insurgent America*, New York 1935 and New Edition 1938). For a popular statement of this view see Duffus, R. L., "Our Backbone: A Middle Class," *The New York Times Magazine*, Dec. 12, 1937.

P. 251, lines 10-17. Cf. House, F. N., *The Development of Sociology* (McGraw-Hill, New York 1936), ch. xxv.

P. 251, lines 25-29. A good sample of the more recent European "class" research has been translated. See the studies of Emil Lederer, Erich Engelhard, Jacob Marschak, Emanuel Januschka, J. Nothass, and Sven Riemer, published by the New York

State Department of Social Welfare and the Department of Social Science of Columbia University, conducted under the auspices of the Works Progress Administration.

P. 252, lines 1-2. See Dollard, J., *Caste and Class in a Southern Town* (Yale University Press, New Haven 1937); Warner, W. L., "American Caste and Class," *American Journal of Sociology*, Vol. XLII, No. 2 (Sept. 1936), pp. 234-237; Johnson, C. S., "The Concept of Caste and Class in an American Industry," *American Journal of Sociology*, Vol. XLII, No. 1 (July 1936), pp. 55-65; Powdermaker, H., *After Freedom* (Viking, New York 1939).

P. 252, line 3. Lynd, R. S. and H. M., *Middletown* (Harcourt Brace, New York 1930), and *Middletown in Transition* (Harcourt Brace, New York 1937).

P. 252, lines 6-8. Corey, L., *The Decline of American Capitalism* (Covici Friede, New York, 1934) and *The Crisis of the Middle Class* (Covici Friede, New York 1935).

P. 253, lines 16-20. Cf. Bukharin, N., *Historical Materialism* (International Publishers, New York 1933) especially ch. viii.

P. 253, lines 28-30. Corey, *loc. cit.*, "solves" the American "inconsistency" between sharp economic class lines and the dominance of middle class consciousness by naming the latter a "cultural lag." See especially *The Decline of American Capitalism*.

P. 253, lines 31-32. The distinction between the *socioeconomic* and *sociopsychological* meanings of class is explicitly developed by Goetz A. Briefs in *The Proletariat* (McGraw-Hill, New York 1937); see especially chs. iii and iv. Cf. the analysis in terms of the "objective" and "subjective" approaches by Mombert, *loc. cit.*

P. 253, lines 32-34. The *sociopsychological* meaning of class is illustrated today in the sociology of R. M. MacIver and the semi-popular work of A. M. Bingham. See MacIver, R. M., *Society* (Farrar and Rinehart, New York 1937), ch. ix; Bingham, *loc. cit.*, especially pp. 52, 65 of the New Edition.

P. 254, lines 11-14. Briefs, *loc. cit.*

SELECTED BIBLIOGRAPHY

CHAPTER ONE

Beard, C. A. and M. R., *The Rise of American Civilization* (Macmillan, New York 1930). One vol. edition, vol. ii.

Bradbury, W., unpublished manuscript on Veblen's class theory, Columbia University.

Chamberlain, J., *Farewell to Reform* (Day, New York 1933), Second Edition.

Commons, J. R. and others, *History of Labour in the United States*, 4 vols. (Macmillan, New York 1918), vol. ii.

Corey, L., *The Decline of American Capitalism* (Covici Friede, New York 1934).

———, *The Crisis of the Middle Class* (Covici Friede, New York 1935).

David, H., *The History of the Haymarket Affair* (Farrar and Rinehart, New York 1936).

Dombrowski, J., *The Early Days of Christian Socialism in America* (Columbia, New York 1936).

Dorfman, J., *Thorstein Veblen and His America* (Viking, New York 1934).

Gillin, J. L., "The Development of Sociology in the United States," *Publications, American Sociological Society*, Vol. XXI (1926).

Hacker, L. M., "Lloyd, Henry Demarest," *Encyclopaedia of the Social Sciences* (Macmillan, New York 1930).

Hacker, L. M. and Kendrick, B. B., *United States Since 1865* (Crofts, New York 1933).

Hertzler, J. O., "Bellamy, Edward," *Encyclopaedia of the Social Sciences* (Macmillan, New York 1930).

Hicks, G., *The Great Tradition* (Macmillan, New York 1935), Revised Edition.

Homan, P. T., *Contemporary Economic Thought* (Harpers, New York 1928), pp. 105-192.

Johnson, A., "Veblen, Thorstein Bunde," *Encyclopaedia of the Social Sciences* (Macmillan, New York 1930).

Kallen, H. M., *Individualism—An American Way of Life* (Liveright, New York 1933).

———, "Reformism," *Encyclopaedia of the Social Sciences* (Macmillan, New York 1930).

Lloyd, C., *Henry Demarest Lloyd, 1847-1903;* a Biography (Putnam, New York 1912), vol. ii, ch. xxv.

Odum, H. W., ed., *American Masters of Social Science* (Holt, New York 1927).

Palm, F. C., *The Middle Classes Then and Now* (Macmillan, New York 1936).

Parrington, V. L., *Main Currents in American Thought* (Harcourt Brace, New York 1930), vol. iii, *The Beginnings of Critical Realism in America 1860-1920.*

Shannon, F. A., *Economic History of the People of the United States* (Macmillan, New York 1934).

Simons, A. M., *Social Forces in American History* (Macmillan, New York 1911).

Small, A. W., "Fifty Years of Sociology in the United States," *American Journal of Sociology*, vol. XXI (1926).

Tugwell, R. G., "George, Henry," *Encyclopaedia of the Social Sciences* (Macmillan, New York 1930).

CHAPTER TWO

Barnes, H. E., "Two Representative Contributions of Sociology to Political Theory: The Doctrines of William Graham Sumner and Lester Frank Ward," *American Journal of Sociology*, Vol. XXV, No. 2 (1919).

Bodenhafer, W. B., "The Comparative Role of the Group Concept in Ward's *Dynamic Sociology* and Contemporary American Sociology," *American Journal of Sociology*, Vol. XXVI, Nos. 3, 4, 5, 6 (1920-1921).

Dealy, J. Q., "Lester Frank Ward," *American Masters of Social Science*, ed. H. W. Odum (Holt, New York 1927).

Dealy, J. Q., and Ward, L. F., *A Text-Book of Sociology* (Macmillan, New York 1905).

Ellwood, C. A., *A History of Social Philosophy* (Prentice-Hall, New York 1938) ch. xxix.

Gumplowicz, L., "An Austrian Appreciation of Lester F. Ward," *American Journal of Sociology*, Vol. X, No. 5 (1905).

"Lester F. Ward," *American Journal of Sociology*, Vol. XIX, No. 1 (1913).

Small, A. W., "Fifty Years of Sociology in the United States," *American Journal of Sociology*, Vol. XXI, No. 6 (1916).

Stern, B. J., "Ward, Lester Frank," *Encyclopaedia of the Social Sciences* (Macmillan, New York 1930).

———, ed., "Giddings, Ward and Small: An Interchange of Letters," *Social Forces*, Vol. X, No. 3 (1931).

———, ed., "The Letters of Albion W. Small to Lester F. Ward," *Social Forces*, Vol. XII, No. 2 (1933); Vol. XIII, No. 3 (1934); Vol. XV, Nos. 2 and 3 (1936).

———, ed., "The Ward-Ross Correspondence, 1891-1896," *American Sociological Review*, Vol. III, No. 3 (1938).

———, ed., *Young Ward's Diary* (Putnam, New York 1935).

Ward, L. F., *Dynamic Sociology*, 2 vols. (Appleton, New York 1910), 2nd edition. (Originally published 1883.)

———, *The Psychic Factors of Civilization* (Ginn, Boston 1906), 2nd edition. (Originally published 1893).

———, *Outlines of Sociology* (Macmillan, New York 1898). This work also appeared in twelve issues of the *American Journal of Sociology*, Vols. I, II (1895-1897).

———, *Pure Sociology* (Macmillan, New York 1911), 2nd edition. (Originally published 1903).

———, *Applied Sociology* (Ginn, Boston 1906).

———, *Glimpses of the Cosmos*, 6 vols. (Putnam's, New York 1913).

———, "The Sociology of Political Parties," *American Journal of Sociology*, Vol. XIII, No. 4 (1908).

———, "Social Classes in the Light of Modern Sociological Theory," *American Journal of Sociology*, Vol. XIII, No. 5 (1908).

———, "Discussion of T. N. Carver's 'The Basis of Social Conflict,' " *American Journal of Sociology*, Vol. XIII, No. 5 (1908).

CHAPTER THREE

Barnes, H. E., "William Graham Sumner," *Sociological Review*, Vol. XIV, No. 3 (1922).

———, "Two Representative Contributions of Sociology to Political Theory: The Doctrines of William Graham Sumner and Lester

Frank Ward," *American Journal of Sociology*, Vol. XXV, No. 1 (1919).

Chamberlain, J., *Farewell to Reform* (Day, New York 1933), Second Edition, pp. 9-17.

"Comments, William Graham Sumner," *Yale Review*, Vol. XIX, First Series (1910).

Cooley, C. H., "Sumner and Methodology," *Sociological Theory and Social Research* (Holt, New York 1930).

Ellwood, C. A., *A History of Social Philosophy* (Prentice-Hall, New York 1938), ch. xxviii.

House, F. N., *Development of Sociology* (McGraw-Hill, New York 1936), ch. xxiii.

Keller, A. G., *Reminiscences (Mainly Personal) of William Graham Sumner* (Yale, New Haven 1933).

Park, R. E., "The Sociological Methods of William Graham Sumner, and of William I. Thomas and Florian Znaneicki," *Methods in the Social Sciences*, ed. S. A. Rice (University of Chicago, Chicago 1931).

Starr, H. E., *William Graham Sumner* (Holt, New York 1925).

Stern, B. J., "Sumner, William Graham," *Encyclopaedia of the Social Sciences* (Macmillan, New York 1930).

Sumner, W. G., *What Social Classes Owe to Each Other* (Harpers, New York 1920). Originally published 1883; also published by Yale Uni. Press, New Haven 1925.

——, *Folkways* (Ginn, Boston 1911). Originally published 1907.

——, *War and Other Essays*, ed. A. G. Keller (Yale, New Haven 1911).

——, *Earth Hunger and Other Essays*, ed. A. G. Keller (Yale, New Haven 1913).

——, *The Challenge of Facts and Other Essays*, ed. A. G. Keller (Yale, New Haven 1914).

——, *The Forgotten Man and Other Essays*, ed. A. G. Keller (Yale, New Haven 1918).

——, *Essays of William Graham Sumner*, 2 vols., eds. A. G. Keller and M. R. Davie (Yale, New Haven 1934).

——, "The Bequests of the Nineteenth Century to the Twentieth," *Yale Review*, Vol. XXII (1933).

Sumner, W. G. and Keller, A. G., *The Science of Society*, 4 vols.; M. R. Davie co-author of vol. iv (Yale, New Haven, 1927), vols. i, ii, iii.

Ward, L. F., "Prof. Sumner's Social Classes," *Glimpses of the Cosmos*, vol. iii (Putnam's, New York 1913).

Chapter Four

Barnes, H. E., "The Place of Albion Woodbury Small in Modern Sociology," *American Journal of Sociology*, Vol. XXXII, No. 1 (1926).

——, "Discussion of Small's *The Future of Sociology*," *Papers and Proceedings, American Sociological Society*, Vol. XV (1920).

Goodspeed, T. W., "Albion Woodbury Small," *American Journal of Sociology*, Vol. XXXII, No. 1 (1926).

Hayes, E. C., "Albion Woodbury Small," *American Masters of Social Science*, ed. H. W. Odum (Holt, New York 1927).

House, F. N., "A List of the More Important Published Writings of Albion Woodbury Small," *American Journal of Sociology*, Vol. XXXII, No. 1 (1926).

——, *Development of Sociology* (McGraw-Hill, New York 1936), chs. xx, xxi.

MacLean, A. M., "Albion Woodbury Small: An Appreciation," *American Journal of Sociology*, Vol. XXXII, No. 1 (1926).

Small, A. W., *General Sociology* (Uni. of Chicago Press, Chicago 1905).

——, *Adam Smith and Modern Sociology* (Uni. of Chicago Press, Chicago 1907).

——, *The Cameralists* (Uni. of Chicago Press, Chicago 1909).

——, *The Meaning of Social Science* (Uni. of Chicago Press, Chicago 1910).

——, *Between Eras: From Capitalism to Democracy* (Intercollegiate Press, Kansas City 1913).

——, *Origins of Sociology* (Uni. of Chicago Press, Chicago 1924). (First published serially in *The American Journal of Sociology* as "Some Contributions to the History of Sociology," 1923-1924).

——, "The Beginnings of American Nationality," *Johns Hopkins University Studies in Historical and Political Science*, ed. H. B. Adams, Vol. VIII (1890).

——, "Some Demands of Sociology Upon Pedagogy," *American Journal of Sociology*, Vol. II, No. 6 (1897).

——, "The Sociologists' Point of View," *American Journal of Sociology*, Vol. III, No. 2 (1897).

——, "The Meaning of the Social Movement," *American Journal of Sociology*, Vol. III, No. 3 (1897).

——, "The Significance of Sociology for Ethics," *The Decennial*

Publications of the University of Chicago, First Series, Vol. IV (1903).

———, "The Subject Matter of Sociology," *American Journal of Sociology*, Vol. X, No. 3 (1904).

———, "Socialism in the Light of Social Science," *American Journal of Sociology*, Vol. XVII, No. 6 (1912).

———, "The Present Outlook of Social Science," *American Journal of Sociology*, Vol. XVIII, No. 4 (1913).

———, "A Vision of Social Efficiency," *American Journal of Sociology*, Vol. XIX, No. 4 (1914).

———, "Shall Science Be Sterilized?" *American Journal of Sociology*, Vol. XIX, No. 5 (1914).

———, "The Ford Motor Company Incident," *American Journal of Sociology*, Vol. XIX, No. 5 (1914).

———, "The Social Gradations of Capital," *American Journal of Sociology*, Vol. XIX, No. 6 (1914).

———, "The Evolution of a Social Standard," *American Journal of Sociology*, Vol. XX, No. 1 (1914).

———, "The Bonds of Nationality," *American Journal of Sociology*, Vol. XX, No. 5 (1915).

———, "National Preparedness—American," *American Journal of Sociology*, Vol. XXI, No. 5 (1916).

———, "Fifty Years of Sociology in the United States," *American Journal of Sociology*, Vol. XXI, No. 6 (1916).

———, "The Church and Class Conflicts," *American Journal of Sociology*, Vol. XXIV, No. 5 (1919).

———, "The Sociology of Profits," *American Journal of Sociology*, Vol. XXX, No. 4 (1925).

———, A. W. and Vincent, G. E., *An Introduction to the Study of Society* (American Book Co., New York 1894).

Stern, B. J., ed., "The Letters of Albion W. Small to Lester F. Ward," *Social Forces*, Vol. XII, No. 2 (1933); Vol. XIII, No. 3 (1934); Vol. XV, Nos. 2 and 3 (1936).

Wirth, L., "Small, Albion Woodbury," *Encyclopaedia of the Social Sciences* (Macmillan, New York 1930).

Chapter Five

Abel, T., "The Significance of the Concept of Consciousness of Kind," *Social Forces*, Vol. IX, No. 1 (1930).

A Bibliography of the Faculty of Political Science of Columbia University 1880-1930 (Columbia Uni. Press, New York 1931).

Giddings, F. H., *The Theory of Socialization* (Macmillan, New York 1897).

——, *The Elements of Sociology* (Macmillan, New York 1898).

——, *The Principles of Sociology* (Macmillan, New York 1920). Originally published 1899.

——, *Democracy and Empire* (Macmillan, New York 1900).

——, *Inductive Sociology* (Macmillan, New York 1901).

——, *The Western Hemisphere in the World of Tomorrow* (Revell, New York 1915).

——, *Americanism in War and Peace* (Clark Uni. Press, Worcester 1917).

——, *The Responsible State* (Houghton Mifflin, Boston 1918).

——, *Studies in the Theory of Human Society* (Macmillan, New York 1922).

——, *The Scientific Study of Human Society* (Uni. of North Carolina Press, Chapel Hill 1924).

——, *Civilization and Society* (Holt, New York 1932).

——, "The Persistence of Competition," *Political Science Quarterly*, Vol. II, No. 1 (1887).

——, "The Natural Rate of Wages," *Political Science Quarterly*, Vol. II, No. 4 (1887).

——, "The Cost of Production of Capital," *Quarterly Journal of Economics*, Vol. III (July 1889).

——, "The Theory of Capital," *Quarterly Journal of Economics*, Vol. IV (Jan. 1890).

——, "The Province of Sociology," *Annals, American Academy of Political and Social Science*, Vol. I (1890).

——, "The Ethics of Socialism," *International Journal of Ethics*, Vol. I (1891).

——, "Sociology as a University Study," *Political Science Quarterly*, Vol. VI, No. 4 (1891).

——, "The Nature and Conduct of Political Majorities," *Political Science Quarterly*, Vol. VII, No. 1 (1892).

——, "The Ethics of Social Progress," *International Journal of Ethics*, Vol. III (Jan. 1893).

——, "The Relation of Recent Economic Theory to Profit Sharing," reprinted from *Employer and Employed*, Boston (1893).

——, "The Relation of Sociology to Other Scientific Studies," *Journal of Social Science*, Vol. XXXII (Nov. 1894).

——, "Is the Term 'Social Classes' a Scientific Category?" *Proceedings, National Conferences of Charities and Correction* (at New Haven), Boston 1895.

——,"The Destinies of Democracy," *Political Science Quarterly*, Vol. XI, No. 4 (1896).

——, "The Economic Ages," *Political Science Quarterly*, Vol. XVI, No. 2 (1901).

——, "Sociological Questions," *The Forum*, Vol. XXXV (Oct. 1903).

——, "The Concepts and Methods of Sociology," *American Journal of Sociology*, Vol. X, No. 2 (1904).

——, "A Theory of Social Causation," *Publications, American Economic Association*, Third Series, Vol. V (1904).

——, "The Laws of Evolution," *Science*, Vol. XXII (1905).

——, "The Basis of Social Conflict," *American Journal of Sociology*, Vol. XIII, No. 5 (1908).

——, "The Contradictions of Ideas and Beliefs," *American Journal of Sociology*, Vol. XIII, Nos. 5 and 6 (1908).

——, "The Quality of Civilization," *Papers and Proceedings, American Sociological Society*, Vol. VI (1911).

——, "The Relation of Social Theory to Public Policy," *Special Bulletins of American Association for International Conciliation*, No. 58 (New York 1912).

——, "The Changing Attitude Toward War," *Special Bulletins of American Association for International Conciliation* (New York Sept. 1914).

——, "The Child as a Member of Society," *Teachers College Record*, Vol. XVI, No. 5 (1915).

——, "The Democracy of Universal Military Service," *Annals, American Academy of Political and Social Science*, Vol. LXVI (1916).

——, "Social Control in a Democracy," *Papers and Proceedings, American Sociological Society*, Vol. XII (1917).

——, "What the War Was Worth," *Independent*, July 5, 1919.

——, "Pluralistic Behavior," *American Journal of Sociology*, Vol. XXV, Nos. 4 and 5 (1919-1920).

——, "A Theory of History," *Political Science Quarterly*, Vol. XXXV, No. 4 (1920).

——, "Unemployment—The Views of a Sociologist," *Independent*, Oct. 8, 1921.

——, "Societal Variables," *Journal of Social Forces*, Vol. I, No. 4 (1922).

——, "Resurgent Middle Class" (Book Review), *The New York Times*, Dec. 31, 1922.

——, "Social Work and Societal Engineering," *Journal of Social Forces*, Vol. III, No. 1 (1924).

——, "Patriotism," *Teachers College Record*, Vol. XXVI, No. 6 (1925).

——, "Is There a Class Psychology?" *Journal of Abnormal and Social Psychology*, Vol. XXI (1926).

——, "Alternatives Seen as Basic Economic Facts," reprinted from *Economic Essays in Honor of John Bates Clark* (Macmillan, New York 1927).

——, "Sociology as a Science," *The Scientific Monthly*, Vol. XXV (Oct. 1927).

Gillin, J. L., "Franklin Henry Giddings," *American Masters of Social Science*, ed. H. W. Odum (Holt, New York 1927).

Lichtenberger, J. P., "Franklin H. Giddings: An Appreciation," *Journal of Applied Sociology*, Vol. IX, No. 5 (1925).

Northcott, C. H., "The Sociological Theories of Franklin H. Giddings," *American Journal of Sociology*, Vol. XXIV, No. 1 (1918).

Stern, B. J., "Giddings, Franklin Henry," *Encyclopaedia of the Social Sciences* (Macmillan, New York 1930).

Tenney, A. A., "Franklin H. Giddings," *Columbia University Quarterly*, Vol. XXIII.

Ward, L. F., "Principles of Sociology," *Annals, American Academy of Political and Social Science*, Vol. VIII (1896).

CHAPTER SIX

Angell, R. C., "Cooley's Heritage to Social Research," *Social Forces*, Vol. VIII, No. 3 (1929).

Cooley, C. H., *Human Nature and the Social Order* (Scribner's, New York 1902). Also revised and enlarged edition, 1922.

——, *Social Organization* (Scribner's, New York 1909).

——, *Social Process* (Scribner's, New York 1918).

——, *Life and the Student* (Knopf, New York 1927).

——, *Sociological Theory and Social Research*, Introduction and Notes by R. C. Angell (Holt, New York 1930). This volume contains most of Cooley's articles and papers.

——, "The Social Significance of Street Railways" (abstract only), *Publications of the American Economic Association*, Vol. VI (1891).

——, " 'Nature *versus* Nurture' in the Making of Social Careers,"

Proceedings of the National Conference of Charities and Corrections (1896).

——, "The Process of Social Change," *Political Science Quarterly*, Vol. XII, No. 1 (1897).

——, Discussion of Giddings' Paper, "A Theory of Social Causation," *Publications of the American Economic Association*, Third Series, Vol. V, No. 2 (1904).

——, "A Primary Culture for a Democracy," *Publications of the American Sociological Society*, Vol. XIII (1918).

——, "Heredity or Environment," *Journal of Applied Sociology*, Vol. X, No. 4 (1926).

Cooley, C. H., Angell, R. C., and Carr, L. J., *Introductory Sociology* (Scribner's, New York 1933).

Hamilton, W. H., "Cooley, Charles Horton," *Encyclopaedia of the Social Sciences* (Macmillan, New York 1930).

——, "Charles Horton Cooley," *Social Forces*, Vol. VIII, No. 2 (1929).

Mead, G. H., "Cooley's Contribution to American Social Thought," *American Journal of Sociology*, Vol. XXXV, No. 5 (1930).

Wood, A. E., "Charles Horton Cooley: An Appreciation," *American Journal of Sociology*, Vol. XXXV, No. 5 (1930).

CHAPTER SEVEN

Ross, E. A., *Social Control* (Macmillan, New York 1901).

——, *Foundations of Sociology* (Macmillan, New York 1905).

——, *Sin and Society* (Houghton Mifflin, Boston 1907).

——, *Changing America* (Century, New York 1915), copyright 1908; also published 1912.

——, *Social Psychology* (Macmillan, New York 1921). Originally published 1908.

——, *The Social Trend* (Century, New York 1922).

——, *The Russian Soviet Republic* (Century, New York 1923).

——, *World Drift* (Century, New York 1928).

——, *Seventy Years of It* (D. Appleton-Century, New York, 1936).

——, *Principles of Sociology*, Third Edition (D. Appleton-Century, New York 1938). First Edition, 1920; Revised Edition, 1930.

Stern, B. J., ed., "The Ward-Ross Correspondence," *American Sociological Review*, Vol. III, No. 3 (1938).

INDEX

42136